Complex Systems in the Social and Behavioral Sciences

Complex Systems in the Social and Behavioral Sciences

Theory, Method and Application

Euel Elliott and L. Douglas Kiel

University of Michigan Press
Ann Arbor

Copyright © 2021 by Euel Elliott and L. Douglas Kiel
All rights reserved

For questions or permissions, please contact um.press.perms@umich.edu

Published in the United States of America by the
University of Michigan Press

Manufactured in the United States of America
Printed on acid-free paper

First published June 2021

A CIP catalog record for this book is available from the British Library.

ISBN 978-0-472-07488-4 (hardcover: alk. paper)
ISBN 978-0-472-05488-6 (paper: alk. paper)
ISBN 978-0-472-12892-1 (ebook)

Contents

List of figures vii

List of tables xi

Introduction 1
Euel Elliott and L. Douglas Kiel

Part 1 Social Systems Levels and Complexity 31

1. Group Dynamics: Adaptation, Coordination and Synchronization 33
   Stephen J. Guastello

2. Complexity Science and the Organization Sciences: 1999–2018 64
   Kevin J. Dooley

3. Complexity Science and the Study of Armed Conflict: A Narrative Review 83
   Maxime H.T. Stauffer

Part 2 Complexity, Computation and Artificial Intelligence 109

4. Novelty Production and Evolvability in Digital Genomic Agents: Logical Foundations and Policy Design Implications of Complex Adaptive Systems 111
   Sheri M. Markose

5. The Game of Go: Bounded Rationality and Artificial Intelligence 157
   Cassey Lee

Part 3 Simulating Complexity: Agent-Based Modeling   181

6. Agent-Based Modeling: Challenges and Prospects   183
   L. Douglas Kiel, John McCaskill, James Harrington and Euel Elliott

7. An Agent-Based Model of Obesity and Policy Implications   204
   Saikou Y. Diallo, Christopher J. Lynch, Jose J. Padilla and Ross Gore

Part 4 Scaling and Self-Organization   239

8. It's About Time   241
   Bruce J. West

9. Lessons from Collective Intelligence   263
   William Sulis

Part 5 Philosophy of Science and Epistemology   299

10. Philosophy of Science, Network Theory and Conceptual Change: Paradigm Shifts as Information Cascades   301
    Patrick Grim, Joshua Kavner, Lloyd Shatkin and Manjari Trivedi

11. Complexity and Knowledge   326
    J. Barkley Rosser, Jr.

12. Biological Hypercomputation: Social and Political Implications   343
    Carlos Eduardo Maldonado

    References   365

    Contributors   415

    Index   421

Digital materials related to this title can be found on the Fulcrum platform via the following citable URL: https://doi.org/10.3998/mpub.10155018

Figures

1.1 Twin Curves for Implicit and Explicit Learning Dynamics with Chaotic Onset and Asymptotic Stability at the Conclusion of a Self-Organizing Process 45

1.2 Coordination Acquisition during Four Rounds of an Intersection Task with Verbal and Nonverbal Conditions 47

1.3 Electrodermal Time Series From a Group of Seven Experimental Emergency Response Team Members Competing Against One Opponent (GSR 8) 56

4.1 Gödel Meta-Representation (Rogers 1967) and Mirror Systems in Immuno-Cognitive Systems 127

4.2 Gödel Incompleteness Result in Miniature: An Illustration of Mirror Mapping in Thymus Medulla of Gene Codes that are Theorems in Genomic Systems 130

4.3 Price Trends and Winner Determination 143

4.4 The Structure of the European Exchange Rate Currency Peg. Exchange Rates Against the Deutschemark for the Belgian Franc, French Franc, Danish Krone and British Pound Sterling, July 1992–July 1995 (indexed at 100 from July 1992) 148

5.1 Tree Diagram for Player 1's First Move for a 9x9 Go Board 166

5.2 Tree Diagram for the First Moves of Players 1 and 2 for a 9x9 Go Board 167

5.3 Go and Cellular Automata 171

5.4 Four Classes of Cellular Automata 172

- 7.1 Heat Map of Experimental Results Examining Calories in and Energy Expenditure 228
- 7.2 The Results of Thirty-Year Projections for States with High (Alabama and West Virginia), Medium (Minnesota), and Low (Colorado) Levels of Overweight and Obese Populations 230
- 7.3 A Thirty-Year Projection of the Percentage of Nebraska Residents that are Overweight and Obese 234
- 8.1 The Average Heart Rate in Beats per Minute for 16 Animals: From the Fastest—Hamsters—to the Slowest—Large Whales—with Humans in the Center of a Logarithmic Scale 244
- 8.2 Regular Transition between the Two States of the Individual in Operational Time (Upper Curve) and the Subordination of the Transition Times to an IPL PDF to Obtain Chronological Time (Lower Curve) 257
- 10.1 Modeling Progressive Integration within a Network 304
- 10.2 Spreading Falsification within a Popperian Model 305
- 10.3 Distribution of Cascade Sizes in Popperian Networks of Characteristic Degree 0.5 (Top) and 1 (Bottom) 306
- 10.4 Distribution of Cascade Sizes in Popperian Networks of Characteristic Degree 1.5 (Top) and 2 (Bottom) 307
- 10.5 Formation of a Giant Component as a Percentage of a Network at Different Degrees within an Undirected Random Network 308
- 10.6 Cascades of Fully Tipped Nodes in a Kuhnian Network of Characteristic Degree 1, with One Anomaly Passed to Neighboring Nodes at Threshold 310
- 10.7 Cascades of Fully Tipped Nodes in Kuhnian Networks of Characteristic Degree 2 (Top), 3 (Middle) and 4 (Bottom), with One Anomaly Passed to Neighboring Nodes at Threshold 312
- 10.8 Cascades of Affected Nodes in Kuhnian Networks of Characteristic Degree 1, 2, 4 and 6 (from top to bottom), with Full Anomaly Thresholds Passed to Neighboring Nodes 313
- 10.9 Scientific Change within a Popperian Model over Time 315

10.10 Scientific Change within a Kuhnian Model over Time, Using Transfer of a Single Anomaly   316

10.11 Wigmore's (1913) Outline of Legal Reasoning in Terms of a Directed Graph   317

10.12 Distribution of Cascade Sizes in Directed Popperian Networks of Increasing Degree   318

10.13 Distribution of Cascade Sizes in Directed Kuhnian Networks of Increasing Degree   319

10.14 The Bow-Tie Diagram of Components in a Directed Graph   320

10.15 Formation of Strongly Connected Components, In-Component and Out-Components as a Percentage of a Network at Different Degrees within a Directed Random Network   320

10.16 The History of Science in Popperian (Top) and Kuhnian (Bottom) Models Using Directed Conceptual Networks   321

10.17 Comparative Cascade Sizes in Popperian Networks of Fifty (Top) and One Hundred (Bottom) Nodes   324

10.18 The History of Science on a Kuhnian Directed Model   324

Tables

1.1 Matrix Populated with Autocorrelations of Physiological Time Series on the Diagonal   56

4.1 Methodological Differences: G-T-P Immuno-Cognitive Systems vs. Mainstream Cognitive Decision Theories   139

4.2 Gödel Logic on Liar-Like Structures (the Agent Who Negates What Can Be Predicted), Surprise Strategy and Undecidable Dynamics vs. Lucas (1972, 1976) on Policy Ineffectiveness, Strategic Use of Surprise and Lucas Critique   145

5.1 Four Categories of AI Definitions   160

5.2 Rationality, Bounded Rationality and AI   162

5.3 The Complexity of Board Games   163

7.1 Complete List of Parameters for the Model of Obesity   214

7.2 Results of the Sensitivity Analysis Experiments Using One-Way ANOVA   218

7.3 Percent of Experimental Data Points that Fall Within the Historical Confidence Interval of the CDC Data   220

7.4 Monte Carlo Results for Percentage of BMI ≥ 25 Populations over Thirty Years   222

7.5 Comparison of Experimental Data to Finkelstein et al. (2012) at the National Level for Adult Populations with BMI ≥ 30   224

7.6 Comparison of Experimental Outputs to Trust for America's Health and Robert Wood Johnson Foundation (2012) Projections for BMI ≥ 30   225

7.7 Experimental Results for Overweight and Obese Classifications when Conducting Experiments to Attempt and Match Each State's Thirty-Year Projection against Colorado's Projected Obesity Percentage   231

7.8 Experimental Results for Severely Underweight, Underweight, and Normal BMI Classifications in 2040   232

7.9 Nebraska Experimental Outputs   235

12.1 Two Ways of Understanding Complexity   346

12.2 Timeline toward Biological Hypercomputation   351

Introduction

Euel Elliott and L. Douglas Kiel

In the last twenty-five years, scholars across the social and behavioral sciences have applied the growing body of literature, now called the complexity sciences, to a variety of human phenomena. Early work in this field focused predominantly on "chaotic dynamics" (Kiel and Elliott 1996), or the deterministic yet uncertain mathematical dynamics of discrete systems. During this period, the intellectual evolution of these studies has resulted in a more expansive focus on total system dynamics, with particular emphasis on the necessary adaptive capacities of complex living systems. The knowledge produced in the natural sciences, traditionally viewed as the "harder" sciences, has not been replicated in the social and behavioral sciences for more reasons than just the mathematical intractability of the human realm. The inherent change, innovation and necessary adaptability of human social system behavior creates challenges of complexity that force scholars to rethink not only our mathematical formulations for understanding social systems and behavior but also our epistemological bases for grasping the dynamics of the array of interactions typifying human actors and the biopsychosocial influences that drive their multitudinous behaviors.

Social and behavioral scientists have recently developed new intellectual frameworks and methods for better understanding the evolving mechanisms that produce adaptive capacities in complex systems. Researchers have discovered a vast array of phenomena in the biological and physical, as well as in the social and economic worlds that behave in a manner that requires a different set of assumptions than those upon which a linear world view were based. The prior focus on "chaotic dynamics" has been subsumed in the past two decades or so by the sciences of complexity and complex systems, whereby chaotic dynamics have to be understood as being only a part of a more encompassing set of processes governed by principles of emergence, self-organization and self-organized criticality.

Research by Kauffman (1993, 2000), Holland and Miller (1991) and others is consistent with the findings noted above. It is also worth pointing out that, paralleling these new perspectives in the physical, natural and social sciences, the earlier fundamental paradigm shift in mathematics was critical. Gödel's startling revelations as to the incompleteness of certain formal systems and the parallel research by Church and Turing regarding the limits of computability added to the new perspective, as we discuss later.

The complexity sciences, as do all sciences, seek to identify stable patterns and universal behavior across known systems to enhance basic knowledge and better confront, if not solve, human problems. The inherent diffusion of knowledge within disciplines and the balkanization created by these disciplinary boundaries require new approaches that can be provided by the complexity sciences and its approaches to understanding a wide range of phenomena.

Since the publication of *Chaos Theory in the Social Sciences* in 1996, there have been important theoretical and applied breakthroughs in the area of what we refer to as complex adaptive systems (CAS). Today, what we used to call chaos theory—or, to be more precise, nonlinear chaotic dynamics—can be considered a subset of the larger and more expansive area of CAS. CAS—which are typically defined as phenomena characterized by many interacting parts where changes in one element of the system affect other elements—and the behavior of the system as a whole cannot be inferred from any of the individual components. CAS are capable of exhibiting behavior that is highly nonlinear and unpredictable but clearly cannot be described as random. This volume examines the still rapidly developing field of CAS, exploring topics such as emergent phenomena or the tendency for complex, ordered behaviors to emerge from very simple beginnings.

Complex Systems in the Social and Behavioral Sciences is organized into five sections. We discuss the chapters in more detail near the end of this introduction, but here we briefly describe the basic thrust of each. One might ask, why five sections? One obvious way of organizing the volume would be to simply provide a section on theory and a separate section on applications. However, given the expansion of research and the vibrant and variegated contributions by scholars from so many disciplinary and multidisciplinary areas, we thought it made sense to offer a more granular and nuanced structure for the volume. Of course, no organizational scheme is perfect, and given the nature of the research in complexity science with so many areas that overlap with each other, it is not possible to develop an organizational structure to the book that could not be challenged in some way. However, we think the contributions, for the most part, organize rather comfortably into five parts: (1) Social Systems Levels and Complexity; (2) Complexity, Computation and Artificial Intelligence; (3) Simulating Complexity: Agent-Based Modeling; (4) Scaling and Self-Organization; and (5) Philosophy of Science and Epistemology. These categories roughly correspond to what we view as some of the key broad research areas in the field and are consistent with the thrust of the individual contributions to this volume.

The title of this book refers to the application of complexity theory in the social and behavioral sciences, yet readers will notice below that our contributors address topics that range from our understanding of diabetes and obesity to the dynamics of insect colonies, to discussions of computational issues and artificial intelligence (AI). One might plausibly ask, why these topics in this particular research effort? However, the study of CAS over the years is replete with efforts to demonstrate what has been called the "unity of knowledge." It is the idea that all fields can be understood, at least at some level, within certain overarching theoretical frameworks. This is in part what entomologist Edward O. Wilson (1998) meant by the term "consilience," which was also the name of his book in which he discussed the importance of achieving a common understanding among and across all scientific fields. In other words, what Wilson and others have advocated is a true interdisciplinary or transdisciplinary approach to understanding phenomena, whether we would describe them as being in the natural or social worlds, or for that matter whether they lie in abstract areas of mathematics or computer science.

The organization of this volume proceeds as follows: the first part, Social Systems Levels and Complexity, addresses the issues of complexity and its role in better understanding human interactions at different levels of analysis. This section explores applications of complexity sciences at the group, organizational and supra-national levels. The chapters by Stephen Guastello and Kevin Dooley offer important contributions to the study of organizational behavior. While Guastello (chapter 1) examines different types of group dynamics within what is known as the Nonlinear Dynamical Systems (NDS) framework, Dooley (chapter 2) explores how complexity science has been applied in a range of fields and applications in the organizational and management literatures. The third chapter in this part is Maxime Stauffer's contribution on the importance of complexity science for understanding the nature of armed conflict between international and intra-national actors as he explores the variegated and rich literature in this area. His contribution helps us to understand complex system-level effects at the level of the nation-state and the "international" system.

Part two, Complexity, Computation and Artificial Intelligence, addresses issues of computation and artificial intelligence and their relationship to CAS. Here, the work of Sheri Markose and Cassey Lee, using cellular automata theory, offers some very important insights. Markose (chapter 4) explores how novelty production among digital agents is possible. Importantly, Markose argues that conditions from classical recursive theory are found only in digital genomic systems and are not yet a part of artificial intelligence, although this bio-inspired genomic machinery might someday be adapted by AI systems. Our other contributor in this area, Cassey Lee (chapter 5), demonstrates crucial insights into artificial intelligence, bounded rationality and decision-making. The intersection between CAS and computation, and artificial intelligence, is among the most important topics in the literature, and it addresses important questions of the nature of intelligence and the limits of computation.

While the first two parts address broad-gauge theoretical concerns, beginning with part three, Simulating Complexity, we pivot to more applied areas in which CAS offers important insights. One critically important methodology for studying CAS is agent-based modeling (ABM). With the vast expansion in computing power and software development we have witnessed over the last few decades, simulation using ABM and other related approaches, such as cellular automata, has become an impressive tool for researchers. ABM is basically specifying, for each "agent"—which are merely lines of computer code—certain behaviors that the agent will perform under particular conditions and when interacting with other agents. ABM exemplifies, in many respects, the notion of complexity emerging from very simple rules. In other words, it represents the process of "emergence." Two of our chapters are devoted to ABM. Chapter 6, by L. Douglas Kiel, John McCaskill, James Harrington and Euel Elliott, provides a broad overview of ABM and introduces the reader to the topic. The next chapter (7), by Saikou Diallo, Christopher Lynch, Jose Padilla and Ross Gore, utilizes a very large number of agents to examine patterns in obesity and possible future public policies for its mitigation and prevention. The point here is that modeling with very large numbers of agents provides for a more granular analysis that might be missed if fewer agents with fewer possibilities specified for interaction were employed.

Part four, Scaling and Self-Organization, addresses issues related to the mathematical properties of CAS. To what extent can the phenomenon of scaling, by which complex systems exhibit self-similar behavior, be of use in understanding other phenomena? What do allometric relationships tell us about scaling and CAS? Bruce West (chapter 8) sheds important new light on this highly relevant area of concern for the social and behavioral, and indeed, the living sciences, while William Sulis (chapter 9) focuses on the important question of collective intelligence and the issue of emergence. We discuss the individual contributions to this volume below in more detail. However, in an effort to tie the themes discussed in individual chapters with some of the broader questions in the extant research, we offer a more expansive discussion of what we consider some of the more interesting questions in the complexity literature that serve to illustrate the breadth and depth of current work and, at the same time, are relevant to many of the chapters in this volume.

The final section of *Complex Systems in the Social and Behavioral Sciences* concerns itself with broader issues of epistemology and philosophy of science within the context of complex adaptive systems. How do CAS affect our ability to acquire knowledge? What special insights can we glean in this area by studying such systems? The chapter by Patrick Grim, Joshua Kavner, Lloyd Shatkin and Manjari Trivedi (chapter 10), and the contribution by J. Barkley Rosser, Jr. (chapter 11) address crucial epistemological and ontological issues. Finally, Carlos Maldonado (chapter 12) discusses hypercomputation and how biological entities force us to think beyond our traditional assumptions of computation and learning. Maldonado makes the case that creativity and innovation are non-algorithmic in character.

What are Complex Adaptive Systems?

The study of what are commonly referred to as complex adaptive systems is relevant for understanding a sweeping array of phenomena in the behavioral, life and social sciences. The presence of complex systems poses unique challenges for scholars studying CAS and seeking a better understanding of their dynamics at different levels of aggregation. CAS also pose important challenges for those who seek clarity on important issues related to computational complexity.

CAS are typically characterized by multiple entities (sometimes termed actors or agents) interacting in dynamic ways consistent with evolutionary principles as their behavior adapts and evolves over time in response to their environment and the behavior of other actors or agents. Moreover, CAS are characterized by complex, macro-level phenomena emerging from interactions occurring at the level of the individual agents. This implies that CAS can exhibit self-organizing and emergent behavior. This behavior is self-organizing in the sense that the behavior of the system is not pre-determined or otherwise guided through some top-down, hierarchical control mechanism; it is emergent in that the behaviors arise from the functioning of the system itself and do not rely on any external agents or forces in order to evolve. There are numerous examples of CAS, including the biosphere (Hinkelmann et al. 2011), many kinds of group-based behaviors (Axelrod 1981, 1987, 1997), cultures, various aspects of global economic dynamics (Dawid and Neugart 2011), international politics (Cederman 1997) and segregation dynamics (Schelling 1971), among others (see Bonabeau 2002).

The interactions taking place within a CAS may be simple or complex (or more frequently both), but they are always abundant and typically characterized by complex, nonlinear feedback processes. CAS typically operate in non-equilibrium conditions and thus are constantly evolving into new states rather than simply maintaining the status quo. Many CAS also exhibit self-similar or fractal properties. In other words, CAS phenomena are frequently scale-invariant (i.e., patterns observed at the micro-scale are replicated at the macro-scale; see Mandelbrot 1997). Thus, scaling patterns and relationships are an important aspect of the literature on complex systems. Bruce West's chapter on allometric patterns is indicative of this research.

Importantly, CAS are characterized by positive feedback processes that run counter to the more typical negative feedback effects with which we are familiar (G. West 2017, 299). Common negative feedback systems involve the muting of signals over time (i.e., the consequences of some action or event reduce as that action or event recedes into the past). In contrast, at least some of the feedback processes taking place within CAS exhibit positive feedback, where consequences become more significant over time or, in other words, where the signal is amplified rather than muted, as would be the case with negative feedback. This is important because scholars in the social and other sciences have tended to think in terms of linear, negative feedback regimes.

All of the above is well-known to nearly all behavioral and social scientists, most of whom work in one fashion or another with the normal distribution or its progeny on a daily basis. The difficulty that arises for those of us who are interested in CAS is that the statistical properties of such phenomena do not necessarily reflect those of the normal distribution. The fact that CAS, or perhaps one should say the agents or components of CAS, are interacting with each other through various feedback processes means that observations are not independent—one observation depends upon the properties of other observations. A common feature of CAS is that the statistical distributions that best describes such phenomena are fat-tailed (Mandelbrot 1997; Johansen and Sornette 2001). Such distributions have important implications for assessing risk, including those in financial markets (Taleb 2007) and geopolitical risks (Bremmer and Keat 2009). An important point to be made about fat-tailed distributions is that some of these distributions exhibit yet another property: evidence suggests that certain phenomena exhibit a power law decay in their tails. Power laws describe a functional relationship between two quantities so that a one-unit change in one quantity results in a proportional change in another quantity, independent of the initial size. It appears that a very large number of phenomena can be described by power laws over a wide range of magnitudes. Allometric scaling laws among biological variables are among the best-known scaling laws in nature (West, Brown, and Enquist 1997). Within the social and behavioral sciences, the population size of cities has been famously described as exhibiting a power law function (Newman 2005).

Agent-Based Modeling: Simulating Complexity

The nature of CAS requires new ways of thinking about how to better understand and model their behavior. Agent-based modeling provides one such approach and is discussed in greater detail in the chapter by Kiel, McCaskill, Harrington and Elliott. Another approach is through the application of cellular automata (CA), which is addressed later in this chapter and in the contributions by Lee and Markose, and which are extensively discussed in Wolfram (2012). Both CAS and ABM focus on multiple agents interacting with their environment and with one another, both allow for complex feedback loops that impact future agent behaviors, and both allow the behavior of the system to evolve from the conglomeration of the actions of the individual agents. These similarities make ABM a natural choice for modeling CAS.

ABM consists of agents interacting in simulated time and space. In the object-oriented computer programming motif, agents are simply instances of an object of type "agent." An ABM can consist of multiple types of agents, and there can be one (or more) instance of each type of agent. Each agent has certain properties that can change over time, or as a result of some action taken by the agent, or as a result of interactions with other agents and their environment. Epstein and Axtell (1996) provide an excellent introduction to ABM and the construction of simple artificial societies. A more expansive discussion is seen in Epstein (1999; 1997).[1]

Each agent in an ABM exhibits a certain behavior based on its current properties and the ways it is currently interacting with other agents and its surrounding environment. Changes in agent behavior can reflect learning on the part of the agent. Note that most ABMs employ at least some amount of stochasticity; while many agent properties and behaviors are largely deterministic, others are allowed to include random elements.

---

1. Another very well-known application of ABM has come to be known as the Anasazi project (Axtell et al. 2002). This model was developed to generate insights into the disappearance of the Anasazi Indians who lived in the US Southwest for hundreds (or possibly thousands) of years until their disappearance prior to the arrival of Europeans. Using ABM, researchers have developed extremely useful and insightful explanations of how the complex interplay of culture and environment explain the disappearance of the Anasazi. These explanations may not have been generated using more traditional social science methodologies.

These random variations are employed to capture the vagaries of the real world.

Other research has focused on the emergence of actors in the international system, as well as other political processes and interactions (Cederman 1997). Agent-based models have yielded new insights into dynamics and have led many economists to rethink the methodological underpinnings of their field. Some scholars, such as Velupillai (2010), have called for a fundamental revolution in economics that would move the field away from the traditional deductive and mathematically formalized framework toward a computable and algorithmic foundation. Agent-based models could play a key role in any such computable foundation, given the generative and emergent properties of such simulations (see Epstein 2006).

ABMs also have important implications from a classical computation perspective. As Epstein (1999) emphasizes, agent-based models may provide insights into "hard" social problems that are not effectively computable in polynomial time. We discuss the issue of computability and the ability or inability to compute certain problems later in our discussion of the P-NP problem. We note, however, that Axtell (2005), whose work we discuss later, uses agent-based models to demonstrate that certain market equilibrium solutions are computationally hard; in other words, they cannot be computed in polynomial time.

ABMs are not without their critics. A fundamental criticism of ABMs and simulation in general is that simulation model formulations and outcomes are not typically given in mathematical terms, thus making it difficult to bring the tools of mathematical analysis to bear. But as Epstein (2006) notes in an important contribution, the distinction between agent-based and equation-based models is illusory (see also Hinkelmann et al. 2011). Epstein (2006) observes that every ABM is a computer program and, as such, is Turing computable. Therefore, "for every Turing machine there is a unique corresponding and equivalent partial recursive function" (55). These functions are usually highly complex and so difficult to interpret that analysis of them is seldom productive; nevertheless, they do exist. Consequently, ABMs (and, as Epstein argues, generative models in general) are indeed deductive, but deductive models are not necessarily generative in character (Epstein 1999, 44).

Generative social science, or small-world simulation, makes no assumptions regarding a singular, correct worldview. There is no reality outside of the agents and the world that has been created, and within which agents and their world coevolve. ABM allows for the modeling of individual agents whereby each agent is essentially computer code specifying the possible behavior of the agent in the presence of different environments and different agents (Dean and Elliott 2017a). ABM assumes that each agent has only a "local observer view," in which agents respond to adjacent agents and the immediate environment. Moreover, as noted above, agents are capable of using decision rules that relax traditional assumptions of classical logic (Borrill and Tesfatsion 2011, 230). In particular, it is not necessary in this world for the Law of the Excluded Middle to strictly apply (see Brouwer 1913; Dean and Elliott 2017b). Agents can simultaneously believe A, not A, or they can be uncertain. We suggest that agents could, in theory, possess contradictory beliefs about a topic, just as individuals in the real world can hold contradictory beliefs. So there needs to be a means of accounting for such phenomena. As Borrill and Tesfatsion (2011) note,

> ABM agents can have uncomputable beliefs about their world that influence their interactions. These uncomputable beliefs can arise from inborn (initially configured) attributes, from communications received from other agents, and/or from the use of non-constructive methods. … These uncomputable beliefs enable agents to make creative leaps, to come up with new ideas about their world.
>
> (230–231)

ABM allows us to utilize elements of nonstandard logic and mathematics. To date there have been, with a few notable exceptions (including Borrill and Tesfatsion 2011; Chaitin, Doria, and da Costa 2012; Koppl et al. 2014; Velupillai 2005, 2007, 2010), suggestions that the behavioral and social sciences could benefit from incorporating new perspectives drawing from non-classical logic and mathematics. We make the case that allowing for the incorporation of nonstandard perspectives can provide new insights into the study of CAS. Smolin (2001) recognized that multiple observers trying to understand such phenomena face the problem of the "god's eye view" perspective versus a "local observer view" perspective in which any observer can only have knowledge about phenomena in their immediate space (Smolin 2001; Borrill and Tesfatsion 2011).

Future research endeavors may benefit from a greater appreciation of intuitionist logic and constructivist mathematics and how they contribute to the study of CAS by offering more realistic standards of proof than would otherwise be the case under classical logic. It is clear, as Smolin (2001) notes, in advocating the application of topos theory to the social sciences, that:

> Here in the real world we almost always reason with incomplete information. Each day we encounter statements whose truth or falsity can be derived on the basis of what we know. ... We recognize, almost explicitly, that different observers have access to different information. ...We also allow ourselves to change our minds or become convinced of a new proposition without adding information to our set of observations.
>
> (31)

Although it is beyond the purview of this essay, topos theory extends and deepens the earlier advances made in intuitionist logic described above (Smolin 2001). Generally speaking, a topos (or topoi) is a type of category that behaves like a category of sheaves of sets on a topological space, where a sheaf provides a means of formalizing the description of a problem in a topological space even where a "true" topological foundation is lacking. Topos theory may also have important implications for understanding a range of human interactions and offer important insights that may not be available under certain classical assumptions.

In addition, category and graph theory are making important contributions to a constructivist-derived social sciences. The former allows us to develop an understanding of the equivalence between one category of sets and another, and how applications ranging from biology to music and philosophy have important topos-theoretic content (Leinster 2014). Graph theory also contains important topos-theoretic elements. It is a crucial mathematical tool in the treatment of network theory and is useful in developing a deeper understanding of agent-based modeling (Borill and Tesfatsion 2011). Graph theory has important connections to the conundrum of the polynomial versus nondeterministic polynomial time problem, or the P-NP problem (Bondy and Murty 2008), discussed later in this chapter.

Gödel, Turing and Complexity

Issues of computation and its limits and artificial intelligence are increasingly important elements of our understanding of CAS. The pathbreaking work of Gödel, Turing, Church and others fundamentally shaped our understanding of computational complexity and its implications. Gödel and Turing each approached the problem of computability from different directions, yet their joint contributions to understanding the fundamental ability to comprehend the nature of reality is immense. Gödel proved that not all problems in mathematics that have an arithmetic foundation are provable within the framework of that system (see Chaitin, Doria, and da Costa 2012; Dawson 1997; van Heijinoort 1967; Doria 2017).

Gödel's breakthrough provided a crucial foundation for Turing (1937b), who demonstrated that there are limits to the ability of any computer (what he termed "decision problems") to solve certain mathematical problems using deterministic algorithmic routines. No computational device, or what Turing called a Turing machine, could compute certain algorithmically expressed problems and at the same time be able to provide a rigorous proof of the results. Any problem can be solved, if given enough time, in terms of this binary logic. Turing proved any problem could be computed, but, consistent with Gödel, a proof of the accuracy of the computation was beyond the ability of the universal computer.

We know that some problems are computationally more complex than others. While an extended discussion of P-NP is beyond the purview of this volume, it should be noted that it is one of the outstanding unsolved problems in mathematics, and probably the single most outstanding problem in the area of computational theory. The P-NP problem has to do with the solvability of certain kinds of problems within certain time parameters by a computer. Some tractable problems (P) can be solved in polynomial time where the running time of the computer is upper-bounded by a polynomial expression in the size of the input for the algorithm. In other words, a general algorithm for the problem can be devised. In contrast, NP, or non-deterministic polynomial problems, allow for a correct answer to be verified, although no general algorithmic routine is known to exist (Cobham 1965; Ladner 1975; Kleinberg and Tardos 2006, 464). Among the NP-type problems are those designated NP-hard, or the most computationally difficult to solve, and among NP-hard problems are those designated as NP-complete. Were a general algorithm or solution to be identified for them, it would mean all such problems could be solved using a general algorithm.[2]

There are important implications for policymakers related to the P-NP problem. As da Costa and Doria (2005) point out, the central problem of economic planning is the allocation problem. Yet, they show it is impossible to compute the equilibrium price ahead of time. It is impossible for an efficient global policymaker to exist. Equilibrium can be reached, but it is not possible to know *a priori* what that equilibrium point might be. Markets work, however, because it is not necessary to compute *a priori* equilibrium in advance since markets evolve toward equilibrium. This is in contrast to the social planner who must have advanced knowledge of their subject (see also Velupillai 2007).

While it may not be possible for a single social engineer or Walrasian auctioneer to compute a market equilibrium price in a Walrasian model of an exchange economy, other possibilities exist. Axtell (2005) demonstrates that the prevalence of decentralized exchange overcomes the problem of computational intractability where only the price of a single good is computed. Axtell utilizes agent-based modeling in drawing his conclusions and illustrates the important links between ABM and issues of computational complexity involving the P-NP problem. However, in an economy with literally millions of goods, it seems unlikely that any polynomial solution could ever be found. The problems posed by computational complexity are very similar to those described by Hayek (1948) and what he called the problem of knowledge in society (77–91). There can, according to Hayek, be no effective central economic planner because the knowledge necessary for effective planning is dispersed over countless individuals and organizations.

---

2. A finding that P and NP are equivalent would strengthen the arguments of those who believe that the foundations of artificial intelligence exist in the ability to develop algorithmic procedures for the solution to problems (i.e., intelligence tends to be of an algorithmic character). Conversely, a finding that P is not in NP would clearly set back that line of thinking. Importantly, da Costa, Doria and Bir (2007) offer a fundamentally different approach to the problem and suggest that P = NP is consistent at a meta-mathematical level with Peano arithmetic. They expect that a proof of the consistency of P = NP formalized within a powerful axiomatic system will be provided (da Costa, Doria, and Bir 2007, 1239).

Issues of computational limits also have major implications at the level of individual decision-making. Humans make decisions under extraordinarily complex environmental contexts and thus are confronted with truly daunting challenges. The standard argument made by mainstream economists has been the utility maximization model (Becker 1976). A mainstay of economic analysis for much of the twentieth century, it assumes that individuals have the computational skills to be able to optimize in whatever environment they find themselves. Such optimizing requires adherence on the part of the decision-maker to certain canons of logic, including, critically, the ability to select a maximal set of alternatives. But do most of us, at least under many circumstances, behave in this fashion? How do we actually decide? The traditional approach assumes, at least for the sake of mathematical tractability, that individuals exhibit a comprehensive, or unbounded, rationality in which utility maximization lays at the heart of the mainstream economists' toolkit of assumptions.

The preceding discussion suggests that an alternative approach to decision-making is necessary, and that it should be grounded in computational complexity theory. Over the last few decades, the standard model of economists has been challenged. Beginning with the work of Herbert Simon (1955, 1957), who pioneered research into human decision-making, and continuing through the work of Kahneman and Tversky (1979, 1996) and later Gigerenzer (2008a, (2008b; Gigerenzer and Brighton 2009), alternative models have been proposed that can be described as cognitive behavioral economics. The finer details of this research are beyond the scope of this paper. However, the fundamental assumption of all these models is that individuals possess cognitive limitations. It says that individuals act with agency, but the complexity of the task environment creates challenges that our cognitive architecture cannot handle. Thus, we develop alternative strategies for decision-making. For example, we limit the number of alternatives from which to choose; we develop satisficing rather than maximizing strategies. Relatedly, we develop cues or heuristic devices (cognitive roadmaps) to guide our decision-making due to the fundamental constraints of human cognition, time and informational resources.

Velupillai and Kao (2014) argue that Simon's overall approach to cognitive behavioral economics is "underpinned by a model of computation, highlighting the complexity of chemical decision processes on the basis of computational complexity theory" (40). They show how theorems developed by Simon provide a foundation for understanding the cognitive constraints individuals face with regard to bounded rationality (i.e., the complexity of the problems faced is greater than the individual's ability to solve those problems). The use of satisficing rather than optimizing strategies, the use of procedural as opposed to substantive rationality, and the reliance upon heuristics, or "cognitive roadmaps," for decision-making are critical features of alternative approaches to the traditional utility-maximization model.

Importantly for our purposes, we can hypothesize that the time constraints imposed on individuals reflect the constraints imposed by NP problems—the very definition of NP (that certain problems cannot be computed using an efficient algorithm in some tractable amount of time). Also, complexity issues arise not just from the standpoint of time complexity but from space complexity as well. That is, "the amount of information minds can process at a given moment is severely limited" (Velupillai and Kao 2014, 48).

Another important related area that has implications for individual decision-making is Valiant's (1984, 2013) research in "probably approximately correct" or PAC learnability. Based upon Valiant's pathbreaking research, PAC learnability integrates machine learning, evolutionary theory and computational complexity. Valiant argues that evolution can be explained as algorithms that interact with and benefit from their environment. For instance, the human genome evolves in ways that allow us to interact with our environment, but the process is accelerated by natural algorithms that improve the prospects for survivability. These algorithms accelerate evolution and do so in ways that can be solved in polynomial (P) time. These mutations are in contrast to other features of evolutionary learning that impose greater burdens on learning and that may be NP, or that require much greater computational capacity. The way we make decisions today is based on a long process of natural selection in which certain algorithms for learning are favored over others.

Gilboa, Postlewaite and Schmeidler (2008) suggest, unlike standard assumptions, that people have probabilistic beliefs over any source of uncertainty (consistent with Bayesianism): "There are many instances in which people adjust their beliefs in the face of arguments that do not present new information but suggest that different conclusions should be drawn from the same body of knowledge" (186; see also Aragones et al. 2005).

Moreover, due to computational complexity problems, such learning may be unavoidable even with rational agents. Since we are not only observers within the world we seek to describe, but also participants capable of affecting the truth or falsity of statements we make about the world, a new approach to standards of proof is worthy of consideration.

While the notion that certain processes, both market and otherwise, cannot be described algorithmically might seem disappointing, it is actually the opposite (Koppl et al. 2014). The absence of algorithmic approaches forces new ways of thinking and enables new ideas. In this sense, Koppl et al.'s (2014) arguments are very similar to those of Maldonado. Markose's research (2004, 2017) also addresses the question of actor innovation and novelty production. She shows how a heavy dose of mechanism is needed in the form of Gödel meta-mathematics, which permit computational agents involved in an adversarial game to implement a novelty or surprise in the form of a syntactic object that lies outside enumerable sets as the Nash Equilibrium of the game. While more will be said in the later discussion of Markose's chapter, it is critical to note that Markose identifies the *sine qua non* of CAS with the Type IV dynamics of the Wolfram–Chomsky schema whereby only systems capable of producing novelty qualify to be CAS.

Beyond the Classical Turing Machine

We have assumed in this essay that all computation is consistent with traditional Turing machines and that computation is done within a closed-box transformation of inputs consisting of random numbers or finite strings into outputs. According to the orthodox view, such machines capture all computation. This view, the strong Church–Turing Thesis, rejects the possibility that other kinds of machines more expressive than Turing machines are possible.

Some theorists argue that hypercomputation that goes beyond the abilities of a Turing machine are possible. Such hypercomputers might be able to compute solutions to problems such as NP-hard problems or perhaps even problems considered non-computable. Such hypercomputation systems might take different forms, ranging from quantum computers, whereby the traditional logic that a logic gate can only take one position at a time—"one" or "zero," "yes" or "no"—to allowing it to be in both positions simultaneously. Such a computational device could, in theory, easily compute problems that would otherwise be unsolvable. Other approaches that are consistent with hypercomputation incorporate the idea of interactive computing. Rather than the closed box view of computing consistent with the traditional Turing machine, computation is an ongoing interactive process. Communication with the outside world occurs during computation, not before or after computation. Some (e.g., Goldin and Wegner 2008) argue that such interactive computing radically reinterprets the strong Church–Turing Thesis. Such a theoretical framework is also consistent with the concept of biological hypercomputation—that living systems are essentially computational systems that go beyond Turing computation. This "non-classical" hypercomputation incorporates the concept of an organism's interacting with its environment. It must be noted that Markose (2017, and the present volume) categorically abjures an anti-machine view of novelty production and indeed shows that immuno-cognitive systems manifest conditions that embed Gödelian incompleteness, thereby permitting endogenous novelty production.

Hypercomputation might very well be capable of computing market processes (Bartholo et al. 2009; Maldonado and Gómez 2014). Hence, we might be able to determine *a priori* algorithmic procedures for computing market equilibrium. The critical question that arises is, can such machines perfectly emulate interactions that generate novelty and creativity? Does the very act of computing certain heretofore non-algorithmic processes disrupt, in some fashion, the creative process as described by Koppl et al. (2014)? Or, could such a system emulate or possibly even improve upon the creation of novelty and creativity?

Another intriguing concept is whether markets, and perhaps other social processes, are not themselves hypercomputers, only we—at this stage of our technology—are unable to recognize them as hypercomputation. Hence, one could argue that markets are essentially hypercomputers computing themselves. Of course, this thinking runs us into some very deep issues relating to the problem of self-reference, which does not go away merely because of vastly expanded computational ability. In other words, the problems identified by Gödel do not disappear in the presence of a hypercomputational environment.

This is not to say that other kinds of social or biological systems might not be computable. One could certainly imagine that ant colonies and other highly organized insect societies may possess attributes that would allow the evolution of their worlds to be computable. Indeed, any non-human society, the behavior of whose agents are highly deterministic due to evolutionary and environmental pressures, may be computable in ways that human societies are not, or at least may possess attributes that are computationally tractable (i.e., can be computed in polynomial time, at least over some limited, finite time period).

Overview of Chapters

Part I: Social Systems Levels and Complexity

From an intellectual history perspective, the current study of complex systems must be viewed as a continuation of the study of and lessons learned from the evolution of general systems theory (von Bertalanffy 1968). General systems theory offers a means to examine the hierarchy of living systems ranging from the expression of genes to the global system of nation-states (Miller 1978). Perhaps it is this seemingly infinite assemblage of systems and system levels that produces both the complexity and the intractability of the social and behavioral sciences. It is a primary challenge of these fields to connect and understand the interactions between the micro (group), meso (organizational) and macro (supra-national) levels of analysis. The three chapters in this section of the book examine each of these levels of analysis.

During the early days of the exploration of chaos theory in the social sciences in the 1990s, organizational thinkers began to apply that paradigm to topics ranging from organizational strategy (Stacey 1992), to organizational change (Kiel 1993) to the adaptive requirements of organizations themselves (Dooley 1997). The evolution of this thinking toward a more comprehensive model of the sciences of complexity has now generated a large body of literature in the organizational sciences. Much of this literature focuses on the challenges of change in an increasingly complex world. The contributions in this volume examining systemic, group and organizational dynamics by Stephen Guastello, Kevin Dooley and Maxime Stauffer reveal the analytical tools now available to us via the complexity paradigm and a broader view of how this paradigm has influenced the literature of organizational management.

Stephen Guastello's "Group Dynamics: Adaptation, Coordination and Synchronization" captures three components of group dynamics for which nonlinear dynamic processes have been studied recently, all of which involve group performance: adaptive behavior, team coordination and workload physiological synchronization. The chapter begins with a general theme that group performance contains inherent variability that results from underlying deterministic processes. The principle of optimum variability reflects the right amount of variability needed to adapt to a wide range of circumstances and involves an interplay between the minimum entropy principle and Ashby's Law of Requisite Variety. The dynamics of each group component are examined, and the implications for our understanding of human groups as complex adaptive systems are discussed. Guastello's work represents the archetype of the application of experiments and emerging analytical tools to understand the nonlinear dynamics of human group interactions.

Kevin Dooley's chapter, "Complexity Science and the Organizational Sciences: 1999–2018," explores applications of complexity science to organizational change and adaptation. Dooley examines how complexity science has been interpreted and applied in terms of organizational change, leadership, strategy, marketing and communications as well as supply chain management, entrepreneurship and management information systems. Using Kuhn and Abbott's models of scientific and disciplinary evolution, he illustrates differences between different disciplines in terms of how the complex systems framework is utilized, and its implications for the future.

The use of CAS as a framework for studying armed conflict has a substantial history. Maxime Stauffer explores the issue in "Complexity Science and the Study of Armed Conflict: A Narrative Review." Armed conflict is notoriously difficult to study. Combined with the paucity of reliable, timely and sufficiently disaggregated data amenable to comparison across units, conflicts are typically characterized by multiple, heterogeneous actors, social ties and group allegiances that shape and are, in turn, shaped by violence, population movements, the absence of clear front lines (particularly in the case of now widespread intra-state war), and a diverse set of causal factors that by no means remain constant.

Stauffer argues that these factors bear all the hallmarks of a complex system. This chapter begins by exploring why complexity science lends itself to the study of armed conflict, and then goes on to survey the contributions—past, present and future—made by complexity science in this domain. Stauffer traces the application of complexity theory, beginning with seminal work on power laws of wars in the 1960s, conflict outbreak and chaos, and "world models," to today's evidence-driven agent-based models. He also examines potential future applications of complexity science to the study of armed conflict, demonstrating how the progression of approaches may be understood as a logical reaction to the evolution of armed conflict itself, innovations in data collection and analysis, and a clear trade-off between increased knowledge about specific cases—now far more complex—and generalizability.

Part 2: Complexity, Computation and Artificial Intelligence

As we discussed earlier in the chapter, there are many aspects of computation related to the study of complex systems, and they are relevant to our understanding of artificial intelligence. Complex systems can themselves be described as computations, and in many cases, they can be described by a computer program of a given length. The longer the program, the more "complex" the system that is being described. This does not necessarily mean that the system is more difficult to compute because caching allows for a computer program to run more efficiently—certain repeated routines can be handled with less effort in a system that retains certain information. The earlier discussion of the P-NP problem describes the difficulty in finding general solutions to algorithms that may describe important elements of a complex system.

While artificial intelligence is obviously related to computational capabilities, they are not one and the same. AI may be described as belonging to a subset of computational capabilities by some system. Computing power does not equal intelligence; thus, one of the most fascinating aspects of the study of CAS is the question of how AI, as defined by the ability to perform in ways that go beyond predetermined lines of code, can be attained. How can complex systems compute in ways that yield surprises and innovation? Given that complex systems are themselves phenomena that exhibit uncertainty and surprise in their behavior and evolution, how can our understanding of computation, and even AI, tell us more about these systems?

The first contribution in this section is the chapter by Sheri Markose, titled "Novelty Production and Evolvability in Digital Genomic

Agents: Logical Foundations and Policy Design Implications of Complex Adaptive Systems." We know that novelty and innovation, or "surprises" that defy prior behavior or processes, are common in biological and human systems. But while novelty production is consistent with the behavior of complex adaptive systems, there is no consensus on what exactly provides the mechanism for allowing novelty to be produced. Markose seeks to provide answers to these questions. She abjures, contrary to Maldonado, an anti-machine view of novelty production and contends that it is not necessary to go beyond classical recursive function theory and Gödel's incompleteness result to achieve novelty production consistent with her findings regarding genomic systems. Extending her research (Markose 2004, 2017) where she has shown that the Gödel-Turing-Post (G-T-P) conditions are critical for understanding novelty in varying contexts, Markose shows how the G-T-P conditions for self-reference and self-representation necessary for the encoding of the Liar (rule-breakers) can lead to a digital agent engaging in innovation by reporting itself to be under attack. Thus, systems established on the basis of predictable, deterministic rules are subject to demise by the archetype of the Liar, who can negate or falsify what can be predicted.

Markose shows that only in a consistent formal arrangement, what she calls a G-T-P cognitive system, can there be an endogenous production of surprises or innovations. This takes the form of an arms race in which the adversaries coevolve new phenotypes. Parties cannot withdraw from coevolution and pre-commit to predictable rules without being wiped out. What is especially compelling about her contribution is her demonstration of its relevance to Kantian principles of political economy and the systemic failures evident in the financial crisis of 2007–2008, and how authorities' commitment to fixed rules, consistent with her theoretical findings, gave the rule-breakers (Liars) opportunities to game the system.

The purpose of Cassey Lee's chapter, "The Game of Go: Bounded Rationality and Artificial Intelligence," is to examine the nature and relationship between bounded rationality and artificial intelligence. Within the context of recent developments in the application of artificial intelligence to two-person games with perfect information, such as Go, Lee incorporates bounded rationality assumptions into his models. This is an assumption that is not typically made in such game theoretic models, but that adds a critical element of realism to the games, given that bounded rationality is inextricably linked to the nature of the problem to be solved. Thus, Lee draws upon the findings of Simon (1955), Kahneman and Tversky (1979, 1996) and Thaler (2018) among others in developing his models. Using CA, he shows that the undecidability of CA evolution suggests that, even though artificial intelligence programs may achieve superhuman capabilities in games like Go, it is not possible for them to solve the game in a way that produces global optimality. Lee's conclusions have important insights into the nature of rationality and of artificial intelligence. It should be noted that both Markose and Lee utilize the Wolfram-Chomsky Type IV cellular automata dynamic in framing their arguments (see Markose 2004, 2017).

Part 3: Simulating Complexity: Agent-Based Modeling

Social scientists have endeavored to simulate complex social relations at least since the early days of the rise of modern computing. Jay W. Forrester's groundbreaking work in the 1960s examined the emergent dynamics that may drive the expansion and contraction of industrial (1961) and urban systems (1969) and helped set the stage for the advances in simulation that would come later.

The rise of agent-based approaches to social simulation in the 1990s offered a means to use the framework of the complexity of emergent behaviors and the adaptive nature of complex adaptive systems to develop "artificial societies" in a computer. Improvements in software technologies in both the application development side and in the production of graphics greatly expanded applications of the field of agent-based simulation. We can now think of "complexity in a bottle," as such simulations seek to develop evolutionary agents adapting to social landscapes and creating emergent and novel behavior. The rise of rigorous agent-based modeling evidenced in journals, such as the *Journal of Artificial Societies and Social Simulation*, is now an essential element of the study of complex social systems.

The chapter by Kiel, McCaskill, Harrington and Elliott in this volume, "Agent-Based Modeling: Challenges and Prospects," explores current challenges and prospects for agent-based modeling. Issues of verification and validation remain essential challenges for the production and outcomes of ABM. The challenge of embedding learning into agent behavior to invoke increased realism into simulations creates new opportunities to establish realistic dynamics in these simulated environments. The real possibilities of applying big data, and even data from human biosensors, may add to the dynamism and realism of agent-based modeling. While agent-based modeling has yet to reach its potential as a source of public policy information, better coordination with the public policy community may help to enhance the prospects for ABM as a means for moving from simulation to practical policymaking.

Diallo, Lynch, Padilla and Gore, in their chapter "An Agent-Based Model of Obesity and Policy Implications," use a very large agent-based model to examine overweight and obesity variations in adults. To demonstrate the utility of modeling and simulation for future policy, the authors present a computational model of overweight and obesity in adults as a function of energy intake and energy expenditure to examine future policies for obesity prevention. Energy intake depends on the type and quantity of food that individuals choose to eat. Energy expenditure is largely dependent on one's desire to exercise, type of work, choice of travel method and access to recreational facilities. While preferences exist, individuals are usually limited to the food and exercise opportunities they have access to at home and at work or within a certain distance from these places. The authors apply this model to all fifty states in the United States to identify families of policies capable of reducing obesity and overweight levels in the next thirty years for each state. The model suggests that, while each state needs its own policy, workplace-mandated exercise combined with active travel means are the factors with the greatest potential for reducing the obese and overweight populations.

Part 4: Scaling and Self-Organization

Two of the principal concepts of complex systems are scaling and self-organization. Scaling simply refers to how things change with size. For social and behavioral scientists, scaling involves the understanding and analysis of scaling issues ranging from small cities to large metropolitan areas; on the behavioral side, they include anything from the behavior of small groups to that of a nation-state. Scaling, as an analytical concept, seeks to identify the commonalities within a phenomenon between units at varying scales of size.

Self-organization refers to the tendency of complex systems to produce emergent behavior that, in itself, creates organization and novel structure.

The rise of a seemingly small urban area to become a large metropolitan city reveals a level of self-organization requiring history and energy to produce new forms of organization and complexity. The constituent parts of the metropolitan area each emerge via agreed-upon systems of transportation, culture and rules to create the organization of the metropolis. This collective intelligence, both tacit and explicit, serves to create novel, emergent forms of order.

A fundamental quest of all of science is to identify universal principles consistent across all phenomena of interest or even within a discipline. The study of complex systems also seeks to discover such universals. These universals, with regard to scale and self-organization, afford the complexity sciences multidisciplinary and interdisciplinary lenses to seek such universals across the boundaries of scientific disciplines. The chapters by Bruce West and William Sulis in this volume represent such efforts. Both West and Sulis use biological examples to examine the concepts of scaling and self-organization.

The relevance of these biological examples is their commonality with the realities of scaling in human phenomena, such as cities and organizations. West examines scaling phenomena in the heartbeats of mammals of various sizes to help us understand physiological scaling across species. Sulis explores the seemingly mindless behavior of ants to reveal how the apparently unguided behavior of individual ants results in the amazing self-organization of an ant colony. Self-organization occurs without any apparent guiding force. The ants act as individual agents, yet they produce organized complexity on various scales. This work hearkens back to Herbert Simon's (1969) earlier references about the similarities between the routine behaviors of ants and the routines of humans. We humans follow consistent paths in our daily activities: we rise in the morning and sleep at night and refuel on a timed and consistent basis. From a view from outer space, the routine pathways of humans and ants would not appear much different at all.

Bruce West's contribution, "It's About Time," provides a fascinating explanation of allometric phenomena. Allometry relations are ubiquitous across the sciences and their origins are as varied as the disciplines in which they have been uncovered. To briefly review, allometry explores the relationship of the body size of organisms to their shape, anatomy, physiology and behavior. It has both applied and theoretical elements. It explores the phenomenon of scaling, in which allometric patterns may follow certain kinds of statistical laws, including power laws. West explores the hypothesis that allometry is entailed by complexity, as manifest in the flow of information generated by the simultaneous—but unbalanced—growth in the functionality and size of a network. For concreteness we focus on the time experienced by processes in living systems and hypothesize that it is fundamentally different from the time governing physical processes in inanimate systems. The time experienced by a living system has been empirically shown to be tied to system size by means of an allometry relation—a nonlinear relation between physiologic time for an underling physiological process, such as the beating of the heart, and a living system's average total body mass. The generic form of allometry relations are shown to be dependent only on the scaling properties of the statistics, as determined by the fractional probability calculus and not by any specific interaction mechanism. The scaling solution to a fractional phase space equation, for the probability density in mass and time, is shown to entail such an allometry relation.

William Sulis's essay, "Lessons from Collective Intelligence," addresses what we observe as the appearance of apparently intelligent behavior, which emerges from the behavior of agents absent the existence of apparent top-down control or influence. The behaviors of insect colonies, such as bees or ants, represent prototypical examples. As Sulis points out, such collective behavior seems to occupy a kind of middle ground between mob-driven behavior and strict hierarchical control with a single decision-maker. Moreover, the individual agent within the collective may appear to act non-rationally even though the behavior of the collective seems highly rational, a finding that has led to a revolution of research into collective intelligence systems.

Sulis examines what we can learn from the behavior of natural and artificial collective intelligence systems, and how we can develop better theories of collective behavior within a CAS framework. Sulis's research is particularly interesting and important given the challenges posed by such systems to more "traditional" statistical methodologies, including differential and statistic differential equations. The development of formal models of behavior, including the Process Algebra and Fractal Functionality approaches, are critical to Sulis's arguments and illustrate the importance of theory development and hypothesis testing in this fascinating area of research.

Part 5: Philosophy of Science and Epistemology

We conclude *Complex Systems in the Social and Behavioral Sciences* with a discussion of the most wide-ranging philosophical elements of CAS theory. The chapter by Grim et al., "Philosophy of Science, Network Theory and Conceptual Change: Paradigm Shifts as Information Cascades," addresses some of the most critical philosophical issues related to CAS. Philosophers have long tried to understand scientific change in terms of a dynamic of revision within "theoretical frameworks," "disciplinary matrices," "scientific paradigms" or "conceptual schemes." No one, however, has made clear precisely how one might model such a conceptual scheme, nor what form change dynamics within such a structure could be expected to take. The authors take some first steps in applying network theory to the issue, modeling conceptual schemes as simple networks and the dynamics of change as cascades on those networks. The results allow a new comparison of two traditional approaches—those of Popper and Kuhn—and introduce the intriguing prospect of viewing scientific change using the metaphor of self-organizing criticality.

This section of the volume continues with J. Barkley Rosser, Jr.'s contribution, "Complexity and Knowledge," which explores the difficult epistemological problem in the study of CAS. At one level, there is the problem of simply discerning whether a given system contains a complex nonlinear dynamical structure or is a simple linear system buffeted by exogenous stochastic processes. The social and behavioral sciences have tended to assume the former. Since chaotic systems exhibit sensitive dependence on initial conditions, or the "butterfly effect," even small changes in the value of a parameter or in the value of a variable at a starting point can lead to very different dynamic paths of the system. This fact underlies the problem that econometric tests for the presence of chaotic dynamics lack usable measures of statistical significance, a challenge that has frustrated many empirical researchers in the area of complex dynamics.

Moreover, there is the distinction between epistemological and ontological matters in the analysis of nonlinear dynamical systems, with this problem expanding when such systems evolve in an adaptive manner. Epistemological problems are simply those of knowledge: how do we know things? Ontological problems involve the nature of underlying realities. Thus, when many economists see dynamics that do not seem to be ergodic over time, there is a problem of determining if this non-ergodicity is due to a fundamental ontological reality, or if the observer is misguided by the complexity of the system into failing to be able to identify properly an underlying ontologically ergodic system. This is a much-debated problem that remains unresolved and is especially difficult for complex adaptive systems.

The third and final chapter in our last section is Carlos Eduardo Maldonado's "Biological Hypercomputation: Social and Political Implications." The thrust of Maldonado's arguments fit comfortably within the discussion of epistemology and its relationship to complex systems because Maldonado is essentially addressing questions of how we come to respond to our environment. Hypercomputation, as described earlier, refers to models of computation that produce outputs that are not Turing computable. Maldonado discusses one particular type of hypercomputation known as biological hypercomputation, or BH.

BH addresses computational processes ranging in scale from genes and bacteria to humans and the biosphere. Maldonado argues that the implications of BH are that organisms at any scale do not process information like a Turing machine in the sense of the Church–Turing Thesis. In other words, they process information non-algorithmically, and by implication, creativity and innovation are non-algorithmic. This contrasts with the earlier contribution by Markose who demonstrates that genomic intelligence that evolved toward protecting the genomic code from biotic hackers possesses recursive machinery allowing for self-referential identification of the hostile other using the Godel Sentence, and thus, novelty production. Maldonado approaches the problem from the standpoint of systems that increase, rather than limit, degrees of freedom and, in that regard, makes a critical distinction between systems science and complexity science. Maldonado makes a compelling case that, whereas human culture is defined by laws, norms, commandments, tactics and strategy, examining biological entities as non-algorithmic information processors provides a new way to look at the world.

Concluding Comments

This volume seeks to provide insights across the intellectual journey from the recognition of the relevance of chaotic dynamics to social and behavioral systems to those of the more expansive and inclusive sciences of complexity. To fully understand this quarter-century journey, it is necessary to reflect on the evolution of both the social and behavioral sciences. The rise of the social sciences in the nineteenth century resulted in a commitment to positivism that ultimately resulted in a desire not only to emulate the natural sciences but also to create a better world based on the view that an understandable, and therefore controllable, social realm would lead to improving the human condition. The work of Saint-Simon (1821) typifies these nineteenth-century examples. This desire to create a social physics (Sen and Chakrabarti 2014) that would lead to a more "manageable" human realm continues today as some scholars seek to understand and quantify human social dynamics. In many ways, the physics envy of the social sciences continues.

The classic works of B.F. Skinner (e.g., 1971) typify efforts within the behavioral sciences to develop a corollary physics of human behavior. This behaviorist perspective, which sees humans as stimulus response machines subject to operant conditioning, provides analytical simplicity but very clearly limits our appreciation for the complexity and evolving dynamism of human behavior. While our cognitive limitations seek to simplify a complex reality, our deeper analytical and philosophical tools suggest that such simplification may reduce the essential variance and uncertainty necessary for human adaptive responses.

What the sciences of complexity offer us is a deeper recognition that the social and behavioral sciences are simply not of the same character as are the natural sciences. Yes, the quantum perspective informs us that we live in a world of constant movement and change, with the vast majority of this movement and change existing beyond the recognition of our eyesight. But a controlled experiment in a chemistry lab yields consistent results. The dynamism of human behavior and the infinite interactions of human beings in groups overwhelm our analytical tools. The recent problem of replicability in psychological experiments (Lakens 2015) must, to some extent, be the result of the enormity of human factors that confound the production of consistent results, even when the experimental conditions appear consistent.

Perhaps it is best to let natural scientists speak for us when considering the challenges of the social sciences. The biologist E.O. Wilson (1998) noted in his efforts to find "consilience" across scientific disciplines that,

> Everyone knows that the social sciences are hyper-complex. They are inherently far more difficult than physics and chemistry, and as a result they, not physics and chemistry, should be called the hard sciences. They just seem easier, because we can talk with other human beings but not with photons, gluons, and sulfide radicals.
>
> (199)

Or perhaps, more simply, as the eminent physicist Stephen Hawking (2010) noted, "While physics and mathematics may tell us how the universe began, they are not much use in predicting human behavior because there are far too many equations to solve." Perhaps a recognition of the social and behavioral sciences as the "hard sciences" may serve to elevate the social sciences to the level of esteem desired by Saint-Simon (1821). But such elevation does not necessarily equate with solutions. The natural sciences allow us to send devices for space exploration beyond our solar system and to replace a human heart. However, from the realities of the vagaries of the birth lottery, to the apparent inevitability of social conflict, to the global problem of "the commons," our many challenges of adaptation often seem to defy, if not our knowledge, then at least our ability to produce longstanding solutions. The dynamism of the social and behavioral realms is responsible for the amazing novelty and adaptive capacities of our species while also serving as the foundation for a world in which our solutions inevitably create new sets of challenges.

What the sciences of complexity offer the social and behavioral sciences is an analytical and philosophical window from which to appreciate both the uncertainty and the emergent self-organization of the human experience. This uncertainty allows for the creative forces of evolution to adapt to a dynamic environment. The enactment of a socio-physics, even if it were possible, would defy the dynamism and uncertainty that make the human experience interesting and might even destroy the desire for improving the human condition. Complexity science informs us of our inherent limitations to know, but provides comfort by affording us the knowledge that creativity is embedded in the process of socio-cultural evolution.

We think the reader will find this volume enlightening. Of course, our brief synopsis of the contributions to *Complex Systems in the Social and Behavioral Sciences* does not do full justice to the argumenta. So, we encourage readers to take the time to explore all of the chapters in this volume. Readers may also find the bibliography helpful in gaining a better understanding of the extant literature. Much has changed since *Chaos Theory in the Social Sciences* was published more than twenty years ago (Kiel and Elliott 1996), and it is certain that the vast arena of complexity studies will continue to evolve in ways that, appropriately enough, are consistent with the behavior of complex systems.

PART I

Social Systems Levels and Complexity

CHAPTER I

Group Dynamics

Adaptation, Coordination and Synchronization

Stephen J. Guastello

Introduction

This chapter describes three interrelated topics in group or team behavior that have developed from the nonlinear dynamical systems (NDS) perspective: adaptive behavior, coordination and physiological synchronization. The theoretical principles behind all three phenomena have considerable practical relevance for shaping the performance outcomes of work groups and teams. Fortunately, there is a growing awareness of the need for NDS concepts within the conventional group dynamics literature that is currently dominated by linear models and linear relationships. In their comprehensive review of factors related to team performance, Kozlowski and Ilgen (2006) remarked that "teams are complex dynamic systems that exist in a context, develop as members interact over time, and evolve and adapt as situational demands unfold" (78). The empirical work on theoretical principles of NDS in group dynamics has received much less attention, however, in the foregoing literature, and substantial progress has occurred since the time of those publications. This chapter recounts the progress within the NDS paradigm in each of the three areas and integrates the principal findings from the conventional or linear paradigm with those from the dynamical theories of group dynamics. Further expansion on the nature of the paradigm shift can be found in Fleener and Merritt (2007) and Guastello (2017).

The use of "emergence" within the broader research community is consistent with Sawyer's (2005) exposition: interactions among individual group members give rise to a supervenient group-level outcome that is not explicable as simply the result of individual actions. The group-level outcome has a downward influence on the actions of group members. The formation of the group-level outcome is a self-organizing process and constitutes the downward influence.

A "group" in this chapter is defined as a social unit of at least three people with a common interest or purpose, following Caplow's (1956) definition of a minimum group size. The words "group" and "team" are used interchangeably in this chapter inasmuch as the groups that were studied did function as teams, at least when they were functioning effectively. Although teams of two people have been studied in various contexts, the majority of the focus here is on teams of three or more members.

Adaptive Behavior

Background

The central concern is the group's ability to respond effectively to rapidly changing environments. Burke et al. (2006) developed twenty-one propositions for research on team adaptation, each of which was accompanied by a substantial amount of research in the conventional linear mode. The propositions aggregate into seven themes—individual differences, cognition-action stages, multiple feedback loops, self-management, psychological safety, communication and leadership, team orientation—which are explained below. They are followed by the concept of the complex adaptive system (CAS) which is strongly tied to NDS principles and reasoning. The bottom-up phase of self-organization and emergence begins with individual situation awareness, general intelligence, creativity and task knowledge, all of which contribute to group-level situation awareness and eventual task effectiveness (Burke et al. 2006). The sequence of group cognitive and action stages continues with the formation of mental models, plans and actions. Each subsequent stage will have a better result to the extent that the quality of the previous stage is also strong (Burke et al. 2006). In fact, many real-world decisions are dynamic in nature, meaning that the choices that a person or group makes at one juncture affect the options and utilities available for the next decision (Brehmer and Dörner 1993). When the group's task itself is complex or perhaps navigates a non-linear process over time, successful adaptive responses can be especially challenging.

Group cognition processes are enhanced to the extent that the group can work relatively free from the influence of any upper management (Burke et al. 2006). This principle makes use of the finding that autonomous work groups outperform those that have a traditional top-down supervisory structure. Autonomous work groups originated with sociotechnical systems theory, the central premise of which is that work should be rationalized from the point of view of the people who are doing the work, rather than from the view point of the (inanimate) work itself. The best way to divide work among participants is to assemble a group of people who have all the necessary capabilities, present them with the whole job and let the forces of self-organization produce the optimal arrangement of people and tasks (DeGreene 1991).

The self-organizing approach gives the group the flexibility that it needs to adapt to a changing environment. Unconstrained self-organization sometimes produces suboptimal or perverse outcomes, however; better outcomes can be afforded by actively shaping the boundary conditions in which self-organization can occur (Goldstein 2011). Group cognition processes are also enhanced by the level of psychological safety in the work group (Burke et al. 2006). Psychological safety is a climate of trust and mutual respect that fosters interpersonal risk taking.

Mutual performance monitoring, back-up plans, leadership input and communication quality all contribute to the coordinated execution of the adaptive response in the conventional paradigm. The NDS paradigm, however, offers some important qualifiers that are addressed later in this chapter. Similarly, group cognition is enhanced if the group has a "team orientation," by which the members are willing to forego personal interests in service of the collective (Burke et al. 2006). This point is also revisited later in conjunction with social loafing, group self-efficacy and Stag Hunt coordination.

Complex Adaptive Systems

In the long history of organizational psychology, knowledge about specific phenomena was often guided by the assumed answer to the question: What is an organization? The mental model of the organization has evolved during the last century from the bureaucracy, to the humanized versus dehumanized work environments, the organization as a living system, and the organization as a complex adaptive system. The CAS concept, which was first introduced by Gell-Mann (1994), can be applied to any living system, although Dooley (1997) first articulated it as the new dominant mental model of organizations. The perspective incorporates NDS concepts to study patterns of behavior. In doing so, it frames new questions regarding how the system recognizes signals and events in the environment, harnesses its capabilities to make effective responses, changes its internal configurations as new adaptive responses require and interacts with the external environment.

Although Dooley (1997) framed the CAS concept in terms of organizations, there is no loss of meaning by substituting "group" for "organization," especially when one considers that small work organizations and single work teams are often one and the same. The central themes of the CAS are schema and agents, agent interaction, problem-solving and conflict, supervenience of internal order and agent fitness.

Schemata and agents. Group members scan the environment and develop schemata (Dooley 1997). A *schema* (*pl.* schemata) is essentially the same as a mental model, although its history in psychology is much older and places additional emphasis on the actions that could be taken in response to the mental models of the situation (Newell 1991). Schemata define rules of interaction with other agents that exist within the team or outside the team's boundaries (Dooley 1997). A group's schemata are often built from existing building blocks, which are inevitably brought into the group when members arrive. Here we see the role of particular individual differences in job knowledge and other attributes (Burke et al. 2006).

A group's schemata can be indeterminate, observer-dependent and contradictory (Dooley 1997). The integration of individual perspectives on a work situation is not always smooth. Although the individual schemata self-organize into one or more supervenient mental models, individual differences can remain that provide enough entropy for further modification of the schemata. This effect is known as *symmetry-breaking* (Sulis 2009): an errant agent enacts a schema that is different from the dominant ones, other agents replicate it and eventually it, becomes an alternative schema. The alternative schema sometimes becomes dominant, sometimes not.

Schemata change via mutation, recombination and acquisition of new ideas from outside sources. Change occurs in response to both changing environments and changing internal conditions. Indeed there are numerous sources and types of entropy that could arise from changes in client populations, the workforce, demands for products and new markets and governmental regulations (Bigelow 1982; Guastello 2002). The processes of mutation and recombination suggest an analogy between the dynamics of genetics or genetic algorithms and creative problem-solving.

When schemata change, requisite variety, robustness and reliability are ideally enhanced (Dooley 1997). *Reliability* denotes error-free action in the usual sense. *Robustness* denotes the ability of the system to withstand unpredictable shock from the environment. *Requisite variety* refers to Ashby's (1956) Law: for the effective control of a system, the complexity of the controller must be at least equal to the complexity of the system that is being controlled. *Complexity* in this context refers to the number of system states, which are typically conceptualized as discrete outcomes.

From a more contemporary perspective, the number of system states is closely connected to the conceptual complexity of managing them, especially when the complexity of the system increases over time. Boisot and McKelvey (2011) identified three strategies for responding to increasing complexity: *routinizing*, even if it means causing errors by over-simplifying; *maintaining a balance between order and chaos*, where meta-stability occurs; and *behaving as chaotically as the system*, which they likened to running around like a chicken with its head cut off. The meta-stability state is also known as "optimum variability," which is an equilibrium between maintaining sufficient complexity and minimizing the energy required to make the necessary adaptive responses (Guastello 2015). Finding schemata that are more complex than the ones in use requires exploratory learning, whereas simplification relies on crystalized past learning (Boisot and McKelvey 2011).

Agent interaction. As team members interact, there is a flow of information and resources (Dooley 1997). In the early stages of team life, the interaction patterns are often volatile, but they eventually self-organize to enhance collective efficiency, which is in part a reduction in the entropy and uncertainty in how the information flows will occur. The performance of the system can be enhanced by manipulating the levels of decentralization, diversification and specialization of members' roles. The use of symbolic tags (e.g., job titles) facilitates the formation of subunits or specific functions.

Problem-solving and conflict. The feedback loops associated with team cognition sometimes result in the need to change schemata. The potential for intellectual conflict could involve differences between a current schema and a view of external reality, different views of external reality, different views of current schemata or different alternative schemata. The problem-solving strategies could be dialectic or teleological. The *dialectic* strategy compares contradictory ideas and usually seeks to resolve their conflict. The *teleological* mode relates to the design or purpose, and how a system's purpose would unfold or evolve over time (Dooley 1997; Van de Ven and Poole 1995). Teleological discussions require the group to recognize that their current situation is not a static one, but a slice of a drama that has been changing over time, perhaps not smoothly. A collective understanding—mental model—of things evolves and helps matters greatly, although some individuals are substantially more skilled at accurately forecasting or anticipating chaotic events than others (Guastello 2002; Heath 2002).

Irreversibility and emergent order. If it is indeed a complex *adaptive* system, it remains poised on the edge of chaos ready to reorganize itself in response to new demands. The sequence of states through which it reorganizes are relatively unpredictable, although the understood goal of situation awareness is to envision possible future scenarios and states eventually and predict the outcomes of one's control actions (Endsley 1995, 2015); again some people are better at it than others. A team's particular sequence of stages is often subject to initial conditions that contribute to the global unpredictability of the system. The states of team organization are irreversible once they have taken hold and stabilized (Dooley 1997). Although teams can redeploy old schemata, the effect is not the same because of the history and events that accumulated, both within the team and in the environment, during the time that has elapsed.

The dynamics of agent interaction and problem-solving give rise to the development of schemata. Once adopted, they are expected to have a supervenient effect on the further actions of the agents. The supervenient effect presents another reason why group events are irreversible: a schema is deployed or changed against a context that could contain little history or precedent, as in a group's early stages of life, but the same schema might have a different impact within a different context where the schema would be introduced.

Agent fitness. A final feature of the CAS involves agent fitness. The notion of fitness arises from genetic algorithm and related studies. A team might generate many work-related ideas or schemata for their internal operation, but some ideas and schemata will be better than others. *Fitness* is the rating of how good they really are. Similarly, agents have a level of fitness that projects their longevity with the group. It is not the same as a performance rating, but something closer to a person–job fit. It is the subjective response of the agents to their levels of discrepancy between personal schemata and group schemata. Many global and local issues and discrepancies between them could culminate in an agent's level of satisfaction with the team situation.

The probability of a change in a team's schema is a nonlinear function of satisfaction (Dooley 1997). After some destabilization, self-organization reoccurs and stabilizes at new levels of fitness, discrepancy or satisfaction. Importantly, the top-down driving effect is not immutable once it is installed unless there is a rigid one-way flow of information in the group. In all likelihood, informal communication networks could undermine the hegemony of unilateral top-down communication. In the more likely scenarios, symmetry breaking provides the source for sufficient entropy and upward information flow that destabilizes the top-down driver. Rosser et al. (1994) characterized the bottom-up destabilization phenomenon as a "revolt of the slaved variables," which can be particularly strong in hierarchically organized groups (Guastello and Johnson 1999).

Coordination

Coordination occurs in a work team when two or more people do the same task, or complimentary tasks, at the same time. This definition derives explicitly from the economic theory of games (Friedman 1994; Guastello and Guastello 1998; von Neumann and Morgenstern 1953) and encompasses a wide range of situations where individuals must act, but the rewards for task completion are assigned to the group as a whole. Coordination has been variously operationalized as the time delay between a group member's action and another member's contingent action (Brannick, Roach, and Salas 1993), the quality of communication between members of a group (Daily 1980) or performance in a group task wherein members were required to figure out and take correct actions in the correct sequence (Guastello and Guastello 1998).

Shared Mental Models

The conventional explanations for how coordination occurs and sustains in a work team rests primarily on the principle of shared mental models of their tasks, procedures, and group processes (Cannon-Bowers, Salas, and Converse 1993). Shared mental models may be induced by cross-training the group members in each other's roles, or by discussions and presentations of groups' task models (Marks et al. 2002; Matthieu et al. 2000).

Another manifestation of shared mental models can be found in some older studies on experimental cultures. Decision norms can persist in a group even as group members are systematically replaced (Weick and Gilfillan 1971). Conformity pressure supports the persistence of norms.

Nonlinear Dynamics of Coordination

NDS perspectives on coordination involve three related principles. One is the fundamental role of *self-organization*. The second is the *game theory perspective*, which, on the one hand, gives rise to evolutionarily stable states (ESS) that in turn have a supervenient impact on team behavior, and on the other hand specifies local rules of interaction that distinguish a few types of coordination phenomena. The third aspect of NDS appears in the time series for *coordination acquisition* wherein we can observe chaos in the early stages of learning, and self-organization as group learning consolidates. Both explicit and implicit learning are involved, as elaborated below.

Self-organization. One productive area of psychology where the notion of self-organization has been usefully applied is in the understanding of the coordination among muscle groups and limbs in any moving organism (Turvey 1990). It takes far fewer degrees of freedom to account for all the combinations of coordinated limb movements by assuming a system of self-organized internal information flows, compared to a system that relies on an external puppeteer pulling all the strings (Turvey 1990). In other words, the system works efficiently with no leader or *deus ex machina* involved. None of the information flows involved in psychomotor movement are verbal in nature; cognitive processes that are involved in some types of movement are topics of current investigation, however, particularly for groups and teams (Gorman et al. 2017).

Animal models for coordination also support the premises that leadership is not required and obviate any requirement for verbal communication. A flock of birds maintains its structure and its travel itinerary by using only three rules: (a) avoid colliding with flock-mates, (b) maintain the general heading of the flock and (c) stay close to one's flock-mates (Reynolds 1987). In complex physical environments, there is one additional rule: Don't crash into buildings, trees or other fixed objects. The flock has no leader; any apparent leadership role among birds is the result of rotating turns in positions within the flock. Similar dynamics have been observed with schools of fish (Semovski 2001) and continue to be studied in the context of collective intelligence (Sulis 1999, 2009). One could say, however, that events similar to leadership occur when the bird or fish that is most capable of detecting a threatening signal makes the first move that compels the entire group to move (Wilson 1975).

None of the foregoing should be interpreted as meaning that leaders cannot emerge from coordination-intensive groups, as explained later in this chapter. Nor should the foregoing remarks be interpreted as meaning that verbal communication plays no role in team coordination. Rather, the NDS experiments were defined to isolate the role of verbalization.

Game theory. The central premise behind game theory (von Neumann and Morgenstern 1953) is that when interacting agents are faced with options, they will choose options that maximize their own outcomes. The outcomes associated with the options are expressed as *utilities*, and the utilities of any option depend on the options selected by the other agents. Typical experiments do not allow participants to talk while gaming to prevent the discussion from altering the perceived game utilities (Friedman 1994). Furthermore, no leaders are appointed in the typical experiments.

The NDS connection to game theory began with Nash equilibria and *dominant strategies* that agents acquire after many repeated interactions. If games are played by a population of agents (e.g., in a computer simulation) iteratively in a "tournament," a strategy usually dominates in the form of an ESS. The ESS will be close to the Nash equilibrium that applies to a single-exchange game (Maynard-Smith 1982). If we add some complexity to the possible game options and the utilities, and give up the assumption of strict competitiveness, however, the ESS cannot be guessed from prior knowledge of the Nash equilibria. Rather, the ESS becomes highly dependent on initial conditions as they pertain to options and utilities (Samuelson 1997). Thus, ESS experiments are needed to identify the real behavior patterns that form games that emulate real-world problems and decisions.

Game structures that are not strictly competitive offer opportunities for coordination in which the agents simultaneously select a cooperative response as opposed to a competitive or indifferent response (Camerer and Knez 1997; Friedman 1994). *Mixed motivation* games, notably Prisoner's Dilemma, attracted a great deal of attention in psychology and economics because of their counterpoint between cooperative and competitive response options. Two types of *strictly cooperative* games that are considered in this chapter are the Intersection and Stag Hunt.

Learning processes. The literature on organizational learning dates back to the behavioral theory of the firm (Cyert and March 1963). Organizations execute strategies to maximize profits in much the same way as the rat runs to where the largest piece of cheese is most probably located. One contemporary view characterizes an organization's ability to learn as part of what it does to adapt to situations in the sense of what a CAS does (Seo, Putnam, and Bartunek 2004); effective adaptation involves exploratory learning (Boisot and McKelvey 2011).

Allen (2009) identified and evaluated three organizational learning strategies. The first is *Darwinian learning*, which involves the least amount of learning and performance success over time, according to the simulation results. Groups or organizations start with a random action strategy; if its fitness is high enough, the group and the action strategy survive, and the group could evolve to higher levels of fitness. The second learning approach occurs when *all groups imitate* the fittest-looking agent in the terrain. More groups survive and performance is better in the long run compared to Darwinian learning, but they run the risk of imitating another agent in the wrong way or at the wrong time. The population of groups runs a risk of large swings in fitness over time as a result. In the third approach, all groups *learn through experimentation*. Although they might start with a random strategy, they continually explore new ideas, some of which are obtained through imitation; they try some of them, assess the results and retain the action strategies that work best.

The earliest connections between NDS, learning and motivation took the form of catastrophe models (Baker and Frey 1980; Frey and Sears 1978; Guastello 1981, 1995), which characterized learning as a discontinuous process with an underlying bifurcation structure. Indeed, Newell (1991) reported that, although the power law function for simple learning or motor skill acquisition processes was firmly lodged in the psychological literature, it did not account for discontinuities that are inherent in more complex learning phenomena. Discontinuities occur in cognitive automaticity processes wherein the elementary perception–cognition–action elements consolidate into larger, smoother units of behavior (Guastello 2014).

A particular learning curve can be represented as a slice of the catastrophe response surface. The response surface describes the full range of possible learning trajectories, including the possibility that some agents never learn. Learning curves differ with respect to the sharpness of their ascent over time; the underlying catastrophe model indicates that the bifurcation manifold accounts for the sharpness of inflection. A further implication is that the conventional two-dimensional representations of the learning curve loses a lot of information about the differences in the shapes of the learning curves.

Learning curves can be highly irregular and variable, particularly during the acquisition period, and not smooth the way they are usually drawn in textbooks. Hoyert (1992) examined the behavioral response patterns of pigeons in a fixed interval schedule of reinforcement. Although the general shape of the scallops was the same as those reported during the previous fifty years, there were epochs of variability and internal patterning that could not be explained by the schedule of reinforcement alone. A phase diagram (i.e., a plot of ΔX against X for a time series) of the pigeons' responses closely resembled the phase diagrams of chaotic patterns, thus indicating that the micro-level variability was deterministic rather than random variation or measurement error. Analyses using structural equations showed that the variability between intervals could be better accounted for by nonlinear models than by linear models.

The (possible) presence of chaos suggests an eventual transition to a self-organized structure. The learning curve has been characterized as a phase transition whereby a self-organized structure is thought to occur when the asymptote is attained (Vetter, Stadler, and Haynes 1997). Furthermore, the neuron patterns in the (human) brain respond in a chaotic pattern in the presence of novel stimuli, but the neural patterning becomes more regular once learning has occurred (Freeman 2000). The entrained patterns represent basins of attraction. Thus, coordination acquisition would be no different; it would follow a learning curve globally, with an epoch of chaos in the early stages and self-organization culminating in a fixed point later on—if learning is successful. Otherwise, the self-organization and asymptotic stability would not occur.

A small amount of variability in performance still persists after asymptotic stability has been reached. Meanwhile, there is a popular tendency to expect that maximum-performing groups or agents are also highly consistent over time once the asymptote of the learning curve has been reached. A machine will produce that type of result, but it cannot adapt to perturbations from the environment without the intervention of a human. For living systems, the residual variability indicates that there are some degrees of freedom in how the result is produced. Those degrees of freedom allow the system to make new adaptations and develop new levels of performance beyond the first stage of asymptotic stability (Guastello et al. 2014; Mayer-Kress, Newell, and Liu 2009).

Implicit learning. The foregoing examples of learning and NDS processes were mostly confined to the explicit mode of learning. Groups acquire coordination as an implicit learning process, however, which is an incidental learning effect that occurs when an agent is trying to explicitly learn something else (Seger 1994). Although implicit learning was first studied as an individual process, group coordination can be interpreted as an implicit process also. Guastello and Guastello (1998) demonstrated experimentally that coordination within a group of four agents that was acquired while learning one task transferred to subsequent tasks performed by the same group when the coordination rule was changed. Figure 1.1 depicts the twin chaotic learning curves that result.

Reliance on the implicit nature of team coordination, however, is more effective when the team actions are routine; non-routine tasks require explicit planning along with the main task (Rico et al. 2008). This group or organizational form of learning is also known as *situated learning* in some contexts (Dobson et al. 2001; Yuan and McKelvey 2004).

Intersection Experiments

In an Intersection game, an individual's decision to participate in a group activity is required and not assumed for an effective outcome. The objective

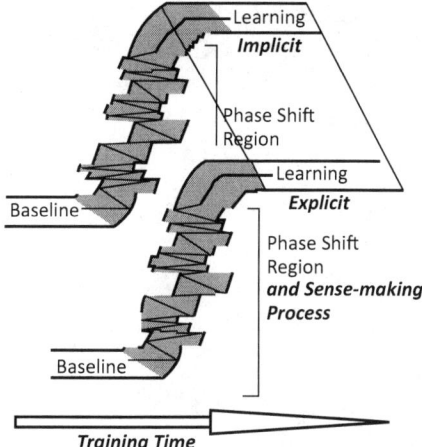

Fig. 1.1. Twin Curves for Implicit and Explicit Learning Dynamics with Chaotic Onset and Asymptotic Stability at the Conclusion of a Self-Organizing Process

is to select an action that facilitates the individual's utilities, which can only occur if the group's utilities are facilitated (Crawford 1991; Guastello et al. 2005; Guastello and Bond 2007a; Guastello and Guastello 1998). A critical feature of the Intersection game is that the agents must figure out what the correct actions are, and in what order they must be taken to facilitate the groups' outcome. The game got its name from the four-way stop intersection on roadways. Each motorist approaching the intersection must figure out which rule is in play for moving through the intersection—which is not always immediately predictable from having memorized state driving laws—when one's turn occurs, and to take one's turn instead of sitting there waiting. Intersection is thought to characterize many forms of work performance in industry, military operations, hospital emergency rooms and the performing arts.

The Intersection game was operationalized as a card game in a series of experiments (Guastello et al. 2005; Guastello and Bond 2007a; Guastello and Guastello 1998). Groups of four participants were dealt five cards from a limited standard deck. Their objective was to play the cards on a table in the correct order to acquire points (utilities), although they had to figure out what the correct sequence was. Four points were awarded to the group if a series of four cards was played correctly, one point if three out of four cards were played correctly and no points otherwise. One round of the game consisted of eight hands of five cards. After one round, the participants were told that the rule changed and they needed to figure out the new rule. There were four rounds altogether, including rounds that switched to a rule that was equal in difficulty to the first rule, and a rule that was more difficult.

The following mathematical model for performance over time was established empirically from the foregoing experiments (Guastello et al. 2005; Guastello and Bond 2007a; Guastello and Guastello 1998):

$$z_2 = \theta_1 z_1 \exp(\theta_2 z_2) + \theta_3, \theta_2 < 0 \qquad (1)$$

$$z_2 = \exp(\theta_2 z_2) + \theta_3, \theta_2 > 0, \qquad (2)$$

where z_i are a time series of performance measures and θ_i are nonlinear regression weights. Equation 1 is the primary function that is extracted from the data. The term $\theta_1 z_1$ denotes a bifurcation effect whereby some groups attain coordination more decisively than others. The term θ_2 is comparable to a Lyapunov exponent; it was usually negative in these experiments, denoting asymptotic stability at a fixed point.

Equation 2 is a secondary function that was extracted from the residuals of Eq. 1. It appeared in conditions where coordination was particularly challenging; θ_2 was positive, denoting chaos. For further elaboration of this nonlinear statistical modeling system, see Guastello and Gregson (2011). A substantial amount of variance was explained by knowing the dynamical process underlying coordination acquisition compared to the conventional linear explanation.

There was transfer of coordination learning from the first round of the game to the second with the rule of equal difficulty, as evidenced by an overall higher mean of points accumulated by the groups. This point was true whether or not the experimental groups were allowed to talk (Guastello et al. 2005; Guastello and Bond 2007a; Guastello and Guastello 1998). The transfer substantiated the implicit nature of coordination learning.

In the experimental conditions where verbalization was varied, verbalizing groups performed better overall than groups that were not allowed to talk, and their learning curves indicated sharper coordination acquisition. Figure 1.2 depicts the performance or learning curves for four rounds of an Intersection game: starting rule, switch to a rule of equal difficulty, switch to a more difficult rule and switch back to the starting rule (Guastello and

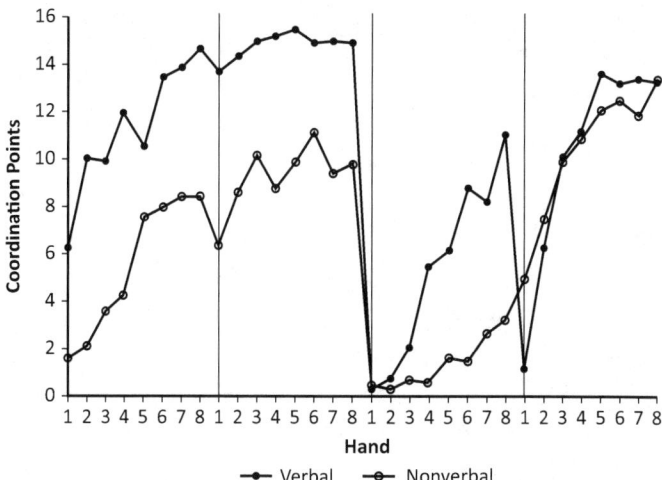

Fig. 1.2. Coordination Acquisition During Four Rounds of an Intersection Task with Verbal and Nonverbal Conditions

Source: Reprinted from Guastello and Bond (2007a, 104) with permission of the Society for Chaos Theory in Psychology and Life Sciences.

Bond 2007a). In another experiment (Guastello et al. 2005), one, two or three of the participants were replaced at the start of the third round of the game with participants who had no prior experience with the game. The transfer of learning effect persisted and performance improved compared to the first round, when one or two participants were changed; changing three out of four was tantamount to starting the coordination acquisition process over again. Interestingly, the ability to talk did not help or hinder the assimilation of new personnel; new personnel apparently had to learn something critical in the nonverbal channel for coordination to occur.

Gorman, Amazeen and Cooke (2010) found, on the other hand, that group performance can be enhanced by exchanging personnel with members of other groups who were already trained and coordinated on the same type of task. The performance improvement might be explained by an elevated sense of interpersonal awareness among the members of the reformed group. More research is required to know for sure why the differences in results occurred.

Even though leadership is not required to produce coordination, leaders can still emerge from coordination-intensive groups. In the third study from the NDS series (Guastello and Bond 2007a), participants completed a questionnaire at the end of the study in which they were asked which member of their group acted most like the leader and who acted second-most like the leader. They were also asked other leadership-related questions about who contributed to the group's problem-solving dialog. The response options allowed the participants to indicate that no one behaved like the leader or made a particular type of contribution. Thirteen groups were allowed to talk during the game, and thirteen were not allowed to talk. Clear leaders emerged from both types of groups, and importantly, the verbalizing groups did not produce more or stronger leaders than the nonverbal groups. The talking and non-talking groups did vary on other points covered in the questionnaire, however.

In spite of the alleged advantages of shared mental models, the NDS studies showed that coordination occurred without prior mental models, discussion, cross-training, verbal communication or leaders. Group members developed their shared mental model through their own observations and interactions with other group members. Similarly, verbalization had its advantages, but it did not have a critical effect on the assimilation of new personnel, and it was not a requirement for coordination to occur. Of course, businesses usually encourage their personnel to talk about the work, but there are times when communication is impossible because of technological faults, geographic dispersal, or other types of interference.

Stag Hunt Games

Stag Hunt is a game where the agents choose between working with the group or working on their own. In other words, an agent can join a group of hunters to hunt stag, or work alone hunting rabbits. The likelihood of a hunter joining the group depends on a comparison of the group's efficacy versus personal efficacy. The expected performance of the group depends on the combined skill and efforts of all the hunters as evaluated by the particular agent. If the agent is savvy enough to determine the extent to which the whole is greater than the sum of its parts, so much the better for that agent.

The agents' levels of individual involvement are observable in the course of the tournament. One can measure either the level of participation or the performance of the group over time as evolutionary outcomes.

The group outcomes can tolerate some individual differences in contributions, but if too few agents take the group action once they join, the overall performance of the group suffers. Two other strands of group research from the conventional medium, social loafing and self-efficacy theory, are relevant here.

Social Loafing

Social loafing is a phenomenon wherein a group of people is supposedly working together for a common goal and sharing a common reward, but some people work a lot harder than others (Geen 1991; Latané, Williams, and Harkins 1979). The disparities in input tend to be greater in larger groups. Possible explanations for the phenomenon include output equity, the free-rider effect, evaluation apprehension and lack of a performance standard.

Output equity is the result of an agent's attempt to work only as hard as other people; if an agent expects the other agents to withhold input, that agent will do so also. The free-rider effect is similar: the agent expects *someone* in the group to solve the problem, so it is beneficial to be part of the group of which the star performer is a member. In the evaluation apprehension explanation, the individual does not expect to perform well, and thus sees a benefit in becoming anonymous in a larger group (Geen 1991). As the group size increases, the agent's contribution becomes a smaller percentage of the total, leading to the reaction, "Why bother? It doesn't make any difference anyway" (Comer 1995). Given the uncertainties about how the other agents are expected to perform, agents might loaf because they really do not know what performance expectations would apply (Geen 1991).

Social loafing can be reduced in work groups by organizing a larger group into smaller units and then identifying some "coordinator roles" to connect the subunits. This solution helps make each person's contribution more visible and proportionately larger (Comer 1995). The solution also produces a hierarchical structure within the work group. A substantial amount of work time can be lost waiting for information to travel up and down a hierarchy, however (Guastello 2002). In those cases, what might appear to be social loafing is not at all related to people not wanting to work; rather, it is the result of a bottleneck falling on one person while others wait for the work to flow in their direction.

Self-Efficacy

Self-efficacy plays an important role in the performance of challenging tasks (Bandura 2001). It is partially the result of past performance, personal evaluations thereof, motivation and belief in one's ability to control one's own behavior and aspects of the situation. It is sometimes the sole determinant of which competitor will win a wrestling match or prevail in other difficult situations (Bandura and Locke 2003). Not only does self-efficacy contribute to constructive reactions that people have to the discrepancies between current situations and their self-set goals, it contributes to proactive responses as well.

Teams also need self-efficacy. A meta-analysis of forty-two effect sizes for the relationship between team self-efficacy and team performance produced a corrected mean r^2 of .17 (Gully et al. 2002). Tasa et al. (2007) illustrated that group self-efficacy might self-organize from the individual agents' experiences by comparing individuals' perceptions of group self-efficacy with feedback the group received about their collective work at several points in time. According to Kenny (1994), members of a newly formed group expend substantial effort learning about other group members' capabilities and likely contributions to the group effort. This sort of information leads to a sense of the team's efficacy, and by virtue of social comparison, one's own efficacy as a team member.

Evolutionary Stag Hunt Games

Stag Hunt games comprise a significant number of team experiences during an emergency response (ER) situation. There are some differences between the economic game of Stag Hunt, a real stag hunt, a situation involving an analogous game against a natural disaster and an analogous game against a disaster that involved a sentient attacker. In a real stag hunt or game against a sentient attacker, there are learning dynamics by both the humans and the prey or protagonist; natural disasters and hypothetical stag are indifferent to the humans' responses. Real-world Stag Hunt situations are not *subgame perfect*, meaning that at each choice point within the game, the options are often not the same, and utilities associated with the players' choices are often not the same. In real-world Stag Hunt situations, the choices facing the group members are always to participate in the group decision to define a strategic option and take action versus not participating. Other than that dichotomy, however, the possible strategic actions available to the group are numerous and the utilities to the group associated with the available actions vary each time the group faces a decision. Thus, the utilities to the individual for staying with the group or dropping out can vary substantially as well.

Guastello and Bond (2004) adapted an experimental task from a board game (*The Creature that Ate Sheboygan*; Simulation Productions, Inc. 1979) wherein an ER team worked cooperatively together, but competitively against an adversary. Four ER teams of four participants (undergraduates) could move game tokens for police, fire, helicopter and military ground troops to reduce the attackers' defenses and eventually finish them off. Attackers were characterized as Godzilla-type monsters who would burn buildings and destroy ER personnel and resources. There were seventeen turns within a game, three games per experimental session and two sessions. Two of the groups worked under conditions of a communication outage during one of the sessions, meaning that they could no longer talk to each other while working.

The performance of both the ER team and the attacker varied over time in several important ways. First, the teams and the attackers improved their performances over time. Thus ESSs are partially the result of learning effects and are thus not linked to the outcomes of single games or exchanges in a simple fashion. Furthermore, the attackers learned how to perform better over two consecutive sessions of three games, which presented an added challenge to the ER teams; this is a feature that distinguishes emergencies that involve sentient attackers from those involving natural disasters. ER teams showed both improvements and drops in performance as they played more games.

Second, the communication outages did not hinder the ER teams' performance (measured in game points), but attackers did better under those conditions. This finding suggests that although team members might be sufficiently well-coordinated with each other to overcome communication impairments, the communication impairments could hinder counter-adaptive responses to the adaptive responses of the attacker.

Videotapes of the games indicated that the number of team members who participated in the decision associated with each move depended on the number of points accumulated by the attacker on the previous turn. This analysis was performed only on one group without the communication outages because of the difficulty in interpreting the tapes. ER team members tended to disengage when the going got tough. This result supported the principle that the efficacy of the group affects the utilities of individual participation, and furthermore that group self-efficacy can fluctuate over time. The nonlinear model for participation was:

$$h_2 = \exp(\theta_1 m_1) + \theta_2 \qquad (3)$$

where h_2 was the number of team members participating on a given turn, m_1 was the Attacker's cumulative score on the previous turn—which was itself nonlinear over time—and θ_i were nonlinear regression weights.

In a later study with the *Creature* game (Guastello, Marra, Castro, Gomez, and Perna 2017), human research assistants recorded the number of team members who participated in a decision on each turn of a tournament of six games with one attacker and ER teams of four members. Performance and participation trends were analyzed for nonlinear properties using an expanded statistical model. For the ER teams,

$$h_2 = \exp(\theta_1 h_1) + \theta_2 \exp(\theta_3 {}^* m_1) \qquad (4)$$

where h_2 was the ER teams' cumulative performance or participation level on a given turn, h_1 was the ER teams' cumulative performance on the previous turn, m_1 was the Attacker's cumulative score on the previous turn and θ_i were nonlinear regression weights. All games from the teams were spliced end-to-end to form longer time series. θ_1 was the Lyapunov exponent associated with teams' performance trends, and θ_3 was the Lyapunov exponent associated with attackers' performance trends. The same equation was used for attackers' time series, except that m_2 replaced h_2 on the left side of the equation.

Advances made by the attackers would dampen participation by the team members. This is an illustration of self-efficacy affecting participation in the group. If the hypothetical hunting team looked like it had a good chance of winning, more hunters would join in. If the prey got away, or fought back too hard, the hunters retreated.

Further analysis showed that performance affected participation rather than the other way around. This finding, although predicted from self-efficacy theory, runs contrary to classical management theory: in the long-term time horizon, the classical notion that participation in decision-making enhances performance may be true, but events in the short-term are a different story.

Dynamics and Group Size

The relationship between group size and group outcomes has been enigmatic in social psychology. For creative problem-solving groups, a group that is large enough would generate a critical mass of useful strategic ideas (Dennis and Valacich 1993; Guastello 2002). From a coordination standpoint, however, a group that is too large would either take too long to make a decision or produce social loafing or other situations where some members work a lot harder than others (Comer 1995).

Another experiment with the *Creature* game (Guastello 2010) considered whether there existed an optimal group size associated with the ER teams' performance curves. The reasoning was: (a) if any group size effect occurred, it would be evidence that a group-level dynamic had self-organized; (b) if results favored larger groups, the critical mass principle was operating; (c) if results favored smaller groups, then social loafing was affecting the larger groups; and (d) if no group size effect occurred, then the task was being performed by the most competent individual and widespread loafing or task incompetence was operating. Groups of four, six, nine and twelve undergraduates (four groups each) played the same board game against an adversary who worked alone. There was a significant main effect for team performance as a function of group size, whereby ER teams performed best and attackers the worst with team sizes of nine and twelve members.

The teams' performance dynamics were chaotic, and the fractal dimension of the series was unaffected by group size (average Lyapunov dimension, D_L = 1.52). Chaos was signified by a positive Lyapunov exponent and was interpreted as an indicator of adaptive capability. Teams' performance on a given iteration was once again negatively affected by the Attacker's performance in the previous turn. The performance dynamics of the attackers were not affected by the progress made by the teams on the previous iteration. Their chaoticity level was generally higher than the teams', although it declined when attackers played against teams of twelve (D_L = 2.00, compared to D_L = 2.67 for smaller groups). The results indicated again that the groups were affected by signs of their own self-efficacy, while individual attackers were not as affected. The attackers seemed to have lost adaptive capability when competing against team sizes of twelve.

Synchronization

Synchronization is often regarded as a special case of coordination, usually representing a situation requiring physical movements that are exactly timed. Synchronized swimming or rowing would be examples. It is also used to describe the mimicry of physical movements, such as postural sway, hand and facial expressions, or speech patterns between two people in a psychotherapy session or an ordinary conversation (Delaherche et al. 2012; Orsucci et al. 2016; Ramseyer and Tschacher 2016).

Numerous studies have shown that autonomic arousal and EEG patterns can synchronize when a dyad or group is engaged in a common activity (Palumbo et al. 2017; Stevens and Galloway 2016). Physiological synchronization occurs through a combination of emotional contagion, empathy, common focus of attention and temporal regularities in the activity or environment (Guastello et al. 2018; Palumbo et al. 2017; Stevens, Galloway, and Lamb 2014). An activity that requires some form of turn-taking among the group members could induce temporal regularity (Guastello et al. 2017).

Principles

More formally, synchronization occurs when two or more oscillating elements of a system are completely in-phase or out-of-phase with each other. Historic examples include two clocks ticking in unison, a tree full of fireflies flashing on and off in unison or two sound waves cancelling each other out. In the prototype situation (Pikovsky, Rosenblum, and Kurths 2001; Stefański 2009; Strogatz 2003), the minimum requirements for synchronization among living or nonliving entities are two oscillators, a feedback loop between them and a control parameter that speeds up the interactive process. The control parameter could take the form of putting the two clocks on a wooden beam (which transfers the vibrations) or taking them off, fireflies responding to a growing number of other fireflies, humans pacing their activity with a metronome (Haken, Kelso, and Bunz 1985) or humans responding to task-relevant stimuli that are presented in random sequences at an increasing rate (Guastello 2016). A *phase lock*, meaning full synchronization, occurs when the speed of the agents' interactions reaches a critical level.

To operationalize the prototype for human systems, one must identify the nature of the oscillators, the feedback loop and the control parameter. In the prototype, the feedback loop is bi-directional. Phase lock can be observed when synchronized movements are trained and the synchronization effect is actually the explicit goal of learning. More often, however, synchronization is an implicit function while other team performance objectives are being achieved explicitly. In human interactions such as conversations, either a one-way or two-way influence is possible (Guastello 2016; Guastello, Pincus, and Gunderson 2006; Levinson and Gottman 1983).

In cases where synchronization of autonomic arousal has been studied, the interpersonal time lag between shifts in arousal levels can vary from one to twenty seconds or longer, depending on the task. Synchronization is generally not phase-locked, and is thus a matter of degree overall. It is also affected by whether the group members are only interacting among themselves, whether they are attending to an external event or whether external forces driving temporal regularity are operating.

Neurological activity adds another level of complexity to the problem of identifying how the elements of a system synchronize. Although individual neurons and neural circuits can be characterized as oscillators, they work in groups and bundles that produce chaotic firing patterns (Whittle 2010). Their effects on each other can be mutually excitatory or inhibitory. Synchronization among chaotic agents can also be pushed into phase lock, however (Stefański 2009). Similarly, the effects of team members on one another can be mutually excitatory or inhibitory (Guastello 2016). Figure 1.3 illustrates a level of synchronization among seven team members competing against an opponent in *The Creature that Ate Sheboygan* (Guastello et al. 2017).

Measurement of Synchronization

Progress with team synchronization research has been slower than studies of dyads due to a lack of an appropriate metric for quantifying synchronization for physiological synchronization within a group of three or more members. Synchronicity for groups has been calculated by a few means: relative synchronicity occurring when the disparity among oscillatory phases

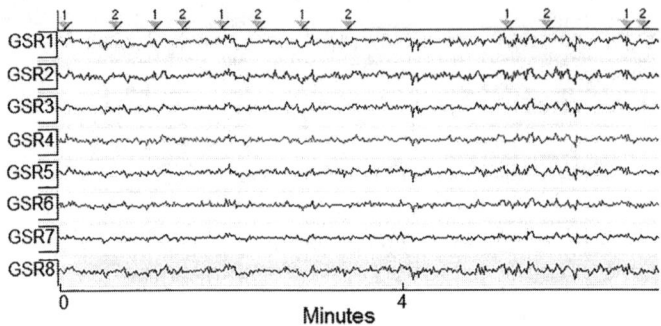

Fig. 1.3. Electrodermal Time Series From a Group of Seven Experimental Emergency Response Team Members Competing Against One Opponent (GSR 8)

Note: Event markers indicate the start of an opponent's turn (1) and the start of the team's turn (2).

Table 1.1 Matrix populated with autocorrelations of physiological time series on the diagonal

		TO				
		P_1	P_2	P_3	... P_n	Driver score
FROM	P_1	AR_1	R_{12}	R_{13}	R_{1n}	ΣR^2_1
Matrix P:	P_2	R_{21}	AR_2	R_{23}	R_{2n}	ΣR^2_2
	P_3	R_{31}	R_{32}	AR_3	R_{3n}	ΣR^2_3
	P_n	R_{n1}	R_{n2}	R_{n3}	AR_n	ΣR^2_n
Empath score		ΣR^2_1	ΣR^2_2	ΣR^2_3	ΣR^2_n	

is minimized (Elkins et al. 2009; Richardson et al. 2012), pairwise recursion plots (Mønster et al. 2016) and autocorrelation and cross-correlation analyses of time series (Guastello et al. 2006; Guastello and Peressini 2017). The choice of analytic approach resides, at least in part, on whether one wants to assume oscillation as a starting point, which would then expand into chaos, or whether a chaotic regime is taken as a starting point that could be reduced to a quasi-oscillatory regime.

Guastello and Peressini (2017) developed a metric (SE) that can be used in conjunction with the types of time series data produced by electrodermal and other biometric sensors. Briefly, S_E is calculated from a set of influences from each member of the group to each other member of the group. The computation begins with the matrix that is populated with autocorrelations of physiological time series on the diagonal (table 1.1). Semi-partial correlation coefficients on the off-diagonal entries show the impact of one person on the other. Matrix entries can be positive or negative coefficients. Negative autocorrelations reflect oscillating functions. Negative off-diagonal elements reflect dampening effects between people rather than mutually exciting effects.

Sums of squared coefficients of the rows and columns are calculated. The person with the largest row total is the *driver*. The person with the largest column total is the *empath*. The reasoning is that a driver has no impact on group synchronization unless other group members are responding to that individual. The correspondence of team members with the empath would reflect the highest synchronization of one person with other team members. The final step calculates a single number, *synchronization with the empath* (S_E), which expresses a global level of synchronization for the group.

The autocorrelations in the matrix diagonal and the standardized regression weights (β_2 in Eq. 2) can be produced by either linear regression (Eqs. 3–4) or nonlinear functions:

$$X_n = \beta_0 + \beta_1 X_{n-j}, \qquad (3)$$

$$X_n = \beta_0 + \beta_1 X_{n-j} + \beta_2 P_{n-j}. \qquad (4)$$

Only linear models were considered in the group dynamics studies with S_E that have been completed thus far. Mathematical simulation studies showed that linear models are sufficient for characterizing pairwise levels of synchrony to the extent that the agents are operating under homogeneous conditions and the time intervals between observations are relatively short (Stefański 2009). Individual time series from a group dynamics study tend to harbor multiple lag lengths that are idiosyncratic to the individuals and particular pairs within a team (Guastello and Mirabito 2018). Thus, the linear relationships are often sufficient when the functions that are synchronizing are chaotic. Although some viable nonlinear functions connecting synchronized agents have been proposed, they require further study. For a worked-out example and numerical analyses that explored the properties of S_E, see Guastello and Peressini (2017).

Team Performance

Researchers have been actively exploring the synchronization of body movements, EEGs, and autonomic arousal of dyads, groups and teams as part of the explanation for team performance (Elkins et al. 2009; Guastello 2016; Henning, Boucsein, and Gil 2001) and the intervening group dynamics that impact the final performance outcomes, such as participation in decision-making (Guastello et al. 2016), team cohesion (Mønster et al. 2016), coordinated action (Richardson et al. 2012; Stevens and Galloway 2016), and adaptive action (Stevens, Galloway, and Willemson-Dunlap 2016). The initial proposition that stronger physiological synchronization was connected to better team performance seemed reasonable for tasks that required short-term repetition (Henning et al. 2001), although it was not immediately clear whether performance produced synchronization or vice versa, or whether the relationship was circular. Later studies diverged toward cognitive tasks and affiliative behaviors with either physiological or behavioral synchronization. The current state of the science relies on studies involving dyads and children along with adult task teams.

Synchronization and affiliation. Synchronization represents an affiliative phenomenon in which two people establish a rapport, hence the robust connection between autonomic synchronization and empathy in dyads (Palumbo et al. 2017). Hove and Risen (2009) showed that behavioral synchronization, which was deliberately manipulated with a finger-tapping task, promoted greater affiliation responses between the research participants and a confederate in the experiment. Participants who were pre-tested for social orientation, in contrast to individualistic or competitive orientation, synchronized with a sixty-second video tape of a person doing arm curls with barbells (Lumsden et al. 2012). The latter two studies together seem to suggest that the affiliation synchronization relationship could be circular.

In more realistic contexts, arousal levels drop in the presence of a romantic partner (Helm, Sbarra, and Ferrer 2012). Distressed couples, in contrast, tended toward higher levels of autonomic synchronization when discussing negative topics (Levinson and Gottman 1983). This finding led to the tentative conclusion that conflict produces synchronization, but that explanation was not generalizable when conflict was experimentally induced (Guastello et al. 2006); autonomic synchronization occurred at approximately the same levels for dyads in a conflict-inducing experimental condition and a non-conflicting conversation. Helm et al. (2012) found more synchronization in romantic couples when a partner had a relatively high level of anxiety, particularly attachment anxiety. Couples with higher relationship satisfaction showed less coupling of emotional states. It would not be clear, however, how these affiliation-synchronization patterns transport to task groups until groups that have very strong affiliative bonds in place are studied.

Mønster et al. (2016) showed that teams of three people, who were initially strangers, reported greater levels of group cohesion after displaying stronger levels of synchronization during a cognitive task. An earlier meta-analysis showed that more cohesive groups were also better-performing groups (Evans and Dion, 1991). Once again, it was not clear whether cohesion produces performance success, success produces cohesion, or the relationship is circular. Lebed and Bar-Eli (2013) suggested that the initial conditions of whether the groups started with affiliative bonds before the task activity began versus joining the task before they had formed any affiliative bonds could produce different patterns of team development.

Synchronization and performance. Henning et al. (2001) first reported a positive relationship between autonomic synchronization and performance for dyads engaging in a repetitive and rhythmic task. Elkins et al. (2009) also reported a positive relationship between autonomic synchronization and performance for larger teams engaged in a computer-based para-military simulation in which the team had to remove snipers from a building. Abney et al. (2015), however, found that dyads performing a cognitive task that involved making structures out of spaghetti and marshmallows performed better if their gross body movements were *loosely* coupled. The last finding could be idiosyncratic to the physical movements required by the task, and not necessarily generalizable to autonomic arousal for cognitive tasks.

The social interactions combined with the task could induce further complications with the synchronization results. Ramenzoni et al. (2011) found that synchronization of movements increased as the task became more difficult over time. Guevara et al. (2017), however, reported that the synchronization–performance link among children decreases over time as the task becomes more difficult, which they thought could be attributable to the task difficulty interfering with the dyadic interaction if it was not interfering with the task itself. They also reported that dyads performed equally well when both parties were contributing equally, or when one person was doing the majority of work. Thus the nexus of participation, social loafing and stag hunt coordination appears to be involved in the process. Vink et al. (2017) reported that, for dyads of children, *less* synchronization in postural sway was associated with better performance on a cognitive task. Children who were more *popular*, however, based on a sociometric survey given prior to the main experiment, were more synchronized.

The foregoing experiments involved dyads or groups working cooperatively on a task. Two studies considered a situation in which an ER team worked cooperatively internally, but competitively against an opponent. Electrodermal response measured autonomic arousal, and synchronization was measured by S_E. In the first study, ER teams of four competed against one attacker (Guastello et al. 2018) in a tournament of six games. S_E was not correlated with performance within a game, but it did increase to the extent that the teams won more games. S_E did not improve as a result of simply playing more games, however; thus, winning was critical to developing synchronization. Similarly, participation improved as a result of winning more games.

In the second study (Guastello et al. 2019), ER teams of four to eight members competed against one or two attackers, depending on the experimental condition. The tournament was divided between two experimental sessions of three games each. There was also a time pressure manipulation that was applied in either the first or second gaming session. S_E was unrelated to team performance, but it was affected by the experimental conditions, most often as interaction effects.

The participants also provided ratings of subjective workload at the end of each session. The NASA Task Load Index ratings (Hart and Staveland 1988) were used to capture individual-level cognitive workload. Individual responses were then averaged across team members to provide a value to correlate with S_E. The Group Workload (GWL) ratings recently developed by Helton, Funke and Knott (2014) are scales that are conceptually parallel to the NASA set, but for the group-level aspects of the activity. The central premise of the GWL is that teamwork involves sources of demand in addition to the individually defined sources. A separate analysis of the workload data from the second ER study showed that both sets of ratings were responsive to the experimental manipulations, although differences in GWL ratings were more localized to the number of attackers (Guastello and Marra 2018). Two workload ratings were correlated with S_E (Guastello, Correro et al. 2018): S_E was stronger in groups that rated coordination demands lower and communication demands higher. The higher communication demands could reflect difficulty in giving everyone a chance to contribute during a limited time allowance, and they could also reflect a heightened awareness of the need for communication among team members.

Stevens and Galloway (2016) reported several studies in which they assessed synchronization in EEG activity among teams of six members engaged in a submarine navigation task. They referred to their phenomenon as *team neurodynamics*, rather than synchronization *per se*, because they were actually examining how the team members went in and out of synchronization with each other during the task. The configurations of EEG matching were calculated at short intervals and represented by symbols. The symbols changed over time, and the amount of change was characterized by an entropy statistic. Of particular relevance here was the finding that better performing teams displayed less entropy during a phase of the task when they needed to maintain a common focus of attention, and greater entropy when they needed to take individual but coordinated action (Stevens et al. 2014).

Another EEG study showed that pseudo-pairs of people could display similar EEG patterns simply because they were subjected to the same experimental conditions (Burgess 2013). Furthermore, autonomic arousal between dyads synchronized when the partners were not interacting, but watching the same video (Golland, Arzouan, and Levit-Binnun 2015). This combination of results led to a study in which it was possible to compare S_E for autonomic arousal in groups that watched a video together, performed an individual cognitive task, then performed a group cognitive task (Guastello, Mirabito, and Peressini 2020). Groups of three to seven members engaged in a survival simulation in which their plane had crashed in northern Canada. They watched a video that explained their survival problem. In the individual task they rank-ordered fifteen items for their relevance to survival. In the group task they discussed their rankings to produce an optimized set of rankings. Performance was measured as the degree to which the team rankings matched those given by experts. No significant differences in S_E were obtained for the three parts of the study overall. Better performing groups, however, showed greater synchronization in the group task and less synchronization during the video and the individual task. In other words, performance was better when they acted as a group in the group task, but retained their individual concentration during the individual task. This combination of higher and lower S_E from the three parts of the study was further associated with GWL ratings for stronger team dissatisfaction, stronger demand for team effectiveness and lower ratings for time-sharing demand.

Summary

Specific NDS concepts and analyses have produced new research questions concerning adaptive behavior, coordination and synchronization that would not have been asked within the ordinary linear framework. The interest in adaptation that is currently shared with the linear community was addressed more vividly by the NDS community a decade earlier. NDS, furthermore, offers a metric for quantifying adaptation levels, and makes use of the concepts of attractors, bifurcations, chaos, turbulence, catastrophe and self-organization for explaining groups' responses to situations. The same concepts appear to explain learning phenomena at the group level and, to some extent, at the organizational level. Although a collective learning theory for humans is still a work in progress, the combination of basic nonlinear dynamics and the group phenomena studied here should continue to bring such a theory into sharper focus.

The primary results to date for team coordination phenomena from the NDS paradigm are: (a) there are several distinct forms of coordination covered in evolutionary game theory, not just one, as tacitly assumed in the conventional perspective; (b) shared mental models of the task and group processes are necessary, but they emerge or evolve extemporaneously as team members make sense of a changing situation; (c) verbal communication is neither necessary nor sufficient for developing team coordination, but it does help considerably; (d) coordination is implicitly learned at the group level, while the task is explicitly learned; and (e) leaders are neither necessary nor sufficient for developing team coordination, but they are likely to emerge anyway.

The primary results to date for synchronization phenomena are: (a) when behavioral synchronization is not explicitly defined by the task requirement, it is reflective of an affiliative process that can be recognized as an aspect of group cohesion; (b) synchronized autonomic arousal is also an affiliative process; (c) synchronized autonomic arousal is really a matter of degree and develops from empathy between coworkers and shared foci of attention; (d) when a team is engaged in a competitive task against an outside agent, shared successes produce improvements in team synchronization rather than vice versa or arising from simply working together for the same amount of time; and (e) in non-competitive tasks, team performance is better when members are not closely synchronized during individual phases of work, but are synchronized during group phases of work.

There are many opportunities for further research. For instance, more types of creative problem-solving, production, coordination-intensive or other types of tasks and groups should be examined, especially in real-world situations. The laboratory teams in the experiments to date were assembled for the purpose of the experiments, thus, the teams did not have any meaningful prior history with each other and probably not much other motivation for joining the group. Real-world groups often have deep and complex histories and a felt purpose, which could affect the social structures and leaders that emerge. Future NDS research should explore historical context variables within a group for their dynamical impact. The same case could be made for more examples of real-world coordination and synchronization research as well.

CHAPTER 2

Complexity Science and the Organization Sciences

1999–2018

Kevin J. Dooley

Introduction: The Roots of Complexity Science in the Organizational Sciences

Complexity science's roots lay in systems theory. Systems theory and cybernetics were initially created in the engineering (physical) sciences in the 1940s as a means to control complicated mechanical systems. While developing the means by which to target anti-aircraft guns, Norbert Wiener created the concept of systems feedback for purposes of teleological control of a system. Wiener and colleagues (1948a) posited that this general approach could be used in any artificial (i.e., human-made) or biological system. Social scientists were quick to recognize the broader theoretical and practical implications of systems theory, as biologist Ludwig von Bertalanffy (1951) developed the first outlines of General Systems Theory in 1951. Systems theory was generally attractive to those social scientists (Easton 1965) who found the existing reductionist paradigm to be problematic.

After its introduction, systems theory developed rapidly in depth and application in the 1960s–1980s. In the engineering domain, Wiener's methods were expanded to be applied to almost every electro-mechanical system in existence. In the physical and social sciences, theorists and experimentalists focused on developing systems theory that was specifically applicable to living systems. Much of that work touched upon how evolutionary processes (including learning), control mechanisms and a system's external environment shape system behavior.

Several system theorists stand out for their later influence on scholars in the organizational sciences. For example, W. Ross Ashby (1956) extended General Systems Theory to clarify the importance of variety in regulation and control of complex systems. Herbert Simon (1947) applied systems theory to administrative (business) organizations to model their evolution and control as the outcome of decision-making. Jay Forrester (1961) applied Weiner's mathematics of control theory to general systems and created the field of system dynamics, which used coupled differential equations to predict the evolution of systems. Maturana and Varela (1972) created the term autopoiesis to explain how living systems maintain and replicate themselves through processes of self-organization. Gregory Bateson (1972) also addressed this self-maintenance as a form of homeostasis, where systems interact with one another in both complementary and competitive ways. Rene Thom (1972) created the field of catastrophe theory, which used nonlinear models to show how complex systems can undergo singularities and hysteresis. Hermann Haken (1984) helped create the field of synergetics, which used thermodynamic principles to discuss how processes of self-organization worked.

In the 1980s, several developments took place that led to a very significant increase in awareness about living, or complex, systems amongst organizational scientists. The Santa Fe Institute was formed in 1984 as an interdisciplinary center to advance the study of complex systems. Out of this came the first popular books published on complexity science (e.g., Waldrop 1992; Lewin 1994), formal definitions of complex adaptive systems and the development of computational methods to simulate complex systems (Holland 1995), and domain-specific studies arguing that systems in their domain were best modeled as complex adaptive systems, drawing contrast to the mechanical and linear systems paradigm that existed in social sciences in general, and organizational sciences in particular. Parallel with this Ilya Prigogine and Isabelle Stengers's ([1984] 2018) *Order Out of Chaos*, which linked changes in complex systems to their state of being "far-from-equilibrium," where small changes in the external environment are adapted to by self-organization to a new dynamical attractor. Per Bak (1996) developed the so-called sandpile model to show how a system at a point of criticality can display extreme sensitivity to small changes.

In 1987, James Gleick's (1987) *Chaos: Making of a New Science* popularized the concept and computational methods of chaos theory and fractals. Chaos theory had been discovered at several points in history, but the book brought the topic to many for the first time, spurring empirical research using nonlinear, dynamical models. While chaos theory and nonlinear dynamics had broad applicability, there was particular focus on whether chaos theory could help improve financial (e.g., stock market) predictions (Taleb 2007). Akin to Forrester's system dynamics, nonlinear modeling and fractals were largely made possible because of the availability of computers, which was accelerating at the time.

As the concepts of complex adaptive systems and nonlinear dynamics became known by a much broader population of scholars and thought-leaders in the 1990s, these concepts were adopted into the fringes of academic and practitioner disciplines. Within the organizational sciences, numerous authors applied nonlinear dynamics and complexity science to organizational sciences. For example, Goldstein (1994) used concepts of self-organization to recommend a different normative approach to organizational change, contrasting with the dominant model at the time of Lewin's unfreeze-move-refreeze model of change. Dooley et al. (1995) and Dooley (1997) explained complex adaptive systems in the context of total quality management and organizational change and drew links between complexity science and other streams of organizational research, such as organizational learning. Stacey (1992), Levy (1994) and Thietart and Forgues (1995) contrasted traditional strategic planning processes to those more aligned with the complexity perspective. Kiel (1993) applied complexity science to government and other institutional processes, and Wheatley (1992) applied complexity concepts to organizational leadership. Eoyang (1997) developed the "container, difference and exchange" model to apply Prigogine's model of self-organization to organizational change phenomenon. Zimmerman and Hurst (1993) applied self-organizational principles to organizational learning processes in health care, and Brown and Eisenhardt (1998) suggested that innovation processes should be managed as complex adaptive systems. Cheng and Van de Ven (1996) modeled organizational data to find chaotic dynamics in organizational routines during new product development. Guastello (1995) used catastrophe theory models to explain human resource and organizational development processes in organizations.

Several organizations were founded in the 1990s to support this increased attention to complexity. The Chaos Network formed in 1988 to gather scholars who were interested in complexity science and organizational change and development. The Society for Chaos Theory in Psychology and Life Sciences began in 1991 and focused on empirical modeling of nonlinear dynamical systems. The Plexus Institute started in 1995 to help health care practitioners apply complexity science to their operations and clinical care. The New England Complexity Systems Institute was founded in 1996 as a think tank for complexity science scholars in New England universities and has done much work on social systems. Specialized journals also started up during this period. The journal *Nonlinear Dynamics in Psychology and Life Sciences* began in 1997 and *Emergence: Complexity and Organization* began in 1999. The American Society for Public Administration formalized the Section for Complexity and Network Studies in 2008, though its roots trace back to the mid-1990s. Interestingly, all of these organizations and journals (except Chaos Network) are still in existence in 2020.

The proliferation of research articles, empirical studies, practical applications and institutions (specialized journals and professional societies) in the 1990s was suggestive of a significant change in theory and practice of organizational sciences—a paradigm shift. In fact, Barker's (1992) book, *Future Edge*, introduced the notion of Kuhnian paradigm change to the world of business in the context of complexity science. The movie *Mindwalk* (Capra 1990) featured a physicist, poet and politician struggling to shed a mechanistic frame and adopt one of holism. At the end of the movie, the protagonist asks, "Is this a turning point?" As a scholar embedded in these activities in the 1990s, I certainly thought so. I would have predicted back then that twenty years later there would be hundreds of organization science scholars, if not the majority, who had changed their mental models and workstreams and would begin their inquiries from the foundations of complexity science, or at least acknowledge such an approach.

This chapter addresses the question: what happened to the use of complexity science concepts after this initial fount of awareness, excitement and foundation building? Can we consider complexity science to be a paradigm shift in the organizational sciences? A period of twenty years, 1999–2018, is examined to assess, in particular, the fields of general management and supply chain management, two business disciplines that were particularly active in first experimenting with complexity science. All relevant papers published in the two disciplines' top journals are identified and analyzed as to how complexity science concepts have been applied. Next, I conduct a deeper review of two specific research topics—complex adaptive supply networks and complexity leadership—and examine relevant papers across relevant journals.

In brief, the answer to the questions are mixed and nuanced, as with complexity science itself. Complexity science has not been a paradigm shift in the classical, Kuhnian sense. Linear and mechanistic thinking is still the foundation for much or most of organizational science, in practice and in theory, but it perhaps is not as dominant as it once was. However, specific ideas in complexity science have become well-linked with certain phenomena of scholarly interest (e.g., emergence and organizational change) and have created significant bodies of knowledge, mostly published in the secondary journals within the disciplines. Moreover, if we view complexity science not independently, but rather as part of a systems theory movement that is now seventy years old, the influence on theory and practice is clearer and significant. These influences will be addressed in greater length in the discussion section of the chapter.

Evolution and Revolution in Scientific Paradigms

Thomas Kuhn wrote *The Structure of Scientific Revolutions* in 1962. In it, he explained that, during a phase of "normal science," a discipline would accumulate knowledge, one study building upon the other. In normal science, scholars share similar assumptions, concepts, definitions and mechanisms in the discipline. There are times, however, when existing theory cannot explain observed phenomena. This becomes a phase when a paradigm shift is possible: an alternative theory that differs fundamentally from an existing theory is proposed and is better at explaining observations. Kuhn (1962) said, "First, the new candidate must seem to resolve some outstanding and generally recognized problem that can be met in no other way. Second, the new paradigm must promise to preserve a relatively large part of the concrete problem-solving activity that has accrued to science through its predecessors" (168). During the paradigm shift, old knowledge and theory would be re-questioned, and assumptions, concepts, definitions and mechanisms would change. Kuhn's model is one of punctuated equilibrium within a discipline.

Kuhn discussed the type of observable behavior that would indicate a paradigm shift had occurred. The new paradigm would be popularized by newcomers, who would intellectually battle the old guard representing the existing paradigm. The new assumptions and mental models get embedded into standard language and definitions and eventually become part of the discipline's standard corpus (i.e., textbooks and other reference documents). New institutions, such as journals or professional societies, form to support the new paradigm, and existing institutions adopt means by which to accommodate or absorb the interests of the new paradigm.

Kuhn did not particularly stress that his model was applicable to the social sciences. In the physical sciences, a truth exists as measurement; in the social sciences, truth is not binary, and reality is interpreted. For example, while agency theory is a much-used theory in management and supply chain management, there is open debate about the validity of agency theory's assumptions about human nature (Donaldson 1990). However, even if agency theory's assumptions are considered weak, organization science scholars will still use it because, at an abstract level, the theory's context (i.e., situations where an agent is working for a principal) is still broadly applicable. Whereas physical science theories substitute for one another across the boundary of a paradigm shift, theories in the social sciences are not overturned as much as they simply fall out of favor.

In line with that idea, Abbott's (2001) model of disciplinary evolution can be thought of as a complexity-inspired update of the Kuhnian model. Abbott uses the concept of fractals to explain how disciplinary evolution creates theoretical or methodological cleavages in a discipline, and development tends to occur through the competition between these two paradigms, or mindsets. These paradigms address the same core problems of the discipline over time, but at any given time one will tend to dominate the other. For example, in the discipline of supply chain management, empiricists and mathematical modelers conceptualize the same business problem or phenomena in very different ways (Dooley 2009b).

Scholarly disciplines involve decisions by scholars who are embedded in a career where they need to demonstrate creativity and novelty.

Abbott says that while established scholars may see benefit and efficiency remaining in the dominant paradigm, some young scholars will tend to find more open territory by working problems from the perspective of the emerging paradigm, creating momentum for a shift. This establishes a cycle: the new paradigm is not so much a new paradigm as an older paradigm that is being reborn with new and updated language and concepts. Abbott's model also suggests that disciplines will tend to compete for which core problems belong to them, and that more successful disciplines will tend to appropriate those core problems away from others. For example, both supply chain management scholars and geography scholars work on the question of "supply chain governance," but there is little interaction between the two disciplines' workstreams. Supply chain scholars seeking to expand their conceptual base may appropriate novel components of geography's approach, and vice versa.

Methods

According to both the Kuhn and Abbott models, a new paradigm (or reborn older paradigm) will manifest itself in the scholarly publications of the discipline. However, an exploration of everything that has been published in management and supply chain management from 1999 to 2018 is infeasible. For that reason, a two-step process was used.

A search was conducted for complexity-inspired publications in the top-ranked journals of each discipline. Top-ranked journals are often more risk averse, thus the presence of complexity science ideas in such journals indicates penetration of those ideas into the core of either discipline. Top-ranked journals also tend to get cited more, so publications in them are more likely to be influential to future scholars' works. I used the *Financial Times* list of fifty business journals (Ormans 2016) that many business schools use as the "A-journal" list. The list was last updated in 2016 and was created using a survey of over 200 business schools. Within each journal, I used the following search terms: complex, complexity, complex adaptive, emergence, self-organization, chaos, chaotic, nonlinear. I examined all search results, reading the title and abstract and the body of paper when there was ambiguity.

The words "complexity" and "emergence" are often used in a vernacular way. Complexity can be interpreted as "many" and emergence as the "beginning of." This use of the words is not misaligned with their deeper meaning in a complexity science context. In many models of complex (adaptive) systems, the number of components that make up a system contributes to its complexity. For example, in a network of "N" people, the number of pairwise couples in the network is a function of N^2, so coordination complexity increases as a quadratic function of N. Equations that quantify the computational complexity of a system usually have some parameter related to the number of components in the system.

Likewise, the concept of emergence in complexity science is similar to its simpler meaning, as it relates to the beginning of a new system, where elements of the new system are somewhat unpredictable. In both these cases, though, the use of the word is the end—further concepts, theories and insight in the paper do not draw from complexity science. Thus, I also looked for references related to complexity science to ensure the paper's relevance to the research question at hand.

The relevant journals searched are listed below with the number of relevant publications found in parentheses. The journals *Administrative Science Quarterly*, *Journal of Management*, *Manufacturing and Service Operations Management*, *Operations Research*, *Organizational Behavior and Human Decision Processes*, *Production and Operations Management*, *Sloan Management Review* and *Strategic Entrepreneurship Journal* had zero relevant articles.

- *Academy of Management Journal* (1)
- *Academy of Management Review* (5)
- *Entrepreneurship Theory and Practice* (1)
- *Journal of Business Ethics* (3)
- *Journal of Business Venturing* (4)
- *Journal of Management Studies* (3)
- *Journal of Operations Management* (1)
- *Management Science* (7)
- *Organization Science* (16)
- *Organization Studies* (6)
- *Strategic Management Journal* (3)

Complexity Science Publications in *Financial Times* Organization Science Journals

In reviewing the relevant papers, I sorted them into categories dependent on the specific theories they drew from. The most common applications of complexity science came from works inspired by Kauffman's (1993) NK rugged landscape model, Prigogine and Stenger's ([1984] 2018) model of change when dissipative systems are in a far-from-equilibrium state (including applications to entrepreneurial dynamics), and Ashby's (1956) Law of Requisite Variety. Some papers also drew from Bak's sandpile model of self-organized criticality (1996) and the modeling techniques of nonlinear dynamical systems (Guastello 1995).

A number of papers used complexity science concepts as a *loose theoretical framework*, arguing that it provided a better theoretical lens than extant theories. Anderson (1999) reviews the application of complexity science to organizational sciences. Key conceptual elements include: agents with schema, self-organized networks sustained by importing energy, coevolution to the edge of chaos and recombination and system evolution. Wong (1999) uses complexity science concepts to argue how Chinese *guanxi* can be conceptualized as a complex adaptive system that uses networks of networks to create a highly adaptive social structure. Peterson and Meckler (2001) use qualitative arguments to explain that immigrant entrepreneurship is like a chaotic system in that it has sensitivity to small changes and can be patterned while seeming random. Colbert (2004) argues that complexity science concepts provide a strategic human resource management extension of the resource-based view by focusing on emergence, unpredictability, agency, and causal ambiguity. Burgelman and Grove (2007) use complexity science as a type of theoretical triangulation, adding a systems theoretic explanation to their game theoretic model of nonlinear strategic dynamics. Groves, Vance and Paik (2008) examine linear and non-linear thinking and its influence on ethical decision-making. Garud, Gehman and Kumaraswamy (2011) use different dimensions of complexity to explain why different innovation processes have different dynamics. Using case analyses, they posit that relational, manifest, regulative and temporal complexity is managed correspondingly by "complexity arrangements" by organizational agents, allowing them to use narrative and discourse to deal with these complexities.

Two papers mainly drew theoretical inspiration from Bak's sandpile model of *self-organized criticality* (1996). The model states that when a complex system is at a state of self-organized criticality (involving its degree of connectedness), small perturbations lead to an inverse power law of observed consequences. Morel and Ramanujam (1999) discuss self-organized criticality and its role in organizational evolution. They use random graph theory to develop propositions about how organizations evolve without depending on a teleological premise. Accard (2018) uses the model to explain how small changes to organizational norms and routines diffuse unpredictably, sometimes leading to no change and sometimes leading to transformational change. Even though these were the only two papers to use the sandpile model explicitly, many other papers that discussed self-organizing phenomena also mentioned it as part of their theory development.

Several papers focused on Ashby's *Law of Requisite Variety* (1956) and the general notion that firms choose to reduce complexity in the environment as a response to complexity misalignment. Most of these papers suggest that a far-from-equilibrium model (Prigogine and Stengers [1984] 2018), which emphasizes complexity absorption over complexity reduction, is a better explanation of many situations. Boisot and Child (1999) argue that China's evolution can be better understood as a case of complexity absorption as opposed to complexity reduction. Ashmos et al. (2002) argue that complexity absorption is an alternative to complexity reduction, and that participation and collaboration are efficient means to conduct such complexity absorption. Boisot and McKelvey (2010) argue that Ashby's Law and the concept of self-organized criticality can provide causal explanations that bridge modernism and post-modernism perspectives. Schneider, Wickert and Marti (2017) posit that organizations can use collaboration complexity as an adaptive mechanism and will choose to do so opportunistically. Specifically, if collaborators exist to reduce the amount of effort and resources needed to appropriately respond, organizations will prefer collaboration to developing internal complexity. Poulis and Poulis (2016) argue that Ashby's Law was misappropriated by management scholars. Their work adapts and extends the model to differentiate low and high levels of environmental and organizational complexity.

Several papers drew inspiration from the area of *nonlinear dynamics*. Dooley and Van de Ven (1999) develop a diagnostic map linking observed nonlinear dynamics to corresponding nonlinear generative models. They conceptualize the causal system by dimensionality and the nature of interaction between causal factors, yielding either periodic, white noise, chaotic or colored noise dynamics. Frank and Fahrbach (1999) develop a nonlinear model of the role of balance and information in decision models. Haxholdt, Larsen and van Ackere (2003) model a deterministic queuing system with feedback and show under what conditions mode-locking or chaotic dynamics can be observed. Linn and Tay (2007) examine behavior in stock market prices that is indicative of nonlinear dynamical systems at a point of self-organized criticality. Their model involves "complex, self-referential learning and reasoning amongst economic agents … traders who reason inductively while compressing information into a few fuzzy notions that they can in turn process and analyze with fuzzy logic" (1165). Farjoun and Levin (2011) use information complexity theory and nonlinear dynamics to argue that industry dynamics can best be understood as a fractal process. In a study of the television industry over time, they demonstrate that the fractal dimension of an outcome indicator (viewership) is more predictive of industry turbulence than the indicator's standard deviation.

Kauffman's rugged landscape (NKC) model (1993) has been a popular theory to use to examine the process of organizational search from a broad number of perspectives. The NK model consists of the number of system components (N) and their connectivity (K). These create a performance landscape that may be smooth (when K is low or zero) or rugged (when K is moderate or high). This causes different adaptive search dynamics when looking for an optimal system configuration. The NKC model, an extension, considers the level of connectivity (C) between coupled landscapes.

McKelvey (1999) used the NKC landscape model to explore the complexity that arises when value chains of firms and their competitors overlap. His simulations suggest that moderate amounts of both internal and external connectivity yield the highest adaptability and fitness. Levinthal and Warglien (1999) applied the NK model to examine dynamics of adaptive search within new product development teams and distinguish the tradeoffs between modular and integral system design. Rivkin (2000) uses the NK model to examine whether complex organizations can be copied. He finds that such copying by other organizations can only be successful if it is coupled with a search and learning strategy.

Mihm, Loch and Huchzermeier (2003) use the NK model to show that in new product development projects, adaptive search may oscillate between solutions and diverge to low performing configurations, and they suggest managerial actions that could mitigate these search dysfunctionalities. Ethiraj and Levnithal (2004) use the NK model to examine optimal product design. They conclude that there is a "trade-off between the destabilizing effects of overly refined modularization and the modest levels of search and a premature fixation on inferior designs that can result from excessive levels of integration. The analysis highlights an asymmetry in this trade-off, with excessively refined modules leading to cycling behavior and a lack of performance improvement" (159).

Rivkin and Siggelkow (2007) adapt the NK model to more fully incorporate complexity-based attributes, such as small-world phenomena, power laws, hierarchies and preferential attachment in networks. Their models suggest that even if N and K are the same, search results can vary by an order of magnitude depending on the nature of the interactions within the complex system. Ganco and Agarwal (2009) use the NKC landscape model to explore performance differences between existing firms who are diversifying versus entrepreneurial start-ups within a dynamic market. The model shows that existing firms will benefit when industry turbulence is high, but start-ups benefit more from learning effects.

Mihm et al. (2010) use a variant of the NK model to explore the role of hierarchy in search. They conclude: "(1) assigning a lead function that 'anchors' a solution speeds up problem-solving; (2) local solution choice should be delegated to the lowest level; and (3) structure matters little at the middle management level, but it matters at the front line; front-line groups should be kept small" (831). Baumann and Siggelkow (2013) use the NK model to examine the tradeoffs between local versus global search in organizational problems. Their findings suggest that the best search strategy and sequencing depends on the nature of the underlying fitness landscape. Billinger, Stieglitz and Schumacher (2014) compare adaptive search behavior of humans in experiments to predictions from Kauffman's NK (1993) model. Their results confirm that humans explore after failure and exploit after success.

Perhaps the most popular theory for organizational scientists is Prigogine and Stenger's ([1984] 2018) model of change in *dissipative systems that are far-from-equilibrium*. Their theory draws upon a thermodynamic model of what happens when a system imports energy from an external source. From the organization theory perspective, the external source is the external environment of the organization. Under normal loads, the system balances the import and processing (dissipation) of that energy; as energy import increases and pushes the system far-from-equilibrium, small perturbations can shift the attractor of the system. This new structure performs the same function but is structurally different, and more capable of dissipating the energy imported.

In some papers, the dissipative model is used for theoretical reasoning. Macintosh and Maclean (1999) use a dissipative model of complex adaptive systems to explain strategic organizational change. They propose a three-stage process model of conditioning: preparing for change and learning, creating far-from-equilibrium conditions and managing positive and negative feedback. They posit that managers can have some influence on the new structures that emerge if they work at the "deep systems" level and use feedback appropriately. Madden et al. (2012) use a far-from-equilibrium model to explain the emergence of organizational capacity for compassion. This includes a personal tragedy acting as a trigger, agents sensemaking and amplifying awareness, and organizing into new organizational routines.

The dissipative, far-from-equilibrium model has also been used in conjunction with case studies, sometimes in the form of event history studies. Chiles, Meyer and Hench (2004) use a dissipative model to analyze the emergence of the entertainment cluster in Branson, Missouri. Their case study maps historical events to four dimensions of the complexity model: fluctuation, positive feedback, stabilization and recombination. Meyer, Gaba and Colwell (2005) examine four case studies of change and evolution in institutional fields and argue that a complexity science lens provides a fuller thick causal narrative than existing linear models of change. They conclude that institutional change is better understood via far-from-equilibrium dynamics.

Plowman et al. (2007) use far-from-equilibrium logic to explain an organizational change event that cannot be easily explained using traditional organizational change logic. They state,

> radical change was unintended, emergent, and slow; destabilizing conditions helped small changes to emerge and become radical;

subsequent actions amplified an initial small change and, though not intended to do so, promoted radical change; finally, the dynamic interaction of amplifying actions, contextual conditions, and small changes led to continuous radical change.

(515)

This is an archetypal description of far-from-equilibrium dynamics.

Chiles et al. (2010) merge complexity science theories of emergence with concepts from Austrian economics and organizational structure theory to develop a model of dynamics in entrepreneurism. They propose "entrepreneurs, by imagining divergent futures and (re)combining heterogeneous resources to create novel products, drive far-from-equilibrium market processes to create not market anarchy but market order" (7). Beck and Plowman (2014) perform an inductive case study of the Columbia space shuttle disaster to explain the emergence of collaboration between government agencies and departments. Their model posits that far-from-equilibrium conditions within trust and identity were coupled with self-organization to lead to relational trust and a collective identity, which led to the temporary interorganizational structure to collaborate within. Girod and Whittington (2015) use complexity science to examine whether organizational change can become discontinuous through accumulation or perturbation. They use an event history analysis of Ford Motor Company to show that incremental continuous change is a causal precursor to discontinuous change—accumulation can lead to a state of criticality where a small perturbation can yield a new self-organized configuration.

Thietart (2016) uses event history analysis to examine the evolution of the multinational firm, Danone, over forty-plus years. He used time series analysis of the event data to identify both periodic and colored noise dynamics. He overlaid these dynamical explanations with qualitative information at the macro and micro levels to develop theories regarding strategic change. For example, one of the derived hypotheses was "An intermediary level of organized sequences of strategic actions at the micro level is necessary for self-organized strategy dynamics to develop at the macro level" (Thietart 2016). As he points out, this is aligned with other models of emergence in entrepreneurial processes (Lichtenstein et al. 2007).

The study of entrepreneurism involves the question of how firms emerge, so the dissipative model has also been applied to the area of entrepreneurial dynamics. McKelvey (2004) argues that theories of entrepreneurial processes would be better tested using agent-based modeling. Such an approach would afford insight into multiple types of causality (material, final, efficient, formal) and multi- and equifinality. Lichtenstein, Dooley and Lumpkin (2006) use event history analysis of a nascent entrepreneur to study the dynamics of events related to vision, strategy and tactics. The three time series experience a change point concurrent with the formal emergence of the firm, and this is defined as the emergence event. Time series analyses indicate that tactical changes led to strategic changes which led to change in vision, a sequence in the opposite direction of what is typically posited in rational change models.

Lichtenstein et al. (2007) suggest that pre-emergence dynamics alone can explain the emergence of new organizations. They draw from models of far-from-equilibrium systems to posit that firms will more likely be created when the temporal rate of organizing is high, the temporal concentration of organizing is low, and the temporal timing of organizing is later. Results from a three-year panel sample of 335 nascent entrepreneurs supported the hypotheses. Schindehutte and Morris (2009) argue that entrepreneurship research needs to adopt a CAS perspective to better address exploration–exploitation, opportunity, newness, micro–macro interaction and dynamics. CAS provides a means to explain fluctuations, irreversibility, nonlinearity and instability, and focuses on form, flow and function. Selden and Fletcher (2015) conceptualize the "emergent hierarchical system of entrepreneurial artifact-creating processes" (603). Their model discusses how loosely coupled artifacts emerge at five levels (sense-making, stakeholder, firm, market, society) and form into a hierarchy, akin to Simon's (1962) model of architectural complexity.

Discussion

First, the results show that complexity-science-inspired publications are a small minority within the disciplines' top-rated journals. There were zero relevant publications in five of the fourteen management journals, and three of the five supply chain management journals; the highest number (sixteen) was in the journal *Organization Science*. Given the number of articles published in twenty years in these journals, we can conclude that complexity science has not been a major part of the corpus of the two discipline's top journals, at least as defined by the *Financial Times* list.

This point, though, must be taken with nuance. Lack of presence within the journals in the *Financial Times* list does not *de facto* mean that complexity-inspired papers are not in some of the "top" journals in management or supply chain management. There are journals not in the *Financial Times* list that are still considered "A" journals by departments and colleges; and of course, there are many secondary journals that were not searched here and are nevertheless an important part of a discipline's corpus. Complexity-inspired work has occurred in both.

For example, only two papers in the *Financial Times* sample address complexity and leadership. Painter-Morland (2008) uses CAS concepts to argue that leadership is relational and distributed throughout the organization. Tourish (2018) examines the literature on "complexity and leadership" and posits that while many papers have adopted new language, the mechanisms they posit are still simple and grounded in the historical "leader as hero" meme. Tourish (2018) suggests, "The key theoretical challenge, therefore, is to proceed from the foundational assumption that leadership cannot be understood so long as it is envisaged as a means whereby powerful actors exercise more or less unidirectional influence on others and on organizational systems" (15).

"Two papers" does not accurately reflect the level of scholarly activity, though. During this time, there was a concerted attempt by complexity and leadership scholars to coalesce and create new theory and studies—the Tourish criticism noted above speaks to the broader work. Uhl-Bien, Marion and McKelvey (2007) published their seminal work in *The Leadership Quarterly*. Their model posits that "three entangled leadership roles (adaptive leadership, administrative leadership and enabling leadership) reflect a dynamic relationship between the bureaucratic, administrative functions of the organization and the emergent, informal dynamics of complex adaptive systems" (298). The paper was part of a special issue on Leadership and Complexity, and other papers included the application of catastrophe theory (Guastello 2007), agent-based models (Hazy 2007) and edge of chaos (Osborn and Hunt 2007). The work also led to a number of conference special sessions and an edited book (Uhl-Bien and Marion 2008).

Similarly, only one paper in the *Financial Times* sample concerned complex adaptive supply networks. Choi, Dooley and Rungtusanatham (2001) propose that supply chains are better conceptualized as supply networks that act as complex adaptive systems. They posit that supply networks are not controlled or designed by any single organization, but are the evolutionary result of a set of make–buy and supplier selection decisions that are made locally by buying organizations within the network. Further, they suggest that the traditional dyad of buyer–supplier is insufficient to understand real-world behavior in supply networks. The paper has over 1,300 citations.

Some papers have drawn from the general framework to develop complexity-specific models (Pathak, Dilts, and Biswas 2007). For example, Pathak, Dilts and Biswas (2007) model the evolution of supply networks using multi-agent simulation modeling. Kauffman et al. (2018) develop the concept of "tinkering" in a complex supply network design to accommodate "unknown-unknowns." However, most of these papers that cite Choi et al. (2001) have appropriated the term "supply network" as an alternative to "supply chain" and conducted empirical investigations using social network (graph) theory and methods (Kim et al. 2011). In this case, the concept of a supply network as a complex adaptive system is attractive, but it is merged back into more familiar theoretical constructs and empirical methods.

Second, it is interesting to note that the complexity theories drawn on by organizational scholars are generally based on non-living systems. Self-organized criticality is based on a model of a sandpile. Ashby's Law of Requisite Variety was initially focused on control of electro-mechanical systems. Kauffman's (1993) rugged landscape model is based on a physics model of electron spin, and chaos and fractals are based on a computational paradigm (even though their connections to natural systems are obvious). Prigogine and Stenger's model of far-from-equilibrium dynamics in dissipative systems is steeped in living systems, but the archetype example that many refer to in the book involves the formation of convection cells in a heated liquid medium. Given that complexity science emerged to some extent as a response to systems theory being primarily focused on non-living systems, this is an ironic outcome.

Third, we can contrast the relative popularity of the dissipative systems model to the use of nonlinear dynamics modeling. Both provide an alternative theoretical frame to the problem they are applied to. Given that scholars are seeking novel theories or methods to apply to mostly existing problems, both approaches would seem to be appealing. The dissipative systems model, however, can be applied as a process model to comprehend qualitative data. It serves as a direct contrast to other process models of change, such as punctuated equilibrium, and the model is fungible enough to "fit" the case. Meanwhile, empirical modeling of nonlinear dynamics requires access to software, expertise with the nuance of the methods, and creates results that are more difficult to interpret in the context of the real system. Organizational data are also often too sparse or noisy to estimate nonlinear models.

Fourth, the impact of complexity science on theory and practice cannot be estimated alone by research publications. Organizations like Human System Dynamics have been training managers and organizational change specialists for over a decade, drawing from Eoyang's model (1997), which is a pragmatic reformulation of the dissipative model. Faculty have introduced complexity science concepts within their business courses, which also affects practice. For example, I have used the rugged landscape model in my "Management of Technology" class for over fifteen years. Students who are engineers and designers have an immediate intuitive grasp of what the model describes, and it helps make real the tradeoffs between modular and integral system design. Business practices today in the "sharing economy" (e.g., Cohen and Kietzman 2014), such as Uber or Airbnb, align directly with agent-based approaches advocated twenty years ago to use distributed control systems to manage complexity.

Conclusion

This chapter sought to answer the question: what happened to the use of complexity science in business research after its initial introduction? I scoped the assessment to management and supply chain management and examined research in both top-rated and other journals. The review suggests that while the presence of complexity-inspired publications is infrequent in the top-ranked journals, there is much activity more broadly, especially involving specific theories. The most common complexity science theories drawn on by organizational scholars were Kauffman's (1993) NK rugged landscape model, Prigogine and Stenger's ([1984] 2018) model of change when dissipative systems are in a far-from-equilibrium state (including applications to entrepreneurial dynamics), and Ashby's (1956) Law of Requisite Variety.

It must be noted, though, that the influence of complexity science on organizational theory and practice cannot be observed only via academic publications. Concepts such as emergence, the butterfly effect (chaos) and networks are part of everyday vernacular of the world. Would these concepts have been as popular without complexity science? We cannot know. But if we widen our time frame—asking not what the impact of complexity science is, but rather what the impact of systems theory and thinking has been—the answer has to be that it has had profound impacts on theory and practice.

Complexity science has not followed Kuhn's model of scientific revolution; rather, it has been a "normal science" extension of systems theory. Just as simple theories seek contingencies to make them more accurate, systems theory was extended with a variety of models that helped it appeal to a new set of scholars and be applied to create novel insights and thick causal explanations. In that context, Abbott's (2001) model of disciplinary evolution is a more appropriate causal explanation. The rigorous application of complexity science concepts and methods has created a niche that several hundred scholars across the business disciplines explore. More broadly, business scholars have appropriated the terms of complexity science and absorbed them into their own existing paradigm—a type of complexity absorption.

CHAPTER 3

Complexity Science and the Study of Armed Conflict
A Narrative Review

Maxime H.T. Stauffer

Introduction

Conflicts, from arms races to revolutions, share an inherent complexity from their causes—attributed to multiple heterogeneous actors, connected by social ties and group allegiances—to their location, diffusion, duration and termination. While the conflict literature, with notable exceptions, pays lip service to notions of complexity, the theories, approaches and data that constitute the body of this work are largely distanced from this approach. Responding to these shortcomings, scholars from disciplines as varied as mathematics, physics, biology and computer science have leveraged techniques and approaches from complexity science and applied these to the study of inter- and intra-state conflict. While this particular research community may not be large, it is nonetheless influential, featuring, for example, the seminal work of Richardson (1948, 1951) on arms race dynamics and the size of wars, or recent research on terrorism that draws on concepts from statistics, biology and physics (Clauset et al. 2007; Bohorquez et al. 2009; Manrique et al. 2018). In political science and international relations, scholars such as Axelrod and Cederman (Axelrod 1984; Cederman 2003), and more recently Gleditsch, Weidmann and

Bhavnani (Clauset and Gleditsch 2012; Weidmann and Salehyan 2013; Bhavnani et al. 2014) have followed suit.

Existing reviews of this field have focused solely on inter-state conflict and agent-based modeling (Cioffi-Revilla 2017; Pepinsky 2005). In contrast, this chapter provides a review of the emergence and evolution of the applications of complexity science to both inter- and intra-state conflicts and extends the analysis to related approaches, such as dynamical systems theory and chaos theory. The goal of this review, however, is not to be exhaustive. Instead, it focuses on the field's key developments and illustrates them with selected pieces of literature. This chapter offers an overview, beginning with past scholarship before turning to current and future applications. Each past, present and future section unfolds as follows. First, the chapter discusses how the theoretical approaches taken by this literature have helped shape the understanding of conflict processes. Second, it documents how these approaches have driven the development and use of new datasets on conflict. And third, it examines advances in the methods used, as a function of technological change and sophistication, to study complex conflict processes.

Complexity and Conflict

The idea of what constitutes a complex system is closely linked to the concept of *emergence*, coined by the English philosopher George Henry Lewes (1875), to imply that dynamics at the system level cannot be understood from the (known) characteristics of its parts. It follows that one aspect of what makes a system complex is not the nature of its constituent parts, but how their interactions give rise to the phenomena observed at the level of the system as a whole. Viewed through this lens, macro-level structures, such as spatial or temporal patterns of violence, are emergent phenomena that arise from the interaction of co-evolving parts—be these individuals, groups, states or institutions—and are not simply additive. This premise stands in marked contrast to what may be termed a *complicated* system comprised of many parts with known properties, from which it is possible to understand and predict system properties or behavior.

Conflict dynamics also tend to be *nonlinear*—that is, seemingly small changes in conflict conditions or minor shifts in momentum may drastically change conflict trajectories or outcomes. Conceptually, this may arise both from the inherently nonlinear character of conflict processes themselves, as well as from a multiplicity of causes.[1] The nonlinear nature of conflict processes can best be understood as arising from intrinsic *feedback loops*—actors and their actions change the conflict environment, which in turn affects their attributes and affinities, decisions, and actions (Beyerchen 1992). For example, the literature on intrastate conflict has advanced this notion in the study of selective vs indiscriminate violence in asymmetric warfare: indiscriminate use of force tends to create new grievances, which in turn increase civilian support and result in more violence, compared to selective use of force (Ellsberg 1970; Schutte 2017). Such systemic feedback loops lead to the intensification of conflict, even if the conflict environment otherwise remains unchanged.

The nonlinear character of conflict dynamics further suggests a high degree of dependence on initial conditions—the notion that decisions made by a few individuals or the particular officer on duty on a given day could dramatically shape the course of a doomsday nuclear confrontation (Saperstein 1984). In a related vein, the actions of actors themselves are highly context-specific—actor characteristics may shape or constrain but fall short of fully determining actions. For example, within a battle, the current trajectory of fighting influences the next, immediate set of decisions to be taken (von Clausewitz 1976). Such dynamic, interconnected conflict processes are notoriously difficult to predict, closely linked to the notion of *analytical blindness* (Poincaré 1912) on the part of analysts, military and political leaders. Conflicts may also be thought of as systems that are not in equilibrium, with parallels drawn to self-organized criticality (Cederman 2003). Such systems undergo a rapid transition from one "state" to another, also referred to as a "phase transition." According to this view, the process by which a particular conflict unfolds is equally, if not more, important than the outcome itself, given that *emergent* macro-level phenomena, such as the size of battles or attacks, arise from dynamics at the micro-level. Research has shown that the signatures associated with this type of critical behavior are robust across countries and types of conflict (Richardson 1948; Clauset et al. 2007).

---

1. See, for instance, Wolfson, Puri and Martelli (1992) who have explored this in the context of balance-of-power and preponderance-of-power theories of international conflict.

Why and *how*, then, does the notion of complexity apply to the study of conflict? Many of today's intra-state conflicts are fought without clear frontlines, against the backdrop of often massive civilian displacement due to the struggle among multiple heterogeneous actors. This implies that the social fabric upon which conflict is fought shapes conflict but is then itself shaped by violence. Similarly, the trajectory of inter-state conflicts arises from a complex interplay of strategic considerations, shifting alliances and, ultimately, the outcomes of individual confrontations on the ground. In other words, conflict dynamics—both inter- and intra-state—are less aptly characterized as *complicated*, bearing the typical hallmarks of *complex* phenomena instead. While the notion of explicitly accounting for the intrinsic complexity of a system may sound simple, in reality it is far more challenging to identify the constituent parts, their attributes and inter-relations, and the underlying mechanisms that give rise to observed outcomes.

The approaches to armed conflict that take the perspective of complexity science share the following features: (1) *formalization* that forces researchers to be explicit about all their modeling choices and assumptions; (2) the use of *computational* and *analytical approaches* that specify how all too numerous, interdependent, micro-level interactions produce emergent macro-level dynamics; and (3) a reliance on *data* to enable a more accurate specification of initial conditions and the ability to validate model outcomes. The combination of the three is what, arguably, sets this scholarship apart, affording a closer representation of the complexity of conflict processes. In what follows, the chapter reviews theoretical contributions and methodological advances—with respect to data and technical approaches—beginning with the past and moving forward in time.

Past: Prior to 2000

The past century witnessed large-scale inter-state conflicts followed by a sharp rise in intra-state or civil conflicts (Gleditsch et al. 2002; Sarkees and Wayman 2010). Before the early 2000s, conflict research largely focused only on the former, given a greater availability of knowledge and information, from official, scholarly or media sources. World Wars I and II shaped a generation of scholars who put primacy on understanding major-power, state- and alliance-centered, ideologically-driven armed confrontation. This focus went hand-in-hand with national research priorities to inform military and defense strategy. Without a doubt, a large part of this effort was also directed at understanding the threat to human existence posed by nuclear arms races.

Theory

Seminal work by Carl von Clausewitz (1780–1831), *On War* (1976), portrays conflict as an inherently nonlinear phenomenon that can only be understood by carefully studying the mutual interdependence of actors (Beyerchen 1992). This understanding of conflict emphasizes understanding psychological feedback loops between opponents: "the course of a given war becomes thereby not the mere sequence of intentions and actions of each opponent, but the pattern or shape generated by mutually hostile intentions and simultaneously consequential actions" (Beyerchen 1992, 67). Additionally, conflict is characterized by friction: in practice, decisions and their resulting actions within an ongoing conflict are interconnected and thus accumulate to a point where conflicts are impossible to manage. The idea is that however much effort is invested in controlling the system, mutual interdependence absorbs these efforts, generating a high degree of disorder and, ultimately, (decision) "noise" (Beyerchen 1992).

This theoretical perspective has two implications. First, the overload of information from unfolding conflict events prevents military leaders from correctly judging the consequences and correctly foreseeing the exact trajectories by which their decisions affect conflict outcomes. Specifically, often seemingly small decisions may lead to large effects, simply because of the high degree of interconnected decision-making—which engages with whom, when and how— within the system and down the chain of command. Researchers face similar constraints when analyzing conflict dynamics *post hoc*, especially if—as usually is the case—only observational data on conflict outcomes are available, and the actual decision cascades remain unobserved. Even if scholars recognized the inherent complexity underlying the conflict dynamics they analyzed, they were limited in their analysis by the lack of granular data, suitable methods and computational power needed to tackle these challenges head-on. Second, and closely related, is the observation that how a conflict plays out also depends on chance—conflict and its specific trajectories are just one of a large number of possible outcomes where each has a certain probability of occurring. This stochasticity implies that specific micro-causes may, purely by chance, play a much greater role in certain settings compared to others. More importantly, it further adds to the analytical blindness that prevents analysts, military and political leaders alike from forming good intuition in the face of complexity (Poincaré 1912).

These limitations consequently gave rise to a literature that readily acknowledged complex systemic dynamics but analyzed them in the abstract, relying primarily on deductive approaches in simplified settings with few (rational) actors. The most prominent line of research focused on the dynamics of arms races with notable contributions by Richardson (1935) and later Saperstein (1984), who modeled the interactions of opponents in volatile settings. Their contribution involved the application of dynamical systems and chaos theory to arms races. In particular, they formulated concrete analytical models that, despite their simplifications, adequately capture the intricate interdependence of actor decisions.

Building on the seminal contribution of Richardson (1948), a growing empirical literature on the relationship between the size and frequency of conflict events suggests strong regularities in the frequency of conflicts of a given size. Across centuries and types of armed conflict, the relationship has been observed to follow a power function. Viewed in this light, the notion of self-organized criticality (Roberts and Turcotte 1998) has seemed equally relevant to conflicts, with similarities to sand piles and forest fires (Bak, Chen, and Tang 1990). Subsequent work on combat dynamics has drawn on mathematical biology, adding the notion of adaptive behavior to the understanding of conflict. Opponents, for instance, attempt to find an equilibrium between launching attacks and losing forces (Epstein 1997). Taken together, these contributions have highlighted the notion that conflicts are nonlinear phenomena and prompted discussion on the degree to which conflict dynamics were deterministic. Additionally, these approaches contributed to the consensus that conflict is a process in which the limited perceptions and information of actors matter, as well as their highly interdependent, dynamic decisions and actions.

While these developments contributed to the understanding of conflict as a complex system, they did not compete against prevailing scholarship in international relations, emerging alongside it instead. The advent of computers shifted this dynamic. For instance, one of the earliest computational models of conflict directly responds to claims made by realist theory (Duffy 1992), and notably shows that the serial assumption does not hold—that more than one conflict can occur at the same time. Other models validated theoretical claims about the influence of democracies on international security (Simon and Starr 2000), or the inverse relationship between trade and conflict (Bearce and Fischer 2002) that is widely discussed in the literature (Doyle 1986; Oneal and Russett 1999; Oneal et al. 1996; Rosecrance 1986). In a nutshell, studies that took a decidedly complex systems perspective made headway on the theoretical understanding of conflict by refuting, validating and expanding theory.

Data

The systematic collection of data on inter-state conflicts forms the foundation of quantitative conflict research. The earliest efforts include data collection on the number of conflicts and their severity in terms of casualties (Richardson 1948, 1960a). Subsequently, the Correlates of War Project became the leading effort with respect to data collection on conflict (Singer 1972, 268). The datasets included machine-readable data about the occurrence of war as well as data on systemic attributes (territory, alliance and trade configurations, capability distributions), dyadic relationships (geographic proximity, diplomatic, geographic and trade bonds) and national attributes (demographic information, military expenditures, industrialization, iron-steel production). The Correlates of War Project also provided data on arms races (Diehl 1983; Gibler et al. 2005; Sample 1997; Wallace 1979).

These data enabled scholars to study, for the first time, the dynamics of inter-state conflict from a holistic systems perspective. Numerous studies set out to statistically confirm the complex, nonlinear nature of conflict dynamics. For example, casualty data from the World War II depicted highly nonlinear patterns (Kuhn 1989; Moffat 2003) as well as fractal properties (Lauren and Stephen 2002). Studies found robust empirical power-law relationships between the intensity of inter-state conflicts and their frequency (Roberts and Turcotte 1998), lending support to earlier findings (Denton 1966; Levy and Morgan 1984; Richardson 1948, 1960b; Rummel 1967) and observed subsequently in work on the intensity and frequency of terrorist attacks (Clauset et al. 2007).

A number of key challenges nonetheless remained for this type of data that limited its practical use. Uneven data availability and reliability across nations (Wallace 1979) together with the fact that data were only periodically available through government reports (Hess 1995) prevented researchers from conducting real-time analyses at a fine-grained temporal scale. Instead, researchers put primacy on mathematical models and broader comparative statistics (Geeraerts 1994).

Methods

Mathematical Models of Arms Races

The chapter previously highlighted the relevance of mathematical modeling in refining one's understanding of conflict. Richardson pioneered the formalization of the behavior of states (Richardson 1935, 1948, 1951, 1960a, 1960b). Specifically, Richardson set out to explain the interaction dynamics of determined choice between, say, states Y and Z. He formalized their respective levels of defense, y and z, as a function of three variables: the perceived ability of other countries to wage attacks and the provocations and threats from other countries; the expense of maintaining defense combined with conflict fatigue; and ambitions and grievances toward other countries. Richardson formalized these relationships with a pair of coupled, first-order ordinary differential equations (Richardson 1951; Hess 1995):

$$dy/dt = -ay + bz + f \qquad (1)$$

$$dz/dt = cy - dz + g \qquad (2)$$

where proportionality coefficients a, b, c and d and the grievances f and g are assumed to be constant.[2]

Richardson's model was innovative, given its ability to formalize a nation's arms race behavior and investigate system stability. His work led to the birth of the field of mathematical international relations, characterized by work on the exact specification of arms race models and their associated parameters (Schrodt 1978), applications to historical case studies (Etcheson 1989; Isard et al. 1988), and various model extensions

---

2. For further explorations and discussions, such as the applications of other mathematical theorems to scrutinize hypotheses, see Siljak (1977). See Ogata (1995) for the use of Lyapunov theorems to study stability and for stochastic differential equations. See Hess (1995) for a broader review of extensions.

(Brito and Intriligator 1982; Gillespie and Zinnes 1975; Gillespie, Zinnes, and Tahim 1976; Simaan and Cruz 1975). Most importantly, Richardson's model highlighted the "inadequacies in theoretical understanding of large-scale behavior ... and in our knowledge of the key parameters which may quantify that behavior" (Hess 1995, 93).

That said, the model also has a number of known weaknesses that include its limited applicability to real arms race dynamics. In particular, the model neglects political, social and psychological processes that underlie such decisions (Anderton 1989; McGinnis 1991; Rapoport 1957). Moreover, the all too "mechanical" nature of the model did not provide guidance to decision-makers. The notion that military expenditures increase exponentially and lead to the outbreak of war was similarly contested, given that such outbreaks did not always occur (Hess 1995; Joyce 1989). More generally, the approach was criticized for its inability to robustly predict the outcomes of historical cases (Etcheson 1989; Isard et al. 1988), the inherent difficulty of defining the meaning of dependent variables and model coefficients across contexts (Anderton 1989), the absence of oscillatory conflict dynamics that were empirically observed (Luterbacher 1975), and its deterministic nature that did not permit for highly nonlinear, chaotic dynamics (Saperstein 1984).

In reaction to these criticisms, Saperstein pioneered the formalization of arms races, taking into account insights from chaos theory (Saperstein 1997, 1995, 1994; Saperstein and Marsh 1988; Saperstein 1986, 1984).[3] His central criticism of mathematical models of arms races, including Richardson's, relates to their deterministic nature: an understanding of present conditions permits the prediction of the future outcomes. Instead, Saperstein suggested that conflict could be perceived "as a breakdown of predictability: a situation in which small perturbations of initial conditions, such as malfunctions of early-warning radar systems or irrational acts of individuals disobeying orders, lead to large unforeseen changes in the solutions to the dynamical equations of the model" (Saperstein 1984, 303). More importantly, he illustrated how the loss of predictability and control could be understood from dynamics at the transition between

---

[3]. Saperstein's work was later extended by several authors, such as Mayer-Kress (1992) and Tomochi and Kono (1998). For conciseness, only Saperstein's contribution is highlighted in this chapter.

peace and conflict, in much the same way as fluid transitions from laminar (predictable) to turbulent (chaotic) flows, an insight he corroborated with historical evidence (Ball 1981).[4]

Mathematical Models of Armed Conflict

Models of arms races analyzed how competition between countries could spiral out of control into armed conflict. Models were equally important to formalize and understand how conflicts themselves play out. Lanchester (1956) and Osipov (1915) independently pioneered this research in the context of inter-state conflict, their work resulting in numerous refinements, including to Richardson's model (MacKay 2015; Panchev and Vitanov 2008). Building on the work of Lanchester and Osipov, Epstein (1997) developed a model of combat based on greater behavioral granularity, which bears additional properties of complex systems, such as nonlinear dynamics and adaptation (Epstein 1985, 1990, 1997).

Epstein proposed two adaptive systems that alter their behavior as a function of their opponent's state and action, and whose interplay generates combat dynamics. Adaptation was modeled by movement and attrition. Initial conditions, such as the prosecution rate and its maximum (e.g., as a function of technology), the maximum withdrawal rate (e.g., as a function of the environment topology or motivations), and the equilibrium attrition rates (e.g., as a function of motivations, importance of a given battle, etc.) were extrapolated from case studies. The model also accounted for the ability of opponents to learn by means of trial and error until they reach their homeostatic targets.

In the aggregate, the model accounted for nonlinear dynamics, generated sophisticated adaptation and was sensitive to initial psychological, technological and environmental conditions. However, it still remained a rather mechanical account of inter-state conflict, one that included many variables but was arguably *reductionist* in how these factors were aggregated.

---

4. Saperstein's model also has its limitations. It is, for example, restricted to two nations that could collapse economically before they can allocate their resources to armaments (Tomochi and Kono 1998). The work has also been criticized for the interpretation that the occurrence of chaos translates into the outbreak of conflict (Intriligator and Brito 1984; Mayer-Kress and Grossman 1989).

Computational Models of Armed Conflict

The advent of computers shifted conflict modeling from a more "mechanical" to an "organic" approach. The use of computers to create simulations of complex social systems started as early as the 1960s but became more widespread in the 1990s thanks to the availability of personal computers. Still, social simulations overall were not widely used in the social sciences. In the eyes of many, they have, to this day, not proven themselves as a quantitative approach (Gilbert and Troitzsch 2005) insofar as a minority of social scientists receive education in computational science, and an even smaller fraction of research explicitly relies on complexity theory.

Computer simulations are essential to the study of complex systems, given their algorithmic nature and emergent properties. For centuries, science relied on induction from experiments and deduction from theory. Simulations make it possible to generate data from theory and permit inductive reasoning in data-scarce contexts (Epstein 2006). Simulations are particularly well-suited for research in the social sciences given that programming languages make it possible to treat parallel processes and interaction dynamics, specify heterogeneous agents, (re-)generate the event trajectories and analyze distributions of histories, run experiments, provide explanation and permit discovery (Gilbert and Troitzsch 2005). A growing number of computer simulations estimate the effects of interventions (e.g., aid, policy) in social systems (Kott and Citrenbaum 2010), or directly study policy-relevant phenomena, such as pandemics, crowd disasters, crime and terrorism (Helbing et al. 2015). Finally, computer simulations are a powerful analytical tool because they allow the integration of large amounts of different quantitative data and complement gaps with theory and qualitative information (Bhavnani et al. 2019; Conte et al. 2012; Janssen and Ostrom 2006).

The first simulations of conflict were very constrained by limited computational power but contributed to international relations theory, nevertheless. In the twentieth century, international relations theory was dominated by realism. Based on deductive game-theoretic models, realist theory makes several prominent claims (Duffy 1992, 242): only one conflict can happen at the time (the serial assumption); states pursue their self-interest and produce as an emergent property a global power equilibrium; actors are treated as alliances of states that make rational choices; only major power actors are taken into consideration; actors have complete and accurate information regarding the power capabilities of one another; all states globally engage in inter-state competition; and conflict outcomes are deterministic and linear based on power disparities between states in conflict. These assumptions allowed realist theory to build a tractable and internally consistent deductive framework. Computer simulations permitted these assumptions to be tested inductively.

Pioneering models (Bremer and Mihalka 1977; Cusack and Stoll 1990) allowed for iterative games, imperfect perception, localized wars, nonlinear and probabilistic relationships, satisficing versus maximizing behavior, and the inclusion of multiple actors. While these initial models implicitly integrated the serial assumption, Duffy (1992) took this further using massively parallel computer architecture. His model included 128 states and 256 parallel worlds and allowed for multiple interactions, effectively relaxing the serial assumption. In contrast, early agent-based models of inter-state conflict and combat focused on theory building (Schrodt 1981). Models designed as a computational response to Lanchester's system of equations portray combat as a complex adaptive system, with the development of a "complexity-based fundamental theory of warfare" as their main goal (Ilachinski 2003, 1997; Moffat 2003). Agent-based models were used to explore self-organized emergent behavior in combat, often providing the military operations research community with easy-to-use combat simulations. In "interaction" mode, the models could be used to test various counterfactual scenarios. In "data-collection" mode, they could generate time series of behavioral data.

Present: 2000–2019

The previous section reviewed key contributions in the twentieth century, highlighting the relevance of embracing a complexity perspective when approaching the study of conflict. The section emphasized, throughout, that there exist aspects of conflict dynamics across diverse topics, from combat dynamics to arms races, that would be impossible to study otherwise. The contribution of this literature was, however, constrained by its focus on inter-state conflict, a lack of more fine-grained empirical data and a dearth of suitable quantitative methodologies. The present literature addresses many of these challenges head-on. Most notably, the theoretical perspective has shifted further to the micro level, focusing increasingly on intra-state conflict dynamics. This shift is also visible in the generation of new, highly disaggregated datasets on sub-national conflict dynamics while embracing novel methodologies suitable for working with these data.

Theory

The overall shift in the theoretical focus in the literature arises from three distinct developments. First, the empirical prevalence of intra-state conflicts over inter-state conflicts is increasingly reflected in a reorientation of the literature toward the study of micro-level dynamics of conflict, civil wars and ethnic violence in particular (Cederman and Girardin 2007). This development may be explained by the significant decrease in the number of inter-state conflicts; the end of the nuclear arms race; the increasing availability of information on intra-state conflict through datasets and media coverage; and a better theoretical understanding of the causes of civil wars and ethnic violence (Kalyvas 2006). Research also increasingly focuses on peace-building and interventions and places a primary geographic focus on conflicts in the Middle East, central Africa and South America.

Second, this overall shift in focus toward the study of intra-state conflict goes hand-in-hand with a push for the disaggregation of micro-level motives (e.g., actors' beliefs, ethnic salience, risk-propensity, and network structures), contextual factors (e.g., physical topology, economic activity, and urban versus rural), and their linkage to macro-level conflict dynamics (e.g., contagion, diffusion, escalation, mitigation and termination of conflict; for a detailed discussion, see Donnay et al. 2014). While many studies in the broader literature do not take a complexity perspective, this overall reorientation favors approaches that make it explicit how complex macro patterns emerge from micro-level interactions. This push for disaggregation is further facilitated by the increasing availability of fine-grained empirical data.

Third, past research relied on frameworks such as chaos theory, dynamical system theory or mathematical biology. They successfully showed how conflict dynamics satisfy the hallmarks of complex systems, but the insights were obfuscated by the plurality of theories contributing to them. In particular, it was not clear whether the complexity of conflict can be understood within a single theoretical framework. The progress in the development of more comprehensive and inclusive theoretical frameworks (Wolfram 1988; Waldrop 1992; Thurner, Hanel, and Klimek 2018) increasingly allows researchers to more readily apply insights from complexity science to their specific questions in the realm of conflict research.

Data

The availability of granular data on conflict dimensions (e.g., location, diffusion, escalation, mitigation, and termination), combatant characteristics and behavior (e.g., identity, resources, interactions), and covariates (e.g., GDP, topology, climate) forms the foundation of a much more disaggregated understanding of conflict. From a complex systems perspective, the availability of these data is paramount to the study of conflict because it allows us to trace the full complexity of the conflict process empirically. Most advances in data development occurred over the past twenty years, and today's focus on intra- rather than inter-state conflicts forces researchers, for example, to dissect individuals' ethnic identity salience, state–civilian relationships or urban–rural dynamics. This development raises the bar on which data are required but also enables much more fine-grained analyses.[5]

Subscribing to the notions of complexity science enables researchers to quantitatively test the complex interactions of (1) the nature of constituent parts' behavior with (2) the characteristics and influence of the conflict "environment," while at the same time enabling the exploration of (3) counterfactual effects of interventions, and (4) tracing macro-level conflict dynamics. This section provides examples of datasets that contribute to this ideal by allowing the specifications of each of these four aspects. The specification of the first three is primordial because they represent the initial conditions from which nonlinear dynamics emerged, with small errors leading to large effects. Therefore, the more accurate these specifications, the more reliable the model outcomes.

Conflict datasets, such as those collected by the Uppsala Data Program (UCDP), the Armed Conflict Location and Event Data Project (ACLED) and the Global Terrorism Database (GTD), offer geocoded information

---

5. For an overview of recent developments in data availability, see Donnay and Bhavnani (2016).

with greater reliability and quality thanks to improved collection and coding procedures (LaFree and Dugan 2007; Raleigh et al. 2010; Sundberg and Melander 2013). The Nonviolent and Violent Campaigns and Outcomes Dataset (NAVCO) provides global coverage of major resistance campaigns from 1900 to 2006 (Chenoweth and Lewis 2013). This dataset dedicates specific attention to the endogenous link between government and insurgent actions, permitting researchers to study reciprocal dynamics, such as reactive violence. GeoEPR offers geocoded data on settlement patterns of politically active ethnic groups and their access to executive government power from 1946 to 2014 (Vogt et al. 2015). AMAR provides data on socially relevant ethnic groups and their component structure worldwide (Birnir et al. 2015). The Non-State Actors (NSA) data contain detailed information on state–rebel group dyads (Cunningham et al. 2013). Leveraging the fact that these data are geo-coded allows, for example, to avoid mixing urban and rural conflicts. The coding of actor types allows the specification of agent attributes and behavioral rules, and the coding of events allows the distinction of different forms of violence, including their characteristics and motivations.

Complementing these data is ever-increasing coverage of conflict covariates, including population density, GDP, education, elevation, road networks, land cover, nigh-time lights, natural resources and climatic conditions. Among others, the use of remote sensing technologies allows the collection of fine-grained satellite data (Witmer 2015). For example, NASA's Shuttle Radar Topographic Mission (SRTM) provides comprehensive data and global coverage on the elevation of grid cells at a resolution of less than one hundred meters (Jarvis et al. 2008). The Gridded Population of the World (GPW) uses detailed, local census data to construct a gridded population dataset (CIESIN 2005). The Natural Resources and Armed Conflict project provides information on natural resources worldwide, including whether and how rebels exploit them (Asal et al. 2016). The Climate Change and African Political Stability Project offers data about the effects of climate change on African and International security, through the collection of various geo-coded data, thus allowing researchers to better understand the context in which conflict may occur.

Moreover, new datasets cover information on conflict mediation, peace agreements and their implementation, peacekeeping operations, and economic and military sanctions. Datasets include the type, location, timing, duration and impact of interventions. Examples include the Civil Mediation dataset (DeRouen et al. 2010), the UCDP Peace Agreement Dataset (Högbladh 2011), the Implementation of Pacts (2012), the Peace Accords Matrix Implementation Dataset (Joshi et al. 2015) and the Power-Sharing Event Dataset (Ottmann and Vüllers 2015). The AidData initiative[6] provides datasets on development finance that can be used to explore the relationship between foreign assistance and intra-state conflict and allow for counterfactual analysis of interventions of how a system reacts to external shocks and stressors.

The increasing availability of these fine-grained empirical data suggests a clear evolution of the field toward enabling empirically driven analyses of conflict. These data, in particular, enable researchers—for a given empirical setting—to trace how the mutual interdependence of conflict actors and their environment gives rise to truly emergent outcomes. In other words, the paradigm shift toward disaggregated research of conflict also represents a significant step forward in recognizing the inherent systemic complexity of conflict processes.

Methods

Modeling Patterns of Insurgent Conflict

This chapter previously highlighted literature that identified a robust power-law relationship between the frequency and severity of conflict. Here, this section starts by discussing two recent mathematical models that derive the emergence of such power-law patterns from specific assumptions about micro-level conflict dynamics. These studies nicely illustrate both the strengths and the potential pitfalls of approaches that subscribe to a complexity perspective.

The first is a simple model of insurgency and terrorism put forward by Bohorquez et al. (2009) that draws on approaches for studying herding dynamics in financial markets (Eguiluz and Zimmermann 2000) and builds on analogies to concepts from ecology. It assumes that an insurgent force can be divided into attack units, each having a respective attack strength proportional to their size. These units are then subject to a process

---

6. See www.aiddata.org.

of coalescence (units merge) and fragmentation (units split up) as part of the ongoing conflict, where the maximal severity of an attack is proportional to their attack strength.

The model was developed as a biologically-inspired mathematical representation of insurgent warfare and terrorism. However, while it successfully captures certain features of conflict dynamics (i.e., the empirical patterns in the size and timing distribution of attacks) the model assumes empirically unrealistic insurgent tactics: attacks are random, unplanned and utterly uncontested by counterinsurgent forces; moreover, coordination between insurgent cells can—in the model—be achieved instantly and without cost. These are strong assumptions that are empirically difficult to substantiate (Clauset and Gleditsch 2012). Additionally, the model is highly over-specified in terms of the number of free, tunable dynamics, thus violating the basic tenet of complexity approaches to maximally reduce explanatory complexity. The interaction dynamics assumed in the model further let it converge rapidly to a fixed end state that is either characterized by complete victory for the insurgents or their complete defeat. These are dynamics that are highly inconsistent with how conflicts play out in reality. Similarly, the model can also not explain dynamic shifts over time, such as the dramatic violence observed in Iraq in 2007 in the context of the US troop surge.

Taken together, this highlights the potential downfalls of such approaches. The fact that *ad hoc* models can explain emergent macro-level outcomes is not a sufficient condition that they indeed represent empirical reality. As long as the mechanisms that give rise to those complex emergent outcomes are not closely aligned with other (often also qualitative) insights on conflict dynamics, this brings scholarship no closer to understanding the inherent complexity of conflict. In other words, one can only effectively fully leverage the strength of complexity approaches if they are both firmly grounded—theoretically and empirically—in the existing literature on conflict.

The model by Clauset, Young and Gleditsch (2007), in comparison, starts from a simple but empirically and theoretically well-founded set of assumptions. They argue that intrastate violence can be understood as arising from a process of competition between insurgent and counterinsurgent forces similar to the logic advanced by inter-state arms race models. In this formulation, insurgent forces attempt to maximize the impact of planned violent attacks, while counterinsurgent forces race to intercept and neutralize these insurgent plots before they can be realized. This very simple model allows us to similarly explain the power laws empirically found on the frequency–severity relationships observed in data on intra-state conflict and terrorism. Clauset and Gleditsch (2012) particularly explore the variation of such power laws in the light of various group sizes and group ideologies. They find that deadlier attacks come from bigger groups because they attack more frequently, not because their attacks are deadlier, and observe this recurrent pattern across ideological groups.

In this way, approaches such as these can offer possible explanations for not only the empirical patterns that one observes, but also the regularity of these patterns; this seems to suggest that explanations across different contexts share some fundamental similarities. This is not to say that there would exist a set of fundamental root causes of conflict—on the contrary. What it does imply, though, is that the underlying mechanisms likely share a set of very general common features (e.g., with regard to the nature of co-dependence of actors, groups or institutions).

Agent-Based Models of Intra-State Conflict

Agent-based models are, by design, useful for inductive modeling that draws on theoretical insights and can thus yield highly relevant insights for further theory building. Present-day agent-based models represent a stark improvement from past models thanks to an exponential increase in computational power. This technological development allows us to model actors with characteristics that more closely reflect the theoretical and empirical understanding of conflict in a changing environment, thus increasingly capturing the full complexity of conflict dynamics. The seminal work of Cederman (2003) that provides a complexity-based explanation for the size of inter-state wars is an excellent example of this.

The increasing availability of fine-grained data allows us to additionally empirically ground such models and test specific mechanisms under conditions that closely represent a given real-world context. Geographical information systems (GIS) and specialized software enable this close geographic integration, including information on the location of violent events, but also key covariate and explanatory dimensions. And it is closely related to the fundamental tenets of the complexity approach, the ability to use empirical data to endogenize the complex empirical context in which complex system dynamics play out. This methodology allows the modeler to better account for path dependence and the sensitivity to a system's initial state.

The following paragraphs illustrate this using three recent models of ethnic violence that all rely on the same three types of data: geography of the case study, disaggregated data on the geographic location of ethnic groups and population density, and geo-coded data of violent events (Bhavnani and Choi 2012; Bhavnani et al. 2014; Weidmann and Salehyan 2013). All three models explore the link between ethnic geography and violence at a sub-national level, but with different sets of mechanisms. The following discusses their mechanisms first, continues with their empirical settings and concludes with their added value.

The first model, by Bhavnani and Choi (2012), relies on the same logic as the seminal work of Epstein (2002) on civil conflict dynamics. Extending his work with explicit theoretical underpinnings, they study the interactions between civilians and either the Taliban or the US-led coalition that compete for territorial control in Afghanistan. Depending on risk-taking propensity, civilians may choose to collaborate with one of the two political actors, remain neutral or denounce other civilians from another ethnic group. The political actor, within vision, then detects civilians and assassinates them. Weidmann and Salehyan (2013) explore the relationship between ethnic segregation and urban violence in Baghdad. Agents can belong to one of two ethnic groups, Sunni or Shia, and can be either insurgents or civilians. Insurgents of one group attempt to attack civilians of the other group. The attack's success depends on the local ethnic makeup of the location where they target civilians. Attacks cause fear among the targeted civilians, which leads civilians to consider migration. This mechanism changes the ethnic spatial distribution, which feeds back in the likelihood of violence. Bhavnani et al. (2014) also explore the link between segregation and urban violence (in Jerusalem) with one central premise: conditional to spatial proximity, the likelihood of conflict is a function of the social distance between two rival groups, with social distance referring to a variety of inter-group differences within class, ethnicity, religion, race and gender.

The three models are developed on the actual geographical topology of the empirical cases they study (i.e., agents do not interact in a fully artificial environment, but on a map that represents their environment). This method is used to fully endogenize the geographic location of ethnic groups, which is a central variable driving violence dynamics—this is in contrast to many prior such models that use artificial grids with no relationship to empirical settings (Epstein and Axtell 1996; Schelling 1971). Lastly, they generate violence dynamics through a selected set of mechanisms and use disaggregated data on the location of violence events to calibrate the model trajectories and validate the model outcomes. As a result, these models can more confidently evaluate whether their selected mechanisms may be plausible explanations for violence dynamics observed in empirical data, including how violence dynamics evolve throughout the simulation and whether they align with empirical dynamics. These models thus make a significant contribution to the complexity science approach to the study of conflict because they allow drawing conclusions about emergent dynamics while fully endogenizing key explanatory factors.

Leveraging this unique approach, they can provide relevant insights into the inherently complex dynamics of civil conflict. For instance, in the context of Afghanistan, the work of Bhavnani and Choi (2012) shows, among other results, that political actors are more likely to attack civilians in heterogeneous areas, where members of one ethnic group are exposed to members of a rival group, and that violence targeting civilians occurs with higher frequencies where one political actor exercises hegemonic but incomplete territorial control. In the context of Baghdad, the model of Weidmann and Salehyan (2013) finds that civilians' desire for safety is a sufficient mechanism to create a marked degree of ethnic segregation, and that a higher degree of segregation is inversely correlated with the level of violence. The model notably provides nuances to the debated effect on the violence of the US surge because ethnic segregation was almost complete at the time of the surge, which perhaps caused the violence to decline, rather than the surge itself. The model on urban violence in Jerusalem (Bhavnani and Choi 2012) confirms the importance of segregation in violence dynamics and presents systematic comparisons of policy-relevant counterfactual scenarios of the Clinton Parameters, a Palestinian Proposal and the situation back in 1967.

The two models of urban violence are thus particularly good examples of the usefulness of complexity science—and especially computational models—to support future decision-making. However, increasing policy-relevance and contextual accuracy presents a trade-off between internal and external validity. The computational models reviewed in this chapter correspondingly exemplify the trend observed in the literature: complexity science can provide broad insights on the general features of complex systems, or very specific insights on select empirical contexts (Mitchell 2009).

Future Directions

The contributions of complexity science to date make a strong case for the relevance of this approach to the study of armed conflict. The literature in the last two decades has, as discussed in the previous section, largely focused on realizing more disaggregate analysis through advances in theory, data and methods. These developments have significantly increased the ability to trace out relevant and highly complex inter-dependencies at a level of analysis and empirical resolution that has enabled novel insights into intricate co-dependent dynamics. While it has tackled many relevant challenges head-on, there remain a number of very promising and highly relevant areas of research that will likely shape the trajectory of the field in the near future.

Theory

New topics related to conflict and warfare continuously arise. This notably includes the emergence of autonomous weapons; the risk of devastating biological attacks (see Carley et al. 2006); the need to better clarify the link between climate change and conflict (see Landis 2014); the possibility of great power conflicts; urban violence dynamics (see Raleigh 2015); and the relationship between humanitarian assistance and conflict. Complexity theory, together with computer simulations, may provide relevant insights on these complex topics.

Agent-based models are, and must be, theory-driven because there is usually not enough clear empirical evidence on the variety of individual and environmental mechanisms that such models aim to capture. However, the way agent-based models rely on theory can still be significantly improved. For instance, most models of inter-state conflict implicitly or explicitly rely on theories attached to the realist school of thought, while other schools include neoliberalism and constructivism, and a dozen alternatives. It is paramount that scholars develop clearer rules and conventions on how these theories are formalized and translated into their models. Researchers should at least state their ontological orientation explicitly (Pepinsky 2005), thus clarifying the kind of contribution they intend to make.

The contribution of complexity science to the study of conflict made a step toward empirically grounded, case-specific models that yield policy-relevant insights. Arguably, future studies should tackle policy-relevant issues and focus on models explicitly built to enable giving policy recommendations based on model results. Note that this development also entails that researchers provide the right nuances to such recommendations, allowing decision-makers to acquire a more granular understanding of the cases at hand while clearly communicating possible caveats and the scope of the insights derived. Such efforts also presuppose progress in data visualization and the creation of platforms to support decision-making.

Data

Complex systems are highly dependent on their contexts because they provide initial conditions that crucially influence system dynamics. The only way to model specific contexts and validate result is, therefore, to rely on a variety of data to support the empirical specification of mechanisms as much as possible. Fortunately, techniques such as agent-based models are well-suited to incorporate quantitative data on micro-level interactions (e.g., ethnic salience), environment (e.g., vegetation) and macro-level properties (e.g., number of casualties). Most importantly, researchers can also integrate qualitative data collected through fieldwork and expert surveys to fill the gaps. Taking this approach includes anchoring "soft" variable relationships in a more nuanced understanding and providing context needed to interpret model results properly. Agent-based models and other techniques can thus benefit significantly from the future availability of even more such data.

Remote sensing technologies are becoming more widely available and provide information on troop movements, damage to communities and property, one-sided violence, mass atrocities, population displacement, economic activity and humanitarian crises (for an overview, see Donnay and Bhavnani 2016). However, these technologies also have limitations, such as their high cost, their lack of reliability during conflict and the need for specific knowledge to process remote sensing imagery. Further expertise in remote sensing technologies to understand conflicts and their ramifications to other phenomena is a crucial future step.

There is a vast amount of new data subsumed under the label of "big data" that may unlock a great untapped potential for computer simulations of conflict and other social phenomena (Nanetti and Cheong 2018). These data include information from social media, archives of news media reports, economic data and various other primary and secondary sources that are machine-readable and often superior in terms of the temporal specificity and resolution as compared to human-coded data. For example, social media data provide a continuous stream of data on sentiments, actions and interactions in near-real-time and at a very granular level. Current challenges include the technical capacity required to process such data and the lack of concrete applications that testify to their usefulness. Other challenges include the accuracy and reliability of such data and an unclear threshold of when researchers can decide whether or not to rely on such data. Lastly, social media data from, for instance, Twitter is not a comprehensive or randomly generated data source, and only 1% of tweets are geocoded (Donnay and Bhavnani 2016).

Methods

Past and current agent-based models attempt to capture agents' limited perception, bounded rationality and individual complexity. However, they still derive decision-making largely from relatively simple utility functions. This approach does not allow researchers to model rich, heterogeneous, individual-level reasoning or, in particular, the dynamic adaptation of actor decision-making. In other words, current models tend to overlook or oversimplify the true complexity of human behavior in decision-making (Pepinsky 2005). Further work encompassing emotions, biases and heuristics, and the formalization of bounded-rationality, is therefore likely needed for a more extensive behavioral account of agents involved in conflict. Insights from neuroscience, behavioral psychology and new data sources, such as social media, psychological experiments or interviews, may provide a solid empirical basis to model more realistic decision-making profiles.

The application of machine learning has made great strides in recent years in the context of data analytics and related to learning and modes of cognition. Correspondingly, there are at least two main avenues in which these techniques can help empower the study of conflict from a complexity perspective. First, major improvements in machine learning approaches allow the automatic extraction of information, especially from image data (see Mnih et al. 2016). This progress will help to significantly improve the scope and coverage of data on conflict covariates—in particular, in the context of remote sensing data discussed above. Second, advances in the domain of machine learning and artificial intelligence can directly help inform how agents learn in complex settings. These developments are particularly relevant for the increasingly realistic agent-based models mentioned before. A key challenge here remains—to derive heuristics that enable agents to also react to situations they had not previously encountered. Works like the study by Miconi et al. (2018) chart a way forward using methods inspired by biological processes of learning.

To conclude, this chapter advances that future applications of complexity science approaches will move toward an even more explicit policy-relevant focus aided by advances in data and theory. Lastly, a stronger focus on actor behavior and cognitive complexity, paired with a more explicit statement of models' ontological orientations, will advance the contribution of computational models to the study of conflict phenomena.

Conclusion

Scholars have widely studied armed conflicts because of their political relevance, humanitarian importance and peculiar nature as a systemic outcome. This chapter reviewed how complexity science lends itself to the study of armed conflict and how the approach evolved and matured, giving birth to today's empirically grounded computational models.

Using complexity science to study armed conflict has yielded numerous insights, including:

- conceptual insights on how to look at conflict, portraying dynamics as nonlinear and emerging from the co-evolution of its constituent parts;

- theoretical contributions by refuting claims, validating others and expanding the body of theoretical insights that guide today's scholarship thanks to mathematical and computational models;
- general empirical laws of conflict, such as the power-law relationship between its intensity and frequency; and
- empirical contributions in specific contexts, such as the inverse relationship between segregation and violence in Jerusalem and Baghdad.

These contributions were possible through a unique combination of approaches that characterize complexity science:

1. Complexity theory allows scrutinizing conflict dynamics and offers a less coarse account of how they emerge.
2. Reductionism forces scholars to state their assumptions explicitly, focus on the most critical variables and thus reduce the size of explanatory complexity.
3. Computation enables modelers to inject dynamism into static theories and perform inductive research on data-scarce questions.
4. The use of detailed data on micro-level dynamics as well as on events of violence allows the specification of models' initial conditions and validation of model results.

Technological developments over the past two decades have contributed to the increasing relevance and explanatory power of complexity science and will do so in the future. However, it is essential to highlight shortcomings and possible failure modes related to the difficult task of modeling conflict. Too many models discard existing theories or are based on implicit theoretical underpinnings. Similarly, many models showcase great technical contributions but feature mechanisms that are merely empirically founded. Therefore, scholars must formulate mechanisms with more systematic theory selection and empirical rigor. Only then can complexity science predict conflict dynamics and increase the likelihood of success of peace-building interventions. This chapter hopes to offer scholars a reference piece and starting point for envisioning the most promising and logical future avenues of research.

PART 2

Complexity, Computation and Artificial Intelligence

CHAPTER 4

Novelty Production and Evolvability in Digital Genomic Agents

Logical Foundations and Policy Design Implications of Complex Adaptive Systems

Sheri M. Markose[1]

Introduction

There have been extensive surveys on what many have purported to be complexity economics and complexity sciences (Holt et al. 2011; Colander 2000). However, few if any of them have singled out novelty production and "surprises"—such as radical disruption of structures and uncertainty of outcomes that exceed a known set of outcomes—as being significant to complex phenomena.[2] Some of the exceptions here are Casti (1994),

---

1. Acknowledgements: I'm grateful for discussions with Bud Mishra (Director, Courant Institute, NYU), Will Casey and Yang Cai (Software Engineering Institute, CMU), who invited me to give a Keynote Speech at the 2019 Bio-Inspired ICT Conference at Carnegie Mellon University. This gave me an opportunity to explore further the evidence for the conjecture that the G-T-P logic is almost exactly hardwired in the immuno-cognitive systems of advanced eukaryotes, equipping them for novelty production and complex interactions. I'm grateful to Mikhail Prokopenko for seconding my view that much of this is exactly like it says on the tin of Recursion Function Theory. The longstanding influences on me have been listed in Markose (2017) and will not be repeated here, Roman Frydman being an exception.
2. The following characteristics have typically been listed as being pertinent for complexity sciences: non-linear dynamics, power laws and fat-tailed extreme events, socio-economic

Albin (1998), Witt (2007), Foster (2005) and Baumol (2002, 2004). Baumol (2002, 2004), in keeping with Schumpeter's (1934) vision of "creative destruction,"[3] has extensively discussed and documented the role of the relentless Red Queen-type[4] strategic arms race in innovation by firms of products and processes in capitalism, which he claims is not addressed in mainstream economics. Witt (2007) states that "the emergence of novelty is a driving agent in evolution … and … the backbone of (economic) development and growth. Despite its central importance, the emergence of novelty is largely a blind spot in economic theory" (1).

The theoretical impasse on novelty production has not been confined to economics. The problem, however, of not addressing what many regard to be the über and Machiavellian intelligence behind novelty production in economic systems is that it has severe pragmatic consequences. These manifest as radical disruption in aspects of socio-economic systemic failure from regulatory arbitrage and gaming of the system with innovative rule-breaking strategies and as structure-changing dynamics from technological arms races with winners and losers. While trust, cooperation and defection strategies are discussed at length in standard game theory frameworks, in a recent 2,000-page volume on the foundations of behavioral economics (Dhami 2016) that is encyclopedic in its scope on extant models on economic behaviors, there is no mention of how agents "think outside the box" by pursuing creative behaviors, such as novel strategic innovation or arms races. Romer (2016), in having critiqued the multitude of exogenous random shocks that typically model "surprise" or innovation in the mainstream

---

    interconnectedness and network models, fractality, self-organization and emergence. A large class of spectacular phenomena can only emerge or self-organize, such as pattern formation in schools of fish or flocks of birds and even racial segregation, as in the Schelling (1971) model. There is no doubt that it is important to understand tipping points and sudden phase transitions in non-linear models.

3. The Schumpeterian view (1934) is that the "perennial gale of creative destruction" in capitalism, during which new products and processes dislodge old ones, is a far more important force than optimization within extant sets of technologies and the Neoclassical model of efficiency with price competition among existing firms and products.

4. The Red Queen, the character in Lewis Caroll's *Alice Through the Looking-Glass* who signifies the need "to run faster and faster to stay in the same square," has become emblematic of the outcome of competitive co-evolution for evolutionary biologists in that no competitor gains absolute ground. Baumol (2002) shows how Red Queen-type arms races in product or process innovation are undertaken by firms to ward off erosion in market share due to competitors.

macroeconomic framework, has compared the model of white-noise shocks to the discredited phlogiston, or theory of fire as a material substance. This is arguably no different from the pre-Barbara McClintock (1984) state of gene science, which had to resort to random mutations as the sole basis of diversity in evolution. McClintock (1984), in her Nobel-prize-winning discovery of transposable elements of viral software in the genome that perform basic recursive or digital operations of scissor-paste and copy-paste,[5] has ushered in the notion of the dynamic genome that creatively responds with the exaptation of already extant functional gene codes to produce viable and novel solutions under conditions of stress. This, along with recent advances in molecular biology, have dislodged the view that random mutation in the form of replication or transcription errors form the primary basis of diversity and genomic change in evolution (Noble 2017; Shapiro 2013,2017; Amaral et al. 2008; Mattick 2011; Ben-Jacob 1998).

The objective of this chapter is to follow the long legacy of the so-called Wolfram-Chomsky schema (see Markose 2004, 2005, 2017) to reboot the *sine qua non* for complex adaptive systems (CAS) in terms of the production of novelty and surprises. This coincides with the Type IV structure changing undecidable dynamics. Types I–III dynamics do not produce novelty, and in sequence, they achieve limit points, limit cycles and chaotic dynamics.

Recent work of Prokopenko et al. (2019)[6] and Markose (2017) show that only systems with digital agents, operating on encoded information, that have achieved what can be called the conditions of computational universality associated with the epochal work of Gödel (1931), Turing (1937b) and Post (1944; G-T-P hereafter) can produce this tall order

---

5. McClintock (1984) described the genome "as a highly sensitive organ of the cell, monitoring genomic activities and correcting common errors, sensing the unusual and unexpected events, and responding to them, often by restructuring the genome" (198).
6. Digital systems capable of Type IV dynamics famously have been given a visual representation in the Wolfram Rule 110 for cellular automata (CA), with irregular structure changes and novel patterns that do not repeat periodically. Prokopenko et al. (2019) associate such novelty generation with Gödel undecidability and incompleteness results. The authors state: "while the key role played by self-reference in proofs of undecidability in various computational frameworks is beyond doubt, its precise use in dynamical systems, and CAs specifically, has not been demonstrated explicitly" (136). They aim to reconstruct the key element of a self-referential format of the negation/inverter machine in a Gödel-type proof for CAs that are capable of novelty-producing Type IV dynamics.

of Type IV dynamics that endogenously produce novel objects and/or phenotypes that were not previously there. The constructive or syntactic generation of the novel objects can be contrasted with statistical white noise as the model of innovation or surprise. The former is characteristic of complex systems like evolution and capitalism, respectively, with signature phenotypical and technological Red Queen-type arms races in innovations. In keeping with Wigner's famous quip (Wigner 1960) on the unreasonable effectiveness of mathematics, Markose (2019, 2021) has given evidence, some of which will be reviewed here, of how the following G-T-P conditions are found to be ubiquitous in digital genomic systems, acquired over the course of evolution, and to form the foundations of intelligence.

The G-T-P conditions needed for novelty production are:

(i) Recursive operations[7] on encoded information, including the machine execution of codes and their generation and storage with each encoded unit of information indexed by unique alpha-numeric identifiers.

(ii) There is a distinct domain of offline recordings and simulation in a formal Gödel meta-mathematics, organized in a tuple of a code centered self and the other. There is a bijective mapping between the offline "mirror" system and the online machine executions of the same codes. This mapping of the mirror system will be called the **Self-Rep**, for self-representation, and so-called diagonal operations, which involve machines running their codes, are called **Self-Ref**, for self-referential recursive operations. These terms were popularized by Hofstadter (1999).

(iii) The identification of the logical archetype of the Liar, involving the negation operation on what can be predicted. This is encoded in a self-referential syntax of the famous Gödel sentence.

Markose (2017) lays the groundwork to show how these are the three G-T-P conditions necessary for novelty production in what can be

---

7. General recursive functions include all elementary arithmetic, logical operations and functions obtained from substitution, iteration and recursion. In the latter, functions call on themselves and use inputs that are outputs from previous calculations (see Cutland 1980 and Rogers 1967, which are well-known textbooks on this).

called a "Genomic Nash Equilibrium." What may be considered to be esoteric concepts in the foundations of mathematics are ubiquitous in the immuno-neural cognitive system and, hence, have applicability far beyond the context in which they were originally developed. In Markose (2017), the discovery of mirror neurons by the Parma Group (see Gallese et al. 1996; Rizzolatti et al. 1996; Fadiga et al. 1995), relating to parallel expression or encoding in an offline environment in the cognitive neurophysiology of the brain of online machine executions from the motor and sensory cortex, has been identified with the G-T-P condition (ii). The Parma Group identifies this mirror system as the basis of social cognition in that recognition of actions of others is facilitated by the reuse of codes from neuronal firings from agents' own motor activity. I show how the well-known textbook exposition of Rogers (1967) for the G-T-P condition (ii) utilizes a two-place Gödel substitution function, which provides a setting that can incorporate the self and the other as a means of achieving social cognition and social interaction based on the reuse of codes from machine executions of motor activity by self. The experiments of Scott Kelso and his group (Tognoli et al. 2007; Naeem et al. 2012) that discovered offline encoding of negation of predicted actions as part of the mirror neuron system were cited in Markose (2017) as providing key evidence for the necessary G-T-P logical condition (iii) in the cognitive-neural system to achieve the capacity to "think outside the box" and be capable of novelty production.

It was in Markose (2019)[8] that evidence was first given for how, since the Big Bang of Immunology (Janeway et al. 2005) associated with the adaptive immune system (AIS) some 500 million years ago in the lineage starting with jawed fish, the immuno-cognitive machinery in genomic

---

8. Around 2014, I became familiar with the discoveries of the Parma Group on the mirror neuron system and the relevance of G-T-P condition (ii) for social cognition and the mutual mentalizing model, thereof. However, the presence of the mirror system in the Thymus Medulla of the adaptive immune system became known to me only about late 2017. This was incorporated in the keynote talk I gave at the 2019 Bio-inspired ICT (BICT) Conference at Carnegie Mellon. It was in a conversation with Bud Mishra of the Courant Institute in November 2018 that I coined the epithet "Genomic Nash Equilibrium" to underscore the point that endogenous novelty production that is ubiquitous in code-based genomic systems is also unique to them. In other words, to date, the endogenous novelty production of genomic systems that is G-T-P based is not yet a property of Artificial Intelligence.

systems acquired the latter two G-T-P conditions necessary for novelty production. Note, the first G-T-P condition is a given with the digitization of inheritable information for life. The major implication of the fact that inheritable information is code with an almost universal four-letter base of known genomic systems is that, while relatively error-free digital copies can be produced, the Achilles heel of such digital systems is that they can be hacked by other biotic digital agents. Thus, in genomic digital systems, the Gödel archetype of the Liar can be identified as the hacker. All formal systems that have rules with predictable outcomes can likewise be destroyed. What is of significance here is the discussion on how G-T-P logic throws light on the very unique intelligence of biotic gene-based digital systems.

It is known that, with the adaptive immune system, which led to the eukaryote and mammalian radiation, the methods of immune defense added cyber security to detect malware that attacks the genomic software. This is over and above the extensive analog defenses[9] in place with the innate immune system. There is now ample evidence that the Thymus Medulla remarkably expresses copies, in an *offline* environment, of about 85% of the genome (Danan-Gotthold et al. 2016) that involves codes of programs that halt in the ribosomal self-assembly of somatic and regulatory domains, viz., "theorems" in the system. Expression of tissue-specific gene codes in an offline environment of the Thymus Medulla in self-referential form, often called promiscuous gene expression (Kyewski and Klein 2006), will be shown to be a textbook case of Gödel formal systems, in particular, G-T-P condition (ii). The large-scale recombinant recursive machinery called the V-D-J (variable-diversity-joining) of the adaptive immune system permits an extensive search in the domain of possible reactive pathogen software to the gene codes, presented in a self-referential way, to simulate putative attacks or changes to the gene codes.

Markose (2019) finds that the recursive machinery that underpins the mirror systems with self-referential mappings for the identification of the other, especially of hostile agency, viz., G-T-P conditions (ii) and (iii), are identical for the adaptive immune system and the cognitive mirror

---

9. Analog defenses of the innate immune system include setting up barriers, toxicity, raising temperature by inflammation and ingestion by phagocytes.

neuron system.[10] Thus, we have growing evidence that the G-T-P conditions, in particular the Gödel sentence, far from being a funky and esoteric construction in the foundations of mathematics, are ubiquitous in the immuno-cognitive code-based genomic systems. Effectively, the Gödel sentence allows for a code in a G-T-P-based immuno-cognitive system to self-report that it is under attack or being hacked. In the absence of this "thinking outside the box," strategic innovation and an arms race in novelty production are not possible.

In the context of extended phenotypes, to use a term coined by Dawkins (1989) to refer to artefacts developed external to the organism, humans equipped with cognitive G-T-P machinery will both embrace the Liar strategy and identify the same in others as they aim to falsify or negate predictable or computable rules and are primed with the "smarts" for protean and innovative behaviors. This, as will be shown, has far-reaching implications for the vulnerability of predictable rules and formal systems.

The main point of departure between the G-T-P games with Genomic Nash Equilibrium (Markose 2017) and standard game theory is that, in the latter, the action set is fixed and given and it is asserted that there is no Nash equilibrium that generates surprises or novelty.[11] The question that Binmore (1987) seminally asked comes to the forefront: can the scope of strategic behavior be restricted to a system that is logically closed and complete in view of the Gödel archetype of the Liar or contrarian qua hacker? The flawed foundation of extant game theory is that there is no option of exiting from given action/choice sets and, in the absence of inherent Gödel incompleteness in the socio-cognitive machinery with putative novelty that lies outside listable action sets, the only indeterminism is randomization

---

10. There is a long legacy at least since Irun Cohen (1992) on the so-called cognitive immune system theories of intelligence in which internal self-image is the basis of the "other." Many, like Nataf (2017), Kipnis (2017), Kipnis et al. (2012) and others, make the link between how the immune system became "smart" and the possible similarities in biomolecular processes underpinning neural activities relating to cognition, communication and signaling, social cognition and even behavioral traits (Lopes 2017). Miller (2018) goes further and characterizes all biotic elements to be cognitive components imbued with self-referential sensory perception of the "other." Of course, what is missing in the above narratives is the precise G-T-P recursive machinery at work.
11. Bhatt and Camerer (2005) succinctly state this: "in a Nash equilibrium nobody is surprised about what others actually do, or what others believe, because strategies and beliefs are synchronized, presumably due to introspection, communication or learning" (425).

between known alternatives. In G-T-P games, radical indeterminism in the form of Gödel incompleteness follows in a Nash equilibrium with surprise strategies that map outside extant action sets to avoid logical inconsistency and strategic failure.

In fact, failure of a player in a two-person adversarial G-T-P game only occurs when the Liar qua hostile agent wins *out of equilibrium* as the formal structure of the game involving the Liar is not acknowledged by the other player, indicating there is a false belief. In other words, a record of being attacked is not sufficient; the self-referential record of the hostile agency of the other is also needed for a code to self-report that it is under attack. This yields a diagonal formulation for which the machinery of the Second Recursion Theorem (Rogers 1967) is needed to determine the Nash equilibria of the game as fixed points of recursive strategy functions being used by the G-T-P players. The important point is that, where the encoding of such fixed points involving the Liar can be achieved, their undecidability is a theorem in the G-T-P cognitive machinery. The recursive best response functions, thereafter, can only take the form of Emil Post's (1944) productive function, which implements novel objects that map outside of all listable sets, viz., a surprise strategy in the Nash equilibrium of the game. This has an inherent "productive" structure of an arms race in innovation that permits co-existence of adversarial agents as part of the Nash equilibrium in G-T-P games.

Further, what is significant is that the incompleteness of the system that permits endogenous novelty production in the form of new syntactic objects implies that the code-based information processing is strictly in accordance with Gödel formal systems (see Smullyan 1961); that is, in the absence of logical consistency, incompleteness is not possible. With the organizing principle behind endogenous novelty production being logical consistency, this rules out the position of those who focus solely on recursive recombinant machinery for variety (Beinhocker 1961; Holland 1995). The partial adoption of the recursive or computation framework typically dispenses with the stock-in-trade features of code-based dynamics of self-reference (Self-Ref), self-representation (Self-Rep), the necessity of Liar-like viral software, recursive function fixed points and incompleteness with the productive function-based (Post 1944) arms race in novelty production.

Doyens like Gregory Chaitin (2012, 2013) have underscored the role of code-based models as opposed to equation-driven ones for evolutionary innovation. However, being wedded to the pre-McClintock (1984) era of gene science and evolution, the Chaitin metabiology[12] purports to model random mutation in software as the sole driver of new forms. Hence, Chaitin, despite making the digital basis of DNA central, dispenses with the ingredients of G-T-P to do with Self-Rep/Self-Ref as being essential to novelty production and incompleteness. The prototypes of this in genomic evolution are the mirror systems in the Thymus Medulla and the mirror neurons in the brain.

Sections 2 and 3 of this chapter elucidate further the above outlined G-T-P logic behind novelty production in genomic adaptive immune systems and in the human mirror neuron system. Section 4 discusses some implications of G-T-P logic-driven über intelligent agents for regulator–regulatee arms races and policy design in general. Here, one is confronted by those, like Foster (2005),[13] who are interested in novelty production but show a disinclination to invest in G-T-P logic and computation theory. Durlauf (2012), who surveys complexity economics in the context of policy, acknowledges his lack of knowledge of the G-T-P logic behind novelty production and hence is not familiar with the archetypes of G-T-P logic to do with self-reflexive mappings and the challenges posed by contrarian or Liar-like negation to predictable trends and formalistic rules. Also, despite his survey of some agent-based stock market models (that purport to generate boom–bust cyclical dynamics), Durlauf (2012) is silent about what can be regarded to be Complexity Economics 101, which is the seminal insight of Arthur (1994) that, in many real-world games, like stock market games, contrarian anti-herding strategies go against predictable trends and, being in the smallest minority, produce the best winning strategies.

---

12. Chaitin's critics have noted that in terms of implementation, the so-called "creative" aspects of the accretion of new and different software ends up being teleological in that only improvements to an n-bit Busy Beaver Function are sought (see Siedlinksi 2016).
13. Foster (2005) stated: "Contributors to this literature have developed a 'meta-mathematics' that can be used to generate models with evolutionary properties, i.e., a capacity to generate 'surprises'. However, although these mathematical developments seem to be fundamentally important, they tend to be only loosely connected with less formal ideas and insights in evolutionary and institutional economics that have been around for decades."

This contrarian payoff structure, analogous to the Liar in G-T-P logic, results in the impossibility of a unique computable rational expectation, which leads to heterogeneity of meta-models for prediction and, with it, endogenous cyclic dynamics that follow.

The far-reaching and deleterious consequences of a four-decades-long macroeconomic policy orthodoxy displays this blind spot on G-T-P logic for CAS; if the rule-breaking Liar-like agents cannot be eliminated, then predictable rules are vulnerable and regulators should be prepared to coevolve, innovate and "do running repairs."[14] Thus, despite the highly influential thesis by Robert Lucas (1972, 1976) on the necessity of surprises in policy in view of the Liar-like negation of what is predictable and problems of meta-measurements with econometrics of identifying behaviorally altered structure changes, the similarity of the Lucasian postulates with G-T-P logic for CAS was missed. Further, apart from Goodhart (1994), nobody queried how predictability can be prescribed as a norm in policy when the first Lucas premise is that predictability can lead to policy failure. Perhaps because of the special case that Lucas conceived of in which "surprise" was embedded as inflation prediction errors,[15] which seems both "bad" and bizarre for a policymaker to do, the logical and strategic necessity of surprises was not explored in any foundational setting. Instead, extensive literature that subsequently developed on the basis of the papers by Kydland and Prescott (1977) and Barro and Gordon (1983) aimed at vitiating surprises by an advocacy of pre-commitment to predictable rules.

The Lucas thesis on policy ineffectiveness and the necessity of policy "surprises" along with Goodhart's Law on indeterminism and policy failure will be shown to have a close bearing on A.O Hirschman's (1991) famous rhetoric of reaction based on futility, perversity and jeopardy arguments

---

14. This is a phrase coined by Paul Tucker in a 2011 speech (see Tucker 2011). The notion of running repairs to regulation illustrates the erstwhile pragmatism of common law countries like the UK.
15. The notion of a surprise strategy appears in the so-called Lucas surprise supply function, often defined as follows: $y = y^* + b((\pi - \pi^e) + \varepsilon$. This says that output, y, will not increase beyond the natural rate, y^*, unless there is "surprise" inflation ($\pi - \pi^e$), which is the prediction error from expected inflation, π^e. The idea here is that the private sector contravenes the effects of anticipated inflation, viz., the neutrality result. Hence, it is intuitively asserted that authorities who seek to expand output beyond the natural rate need to use surprise inflation.

for why expedient policies aiming to achieve specific outcomes, narrowly justified, could suffer these categories of failure. The Kant (1965) and Hayek (1960, 1967) thesis on the primacy of end-neutral legal rules on avoiding coercive imposition of socio-economic laws that fulfil predetermined outcomes will be briefly reviewed here.

I will outline the serial failure of monetary and macroeconomic institutions that were predicated on a pre-commitment to fixed policy rules to vitiate the Lucas surprise strategy. Thus, first was a serial collapse of currency pegs in the 1980s, and then the exclusive focus on an ad hoc inflation target. In many cases, the latter was imposed by statute and aimed at tying the hands of regulators in Western central banks (Markose 2013). This led to an almost near-collapse of the global financial system with the 2007 Great Financial Crisis. Regulators were alarmingly oblivious of the financial arms races (Haldane 2012), many triggered by perverse incentives from the Basel banking regulation, when over US$16 trillion of securitized assets and US$60 trillion of credit derivatives were part of strategic innovations for purposes of gaming the system. The latter triggered self-reflexive forces of financial behaviors that would spell system failure. I argue that this was the consequence of blind spots in mainstream game theory and policy framework that are oblivious of the über G-T-P intelligence behind endogenous strategic innovation.

G-T-P Logic Condition (ii) and Evidence from Genomic Evolution of Self-Ref and Self-Rep

Arguably, evidence for and understanding of G-T-P condition (i) as the model of computation is widespread. There is extensive evidence, starting with the Nobel-prize-winning work of Günter Blobel, on the prevalence of unique identifiers for biotic elements. In twenty-first-century nomenclature, the latter feature can be described as self-assembly of digitized materials in the ribosomal machine execution of gene codes to produce 3-D prints of the somatic and regulatory structures (Gershenfeld 2012). Further, the Turing machine models of bio-molecular computing evidenced in ribosomal RNA are well known (Shapiro 2012; Verghese et al. 2015), and the literature abounds with many metaphors regarding the digitalization of inheritable information. In contrast, what appears to be less well understood is how G-T-P conditions (ii) and (iii) are fundamental to the evolution of genomic systems and how they were acquired in the course of evolution.

In this section, I elucidate the G-T-P condition (ii), which is key to bio-intelligent digital systems seen in the Thymus Medula of the adaptive immune system and in the cognitive mirror neuron systems. It is not without reason that the former is called the "Big Bang of Immunology" and the latter the "Great Leap Forward" by Ramachandran (2000). The recursive machinery of the immuno-cognitive system will be shown to entail Self-Rep and Self-Ref operations, which build Gödel incompleteness into the immuno-cognitive machinery.

The paradigm-shifting nature of the so-called promiscuous gene expression in the thymus, which "*mirrors virtually* all tissues of the body" (Kyewski and Klein 2006, emphasis added), is a view that is widely held.[16] The next section shows how the mirror system permits the cognitive system to identify the other and, in particular, the Liar/hacker or the hostile agent in terms of a self-referential mapping.

Online *Self-Assembly with Self-Ref,* Machine Execution and Offline *Self-Rep in Immuno-Cognitive Systems*

The focus here is on how the recursive function mirror operations in the two key genomic neural cognitive and adaptive immune systems take place involving self and other in what is effectively a digital game. The self-agent will be denoted as the host (h) and the antigen as the parasite (p), with the two protagonists strictly being confined to using (total) recursive functions as strategy functions. Thus, expressions of the tissue-specific gene codes in the Thymus Medulla epithelial cells (m-TECs) relate to the Gödel metamathematics that can organize encoded information in offline domains based on ribosomal machine executions of the same. In Markose (2017), an identical recursive machinery is shown to be at work in the cognitive mirror neuron system that records information from the online action-related operations in the motor and sensory/optical cortex. This basal digitized information in the respective immuno-cognitive systems will be shown to be "theorems" of the systems and define the objective of the genomic game as one in which hosts have to retain the genomic identity

---

16. See Derbinski et al. (2001) and Danan-Gotthold et al. (2016).

and somatic integrity of the basal codes in terms of the phenotypes or the outputs generated from them.

Using the well-known system of Gödel numbers (g,ns), integers can uniquely identify gene codes based on the near-universal alphabet of the genome. The set of gene codes representing both protein coding and non-coding (nc) ones is denoted as

$$\mathbf{G} = \{g_1, g_2, \ldots, g_\#\}. \quad (1.a)$$

Any gene code will be generically denoted as g, and # denotes some finite cardinal number. The digital encoding of the finite set of states under which the genes are transcribed is denoted by $\mathbf{S}$, with $s \in \mathbf{S}$ as an element in a finite and countable set of states and other archival information.[17] The set of online action-related data from the motor cortex and sensory optical neuronal firings will be denoted by set $\mathbf{A}$,

$$\mathbf{A} = \{a_1, a_1, a_1, \ldots, a\#\}. \quad (1.b)$$

In the following, while the narrative is primarily in terms of the tissue-specific gene codes in set $\mathbf{G}$ in (1.a) for the mirror system in the adaptive immune system, as the graphics in figure 4.1 show, upon replacing this by set $\mathbf{A}$ in (1.b), we have an identical mirror system for the cognitive mirror neuron system.

Self-Ref Machinery

To represent the online self-assembly of the ribosomal RNA or the non-protein coding transcription machinery, the following notation from Rogers (1967) is used to represent the online machine execution of the gene code:

$$\phi_{\phi_g(g)}(s) = q. \quad (2)$$

Here, the $\phi_g(g)$ in the subscript of the recursive function ϕ that outputs q underscores the online self-assembly, or Self-Ref process (typically denoted

---

17. Note, analog measurements of state variables, such as chemical concentration, temperature, etc., have to be converted into digital code for this to be processed by a digital agent.

as Diag (g) = $\phi_g(g)$), such that the gene encodes a program g that effectively runs its own code. The output q in (2) that follows from the full transcription/translation process produces, respectively, a protein in the case of a coding gene, or an RNA regulatory phenotype based on a non-coding (nc) gene.

Self-Rep Mirror System

The famous *offline* Gödel Meta-Representation system in Thymus Medulla can be given the following format from Rogers (1967, 202–204):

$$\phi_{\sigma(g,g)}(s) \cong \phi_{\phi_g(g)}(s) = q, \textit{iff}\, \phi_g(g) \downarrow . \qquad (3)$$

Here, the diagonal operation of Self-Ref in (2), when a machine runs its own code and halts, denoted by $\phi_g(g) \downarrow$, is bijectively represented in Self-Rep format, as in $\sigma(g,g)$ for the genome in (3). The left-hand side function $\sigma(g,g)$ in (3) modelled along the lines of the Gödel two-place substitution function (see Rogers 1967) has the feature that it names or "signifies" in the offline recording in the Thymus Medulla epithelial cells, m-TECs, the one–one bijective mapping of the machine execution of the gene codes $\phi_{\phi_g(g)}(s) = q$; that is, when the self-assembly machine halts and proceeds to output q, the meta system also faithfully predicts the outcome is q. In Markose (2017), this is taken to be the baseline point of the game when the pathogen does not disrupt host gene codes.

In general, the two-place Gödel substitution function $\sigma(x,y)$ has placeholders from the perspective of self on status of self and status of non-self vis-à-vis self: σ(*status of self, status of non-self vis-à-vis self*). Thus, in the $\sigma(g,g)$ notation in (3), the first place from the left is the record of the host's gene code; an identical g in the second place implies that the host has identified that there has been no alteration of this gene code by the non-self antigen or pathogen, aka the Liar. In other words, the agency of the other is calibrated self-referentially, viz., in terms of self-codes. The diagonal elements $\sigma(x,x)$, in general, have great significance in the *offline* meta system organized in matrix form. As discussed in Markose (2017), only diagonal elements demonstrate Nash equilibria when both status of self and self's identification of non-self status are in sync, with false beliefs and undetected deceit being ruled out. These will be contrasted with non-diagonal elements σ(x,y) or σ(y,x). In general, as one substitutes different values of σ(x,y) for a given state, s, the whole space of potential genomic outcomes that can be brought about by recursive functions, can be explored. There is an important theorem here (see Rogers 1967)[18]: the *g.ns representing σ(x,y) in the meta-system can always be obtained whether or not the partial recursive function $\phi_x(y)$ on the right-hand side of (3), which executes programs, halts.*

The significance of this bijective offline recording device of m-TECs for tissue-specific genes has led Derbinski et al. (2001) to note that "m-TECs may indeed represent an immunological homunculus, in that they mirror and anticipate the peripheral self" (1037). Markose (2019) gives the bio-informatics in terms of the recursive function operations of the V-D-J recombinant machinery, which enables the adaptive immune system to identify putative attacks on the gene codes, $g \in G$, by a self-referential process. Some key elements of this are outlined in the next section as to how the V-D-J recursive machinery trains T-cell receptors to identify malware alterations of the basal gene codes.

In the case of the mirror neuron system and the motor-sensory cortex mappings pertaining to actions, $a \in A$ in (1.b) denotes a generic action code that belongs to the set of actions A that cause canonical neurons to fire with action execution by self (self-codes, for short). This gives immediate and unerring action prediction and inference relating to the other by embodied *offline simulation* of the self-codes as in (3) and discussed further in Markose (2017). In particular, I argue that, unless there is an exhaustive listing of basal self-codes as in the genomic m-TECs and in the cognitive mirror system of motor-sensory activity, the anticipation of algorithmic alterations of self-codes by the other, malware detection in the case of m-TECs and intentionality of the other in cognitive systems are not feasible.

There is growing evidence for, and many non-mathematical accounts of, the mirror mapping in the adaptive immune system of the tissue-specific gene codes. There was an even more elaborate description of

---

18. It is well known by what is called the SMN Theorem or the Parameterization Theorem (Rogers 1967) how new g.ns for recursive operations on extant g.ns can be mechanically generated.

mirroring of online motor and sensory cortex activity[19] with the discovery of the mirror neuron system (MNS) by the Parma Group in the 1980s. Gallesse (2009) and Gallese and Sinigaglia (2011) have characterized the MNS as a common neuronal platform for conducting *offline embodied simulations* for action prediction in the other based on a parallel set of neurons that fire during action execution by one-self.[20] In fact, Ramachandran (2000) made pronouncements that have been regarded as verging on hyperbole:

> mirror neurons would do for psychology what DNA did for biology by providing a unifying framework and help explain a host of mental abilities that have hitherto remained mysterious and inaccessible to experiments. … And that the emergence of a sophisticated mirror neuron system set the stage for the emergence, in early hominids, of a number of uniquely human abilities such as protolanguage (facilitated by mapping phonemes on to lip and tongue movements), empathy, "theory of other minds," and the ability to "adopt another's point of view."

I, of course, fully concur with these views, though my position is that, without the G-T-P framework, much of this may remain mysterious and controversial.

Indeed, despite so-called computational frameworks for cognitive biology (see Fitch 2014)[21] or computational neuroscience, apart from

---

19. The neurons that fire with action execution are called *canonical neurons* (Arbib and Fagg 1998) and correspond to online machine executions by self in the G-T-P logic.
20. Ramachandran (2000) describes this as follows: "It's as if any time you want to make a judgement about someone else's movements you have to run a VR (virtual reality) simulation of the corresponding movements in your own brain and without mirror neurons you cannot do this."
21. Many computational cognitive models rely on Bayesian learning. As stated in Fitch (2014), the recordings from the sensory-visual and motor cortex constitute "a large, complex and ancient set of Bayesian priors (visual, sensory, motor) that constrain inference in any mammalian brain, and are equally operative in the human brain" (357). Bayesian inference is statistical and is a far cry from inference by embodied offline simulation in the G-T-P cognitive system, which also permits novelty generation. See table 4.1 for further differences between the G-T-P cognitive system and Bayesian and other mainstream decision theories.

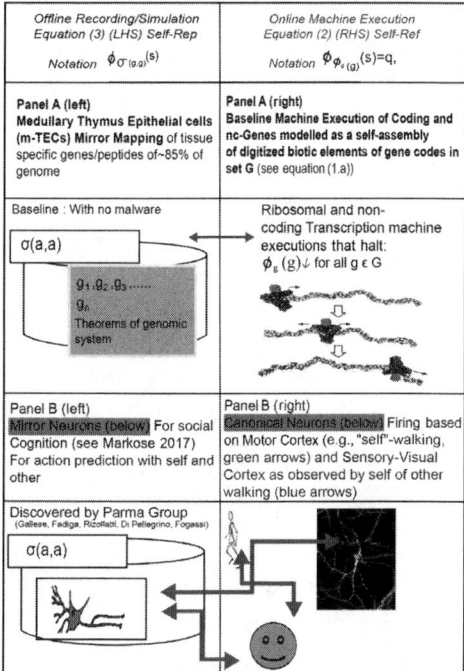

Fig. 4.1. Gödel Meta-Representation (Rogers 1967) and Mirror Systems in Immuno-Cognitive Systems

Note: The figure panels are described as follows: *Offline* mirror systems in Medulla Thymus (Panel A, left) and *Offline* cognitive mirror neuron system (Panel B, left). Respective bijective map of *Online* gene transcription (Panel A, right) and *Online* action execution in motor-sensory cortex (Panel B, right).

Tsuda (2014), there has been no explicit discussion of the role of the genomic mirror systems and the recursive information processing in the G-T-P computational model in equation (3).

Tsuda (2014) identifies how neural systems that need to process a self-referential description use the mirror neuron system as in the mathematics of Gödel's incompleteness theorem:

> When neural systems process a self-referential description, they may first have to make a copy of the object of self-reference and then refer to this copy. This two-stage formulation can be realized

mathematically in the proof of Gödel's incompleteness theorem through the processes of projecting mathematical statements to natural numbers and of referring to meta-mathematical statements by providing mathematical statements about such numbers. The presence of mirror neurons in animal brains or mirror neuron systems in human brains may also be a realization of the above two-stage formulation in brains, because mirror neurons, or mirror-neuron systems, can be activated, not only by behavior in others similar to one's own behavior, but also by one's own behavior.

(365)

However, Tsuda (2014) does not utilize the mirror system for a model of cognition capable of implementing novelty production.

The graphics in figure 4.1 are useful to show an identical recursive machinery based on G-T-P condition (ii) given in equation (3) that is at work both in the mirror system of the m-TECs of the adaptive immune system (Panel A) and for the cognitive mirror neuron system (Panel B). The, respective, self-referential online machine executions (right-hand side) in figure 4.1 are mapped 1–1 to offline Self-Rep that permits meta-inference on self and the other. There are, of course, interesting differences in the processes by which information on the other is conveyed via visual–sensory cortex to the mirror neuron system when external phenotypes are involved in the set **A** (equation (1.b)) and in the case of peripheral antigen receptors and those antigen receptors in the m-TECs. Some details of the latter are given in the next section.

GTP Logic Condition (iii): The Liar Strategy/Malware, Contrarian Structures, and *Who do You Need to Surprise?*

Self-Halting Machines and Theorems of the Systems

The starting point here is to note that a halting computation is proof by construction. The domain of halting self-referential machines constitutes theorems, in the genomic immune and cognitive systems, respectively, given by the basal sets $g \in \boldsymbol{G}$ and $a \in \boldsymbol{A}$.

The sets G and A can be shown to be the subset of the archetypal creative set C^{22} (see Cutland 1980, 133). The latter is a listable set of all self-referential machine calculations that halt with any $x \in \aleph$, where $\aleph$ is the set of integers. Set C is central to Post's (1944) set theoretic proofs for Gödel incompleteness, and figure 4.2 gives what Cutland (1980, 148) calls the miniature form of the Gödel Incompleteness Theorem, adapted for our case. Thus, in the case of set G of gene codes, we have self-halting codes where the downward arrow denotes halting Turing machines (TMs):

$$G = \{g \mid \phi_g(g) \downarrow; TM_g(g) \text{ halts}; g \in W_g \text{ for all } g \in G\}. \quad (4.a)$$

In some formal systems that are consistent, for every $g_i \in G$, a negation symbol on g_i, as in $g_i^\neg$ will suffice to produce a listable set of non-theorems in the system. The latter set, denoted as $G^\bullet$, is disjoint from the set G; and in figure 4.2, $G^\bullet$ displays the *known* listable set containing "forbidden" and altered malware-infected gene codes. A halting machine execution of $g_i^\neg$ will imply the destruction of specific somatic/tissue of $g_i \in G$ and the phenotype associated with it.

$$G^\bullet = W_{\sigma_n^\neg} = \{g^\neg \mid \phi_{g\neg}(g^\neg) \uparrow; TM_{g\neg}(g\neg) \text{ does not halt} \leftrightarrow \quad (4.b)$$
$$g \in W_g, \phi_g(g) \downarrow\}.$$

The listable set $G^\bullet = W_{\sigma_n^\neg}$ is a subset of the set $C^\neg$ (see footnote 22 and figure 4.2) and has the property explained in Markose (2017), Lemma 3, such that its index $\sigma_n^\neg$ entails a recursive enumeration function $\tau(g_n^\neg) = \sigma_n^\neg$ such that the nth element $g_n^\neg$, indexed as $\sigma_n^\neg$, can only be added to the listable set $W_{\sigma_n^\neg}$, but cannot belong to $W_{\sigma_n^\neg}$.

Figure 4.2 illustrates how the listing in the Thymus Medulla of the self-halting tissue gene codes of the ribosomal machinery are identical to the listing of theorems in a formal system. The listing of non-theorems of the system, which are the so called "forbidden" codes, are those that should

---

22. Set C that represents the "diagonal" set contains the g.ns of those recursively enumerable sets, W_x, that contain their own indexes (see Cutland 1980, 123; Rogers 1967, 62): $C = \{x \mid \phi_x(x) \downarrow; TM_x(x) \text{ halts}; x \in W_x\}$. The complement of C represents the "anti-diagonal" set, which is different from every listable set W_x for all x: $C^\neg = \{x \mid \phi_x(x) \uparrow; TM_x(x) \text{ does not halt}; x \notin W_x\}$.

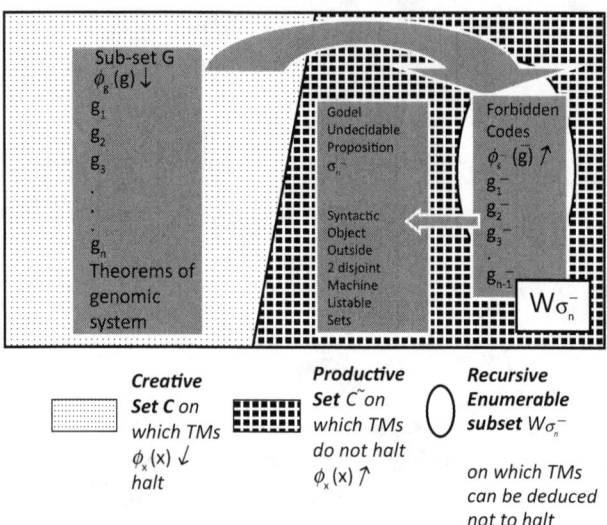

Fig. 4.2. Gödel Incompleteness Result in Miniature: An Illustration of Mirror Mapping in Thymus Medulla of Gene Codes that are Theorems in Genomic Systems

Note: Gödel undecidable proposition $g_n^\neg$ lies outside the listable sets G and $W_{\sigma_n^\neg}$, viz., $\sigma_n^\neg \notin G \cup W_{\sigma_n^\neg}$. Also, $\sigma_n^\neg = g_n^\neg$.

not be executed online in the genomic system as it will produce outcomes antithetical to the original gene codes or theorems of the genomic system. Hence, the forbidden codes belong to the set of non-halting codes, disjoint from the gene codes or theorems of the system.

What is important to note is that the list of forbidden gene codes cannot be exhaustively listed in the set $\mathbf{G}^\bullet = W_{\sigma_n^\neg}$. Moreover, in the miniature formulation of Gödel incompleteness, there will be an altered gene code that is undecidable in the formal system; that is, it is not decidable whether it is a "theorem" in the system or not. With the productive function for set $\mathbf{C}^-$ in Post (1944) being the trivial identity function of the index of the set $W_{\sigma_n^\neg}$, $\tau(g_n^\neg) = \sigma_n^\neg$ is the Gödel undecidable proposition and lies outside the listable sets $\mathbf{G}$ and $W_{\sigma_n^\neg}$, viz., $\sigma_n^\neg \notin \mathbf{G} \cup W_{\sigma_n^\neg}$, as shown in figure 4.2. In the next section, I give details of how malware detection is conducted by the adaptive immune system such that the encoding $g_n^\neg$ can be derived.

Malware/Liar Strategy Function and V-D-J-Based T-Cell Detection of Non-Self Pathogens

We need to bring in the agency of the pathogen qua hacker who can alter the basal gene codes using software. It is useful to assume that the strategy functions for the host and the parasite $f_i, i \in (h,p)$ that can alter the basal information in sets G and A are total computable functions such that g.ns of $f_i, i \in (h,p)$ are contained in set $\mathcal{R}$,

$$\mathcal{R} = \{m \mid f_i = \phi_m, \phi_m \text{ is total computable}\}. \quad (5)$$

The set $\mathcal{R}$ of all total computable functions is not recursively enumerable or capable of being listed by an algorithm. The proof of this is standard (see Cutland 1980, 127). Representing known members of set $\mathcal{R}$ based on sets $\mathbf{G}$ and $\mathbf{G}^{\bullet}$, collectively denoted as $\mathbf{G}^*$, the set $\mathcal{R} - \mathbf{G}^*$ presents a non-listable infinite number of ways for new technologies or phenotypes that can be formed and hence also the potential malware alterations to gene codes. Note, from Markose (2017), the best response Post (1944) productive function is also the surprise strategy function:

$$f_i = f_i' = \phi_m, \text{ such that } m \in \mathcal{R}\text{-}\mathbf{G}^*, i \in (h,p). \quad (6)$$

Markose (2017) has proved that the best response surprise strategy function given by the Post (1944) productive function that maps outside extant listable sets into $\mathcal{R}\text{-}\mathbf{G}^*$ is a Nash equilibrium when this is triggered by a fixed point of the recursive function of the negation or Liar or malware strategy $f_i^{\neg}, i \in (h,p)$, defined in (7.a). Only such innovations will be accorded with the status of strategic innovations. I show how the G-T-P logic can give a plausible model for how the adaptive immune system of the host using V-D-J operations identifies new code-centric threats by pathogens and the resulting somatic hyper-mutation (Noia and Neuberger 2007) associated with novel ways of countering antigenic attacks in terms of surprise strategies.

To understand how T-cells that are released into the periphery from the offline environment of the m-TECs are selected and how they can detect malware using the G-T-P logic, it is useful to define the Liar Strategy, or the non-self malware attack, which occurs online in the periphery. The

Liar Strategy, or malware $f_p^\neg$, aims to change a tissue-specific code of gene self-assembly machine $\text{Diag}(g) = \phi_g(g)$, which produces output q and is recorded accordingly in the m-TEC mirror system as $\phi_{\sigma(g,g)}(s) = q$. As the malware $f_p^\neg$ occurs in the online peripheral tissue-specific code with the code change in g_n denoted as $g_n^\neg$, note the real-time offline mirror recording is in the *peripheral* MHC (major histocompatibility complex) antigen receptors.

The Liar/Malware Strategy $f_p^\neg$

$$\phi_{f_p^\neg \text{Diag}(g_n)}(s) = \phi_{\sigma(g_n^\neg, g_n)}(s) = \phi_{\phi g_n^\neg(g_n)}(s)$$

$$= q^\neg \text{ iff } \phi_{\phi g_n(g_n)}(s) = q \tag{7.a}$$

Thus, the halting online self-assembly machinery as a result of the malware $f_p^\neg$ in (7.a) is:

$$\phi_{g_n^\neg}(g_n) = f_p^\neg \text{Diag}(g_n). \tag{7.b}$$

In (7.a), the effect of taking the malware-altered gene code $g_n^\neg$ with input g_n is to change the output of self-assembly machine Diag (g_n) (on the right-hand side of (7.a)) in the following way: on the left-hand side of (7.a), we have $\neg \phi_{\phi g_n(g_n)}(s) = q^\neg$ if and only if $\phi_{\sigma(g_n,g_n)}(s) = q$ Here, $\neg$ is the "not" or negation symbol. Thus, the malware $f_p^\neg$ in (7.a) produces the opposite of the host's desired outcome.

As noted in Markose (2017) with regard to the Liar strategy, here also the malware/pathogen succeeds only out of equilibrium in (7.a) with the malware $f_p^\neg$ alters the gene code to $g_n^\neg$ under conditions when the host has not yet updated the second place g_n in σ $(g_n^\neg, g_n)$ to reflect self-identification of the agency of the hostile other. On the flip side, from the perspective of the pathogen, the success of $f_p^\neg$ requires that the host is deceived. As is well known, the adaptive immune system can take four to seven days to respond to a tissue code-specific attack by a pathogen. How is this done?

For this, the T-cell receptor must also have g.n $g_n^\neg$ obtained during the training received in the offline m-TEC environment and from which the fixed point of the reactive malware software $f_p^\neg$ on the gene code g_n is obtained.

Bio-Informatics of T-Cell Training

In Markose (2019) it is conjectured that the recombinant V-D-J system of the adaptive immune system imprints the 5×10^7 T-cells that are known to be generated on a daily basis (Kyewski and Klein 2006) with a stochastic selection of g.ns based on the universal genomic alphabet. This is the most spectacular horizon-scanning search process within the set $\mathcal{R}$-$\mathbf{G}^*$ for codes of software that will help the T-cell receptors in their training in the *offline* or virtual environment of the m-TECs. This offline training of the T-cells is for the detection and elimination—in the online environment that immunologists call peripheral tissues—of malware software (non-self-antigen) that is reactive to tissue-specific gene self-codes and their known antigens. The T-cells have to achieve this[23] without attacking self-codes, resulting in autoimmune disease. Extensive discussions are about the so-called elimination of self-reactive T-cells in m-TECs to avoid autoimmune disease. As noted by Wu et al. (2009), with little or no focus on how T-cell training[24] equips T-cells for "self-non-self discrimination ... that ... continues in the periphery after thymic negative selection, ... this is an enigma" (534).

Markose (2019) claims that, in the positive selection of T-cells imprinted with the V-D-J-generated g.ns, only those that are derived from the Self-Rep formatted self-codes in set $\mathbf{G}$ are retained and the others are eliminated; the latter are g.ns for diagonal and off-diagonal terms (of the matrix of meta information, see Markose 2017) not derivable from the g.ns in the set $\mathbf{G}^*$. In the negative selection, partially trained T-cells that generate g.ns for putative malware that is reactive to the g.ns in set $\mathbf{G}^*$, as in (7.a), are eliminated.[25] Partially trained T-cells have signatures like $\sigma(g_n^{\neg}, g)$ in (7.a) and represent machine-halting assembly programs being

---

23. Of the 5×10^7 T-cells that are known to be generated on a daily basis, it is estimated that 1–2×10^6 mature T-cells are released daily into circulation. "The loss of over 95% of thymocytes reflects the stringent selection processes that shape the developing T-cell repertoire" (Kyewski and Klein 2006, 573).
24. As stated by Michael Lotz in his BICT 2019 Keynote, while almost 99.9% of genes are the same for humans, only 6% of T-cell repertoires of different humans are the same. Hence, while some can combat new pathogens, others may not and, hence, succumb to them.
25. It is interesting to note that all V-D-J T-cell codes that are the result of reactivity to known antigen codes in $\mathbf{G}^\bullet$ are virtual clones of more virulent forms of extant pathogens.

executed by the malware and, hence, are dangerous if released online as they will accomplish the negation of the tissue-specific gene code g_n, as shown in (7.a).

The partial training arises from the fact that the host is under false belief that there will be no malware attack when there could be one (in the online environment) and has not identified the function $f_p^{\neg}$, which is the identity of other as the hacker/Liar. For the T-cell training to be complete in the m-TECs, the T-cells must determine a fixed point of $f_p^{\neg}$ and match this with the encoding in the peripheral MHC antigen receptors should there be an attack of the tissue-specific gene codes.

The Gödel Sentence

In other words, the host's immuno-cognitive system must encode the Gödel sentence in (8), which uses the Second Recursion Theorem as follows for the T-cell identification of the malware function $f_p^{\neg}$ on the right-hand side of (8) with the peripheral MHC antigen receptor for the same. Once the host has "synced" with the malware/Liar strategy σ ($g_n^{\neg}$, $g_n^{\neg}$) in (7.a,b), set v to be the g.n of Diag ($g_n^{\neg}$) = σ ($g_n^{\neg}$, $g_n^{\neg}$) = $\phi_{g_n^{\neg}}(g_n^{\neg})$, then, on using the updated version of (7.b) in the fourth equality in (8) below, by construction, v is the fixed point of the malware/Liar function. This yields,

$$\phi_v = \phi_{\sigma(g_n^{\neg}, g_n^{\neg})}(s) = \phi_{\phi_{g_n^{\neg}}(g_n^{\neg})} = \phi_{f_p^{\neg}\sigma(g_n^{\neg}, g_n^{\neg})}(s) = \phi_{f_p^{\neg}(v)}. \tag{8}$$

The index σ ($g_n^{\neg}$, $g_n^{\neg}$) is a very precise self-referential statement of which gene code is under attack and the biotic identity of the pathogen that is attacking it. Further, by construction, this is not a computable fixed point as it will produce a contradiction.[26] Hence, in (8) the output of the game is not predictable. At this juncture, whether the pathogen or host will win is undecidable, once the host has identified the hostile agency of the other.

---

26. On updating (7.a) and (7.b), the Liar/Malware strategy $g_n^{\neg}$ now operates on itself; we have $\phi_{\phi_{g_n^{\neg}}(g_n^{\neg})} = \neg \phi_{\phi_{g_n^{\neg}}(g_n^{\neg})}$, which is a contradiction. Here, we use Roger's Fixed Point Theorem (1967, Section 11.2): all total recursive functions, f, have a syntactic fixed point index v, even if v represents a non-halting computation.

This implies, the Post (1944) productive construction of the set in (4.b) and figure 4.2 follows in that the index for $g_n^{\neg}$ will lie outside two listable or recursively enumerable disjoint sets, respectively, for the "theorems" of the system and the known list of "non-theorems."

In summary, the fixed point in (8) permits the tissue-specific gene code of the host to self-report that it is under attack by a non-self antigen (the hostile other). This plunges the genomic system into a state of radical uncertainty in the form of undecidability. At this point, the adaptive immune system of the host is geared toward countering the malware. For this, a new anti-body must be produced and then applied en masse.[27] The host is compelled by G-T-P logic of the Gödel sentence $\sigma(g_n^{\neg}, g_n^{\neg})$ to adopt the *only* best response function logically permitted by the G-T-P framework, which is the Post (1944) productive recursive surprise function $f_h^!$ defined in (6). The latter will exit known listable sets and adopt an innovative antibody specific to the information in $g_n^{\neg}$, in accordance with the tissue-specific gene code g_n and the nature of the malware attack on it.

It is worth pointing out that this is where extant game theory models that have adopted the computability framework misconstrue the power of the G-T-P results.[28] Incompleteness requires a constructive generation of a "witness" for an undecidable proposition (see Smullyan 1961, chapter 5), which has to utilize a recursive function for this, viz., a Turing machine, that can be proven to map outside of all extant recursively enumerable sets (of gene codes for actions/phenotypes) in that system. This is in keeping with the lay person's intuition about "thinking outside the box," as an

---

27. It is beyond the scope of this chapter to give the detailed recursive bio-informatics behind the somatic hyper mutations (Noia and Neuberger 2007) on B-cells that follow from this point in the host adaptive immune system. The same is the case on how retrotransposon activity can change the germline.
28. For instance, consider the Nachbar and Zame (1996) conclusion that, "for a large class of discounted repeated games (including the repeated Prisoner's Dilemma) there exist strategies implementable by a Turing machine for which *no* best response is implementable by a Turing machine" (111). The Post (1944) set theoretic proof of the Gödel incompleteness result shows that, from fully deducible non-computable fixed points of a game—as in the Gödel sentence in (8)—the *only* best response strategies that can be implemented by total recursive functions, viz., Turing machines, are those that satisfy the property of productive functions that syntactically produce objects that lie outside given recursively enumerable sets.

innovation cannot be confined within extant action/phenotype sets (see Markose 2017).

In Markose (2017, Lemmas 3 and 5), it is shown how a non-trivial recursive reduction function from the indexation of the undecidable proposition from the Gödel sentence in (8), given as $\tau(g_n^{\neg}) = \sigma_n$ in figure 4.2, will produce a Nash equilibrium novelty producing recursive surprise function $f_h^!$. In the case of the adaptive immune system, this takes the form of new antibodies. Corresponding to the set $W_{\sigma_n^{\neg}}$ in figure 4.2, the recursive reduction that implements the surprise strategy function will be indexed as $\sigma_n^!$ such that the surprise strategy set $W_{\sigma_n^!}$ satisfies the consistency requirements of the basal information in figure 4.2; $\sigma_n^!$ can only be added to $W_{\sigma_n^!}$ and cannot belong to $W_{\sigma_n^!}$. This is shown in the structure of a co-evolutionary arms race with innovative antibodies that can ensue as a Nash equilibrium in which both host and pathogen coexist. It can be conjectured that the endogenous recursive reduction operations modelled here govern all RNA regulatory networks so that relays of digital on–off switches satisfy the original basal organization of listable "theorems" in set **G** and from the online genomic machine executions and the non-theorems thereof.

The arms race in the immune system is exactly that—the immune system is primarily evolving its defensive tactics against software hackers that aim to "highjack" the original gene codes to do their bidding. Genomic identity and conservation of some gene codes, which has continued over the millennia, is the remarkable consequence of the immuno-cognitive system being able to put in place a code-centric cyber security. The spectacular horizon scanning done by the adaptive immune system and the decentralized nature of biotic cyber defense are other notable features of the system.

Even though, prior to Markose (2017), there has not been an explicit computational model for meta-representation, deception, detection of deception and so-called social proteanism, a substantial literature addresses this. Many (see Sperber 2000) hold the capacity for meta-representations as *the* prime faculty in humans and adduce from this much credence for the hypothesis of an evolutionary arms race in higher-order meta-representational abilities that has been called "Machiavellian intelligence" by Byrne and Whiten (1988). The evolution of deception in animals and primates in environments with conflicting goals and the detection of falsity have been identified as important landmarks of meta-representational competence in humans (see Baron-Cohen 1995).[29] Miller (1997) has catalogued deceitful behavior to combat situations with the potential for conflict as follows: deceit takes the form of hiding intentions, the deliberate spreading of misinformation and, finally, the development of *protean* strategies based on unpredictable adaptive behavior to escape from hostile agents or rivalrous conspecifics. Miller (1997) and Grammer, Fink and Renninger (2002) cite a co-evolutionary arms race in foundational social interactions, such as human courtship, where deception and proteanism feature.

Further, it can be conjectured that, when the cognitive neuronal system implements the mutual recognition of hostility, negation or deceit, this places the meta-representational system of each agent in a state of chaos corresponding to non-converging calculations elicited by neuronal mappings. Such implications for novelty recognition and production have been cited in Korn and Faure (2003). Remarkably, Korn and Faure (2003), who investigate the role of chaotic dynamics in the neurophysiology of the brain, review the work of Freeman and his collaborators (Skarda and Freeman 1987) and conclude that "chaos confers the (neural) system with a deterministic 'I don't know state' from within which new activity patterns can emerge. ... Chaotic states ... are well designed for preventing convergence and for easy 'destabilization' of their activity by a novel input. ... They are ideally fit for accommodating the neural networks with a new and still-unlearned stimulus" (821).

Extant Strategic and Regulatory Frameworks Relating to Contrarian Oppositional Structures and Innovative Rule Breaking

In this section, I briefly survey the perceived lack of a framework in economics and in political economy, in general, to deal with the logic of opposition or the contrarian, the strategic use of deceit, surprises and rampant

---

29. There is evidence that autistic individuals have difficulty in passing the so-called Sally-Ann test on ascribing false beliefs to others. It has been found that members of this group have dysfunction in their mirror neuron system and, irrespective of high IQ, they have trouble with interpreting others' thoughts and intentions and, hence, social and strategic skills.

technology and strategic arms races in socio-economic interactions. The interesting point is that many notions from Gödel's logic are used intuitively in economic discussions and in popular culture.[30] However, without the investment in the requisite mathematics for the novelty production, the status of these discussions has been hampered by a flawed paradigm of social cognition and strategic interaction dominated by optimization within extant choice sets where the cognitive wherewithal to exit from extant choice sets and innovate is not possible (Binmore 1987).

It is useful here to summarize in table 4.1 the main differences between G-T-P immuno-cognitive systems and mainstream cognitive decision theories. Notions such as reflexivity and self-reference, the contrarian or the Liar and the necessity to exit from extant lists of phenotype and technologies under conditions of radical uncertainty of undecidability are simply missing in mainstream decision and game theory models. This creates serious blind spots in policy-related institutions that have led to severe consequences in the last thirty years, especially in the macro and monetary regulatory institutions of advanced Western economies.

Apropos game theory on strategic behaviors relating to deceit and surprise, Crawford (2003) begins with the elaborate subterfuge involved in the D-Day Allied landings of World War II in order to surprise and wrong foot the enemy. However, Crawford (2003) concludes that, to date, economic "theory lags behind the public's intuition," and "we are left with no systematic way to think about such ubiquitous phenomena" (133). As can be seen in the column on the right-hand side (marked with #) of table 4.1, which covers mainstream cognitive and decision theories, the very concept of a surprise strategy as a Nash equilibrium of a game is missing.

---

30. In Joseph Heller's *Catch 22*, Major Major, who aims to avoid the squaddies, adopts the Liar strategy. He can "win" against any visitor whose arrival is expected or preannounced by simply maintaining that he is not in. The only Nash equilibrium strategy of this game for those who want to see him is to surprise him, as did madman Yossarian who ambushes the Major. Those squaddies who are rule abiding (i.e, those who follow Major's rule that they turn up announced) have given up on seeing him. The only person who is waiting in the antechamber to see the Major is a rookie, Appleby, who has not worked out that the Major is the Liar—an *out of equilibrium* situation, as to turn up announced is simply not rational for anybody who wants to see the Major.

Table 4.1 Methodological Differences: G-T-P Immuno-Cognitive Systems vs. Mainstream Cognitive Decision Theories

Immuno-Cognitive Systems with Inbuilt Gödel Incompleteness and Novelty Production	#Mainstream Cognitive/Decision Models (Primarily Bayesian)
(1.a) Basal information from gene codes and motor-sensory cortex: mapped into offline mirror systems for meta-analysis on self and other. (1.b) Recursion is center stage with Self-Ref and Self-Rep operations. (1.c) Inference by embodied offline simulations that come from reuse of code-based computations (see equation (3) and figure 4.1).	(1.a#) Fitch (2014): The recordings from the sensory–visual and motor cortex constitute "a large, complex and ancient set of Bayesian priors (visual, sensory, motor) that constrain inference in any ... brain." (1.b#) No notion of operations of Self-Ref and Self-Rep. (1.c#) Bayesian inference: statistical.
(2.a) Formalistic and predictable outcomes can be subjected to hostile Liar strategy, viz., predictability can be punished and Liar wins out of equilibrium. (2.b) Non-computability of fixed points with Liar/Contrarian: undecidability and source of heterogeneity.	(2.a#) No archetype of the Liar/Contrarian Instead, game scenarios such as matching pennies used to model opposition (2.b#) No notion of undecidability; Indeterminism takes the form of randomization over known actions
(3) Novelty and surprise manifest as new syntactic objects outside extant listable sets of phenotypes/technology. (3.a) Post (1944) constructive generation of innovation that can be added to a listable set but cannot belong to it. (3.b) Novelty and surprise: Nash equilibrium in G-T-P games with arms races in innovation utilizing the above productive set construction.	(3#) Novelty and surprises: prediction error. (3.a#) The definition of Bayesian surprise "as the distance between the posterior and prior distributions of beliefs over models" (Itti and Baldi 2009). • Random technology shocks (Romer 2016). • Surprise inflation (Lucas 1976). (3.b#) Categorically deny the existence of a surprise as a Nash equilibrium strategy (Bhatt and Carmerer 2005).
(4) Theory of Mind relies on recursive mirror structure of Self-Ref/Self-Rep. (4.a) Agency of other is inferred via recursive function fixed-point methods. Meta recording of Self-Ref takes other to concur with self (4.b) To process deceit, at most, second-order self-referential mapping needed: highest level of computational intelligence with horizon scanning for threats via Godel sentence. (4.c) Organizing principle of encoded information is consistency, without which there cannot be endogenous incompleteness.	(4#) Theory of Mind: No (or optional) mirror structures. (4.a#) K-level reasoning is step-by-step rather than by circular reasoning. (4.b#) Notion of low-level self-referential thinking according to Coricelli and Nagel (2009) is when self disregards the other.

In the next section, I discuss the Arthur et al. (1997) model of self-reflexive price formation in stock markets that makes homogenous rational expectations an impossible result. The agent-based model by Markose, Alentorn and Krause (2004) is used to show how, only when the payoff function rewards those that are contrarian and anti-herd in terms of their decision to buy or sell stock, will the price show endogenous cyclical up-and-down movements. This raises the intriguing prospect that the contrarian structure, well known in the foundations of mathematical logic, is the source of heterogeneity due to epistemic incompleteness, viz., the logical necessity to agree to disagree. Likewise, the seminal inclusion of the necessity of surprise by Lucas (1972) in a policy context in response to regulatees who can contravene predictable policy will be compared to the G-T-P logic in table 4.2 in the following section. Finally, I discuss the widespread and costly failures that characterize Western regulatory institutions due to the doctrinaire way in which pre-commitment to predictable "rules" were instituted starting with the currency pegs in the 1980s on the grounds that they provide an inflation anchor.

Self-Reflexive Stock Market Games, Arthur (1994) and Contrarian/Minority Payoff Structures in Arthur et al. (1997)

In Arthur et al. (1997) the reflexive nature of prices in asset markets was mooted. The best known example of reflexivity, often written about in the popular press, is that of stock market prices:

$$P_{t+1} = g(\sum_{i=1,...N} \beta_{it}(\hat{m}_{it}(P_{t+1}))). \tag{9}$$

Here, P_{t+1} is *the price at t+1* as determined by the strategies β_{it} (to buy or sell) of investors indexed by $i = 1, 2, \ldots N$, based on their respective beliefs $\hat{m}_{it}$ *of the price at t+1*. The market price determination function $g(.)$ is the function that maps from the aggregate net demand (total buy orders less sell orders) at time t. A lucid statement of the problem of self-reference in asset markets can be found in Arthur et al. (1997):

> In asset markets, agents' forecasts create the world that agents are trying to forecast. Thus, asset markets have a reflexive nature in that prices are generated by traders' expectations, but these expectations

are formed on the basis of anticipation of others' expectations. This reflexivity, or self-referential character of expectations, precludes expectations being formed by *deductive means* so that perfect rationality ceases to be well defined.

(22, emphasis added)

Spear (1989) was the first to show that rational expectations involving the belief or forecast function $\hat{m}_{it}$ corresponds to inductive identification by trial and error of the fixed point, a, for the market price function g(.), as in $\phi_{g(a)}(s) = \phi_a(s)$ where s is an encoding of past historical data and other archival information and a is an algorithm for the market price determination function.

Further, pointing out the inherent contrarian or minority nature of the stock market game where payoffs to pure speculative investors are at their maximum if they sell when the majority are buying and vice versa, Arthur (1994) overturned traditional ideas of rationality and showed that it is logically impossible for all investors to have identical/homogenous rational expectations.[31] The contrarian need not only appear in the agency of a player. It can arise from the structure of the payoffs of a game where a player wins only if his actions diverge from that of co-players.

Arthur (1994) noted that asset markets have a contrarian payoff structure; rewards tend to accrue to those agents who are contrarian or in the minority. That is, if it is most profitable to *buy* when the majority is selling and to *sell* when the majority is buying, then if all agents act in an identical homogenous fashion having made predictions from the same meta-model, they will fail in their objective to be profitable. The following example represents a unique homogenous model for prediction, typically called homogenous rational expectations, for how many will buy (e.g., out of one hundred traders): if fifty or more are predicted to buy, then *all* will sell and they will fail to be in a minority. The reverse is also true: if fewer than fifty are predicted to buy, then all will buy and will again fail to be in a minority.

---

31. Formally, assume that there is a unique homogenous forecast function $\forall i, \hat{m}_{it} = \phi_a(s) = P_{t+1} \uparrow$ (i.e., a price increase is predicted). Then, the contrarian strategy, denoted as β_{it}^-, kicks in for all investors, leading them to sell. This results in the market price function to output a price fall, $\phi_{g(a)}(s) = P_{t+1} \downarrow$. In other words, this fixed point is not computable. Rationality in the presence of minority payoff structures generates endemic heterogeneity in strategies.

Any trend movements in prices will be broken down by contrarians who will arise endogenously from untagged agents (Arthur et al. 1997). The lack of effective procedures to determine winning strategies in games with contrarian payoff structures and the impossibility of homogenous rational expectations, cleverly identified by Arthur (1994) in the above informal statement of this problem in stock markets, is typically called the Minority or El Farol game. So unlike the traditional Milgrom-Stokey no-trade results and a cessation of trade under conditions of homogenous rational expectations, there is instead heterogeneity of beliefs and myriad technical trading strategies that endogenously bring about the boom and bust dynamics seen in asset markets.

In Markose et al. (2004), a simple agent-based model in which the stock market game is stripped down to its basics was devised to test whether it is the contrarian/minority payoff structure that induces self-equilibrating up-and-down swings in the stock prices.[32] First, we use the concept of radical uncoupling from Foster and Young (2006) in that traders have no direct way of knowing how to win the game. Agents only have knowledge of payoffs, such as whether they have won (+1 reward) or lost (−1 loss), when they buy or sell one unit of the stock at each time step. There is no constructive way of mapping between individual actions and the winner determination function, which notifies them if they receive a payoff of +1 or −1. Hence, traders seek to learn how to win from neighbors in a social network. Agents differ only in memory, and those with zero memory give random advice, using a toss of a coin, on whether to buy or sell and, hence, have an inherent capacity to give the "best" advice to win the minority game. Agents with longer memory give trend-following advice.[33]

---

32. This agent-based model on the significance of the contrarian payoff structure is given in the first lecture by me in the module, "Computational Market Micro-Structure and Complexity Economics," for an MSc in Computational Economics at the University of Essex. The link to the simulator of the contrarian payoff game can be found at: www.acefinmod.com/simulators/.

33. Agents use reinforcement learning and incrementally break away from those who give bad advice and randomly find new advisors until all agents learn to play the minority or majority game appropriately, when each of these winner determination rules is in operation. Interesting core–periphery network formations emerge. In a minority game, the "gurus" in the hub from whom most traders are taking advice are zero-memory agents. In a majority game, those with long memories become gurus, and traders chase trends in one-way markets.

A: Majority-Wins Rule

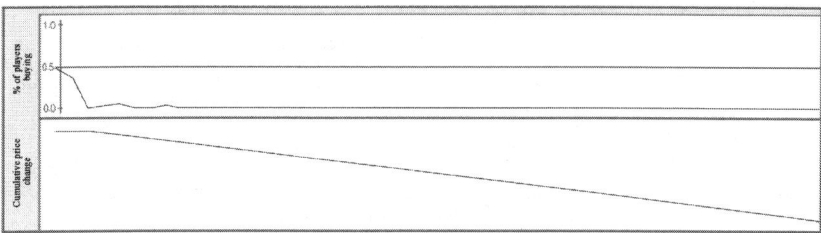

B: Majority-Wins Rule

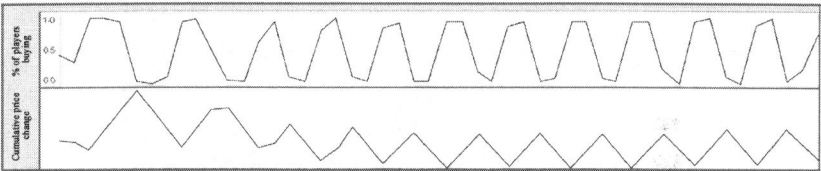

Fig. 4.3. Price Trends and Winner Determination

Note: Rule **A**: When the majority-wins rule applies: the price (bottom panel in **A**) shows a one-way market, either increasing or decreasing. In this case, price is decreasing since everyone is buying (top panel). Rule **B**: When the minority-wins rule applies: the price (bottom panel in **B**) experiences equilibrating up-and-down swings rather than one-way markets.

I report simulation results from these two payoff or winner determination functions: when being in a majority wins the game versus when being in a minority wins. The punchline is that only in a minority payoff game structure—figure 4.3 panel B—does the asset price show self-equilibrating up-and-down dynamics, as the contrarian anti-herding kicks in when price trends form, picking the price up from the trough and bringing the price down from a peak. When the majority-wins payoff function is in place, agents relentlessly follow trends and one-way markets get entrenched, as in figure 4.3 Panel A. This simple model of Markose et al. (2004) is intended to show that contrarian structures, integral to the Gödel logic, are vital in endogenously generating cyclical stock market dynamics.

Lucas's (1972) Thesis on Surprise Policy Strategy and Widespread Policy Failure

A loose amalgam of the three following postulates is well known in the Lucas (1972, 1976) thesis on policy design and these can be seen to correspond closely with issues raised above.

First, policy objectives may be rendered ineffective by strategic behavior of private agents if they can anticipate (i.e., have rational expectations of) or know outcomes of policy. This postulate corresponds to the Liar strategy in G-T-P logic in equation (7.a) when agents can negate what they can predict or compute.

Second, when faced by a private sector with rational expectations, it is necessary for authorities to use surprise strategies to achieve policy objectives. This corresponds to the Nash equilibrium in a G-T-P game in which the only response in the presence of the Liar is to exit from the extant action set and generate novelty.

Third, in what is called the Lucas Critique, Lucas (1976) raised the problem of a lack of structural invariance of optimal behavioral equations due to strategic responses to anticipated policy events that may cause predictive failure in econometric models for purposes of policy evaluation.[34] Typically, mainstream macro-economists do not consider the Lucas Critique to be logically connected to the first two postulates. In contrast, in a G-T-P game, the undecidable dynamics for which there is no finite halting machine that can determine the outcome of the game with the contrarian and with innovations changing structures is the logical consequence of the first two postulates.

Many cite similarities between the Lucas thesis on policy failure and Goodhart's Law. Goodhart's Law (1981) claims that "any observed statistical regularity will tend to collapse once pressure is placed upon it for control purposes." It is basically an empirical rather than theoretical exegesis of what followed when the Tory chancellor, in the mid-1980s, attempted to achieve preannounced nominal monetary targets. As per Goodhart's Law, these monetary variables became more volatile in the period after they were the object of more concerted efforts to control or target them than in any prior period. Fischer (1994) has given Goodhart's Law a wide enough theoretical berth to suggest that any formalistic monetary rule will suffer eventual breakdown. Thus, the general intuition of Goodhart's Law parallels the Lucas Critique (Lucas 1976) in that meta/prediction models

---

34. Lucas (1976) states: "any change in policy will systematically alter the structure of economic models. ... For the question of short-term forecasting or tracking ability of econometric models ... this conclusion is of only occasional significance ... [but] for issues involving policy evaluation, in contrast, it is fundamental" (41).

suffer problems of reflexivity when the outputs of prediction are no longer computable, as the actions based on the prediction will alter outputs.

Table 4.2, items 1–4, show that the trio of Lucas postulates correspond to the conditions that result in the Gödel incompleteness result and a co-evolutionary Nash equilibrium in which novelty and surprises follow.

Table 4.2 Gödel Logic on Liar-like structures (the Agent Who Negates What Can be Predicted), Surprise Strategy and Undecidable Dynamics vs. Lucas (1972, 1976) on Policy Ineffectiveness, Strategic Use of Surprise and Lucas Critique

Postulates of Gödel Logic	Lucas Postulates on Policy
(1) The Liar Strategy: agent who negates what can be predicted. Equation (7.a) states how only what is predicted can be negated. Liar strategy succeeds only out of equilibrium when the identity of Liar is not acknowledged.	(1#) Agents with rational expectations of policy can render it ineffective by negating what can be predicted. The idea that the private sector contravenes the effects of anticipated policy is called the neutrality result.
(2) Markose (2017) and in equation (8) the two-place meta-model records the Gödel sentence in a fixed point of the policy game as one where regulator identifies that the policy has been negated by Liar.	(2#) When faced by regulatees who can negate what can be predicted, it is deemed necessary by Lucas (1972) for authorities to use "surprise" strategies to achieve policy objectives.
(3) Novelty and surprise as syntactic constructions. The Nash equilibrium strategy function that maps from (2) is a surprise one in that no recursive function can remain within the listable set of actions. The Post (1944) production function produces a constructive syntactic object outside of listable sets, as in equation (6).	(3#) Strategy surprise as surprise inflation in Lucas (1972). Lucas couched surprise policy strategy in terms of "surprise" inflation $y = y^* + b(\pi - \pi^e) + \varepsilon$, This says that output, y, will not increase beyond the natural rate, y^*, unless there is "surprise" inflation $(\pi - \pi^e)$ or prediction error from expected inflation, π^e.
(4) Undecidable structure-changing Type IV dynamics implies that no finite meta model with a halting algorithm can list/enumerate the innovation in advance.	(4#) Lucas Critique states: No econometric model can identify innovation-based structure changes that follow from regulatory arbitrage.[a]
(5) Markose (2017) and equation (7.a) show that Liar wins out of equilibrium only if Liar has not been identified. For this, extensive horizon scanning is conducted by immuno-cognitive systems. If Liar/rule breaker cannot be eliminated, either the predictable transparent rule has to be abandoned, or the host has to be involved in a Nash equilibrium of novelty production.	(5#) Consequence of Lucas surprise inflation in (iii) led to the most widespread error of logic and strategy in mainstream macroeconomics. Authorities pre-committed to a fixed rule, abandoned horizon scanning, failed to identify Liar/rule breakers and unilaterally withdrew from co-evolution arms races.

[a] See note 34.

However, table 4.2, item 5, indicates a longstanding misunderstanding by macro and monetary economists of the notion of a "surprise" policy strategy in the Lucas thesis on policy design. If the surprise policy and strategic indeterminism followed to counter regulatees who negate what they can predict, how is it possible that leading economists concluded that systemic stability of the macro-economy can be achieved by simply showing commitment to a fixed rule designed to control inflation?

Most economists show scant awareness of the role of countering Liar-like rule breakers whose success is guaranteed precisely because the regulatory authorities are committed to a fixed formalistic rule and, in some cases, the predictability of these yield free lunches, as we will see in the case of the currency peg debacle to control inflation. Since the 1990s there has been a bandwagon effect of a class of models called monetary game theory models that set aside the Lucas policy postulates and advocate their exact opposite for the conduct of monetary policy. The dichotomous application of the Lucas surprise dictum to policy objectives pertaining to real and nominal sides of the economy is the prominent feature of monetary game theory models that dominated discussions on policy design. Goodhart (1994)[35] was the only economist who smelled a rat and raised the alarm. For real side objectives, the famous Lucasian categories of "dust, ambiguity and uncertainty" (Goodhart 1994, 110) are deemed necessary to achieve policy outcomes. For nominal variables, such as the price level and the rate of inflation, these models hold that commitment to transparent monetary rules, such as that of currency pegs or preannounced inflation targets involving interest rate adjustments, will lead to greater credibility and success in inflation control.

A vast literature on credibility and transparency developed to find means of "tying the hands" and preventing the authorities from using "surprise" inflation. While Rogoff (1985) spoke of the use of reputation without explicit rule, Krugman (1996) argued that a crisis-proof fixed exchange rate lay "with a high cost to abandoning the peg, for example,

---

35. Goodhart (1994), in the format of an open letter to the Governor of the Bank of England, reviews Cukierman (1992). Goodhart suggests that it may be "*silly*" (1994, 144, emphasis in original) that these models have diametrically opposite policy recommendations for policy objectives on real and nominal variables.

a very strong public commitment." The complexity and G-T-P perspective espoused here challenges policy prescriptions of this genre of monetary game theory models summarized in the words of Cukierman (1992): "Precommitment of monetary policy to a pre-announced course is a device for reducing inflation expectations. ... A central bank ... with an unequivocal mandate to focus on price stability, is one institutional device for committing monetary policy. Another device is the maintenance of a fixed parity with the currency of a country that puts high priority on stable prices" (1440).

Pre-Commitment to Fixed Rule to Vitiate Surprise Inflation: The Serial Collapse of Currency Pegs and the Soros Liar Strategy

It is interesting to note that the dramatic demise of the pound sterling tethered to the European Exchange Rate (ERM) currency peg was brought about in 1992 by George Soros, who has openly claimed that fundamental insights from mathematical logic relating to self-reflexivity[36] and the Cretan Liar have served as an inchoate, though powerful, guide to his successful career as a currency speculator (see Soros 1995, 69, 213).

The structure of the currency peg will be seen to provide a classic example of a transparent rule for which the Liar strategy that certifies a no-win for the authorities can be given as formalizable propositions. Figure 4.4, which encapsulates facts on the structure and collapse of ERM currency pegs, gives some credence to the view in Obstfeld (1996) that analyses on currency crises should focus on the "logic" or abstract structure of the game in place rather than just cataloguing the diverse circumstances in each case.

---

36. Indeed, it was a chance meeting with Roman Frydman at the CV Starr Center of NYU soon after the Soros debacle of the pound sterling in 1992 that eventually helped me crack the key element of Gödel logic as to what or who is the Liar. Frydman asked me, since I purport to know so much about Gödel logic, "Why did George Soros claim that he was using the Liar Strategy in his heist on the Bank of England?" The Liar negates and wins from what is predictable/computable (see (7.a)). Ultimately, the Institute of New Economic Thinking (INET) that Soros claimed he was setting up to study reflexivity and Liar-like complex social phenomena, among other heterodox ideas, has shown little or no advance in this direction. After Frydman quizzed me on the Liar Strategy, and having acknowledged the Binmore (1987) seminal insight, my critique (Markose 2001) of Velupillai (2000) focuses on his silence regarding the Liar.

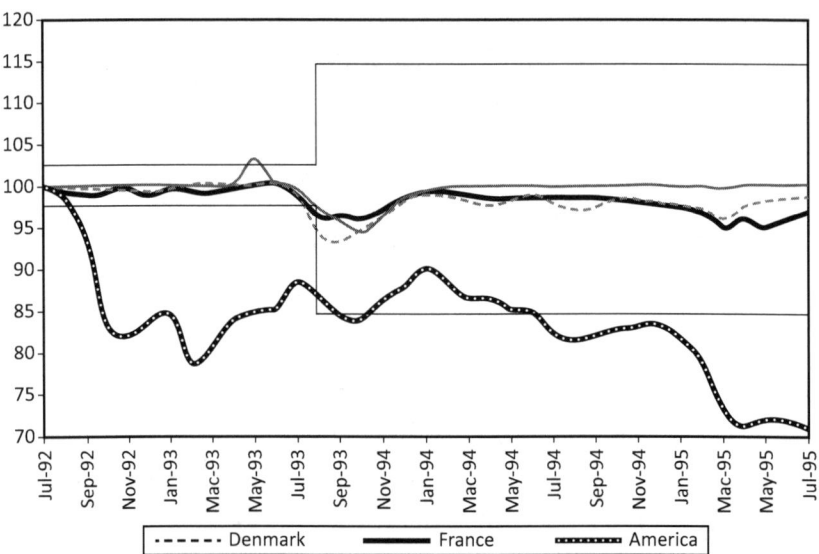

Fig. 4.4. The Structure of the European Exchange Rate Currency Peg. Exchange rates against the Deutschemark for the Belgian franc, French franc, Danish krone and British pound sterling, July 1992–July 1995 (indexed at 100 from July 1992)

Source: *Eurostatistik* April 1993, 1994, 1996, August and October 1995.

Figure 4.4 is useful to state the rules of the ERM currency peg. As shown in figure 4.4, the exchange rates of the pegged currencies were only allowed to fluctuate between ± 2.5%. A central bank inevitably stakes its reputation on its capacity to maintain the parity of the exchange rate of its currency, especially in regard to the lower bound. At that point, taking the case of pound sterling, the authorities were duty-bound to use foreign reserves to buy sterling and/or raise the interest rate and push the exchange rate above the peg.

The stark reality is that no currency peg that operated peg rule has survived, and every failed currency peg was defended *and* suffered speculative attacks. What figure 4.4 shows is that the state of the fundamentals relating to the long-term viability of the parity was neither necessary nor sufficient for speculative attacks. The UK, with a 20% overvalued currency, sustained attacks, as did the other ERM currencies whose parities appear to be virtually unchanged within the pegged regime when it effectively floated. The only material difference in the case with the widening of the bands from ± 2.5% to ± 15% was that it rendered the rule dead letter, and when the conditions of a defense were made ambiguous, the speculative attacks ceased dramatically. This contradicts popular models of the time, which stated that speculators attack when they believe that authorities will *not* defend (Eichengreen, Rose, and Wyplosz 1994; Morris and Shin 1998). This is in stark contrast to the Liar strategy in (L.1, L.2), as shown in figure 4.5.

From condition (L.1), the Liar Strategy attacks took place *after* the authorities had intervened in the forex markets and bought the home currency forward, pushing the forward rates up (see Fung et al. 2000). If the authorities did not buy sterling and defend it, the forward prices would fall and then the Liar/Speculator strategy would no longer be profitable.

Signs that the structure of the game with the Liar was not understood by the authorities are now well recorded. Schooled in the doctrine of transparency and commitment, authorities involved with failed currency pegs, without exception, followed in the footsteps of Norman Lamont, the UK Chancellor, who in the ill-fated defense of the pound sterling in the summer of 1992, worked to remove "any scintilla of doubt about the intentions of the government ... that he and the government were 'going to maintain sterling's parity and ... do whatever is necessary'" (Stephens, as quoted in Eichengreen 1999). Indeed, the greater the defense effort by authorities, the greater are the potential profits for the currency short-seller, as the forward price at which they sell forward is high and the depletion of central bank reserves *signals subsequent sharper devaluations* that enable the speculator to close out by buying back more cheaply than otherwise.

In the standard credibility paradigm, as loss of credibility in the capacity of authorities to defend the parity is seen to be the driving force behind speculative attacks, show of strength and committed defense of the parity is upheld as the optimal strategy. In view of the Liar Strategy for shorting currency, a preannounced defense of the currency peg is never a Nash equilibrium strategy (see (7.a)).

In 1999, after a decade-long serial collapse of currency pegs at great economic cost,[37] Eichengreen (1999) finally sought to break ranks with the official IMF intellectual credo of which he was formerly a part. Eichengreen (1999), with hindsight, calls into question what was considered *de rigueur* on the basis of a very large and influential literature on the conduct of monetary policy that advocated pre-commitment to a transparent formalistic institution, such as the currency peg. In contrast to the prescribed resoluteness by central banks to expend extensive foreign currency reserves in the maintenance of a preannounced parity for the currency at a prespecified discrete point in time, Eichengreen (1999) recommends flexible bands at the first whiff of trouble "before the crunch" comes. To this, Charles Goodhart is reputed to have said: "If at the first whiff of trouble whilst managing a pegged regime, the best response is to preemptively declare a float: Why peg?"

I have argued that the dismal theorizing on the part of economists on formalistic predictable rules comes from the fact that the most prolific and ubiquitous Liar strategy is a closed book to them, as this foundational logical framework is not known to them.

Kant, Hayek and Hirschman: Rules, Principles and Discretion

We are faced with a situation in which economists appear to place their eggs in the one basket of a formalistic rules-based system with little

---

37. Pegged currency regimes, instituted on grounds of providing an inflation anchor, that have suffered systematic speculative attacks leading to a currency crisis and/or economic collapse are the following: Jamaica's 1990 and 1992 ERM crises involving the pound sterling, lira, franc, krona, punt and others; the 1994 Mexican peso crisis; the Thai baht (the second wave of attacks on it); and the Malaysian ringit and the Indonesian rupiah, 1997. In January 1999, the IMF package of US$41 billion was lost in the defense of the dollar peg with the Brazilian real. What constitutes a "successful" speculative attack is contentious. For instance, Krugman (1996) refers to the speculative attack on the krona, which netted what appears to be the largest amount of bank reserves of the ERM currencies to speculators as "an attack that failed when the Swedish government proved ready to defend the currency with very high interest rates" of around 500% (356). Surely, the speculator does not judge his success by whether or not the parity is broken but by how much is netted from the attack and to count on its use as a money pump in the future.

understanding of the vulnerability of formalism to Liar-like gaming that could destroy the system. From the preceding sections, we saw that genomic identity and somatic coherence requires that the basal information in sets **G** and **A** (in equations (1.a) and (1.b)) are offline recordings of predictable rules, respectively, from the ribosomal machine execution of gene codes and the neuronal activity in the motor-sensory cortex. In biotic systems, the models indicate that these code-based predictable rules are given primacy as "theorems" with consistency as an (non-constructive) organizing principle. The biotic system is regulated in a rigorous way in which Liar-like threats are identified by widespread simulation-based and offline horizon scanning in the adaptive immune system, and where the Liar/pathogen cannot be eliminated, the biotic system shows the capacity for an innovation-based co-evolutionary arms race with the hostile agent. This arms race is a Nash equilibrium in which neither party can unilaterally withdraw without facing the destruction of their objectives. However, as I have already noted, as game theory is silent about ubiquitous activities like these, this is also missing in any discussion about policy design in mainstream economics.

It is admittedly less obvious what rules are "theorems" in human-made regulatory systems. Legal formalism and the ideal of the rule of law and not of people are meant to put a brake on arbitrary discretion that arises from excessive leeway on having to interpret the application of the law. But this is predicated on self-evident truths that are "universalizable" (Kant 1965). These, as in the case of the US Constitution, can be taken to be foundational axioms, which are more in the form of juridical principles of a formal legal system. Expectation of equal application without discrimination engenders decentralized litigation initiated by individual litigants who challenge rules for their inability for general implementation. Indeed, rules can be taken down as being "arbitrary" if they encroach on a prior set of libertarian principles of autonomy. These observations lend credence to the hypothesis that, in market societies, decentralized control characterized by the autonomy of the individual decision-maker is achieved by the evolution of a specific kind of legal system that constitutes an end-independent system of rules. The fundamental idea that the autonomy of private decision-making, the freedom associated with market relationships, can only be achieved by a coercive application of those legal rules that are themselves end-independent and universalizable is a Kantian one. In the words of Kant (1965), to develop a deeper understanding of the legal system that co-ordinates actions of autonomous individuals, one must be able to:

(i) ascertain how a legal rule qualifies for universal legislation [see also Kant 1965, 34],
(ii) gauge 'the great and manifold consequences that can be drawn from this law', and
(iii) overcome our astonishment at 'its simplicity (of structure) ... and its authority to command without appearing to carry any incentive with it.' (25)

This Kantian agenda of furthering our understanding of the fundamental rules that coordinate and control market relationships receives the most brilliant and consistent exposition in the work of FA Hayek. In having hypothesized that markets and the libertarian ethic associated with the system are the outcome of the development of a system of control and co-ordination that is (a) informationally decentralized, (b) evolutionary and (c) possessing non-purposive characteristics of an open-ended system, Hayek has undoubtedly challenged the predominant bastions of utilitarian, rationalistic and centralized theories of control. The question is, why should we abstain from using the coercive powers of the state to achieve predetermined outcomes? In Markose (1991), I offer a preliminary investigation of how Kantian end-neutral rules operate to govern market societies. I argue that the expectation of universalizable rules or non-discriminatory application will set in motion a decentralized litigious process in which parties challenge an unjust law.

Hayek's defense of autonomy of action is primarily an epistemic one and is indeed based on his view of cognitive incompleteness in the Gödel sense (see Hayek 1952, 1967). As we possess more knowledge than what can be formalized, especially the uncountable infinite capacity to innovate (see (5)), much of this knowledge is tacit and will be lost to the world without autonomy of action. In classical liberalism, this is what causes tension between the autonomy of the individual and the coercive rules of the state.

The Kantian end-neutral rules do not offer person/place-specific predetermined outcomes, hence, Liar-like rule breaking is also not possible. Likewise, rules such as traffic rules about keeping within speed limits only permit limited opportunities for protean regulatees to game them.

Such traffic rules can be enforced by a system of monitoring. In contrast to Kantian end-neutral rules and traffic rules, economic and financial regulatory rules have specific predicable outcomes and yield economic incentives for regulatees to break them. It is a sign of our times that *ad hoc* rules like the currency peg and inflation targets have been elevated to the status of being "universal," and change or reform to these is considered to be exercising discretion, which is used in the pejorative sense.

In Markose (2017), in the context of a game between regulator and regulatees, regardless of the foundational aspects of the regulatory rules, the latter are considered to be a set of formal rules that, if they can be run with regulatees being rule abiding (i.e., not engaging in malign hacking), produce desirable outcomes for the regulator. However, the status of the Liar as a malign force is problematic in human-made rules-based systems.

The role of contrarian Liar strategies in bringing down financial systems should not be underestimated. The prominent contrarian strategies that have netted vast profits in the context of institutionalized free lunches of the ERM currency peg and the Credit Default Swaps carry trades in the run-up to the 2007 crisis (Markose et al. 2012) have been, respectively, George Soros in 1992 and the protagonists of "The Big Short," including Paolo Pelligrini and John Paulson in 2007. Good institution design should vitiate such opportunities. In fact, the regulatory rules of the Basel Banking Committee that invite such self-reflexive destabilizing forces when regulatees game the system (see Fatouh et al. 2019) have been criticized. In the words of Kane (2010), we must avoid "official definitions of systemic risk that have left out the role of government officials in generating it" (107).

There is, of course, a long line of literature, as in the classic work of Hirschman (1991), where Lucas-type critiques have aptly been called "futility, perversity and jeopardy" arguments against institution building, which deliberately aim to bring about specific and predetermined outcomes in society. Such objectives, when pursued at a collective level, according to this thesis, will result in unintended consequences for society that may nullify the original intent of public action (the futility argument); they may bring about consequences that are opposite those being proposed (the perversity argument); finally, they may "destabilize" the system as a whole (the jeopardy argument). Despite, Hirschman's (1995) original intent to pillory the above as the rhetoric of reaction, he redresses his position and advises policymakers to minimize "the vulnerability of policy proposals on perversity, futility or jeopardy grounds" (61). The idea here is that the rules that aim to stabilize the system self-reflexively[38] end up destroying it.

Clearly, the dominance of the view that macro-stability lies in maintaining a fixed inflation rule has forestalled any scientific advances in the study of the stability of the economic system as a highly interconnected coevolving one in which policy rules have to be carefully designed to avoid unintended perverse consequences. Interestingly, Eichengreen (2010) now concludes: "fundamentally, the (2007) crisis is the result of flawed regulations and perverse incentives in financial markets" (20). Further, in the context of the events leading to the 2007 crisis, Jones (2000) noted a lack of interest in the study of regulatory capital arbitrage entailed in securitization and other financial innovations, regarding which he said, "absent measures to reduce incentives or opportunities for regulatory capital arbitrage over time, such developments could undermine the usefulness of formal capital requirement as prudential policy tools" (37). In the absence of simulation models in the tool kits of most economists, Jones (2000) concluded that it was a lack of data for econometric modelling that prevented academics and regulators from keeping track of activities that undermined stated policy objectives in the Basel II banking regulation.

Slowly, in the post-GFC era, a case is being made at regulatory institutions for simulation-based stress testing policy in terms of the efficacy of the proposed fixed rule before implementation. Questions are being asked about the wisdom of authorities who rely on a fixed rule for inflation for stability of the monetary and economic environment when state-supplied money in retail transactions is being almost fully replaced by digital payments media and a commensurate low rate of inflation in cashless economies.

Conclusion

This chapter has provided evidence that the capacity for endogenous novelty production is not just an artifact of the famous Gödel metamathematics (Prokopenko et al. 2019; Casti 1994). Rather, it is integral to

---

38. Reflexivity of the legal system is enjoying a resurgence of interest (see Deakin 2015; Rogowski and Deakin 2011).

the immuno-cognitive systems of eukaryotes and reaches its apogee with humans with our über intelligence, sometimes called the Machiavellian brain (Ramachandran 2000; Byrne and Whiten 1988). The Big Bang of Immunology (Janeway et al. 2005) and the Great Leap Forward (Ramachandran 2000) characterize immuno-neuronal brain functioning that manifest explicit code-centric digital self-referential mirror systems that permit complex interactions between self and the other, in particular, in the detection of hostile agency and arms races in novelty production. The key mirror systems that implement Self-Ref and Self-Rep in immuno-cognitive systems have been illustrated in figure 4.1.

Further, the advances in molecular biology on the production of variety in evolutionary genomic systems in the post-Barbara McClintock era have revolutionized our thinking that random mutation may not be the primary source of variety in evolution. It is my view, first articulated in Markose (2019), that it is necessary to modify the proposition popularized by Dobzhansky (1973) that "nothing in biology makes sense except in the light of evolution." My take is that nothing in the biotic evolution of complexity makes sense without taking seriously the digitization of inheritable information in the genome. Evidence outlined in the second and third sections above indicates that genomic intelligence, as found in biotic immuno-neuronal systems, takes an elaborate form of distinguishing self and other in a unique framework in which the G-T-P logic is hardwired for decentralized cybersecurity aimed at maintaining genomic identity and somatic coherence.

I have sought to summarize (see table 4.1) the methodological differences between mainstream cognitive decision theories and the G-T-P immuno-cognitive systems. The former do not have the wherewithal to exit outside of given choice sets, and novelty or innovation is typically modelled as white noise prediction error within a statistical framework. G-T-P immuno-cognitive systems utilize code-based embodied simulations and have Gödel incompleteness inbuilt for evolvability and, with it, the capacity to recursively exit from listable sets. Radical uncertainty in the form of undecidability follows self-referential identification of the contrarian/Liar/hacker hostile agency to a baseline action and marks the exit points with the arm race in innovation being a Nash equilibrium with both host and pathogen being able to coevolve. Thus, the cognitive base of the recurring pursuit–evasion-type contests that entail arms races in new behaviors that are as diverse as they are spectacular have been given a new framework.

A key aspect of complex adaptive systems is the capacity of interacting agents to show über intelligence with strong proclivities for contrarian rule or trend-breaking behavior and the production of structure-changing novelty and "surprises." This takes the co-evolutionary form of a Red Queen-type arms race in innovation. I have argued that a regulator–regulated arms race (no different from a parasite–host dynamic) involves monitoring and production of countervailing new measures (comparable to the production of anti-bodies) by authorities in response to regulatee deviations from rules due to the presence of perverse incentives or loopholes. As noted, the blind spots in extant game theory and decision theories have led to spectacular self-reflexive policy-led institutional failures in Western economies. Axelrod (2003) cites system failure in networks, or their lack of robustness, as arising from a situation in which "coevolution is not anticipated." While Axelrod has in mind the arms race between hackers and network developers, I have shown that a fatal oversight in system design is to not take on board the need to constantly address this factor of Liar/hacker-like onslaughts for which simulation-based and real-time horizon scanning are vital. It must be clear to many how my analysis of the dismal failure of mainstream economics in precipitating disastrous systemic failures in Western economies is considerably different to that of other heterodox economists, such as Helbing and Kirman (2013) and Colander et al. (2009). These critiques of mainstream economics remain silent about the blind spots relating to novelty production and the digital foundations of über intelligence.

Perhaps, with the fourth Industrial Revolution driven by code-based digital systems imbued with advanced AI, there may be some added urgency among economists to take digitization and computation theory seriously. Finally, the spelling out of the immuno-cognitive foundations of novelty production in a ubiquitous strategic setting suggests many rich investigative lines for empirical neuro-physiological experiments, extending issues covered in Camerer et al. (2005) and Bernheim (2009). The urgency for these lines of investigation arises from the fact that extant models of strategic behavior cannot account for protean behavior, which is ubiquitous in socio-economic systems.

CHAPTER 5

The Game of Go

Bounded Rationality and Artificial Intelligence

Cassey Lee[1]

"The rules of go are so elegant, organic and rigorously logical that if intelligent life forms exist elsewhere in the universe, they almost certainly play go."

Edward Lasker

"We have never actually seen a real alien, of course. But what might they look like? My research suggests that the most intelligent aliens will actually be some form of artificial intelligence (or AI)."

Susan Schneider

Introduction

The concepts of bounded rationality and artificial intelligence (AI) do not often appear simultaneously in research articles. Economists discussing bounded rationality rarely mention AI. This is reciprocated by computer scientists writing on AI, which is surprising because Herbert Simon was a pioneer in both bounded rationality and AI. For his contributions to these areas, he is the only person who has received the highest accolades in both economics (the Nobel Prize in 1978) and computer science (the Turing

---

1. The author thanks Ooi Kee Beng and Pritish Bhattacharya for comments and suggestions. The usual caveat applies.

Award in 1975).² Simon undertook research on bounded rationality and AI simultaneously in the 1950s and these interests persisted throughout his research career. In 1992, Simon teamed up with Jonathan Schaeffer to publish an article titled "The Game of Chess," which surveyed how boundedly rational humans play chess and how computers are programmed to play the game. In the former case, chess grandmasters were found to be able to remember and recognize chess patterns (chunks) that lead to sound moves. The design of chess computers can vary in terms of the combination of search and knowledge. Five years after the article was published, in 1997, IBM's Deep Blue supercomputer defeated the then reigning world champion, Garry Kasparov, in a six-game chess match.

When this benchmark was achieved in chess, the game of go was considered to be the last remaining challenge in the human-versus-machine competition in AI research.³ The game of go was long considered to be a more complex game compared to chess on account of the number of possible moves from the start of the game. In his survey on games computers, Schaeffer (2000) opined, "it will take many decades of research and development before world-championship-caliber go programs exist" (260). This feat was finally accomplished in 2016, when Google DeepMind's AlphaGo defeated the go world champion, Lee Sedol, 4–1. This watershed event clearly calls for a reevaluation of bounded rationality and AI.

The goal of this essay is to examine the nature and relationship between bounded rationality and AI in the context of recent developments in the application of AI to two-player zero-sum games with perfect information, such as go. This is undertaken by examining the evolution of AI programs for playing go. Given that bounded rationality is inextricably linked to the nature of the problem to be solved, the complexity of the state space of go is examined via a cellular automata (CA) perspective.⁴

---

2. More precisely, the citation for Simon's Nobel prize award was for "his pioneering research into the decision-making process within economic organizations." The one for the Turing Award (jointly with Allen Newell) was for "basic contributions to artificial intelligence, the psychology of human cognition and list processing."
3. The game of go is also known as *Igo* in Japan, *Weiqi* in China and *Baduk* in Korea. It has also been described as the "surrounding game" or "encircling game." For a brief description of the game of go, see Appendix 5A.
4. In terms of topics not covered in this paper that might be worth pursuing in the future, several directions of enquiry are noted. One relates to combinatorial game theory (Albert et al. 2007), the other to the deep links between games and numbers (Conway 2000).

The outline of the rest of this essay is as follows. Section 2 discusses how bounded rationality is related to AI. Section 3 examines the complexity of the game of go from the perspective of bounded rationality. The complexity of go is examined from the perspective of CA in Section 4. Section 5 presents concluding remarks.

The Intertwined Domains of Bounded Rationality and Artificial Intelligence

Bounded Rationality

What is rationality? And in what sense is rationality "bounded"? An agent is **rational** when they make a choice to achieve an objective. In the mainstream economic theory of choice, rationality requires that such a choice be made in a consistent manner. Consistency here refers to the agent having preferences that conform to a set of axioms on completeness, reflexivity and continuity.

Bounded rationality is a departure from the above characterization of rationality as consistency. This point was clearly articulated in the 1950s by Herbert Simon who is often acknowledged as the founder of bounded rationality. In his paper, Simon (1955) argued that humans in the real world experience a number of constraints that limit the applicability of "global rationality" (rationality as consistency). These constraints can be classified as internal constraints (limited computational facilities) or external constraints (limited information about environment). Under such constraints, humans act in a bounded (approximate) rational manner by choosing actions based on heuristics that meet certain aspiration levels. They also learn by gathering information about the environment over time to improve their decision-making processes.

Another approach to bounded rationality focuses on the departure of real-world behavior from "rationality as consistency." Since the 1970s, psychologists and behavioral economists, such as Kahneman, Tversky and Thaler, have employed experiments to discover how people's beliefs and choices differ from the optimal beliefs and choices in rational-agent models (Kahneman 2003; Thaler 2018). Such departures from rationality as consistency characterize how rationality is bounded in reality. Though behavioral economists often cite Herbert Simon as an early pioneer in bounded rationality, their methodology differs from that of Simon in several ways.[5] Behavioral economists employ primarily experimental methods that focus on outcomes (action/behavior). Simon does not rely much on experimental methods. Instead, he presents general observations on how people actually behave (e.g., play chess). Simon is more interested in the cognitive limitations of humans, which also leads to artificial intelligence via the formulation of computational models/machines that simulate boundedly rational human decision-making.

Artificial Intelligence

The 1950s was not only significant for the formulation of bounded rationality by Herbert Simon. This period also saw the emergence of AI as a full-fledged field of research (Nilsson 2010). Simon was an active participant in some of the major AI events during this time, such as the Dartmouth Conference in 1956. At that time, as it is today, AI was fairly heterogeneous methodologically. This can be seen in the four categories of definitions of AI proposed by Russell and Norvig (2010), which continue to be valid descriptions to this day (table 5.1).

In the first category of the definition, AI aims to construct computational machines (models) that possess thinking mechanisms (processes) that are similar to those of humans.[6] These mechanisms include language, knowledge representation (and memory), reasoning and learning. In the second category, machines are merely required to act like humans. They do

Table 5.1 Four Categories of AI Definitions

	Human behavior	Rational behavior
Thinking (mental process)	1. Thinking humanly Machines that think intelligently like humans	3. Thinking rationally Machines that think rationally
Acting (action)	2. Acting humanly Machines that perform activities that humans consider intelligent	4. Acting rationally Machines that act rationally

Source: Adapted from Russell and Norvig (2010, 2), figure 1.1.

---

5. Heuristics are discussed by Herbert Simon as well as Kahneman and Tversky.
6. In this essay, the term "machines" includes hardware and software (programs).

not need to possess human-like mechanisms. In the third category, the focus is on machines that think rationally in terms of being based on mathematical logic. Finally, the fourth category relates to machines that take actions that are optimal (rational) but may not be based on logical reasoning. There is an alternative computational architecture of AI that is not based on mathematical logic but may lead to rational actions.

Hence, computational architecture is another area where there is diversity in AI methodology. In this respect, there are two major approaches to AI, each with its own lineage. Both these approaches were already present during the early years of AI in the 1950s. The first approach is based on mathematical logic, while the second is based on neural networks. Underlying the first approach, also known as von Neumann architecture, is the idea that intelligent action can be modelled using physical symbol systems. The second approach, neural networks, is based on building a computational architecture grounded on our understanding of the human brain, which comprises networks of connected neurons. Learning takes place in neural networks through changes in the strength of neural connections. Though the two traditions or approaches in AI have long been regarded as distinct, there are now attempts to connect them (Kaiser et al. 2017).

AI: Toward Bounded Rationality or Rationality?

The literature on bounded rationality in economics does not usually make any references to AI. Similarly, AI scientists seldom discuss the concept of bounded rationality. Despite this, the two fields are clearly intertwined. Drawing on the earlier discussions on the different types (definitions) of AI research, the approaches that attempt to model how humans think (Definition 1) and act (Definition 2) have to incorporate bounded rationality (see table 5.2). To be human is to be boundedly rational—both human thinking and actions are boundedly rational.

On the other hand, the other two approaches that focus on rationality (Definitions 3 and 4) are not boundedly rational. Computational machines that incorporate processes that are globally rational are a theoretical possibility. This possibility can be framed in terms of the Universal Turing Machine (UTM)—a hypothetical machine that uses a built-in rule table as a guide to read and change an infinite strip tape written with

Table 5.2 Rationality, Bounded Rationality and AI

	Bounded rationality	Global rationality
Thinking (mental process)	1. Thinking humanly Limitations in learning, memory and computation (learning, self-learning)	3. Thinking rationally (super intelligent?) (Universal Turing Machine)
Acting (action)	2. Acting humanly Not globally optimal outcome/action (brute-force search)	4. Acting rationally Globally optimal outcome/action (non-halting UTM) (incomputable)

Source: Adapted from Russell and Norvig (2010, 2), figure 1.1.

symbols (e.g., 1,0). Such a machine can compute a solution to any problem. However, the UTM also demonstrates that it is not possible to tell whether, when or how a UTM will stop computing (i.e., arrive at a solution). This problem—known as the Non-Halting Problem—demonstrates that, although thinking rationally is theoretically attractive, acting rationally is incomputable. In other words, one can design a computer that will search for global optimality but it is not possible to know whether global optimality will be attained.

From the above perspectives, the domain of AI is clearly oriented toward bounded rationality. One way to analyze this issue further is to examine this in terms of the application of AI to board games.[7] This is examined next.

Bounded Rationality and the Evolution of Go-Playing Computers

The links between bounded rationality and AI are most evident in AI research on two-player zero-sum games with perfect information, such as checkers, chess and go. These links are evident during the early years of the founding of game theory and AI. The development of the Min-Max Theorem by John von Neumann in the late 1920s can be traced to the then prevailing interests in set theory and chess within the German-speaking

---

7. Griffiths et al. (2015) provide an alternative discussion on how to relate models from the algorithmic level to the computational level using resource-rational analysis.

mathematical community during this period (Leonard 1995).[8] The contributions of von Neumann straddle both economics (game theory and growth theory) and computer science (von Neumann architecture). Alan Turing (1953)—another founding father of computer science—dwelt on how computers can be used to play chess. Herbert Simon simultaneously conducted research on bounded rationality and chess-playing programs in the 1950s.

As AI developed in subsequent decades after the 1950s, computer scientists continued to use two-player zero-sum games with perfect information, such as checkers, chess and go, as test beds for the application of AI. Progress in the application of AI in this area was often measured in terms of the ability of computer programs to beat world champions. An even more ambitious benchmark was to solve the game completely, which entails proving the result of a perfectly played game. Historically, the progress made in AI applications across board games has been uneven. This is not surprising, as the various types of board games differ in their complexity. Go is often considered to be more complex than chess while chess is more complex than checkers. But how should complexity be defined for such comparisons? In the extant literature, it is defined in two ways. First, space state complexity measures the number of positions that can be reached from the starting position (Bouzy and Cazenave 2001, 44). Second, game tree complexity measures the number of nodes in the smallest tree necessary to solve the game (Bouzy and Cazenave 2001, 44). Table 5.3 summarizes the complexity of various board games using these measures.

Table 5.3 The Complexity of Board Games

Game	Number of positions reachable from starting position	Number of nodes in the smallest tree necessary to solve the game
Checkers	10^{17}	10^{32}
Othello	10^{30}	10^{58}
Chess	10^{50}	10^{123}
Go	10^{160}	10^{400}

Source: Bouzy and Cazenave (2001, 44), table 1.

---

8. These early analyses of chess using set theory are part of the axiomatization movement, *a la* Hilbert, which also influenced the mathematization of economic theories in the 1940s and 1950s.

It is thus not surprising that checkers was the first game for computers to beat world champions. This took place in 1990. By 2007, checkers was completely solved with the discovery of draw as the final outcome of perfect play (Schaeffer et al. 2007). The more complex games of chess and go have not been solved until today. Though later than checkers, computer programs have reached the level of being able to beat world champions—chess in 1997 and go in 2016.

Game-playing computer programs have clearly evolved with advances in computer software (algorithms) and hardware. Appendix table 5a summarizes some of the milestones in the application of AI to games. The progress made in this area has been possible in three key elements: (i) knowledge, (ii) search and (iii) learning. These elements are interrelated, and each will be discussed in the context of AI and bounded rationality.

Knowledge

Specific knowledge about a game is a key element of game-playing computer programs. For board games, this can take the form of historical games played (game database) and a set of expert-based strategies on how a game should be played for different states of the game (specific configurations of the board during play). The game databases for go usually comprise a few hundred thousand games played by professional players.[9] This was made possible by advances in the coding of games in such a way that information in such games can be extracted by computers for analysis and learning. The extraction of information from games requires representation of knowledge. This, in turn, entails the encoding of go knowledge. Muller (2002) suggests that there are two approaches to encode go knowledge, namely, via patterns and structured knowledge representation.

In the first approach, the patterns on the board (go positions) can be matched and compared with patterns in databases associated with good moves (which are identified by human experts). This matching process leads to the generation of moves in the game. The second approach involves a more abstract level of knowledge representation involving tactical and strategic concepts, such as blocks (connected stones of the same color), the type of connections between stones and chains (blocks joined

---

9. A list of such databases is available at: https://senseis.xmp.net/?GoDatabases

by pairwise connections).[10] This approach also draws from human experiences of the game.

From a bounded rationality perspective, the representation of knowledge in go—be it pattern or structural—explicitly involves human intelligence. It is a process of encoding the knowledge for machines as it is understood by humans. Experiments have shown that, when playing board games, humans tend to remember chunks of patterns that are associated with potentially promising moves (Simon and Schaeffer 1992). Given that there are many strategic dimensions and ways of winning a game, knowledge representation also requires an explicit specification of how they are related and whether there should be hierarchies of pattern valuations. These issues are also related to the notion of goals in the search of decision trees.

Search

The second element in AI application to board games is search. Theoretically, two-player alternating games can be represented using minimax decision trees. In classical game theory, such games are solved by computing the minimax in a backward induction setting. However, it is difficult to use this method to solve for the game of go due to the large size of the decision tree.[11] How large is the size of the decision tree for go? A 19x19 go board has 361 grid intersections. After the first player moves, the second player can place their stone in one of the remaining 360 interactions, and so on. Beginner players are sometimes trained with 9x9 boards. The tree diagram for the first and second player using a 9x9 go board is illustrated in figures 5.1 and 5.2. Each node of the tree represents a state of play. After Player 1 moves, Player 2 chooses one of the remaining eighty positions on the board. At this stage, there are eighty nodes connected to each of the eighty-one branches associated with Player 1. Likewise, there are 6,480 branches (or 81 × 80). A crude estimate for the total number of branches for a 19x19 board is 19! = 10^{768}. The actual number of legal branches (moves) is smaller. The number of legal positions for a 19x19 go

---

10. For more detailed explanations, see Muller (2002, 156–159).
11. The minimax tree has two dimensions, namely, breadth (number of options at each stage of play) and depth (the number of game stages of play).

board is huge. The exact size of it remains an open problem (Tromp and Farnebäck 2007).

As it is computationally impossible to undertake a full brute-force search of the entire minimax decision tree for go, the alternative is to search only selected trees (sub-trees). One selective search method that was discovered in the 1960s is the alpha-beta ($\alpha\beta$) algorithm. The alpha-beta algorithm essentially cuts off, or prunes, the minimax decision tree. The lower-bound, or alpha, refers to the minimum value that Player 1 has achieved, while beta is the upper bound denoting the maximum value to which Player 2 can limit Player 1 (Schaeffer 2000). The minimax trees are pruned when alpha exceeds beta. However, the alpha-beta algorithm does have weaknesses—search is limited by a fixed depth, resulting in the size of the minimax tree growing exponentially with search depth (Kishimoto and Mueller 2015). Furthermore, systemic errors can take place but remain hidden.

Another approach to overcome the large size of the decision tree in go is to employ statistical sampling of sub-trees in the games. The Monte Carlo (MC) method overcomes systemic errors by randomizing fixed policies that map states to actions. This is implemented by running a fixed number of simulations from an initial state (board configuration) until the end of the game (Gelly et al. 2012). Such simulations generate expected values for each of the different states.

An important advance in the application of AI to go was the discovery of the Monte-Carlo Tree Search (MCTS) algorithm, which is a hybrid

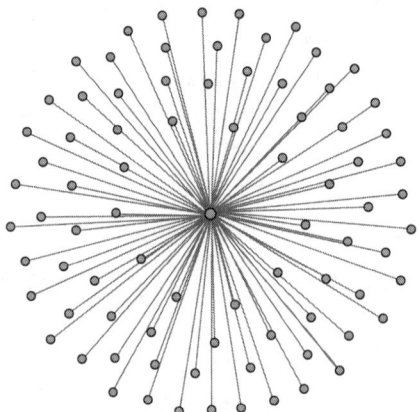

Fig. 5.1. Tree Diagram for Player 1's First Move for a 9×9 Go Board

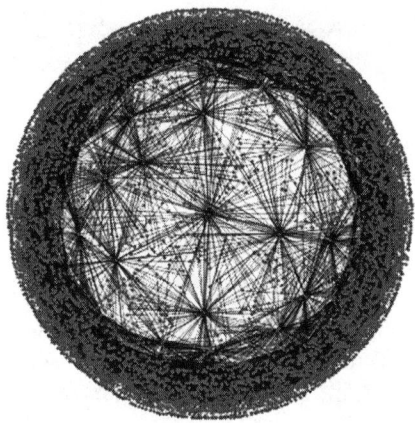

Fig. 5.2. Tree Diagram for the First Moves of Players 1 and 2 for a 9×9 Go Board

approach that combines Monte-Carlo simulations with tree search.[12] The MCTS simulations achieve two things—they "grow" the decision tree and improve the accuracy of the expected values of the nodes. An effective modification of the MCTS algorithm involves the incorporation of an exploration bonus to the expected value in the evaluation (scoring) function. This encourages the exploration of least-tried actions.

It is clearly not possible to undertake a brute-force minimax tree search for global optimality in complex games such as go. AI researchers have attempted to improve search algorithms by limiting search to a subset of trees that lead to approximate global optimality. This was done either by pruning the decision tree searched or by probabilistically sampling and growing the decision trees. Thus, even though the computer programs were designed to act (play) as (boundedly rational) humans, computational limitations constrain the adoption of rational thinking processes (which would have involved minimax brute-force search). It is also important to note that the nature of search algorithms employed are of machine bounded rationality and non-human bounded rationality. Non-human bounded rationality can perform better than human champions (e.g., Deep Blue vs. Kasparov) or poorer than human champions (in go competitions before 2016). The latter was only achieved with further advances in

---

12. See Gelly et al. (2012, 109) for a description of how the MCTS works.

AI that incorporated learning mechanisms, which represent (after knowledge and search) the third important element of AI applications to games.

Learning

Learning entails the acquisition, consolidation and retrieval of information. Though not unique to humans, learning is one of the species's key characteristics. Go players undertake years of learning to become professional players. As discussed earlier, professional go players can use their knowledge to influence the design of go-playing computer programs. Machine learning refers to something else—the learning process undertaken by computers. Even though machine learning has become a key element in computer programs capable of beating world champion go players, learning *per se* is not a new element in AI. Machine learning was already an active area of research in the 1950s but it did not take-off until the 1980s. A key reason for this was the dominance of the logic-based approach to AI and the von Neumann architecture. These trends affected how AI was applied to board games, such as chess and go.

Machine learning can be broadly divided into two types—supervised learning and unsupervised learning. It is often implemented using neural networks in which multiple computing cells or processing units (in the form of hardware or software) are interconnected. The strength of these interconnections, as measured by the value of the synaptic weights, changes during the learning process. An example of supervised learning would be programmers choosing the set of professional go games to train neural networks. Knowledge representation is still needed in the form of specifying what is to be learned. Unsupervised learning is machine learning that involves automatic generation of knowledge. Go programs involving self-play fall into this category of machine learning. Early go-playing programs in the 1990s used a variety of learning approaches—some employed supervised learning, while others used unsupervised learning via stochastic self-play (Bouzy and Cazenave 2001).[13] Despite these developments, go-playing programs using machine learning achieved moderate success as these programs were not strong enough to challenge professional go players, let alone a go world champion.

---

13. Other advances, such as temporal difference learning—a reinforcement learning algorithm—also helped improve go-playing programs in the 1990s (see Schaeffer 2000).

It took another two decades before a go-playing program could finally defeat a go world champion. This took place in 2016 when Google DeepMind's AlphaGo defeated the world champion, Lee Sedol, 4–1 (for technical details, see Silver et al. 2016). In 2017, an even more startling achievement was announced when AlphaGo Zero—an AI program starting from zero knowledge (without human guidance) and based on reinforcement learning—defeated AlphaGo one hundred games to zero (see Silver et al. 2017). Subsequently, a more generalized version of the AlphaGo Zero program was developed (AlphaZero) that was capable of self-learning, and capable of defeating world-champion programs in the games of chess, shoji and go.

The success of AlphaGo is possible due to cumulative advances in AI, such as MCTS and deep convoluted neural network (ConvNet). ConvNet is a deep-learning architecture involving the stacking of multiple layers of neural networks (LeCun et al. 2015). This computational architecture enables multiple levels of representation by extracting different features of an input (e.g., go board configurations). AlphaGo is essentially a hybrid program that first implements supervised learning by training ConvNets on human expert moves in professional games. The outputs from this are then fed into unsupervised (reinforcement) learning that entails stochastic self-play (Silver et al. 2016). The program generates two key outputs: (i) valuations of subtrees (i.e., payoffs), which can be used to reduce the depth of search, and (ii) policy networks, or high probability moves that reduce the breadth of search through sampling of sub-trees.

The next advancement—AlphaGo Zero—is a pure self-play (reinforcement learning) and MCTS search program that does not rely on any human knowledge (Silver et al. 2017). Other characteristics of the program's architecture include raw board representation as inputs, combination of policy and value networks and tree search without growing trees via MC rollouts. Based on the analyses of the games played by AlphaGo Zero, the program clearly exhibits go-playing capabilities that surpass those of human players. Silver et al. (2017) noted that the program is able to rediscover basic, and discover new (non-standard) go knowledge.

What is interesting about AlphaGo and AlphaGo Zero is that, in both programs, "thinking" is boundedly rational in that it is not designed to undertake a full search of the decision tree. These programs are, however, not boundedly rational in the human sense or in the machine sense.

The super-human game play demonstrated by AlphaGo and AlphaGo Zero also demonstrates that machine bounded rationality can lead to super-human artificial intelligence, at least in go playing. However, this is not to suggest that boundedly rational machines are superior to boundedly rational humans in all respects. The two are different. Human bounded rationality is the product of evolution and is physically (biologically) embodied (at least for now). Two lines of enquiries are possible. The first is along the lines of Herbert Simon's research program, which emphasizes cognitive limits (computation, memory). Second, it would be interesting to investigate how humans' bounded rationality along the lines of classical behavioral economics affect their game play.

The game of go is also not a suitable Turing-type test for AI. Simon (1956) has long emphasized the intertwining of bounded rationality and the environment (problem to be solved).[14] The environment of the game of go is finite, fixed and deterministic. It is possible to argue that computers are likely to have the upper hand in discovering universes with deterministic rules, such as in go. To further understand this, it is perhaps useful to explore the complexity of the discrete universe of the game of go.

The Complexity of Go: A Cellular Automata Perspective

The board for the game of go can be represented as a lattice of square cells similar to that of a two-dimensional CA (see figure 5.3). The configuration or pattern of a go board during play corresponds to the state of cells in CA. This leads to the consideration of whether it is possible to think about go in terms of CA and, if yes, what types of insights can be gained from doing so. This should begin with a description of what is a CA.

The CA is a computational model made up of a lattice network of cells. Though the cells are depicted as squares in figure 5.3, the cells of CAs can take other shapes, such as a triangle or hexagon. The significance of these cell shapes lies in the number of neighbors that a cell can be connected to and interact with. Computation is carried through the simultaneous change in the states of cells brought about by local interactions with neighboring cells. Such interactions are specified by a local transition function.

---

14. See Lee (2011) for further elaboration of this view.

For example, in a one-dimensional CA, the state of cell i or c_i at time t+1 can be represented as:

$$c_i(t+1) = c_{i-1}(t) + c_i(t) + c_{i+1}(t) \mod 2$$

where c_{i-1} is the state of cell i's left neighbor, c_{i+1} is the state of its right neighbor and mod 2 is the remainder after division of the sum by 2 (see Schiff 2008, 43). This can be graphically represented as:

| c_{i-1} | c_i | c_{i+1} |

The transition function for a cell $c_{i,j}$ in a two-dimensional CA with interactions with four neighbors (the von Neumann model) can be expressed as:

$$c_{i,j}(t+1) = c_{i-1,j}(t) + c_{i+1,j}(t) + c_{i,j}(t) + c_{i,j-1}(t) + c_{i,j+1}(t) \mod 2$$

The graphical representation for this is depicted as:

The dynamical evolution of the states of CA cells is driven by the rules in the transition function. This has led to the classification of CA into four types:

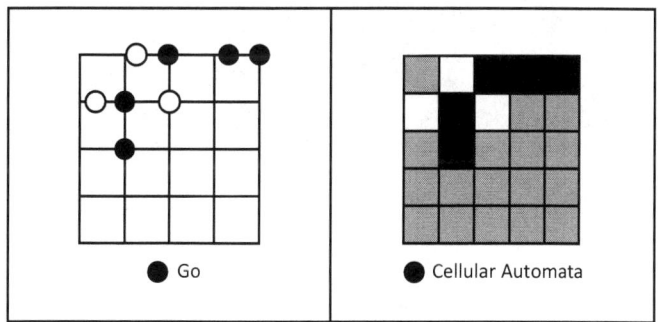

Fig. 5.3. Go and Cellular Automata

- Class I: Fixed Point—where CA cells evolve to a uniformly constant state;
- Class II: Periodic—where CA cells evolve toward continually repeating a periodic structure;
- Class III: Chaotic—where CA cells evolve randomly; and
- Class IV: Complex—where CA cells evolve in such a way that localized structures are produced that move about and interact with each other.

Graphical depictions of the four classes for one-dimensional CAs are presented in figure 5.4.

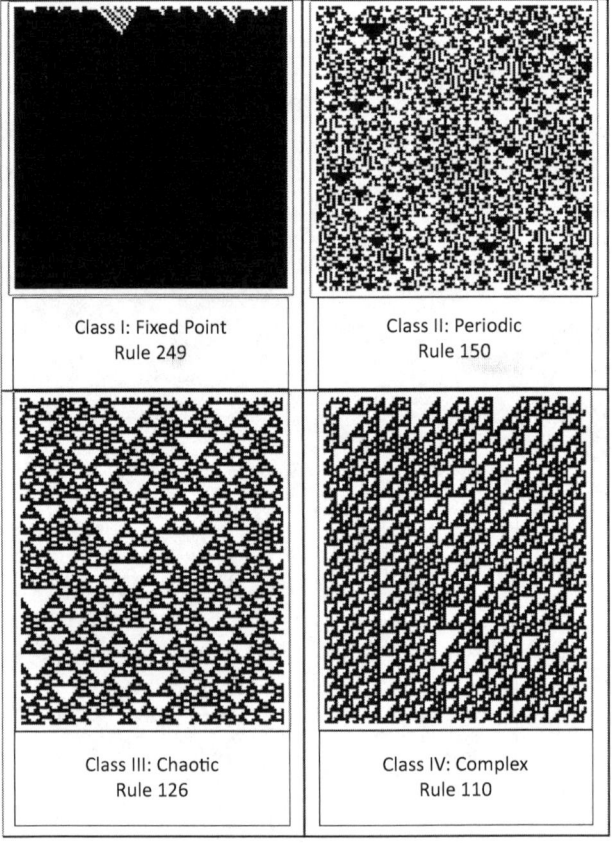

Fig. 5.4. Four Classes of Cellular Automata

Even though researchers have identified four classes of CA, questions relating to long-term evolution of CAs are undecidable (Kari 2012). In other words, while we know there are four classes of CA, it is not possible to *a priori* and comprehensively sort out which rule (transition function) falls into each of the four classes. This is not surprising, as the CA is a universal computing machine and hence is also subject to the Non-Halting Problem identified for UTMs. The implications of this for the game of go are, indeed, intriguing.

The play of go, seen from the CA perspective, is akin to a computational process. Unlike CA, however, there appears to be no equivalent transition function that governs how a go gameplay evolves. The closest to a transition function would be the rules of go and the goal of territorial control. AI programs that engage in self-play explore the landscape of go based on these rules and goal. The undecidability of CA evolution, however, does seem to suggest that even though AI programs may achieve super-human capabilities in go, it is not possible for these programs to solve the game by way of self-play in such a way that they will identify a single self-play game that produces global optimality. Thus, AI machines are always going to be machine boundedly rational, and such machines, while able to defeat boundedly rational human world champions, will intrinsically never be able to solve the game of go.

Conclusion

The game of go was, for many years, the benchmark for the contest between human intelligence and artificial intelligence. The defeat of a go world champion by Google DeepMind's AlphaGo in 2016 has reignited the debate on whether machine intelligence has finally surpassed human intelligence. Given that human intelligence is boundedly rational, how is AI related to bounded rationality? AI researchers have defined AI in terms of a framework that has two dimensions: (i) thinking versus acting, and (ii) human versus rational behavior. If human rationality is characterized as bounded rationality, there is, then, a class of AI that are boundedly rational, either in terms of processes (thinking) or results (acting).

The links between bounded rationality and AI are most evident in the applications of AI in two-player zero sum games with perfect information, such as checkers, chess and go. The three key elements in these applications are knowledge, search and learning. A closer examination of the evolution of go-playing programs along these three elements suggests that these programs are machine boundedly rational in a way that is different from human bounded rationality. The advent of advanced self-playing go programs that do not rely on human knowledge further prompts questions about boundedly rational machines' ability to explore the game-play landscape of go exhaustively. To think about this problem, it might be useful to frame go in terms of cellular automata. In other words, a go gameplay (including self-play) can be thought of as a computational process. The undecidability in CAs seems to suggest that boundedly rational go-playing machines, while able to surpass boundedly rational humans, may not be able to solve the game of go.

Appendix

Rules of Go

Go is a two-player game played on a board with a 19x19 grid. Novice players often train with a smaller-sized board, with 9x9 grids or 13x13 grids. Stones of two colors, black and white, are placed alternatingly at the grid intersections. The game begins with the player with the black stone placing their stone on an empty board. A player can pass their turn at any point of the game, but consecutive (back-to-back) passes ends the game. One or more stones of a given color (say white) is "captured" when it is completely surrounded by stones of the other color (black). Stones that have been placed on the board remain there until they are captured. Players are not allowed to "commit suicide" by placing their stones at intersections that immediately results in their stones being captured by default. Moves resulting in repetitive capture are also not allowed. The game ends when a player resigns or when both players pass their turns consecutively. Note that the person who makes the last move is not necessarily the winner. The winner of the game is the player who controls the most territory at the end of the game. The game can also end in a draw.

Appendix Table 5a Some Key Developments in Game-Playing Computer Programs, Computer Science and Mathematics

Period	Computer checkers	Computer chess	Computer go	Artificial intelligence	Mathematics and statistics
Up to 1930s		• 1845: Charles Babbage first discussed computer program to play chess		• 1937: Claude Shannon's master's thesis containing ideas on Boolean algebra and binary arithmetic	• 1902: Charles Bouton published mathematical paper on Nim • 1913: Ernst Zermelo proved that chess has pure optimal strategies • 1928: John von Neumann proves the Minimax Theorem • 1935: Roland Sprague and Patrick Grundy independently published papers on impartial games
1940s		• 1940s: Konrad Zuse designed chess-playing programs		• 1943: Warren McCulloch and Walter Pitts published paper on neural networks	• 1946: Stanislaw Ulam discovered the Monte Carlo Method • 1949: Richard Guy solved Dawson Chess and re-discovered Sprague-Grundy Theory

1950s	• 1951: Christopher Strachey completed first checkers program • 1952: Arthur Samuel completed his first operating checkers program • 1959: Samuel's paper on a computer program that can defeat strong human players	• 1950: Shannon's paper on chess-playing program • 1953: Alan Turing's paper on a computer program for playing Chess • 1958: Newell, Shaw and Simon's survey paper on computer programs for chess	• 1950: Turing published papers on Turing machine and Turing Test • 1954–1955: Newell, Shaw and Simon developed programming language • 1955: Oliver Selfridge published paper on pattern recognition • 1956: Newell and Simon published paper on Logic Theory Machine • 1957: Frank Rosenblatt invented Percepttron • 1959: Newell and Simon published paper on General Problem-Solving Program • 1958: John McCarthy implemented programming language LISP • 1960s: Alpha-Beta algorithm discovered	• 1953: John Milnor published the first theoretical paper on Partizan games
1960s	• 1963: Samuel's machine-learning program beat a master-level player	• 1960: David Lefkovitz wrote the first go computer program • 1963: H. Remus published the first paper on Computer go • 1968: Albert Lindsey Zobrist's PhD thesis on pattern recognition and go		

(Continued)

Appendix Table 5a (Continued)

Period	Computer checkers	Computer chess	Computer go	Artificial intelligence	Mathematics and statistics
1970s			• 1971: J. Ryder's PhD thesis on heuristic analysis of trees in go	• 1975: Donald Knuth and Ronald Moore's first published paper on Alpha-Beta Pruning	• 1970: John Conway invents Game of Life • 1976: Publication of Numbers and games by Conway
1980s	• 1989: Efforts to design a program to beat world champion began		• 1987: Ing Cup, the international Computer go competition, launched	• 1982: John Hopfield proposed the idea of a network with bidirectional lines • 1985: TL Lai and Herbert Robbins provided an analysis of optimal solution for multi-arm Bandit problem • 1987: Bruce Abramson PhD thesis containing ideas on Monte Carlo Tree Search (MCTS) • 1988: Richard Sutton published paper on temporal difference learning	• 1982: Publication of Winning Ways Vols. 1 and 2 by Elwyn Berlekamp, Conway and Richard Guy

1990s	• 1992: The Chinook program was narrowly defeated by Marion Tinsley—the best-known human checkers player • 1994: Chinook drew with Marion Tinsley • 2007: Schaeffer et al. solved checkers	• 1997: IBM's Deep Blue defeated world chess champion Garry Kasparov	• 1993: Brugmann's report on one-ply Monte Carlo go	• 1998: Publication of paper by Yann LeCun, Léon Bottou, Yoshua Bengio and Patrick Haffner applying convolution networks to document recognition
2000s			• 2006: Remi Coulom paper on MCTS algorithm • 2015: Google DeepMind's AlphaGo defeated European go champion Fan Hui 5–0 • 2016: AlphaGo defeated the world champion, Lee Sedol, 4–1 • 2017: AlphaGo Zero defeated AlphaGo 100–0 • 2018: AlphaGo Zero can play chess, shoji and go at world champion level	• 2002: Peter Auer, Nicolò Cesa-Bianchi and Paul Fischer introduced the upper confidence bound (UCB) for exploration versus exploitation dilemma

Source: Author's compilation based on Bouzy and Cazenave (2001), Muller (2002), Nilsson (2010), Schaeffer (2000) and Sejnowski (2018).

PART 3

Simulating Complexity: Agent-Based Modeling

CHAPTER 6

Agent-Based Modeling

Challenges and Prospects

L. Douglas Kiel, John McCaskill, James Harrington and Euel Elliott

The computer is an essential toolkit for the sciences of complexity. Whether exploring power laws, scaling or the outcomes of nonlinear interactions, it is difficult to imagine the progress of studying complex systems without the modern computer. The computer itself is a complexity generator, as the evolution of the contemporary interconnected and seemingly infinitely complex world is an offspring of the evolution of computer technology. The computer is a foundational technology for not only creating complexity in the current historical era but also for understanding emergent complexity in the social and behavioral sciences.

Over the last quarter century, improvements in computer hardware and software have expanded our abilities to produce sophisticated and more realistic social simulations. The rise of agent-based modeling (ABM), in which agents are imbued with motivational qualities acted out on a defined landscape representing a simulated social environment, now exist across the disciplines of the social and behavioral sciences. ABM fulfills many of the demands of exploring complexity. The ability to imbue such models with nonlinearity and feedback that may produce emergent behavior and spontaneous order make ABM a critical resource for the social and behavioral scientists' exploration of complexity.

This chapter examines some of the prospects and challenges of ABM. We explore the numerous benefits that accrue from such social simulation and identify the numerous challenges that remain in efforts to embody the complexity of the human social and behavioral experience by computer simulation.

One of the enduring challenges of the social sciences is the challenge of experimentation. Experimenting with human groups is inevitably cumbersome. Such experimentation must reasonably represent a sample of size and scale that fits the phenomena under observation. The behavior of human groups is inherently dynamic and thus must be viewed longitudinally if its gamut of outputs and outcomes are to be even minimally understood. Of course, experiments with humans over some reasonable time frame run into intractable issues of resource scarcity, maintaining the viability of the experimental group and a host of ethical concerns. These realities are exacerbated by issues of size, scale and ethics. The extent of the potential nonlinearities and dynamism of human interactions, even among small groups of individuals, further suggests that considerable work is necessary to produce simulations reflective of a dynamic and infinitely complex social reality. Despite challenges related to the validation of agent-based models, ABM provides promising alternatives to the traditional Dynamic Structures General Equilibrium (DSGE) approach that has been standard in the dominant social science fields, such as economics (Guerini and Moneta 2017).

The rise of computing in the 1960s, however, offered a means to use the power of computers to simulate human social interactions. In fact, these were some of the first research areas to use a computer as an experimental petri dish for understanding the dynamics of complex human interactions. Pioneering work in this field was Jay W. Forrester's exploration of industrial dynamics (1961) and urban dynamics (1969). Forrester's work was directly aimed at examining the complex systems of industrial production and urban growth and decline. In his era, Forrester's research was extremely rich. His simulations produced output over time revealing the interconnections and dynamics of industrial interactions and urban networks.

Forrester was more than aware of the challenges of modeling complex human behavior. He clearly understood that modeling complex systems required an appreciation for the inherent nonlinearities in such systems. In *Urban Dynamics*, Forrester (1969) noted, "only by dealing forthrightly with the nonlinearity in systems will we begin to understand the dynamics of social behavior. Nonlinearity is necessary to represent the behavior of complex systems" (108).

Forrester was also appreciative of the counterintuitive behavior of nonlinear social dynamics. His early reflections (Forrester 1969, chapter 6) on such counterintuitive behavior continue to serve as a guide for those who produce simulations of complex human systems. Forrester's recognition of the inherent resistance of complex systems to policy interventions and the challenges of identifying points of influence in the temporal response of dynamic systems to such influences continues today as critical insights for modeling social system behavior. Forrester's work set the stage for the system dynamics approaches that serve as the theoretical foundation for the dynamic modeling typical of contemporary agent-based modeling.

For much of the next thirty years, social simulation relied on the basic characteristics enumerated by Forrester. Advances in computing technology and software allowed the development of more sophisticated simulations incorporating both larger datasets and larger arenas of interaction. For example, the work from the Club of Rome on the limits of growth (Meadows et al. 1972) represents an early attempt to simulate economic dynamics on a global level.

However, this era of simulation lacked one very important ingredient—a more detailed and varied dynamics of the individual-level behaviors and motivations that drive people in social settings. This limitation is most authoritatively dealt with in Epstein and Axtell's (1996) landmark work, *Growing Artificial Societies: Social Science From The Bottom Up*. Epstein and Axtell argued that social science research was fundamentally upside down. Rather than assuming that social phenomena, such as markets or cultural rituals, exist in some social ether and impose themselves on individual behavior, Epstein and Axtell inverted this model. They argued that phenomena, such as markets and social rituals, actually emerge from the multiple interactions of individual actors that we now refer to as agents. It was, in short, the dynamic and longitudinal interactions of agents involving activities, such as barter and exchange, that resulted in the creation of markets rather than markets developing as some top-down and imposed social architecture. Thus, rather than social phenomena being imposed on our models from the top down, Epstein and Axtell taught us to understand that our social systems models should start inductively, based on the interactions of individuals whose behavior may create emergent behavior and spontaneous order. It is important to recognize that the concept of artificial societies best reflects subcomponents of the infinite complexity of human social systems. No scholar yet has fashioned the audacity to take on an ABM of the entirety of a complex human society.

Epstein's approach allowed for the corollary understanding that the social terrain, or what we now refer to as the landscape, must also be considered when examining the dynamics of bottom-up social interactions. For example, the relative resource richness or scarcity of a landscape could determine how agents behave in their efforts to seek and capture resources. This approach provided two new means to consider the interactions of individual agents—the agents' interactions with other agents and interactions between agents and the social landscape they inhabit. Continuing enhancements in computer hardware, software and graphical interface now allow the production of what Epstein referred to as "artificial societies" within the confines of the computer.

Foundational work in many ways set the stage for the growth and continuing expansion of ABM. A voluminous body of literature developed by many outstanding scholars is now devoted to producing artificial societies that represent an efficient and relatively convenient means of conducting social experimentation by computer simulation. The ability to alter system parameters, interject Monte Carlo stochasticism and alter the behavioral motivations of agents provides enormous flexibility in producing models that offer the gamut of likely outcomes under experimental conditions. As John Holland (1992) noted early in the development of such systems, a genuine opportunity for developing social flight simulators capable of informing policymakers was on the horizon.

Academic Communities

To model complex human behavior, academic disciplines are leveraging agent-based models to computationally run simulations of social interactions. These interdisciplinary efforts have the ability to better inform decision-making. While ABM shares commonalities across disciplines, it is important to note that the use, language and method can vary significantly across fields. As Davidsson (2002) notes, agent-based social simulation involves the interaction across three distinct areas: (1) social sciences, (2) computer simulation and (3) agent-based computing. Social scientists use agent-based models to address complex issues across the expansive boundaries of the contemporary social sciences. While the social sciences serve as a cornerstone discipline, the recent expansions of psychology, management and biology in simulations all fill important gaps in our understanding. Of recent interest, the rise of behavioral economics has the potential of improving simulations by adding more realistic assumptions concerning agent "rationality" or the lack thereof. To ensure a bright future, we need more collaboration through interdisciplinary partnerships, better curricula to train future scholars and more research funding. In this section, we briefly summarize seminal research conducted across disciplines and highlight some of the opportunities and challenges facing agent-based simulations.

Sociologists have leveraged ABM to test critical macro theories, such as social stratification (Macy and Willer 2002). One of the earliest seminal studies using ABM was Sakoda's (1971) and Schelling's (1971) simulation on segregation. By the 1990s, there was an abundance of agent-based models due to the aforementioned advances in affordable computing power and open-source software (Bianchi and Squazzoni 2015). Using simulations, researchers were able to examine theoretically critical paradigms, such as cooperation (Axelrod 1997) and collective behavior (Epstein 2002).

Classic simulations, such as Sugarscape, are available on open-source software. Based on an extensive meta-analysis, Bianchi and Squazzoni (2015) found that agent-based models have been used to study important social science topics, including reciprocity (Cohen, Riolo, and Axelrod 2001), ethnocentrism (Hales 2000), commitment (Back and Flache 2006), reputation (Conte and Paolucci 2002), trust (Macy and Skvoretz 1998), innovation diffusion (Van Eck, Jager, and Leeflang 2011; Deffuant et al. 2005), cooperation (Axelrod 1997) and civil violence (Epstein 2002). These represent some of the best examples of high-quality ABM in sociology and political science.

More recently, a growing number of economists, such as Farmer and Foley (2009), argue that experimental designs and advanced econometrics techniques have had miserable prediction performance in unstable environments (e.g., the 2008 recession). Thus, they argue that, to better inform economic policies, economists should employ agent-based simulations as a means to adjust for dynamic and chaotic conditions. While these simulations are better suited to handle more dynamic and unstable conditions, some economists express concerns about unrealistic assumptions embedded in the simulations.

There have been other economic studies in recent years that have used agent-based models to better understand topics, such as the stock market (Thurner, Farmer, and Geanakoplos 2012), electricity markets (Weidlich and Veit 2008) and land use (Brown et al. 2005). These simulations can also be extrapolated to public policy. As Elliott and Kiel (2004) note, "Agent-based models could be used to provide analysts and policymakers with a variety of alternative scenarios in hopes of finding improved alternatives or the outcomes of intended policy intervention." Over time, policy researchers have conducted innovative research on topics that include the optimal allocation of police resources (Weisburd et al. 2017) and energy policy (Pollitt and Mercure 2018).

Given the technical nature of ABM, it is no surprise that computer scientists and engineers are increasingly engaged in this arena (Barbati et al. 2012; Davidsson 2002). In recent years, Macal (2016) finds an increasing trend of agent-based research in both the ACM Digital Library and the IEEE Xplore Digital Library. He argues that programmers are needed in the current environment because existing software packages are not well equipped to conduct more advanced simulations. Yet, this technological divide represents a major challenge facing ABM.

One of the main concerns highlighted by Bianchi and Squazzoni (2015) is the lack of programming and technical skills in the social sciences. This can be worrisome because there is a greater need for cross-discipline collaboration with computer science and engineering. Also, better technical skills will be required to be competitive for grants; for this, it is critical to learn computer languages, such as C++, Java and Python. These languages are the software foundation of most agent-based simulations. For the less technically inclined, there are various software options available to social scientists, including Swarm (Santa Fe Institute), Repast (University of Chicago), MASON (George Mason) and Net Logo (Northwestern University; Bianchi and Squazzoni 2015).

To advance ABM, Farmer and Foley (2009) further that, "this demands serious computing power and multidisciplinary collaboration among economists, computer scientists, psychologists, biologists and physical scientists with experience in large-scale modelling" (686). Agent-based modeling has always been unique in its ability to attract such a heterogenous group of disciplines to solve complex and dynamic problems. Yet, without additional investment in simulation curricula, there is a chance that the development of agent-based simulation will become stagnant. This will require a serious financial investment and better coordination across disciplines both in training and in applyling for research grants.

The Evolution of Agents

As noted above, the joining of ABM and simulation has developed through the synthesis of several disciplines and remains a multidisciplinary field. The idea of agents interacting inside a simulation is a complex one. The basis for this idea is that there are simulation routines running within simulations—whorls within whorls, as Gleick (1987) describes complex systems. The blending of these two attributes was based on the need of economists to blend the world of macro- and microeconomic behaviors. The bridging of these two concepts is not a simple or straightforward one. In the early days of using computers to assist with economic models, the agents were actually what Macal and North (2007) refer to as proto-agents. Those agents have relatively simple behaviors that are aggregations of individual agent behaviors, such as all households or all firms (Hanappi 2017). The models were still focused on the macro level.

Then, evolutionary biologists began to work with models that included von Neumann's Game Theory. These new models were a breakthrough in that they introduced the ability of models to "never rest in equilibrium" (Hanappi 2017, 3). Still, the agents were relatively simple, homogeneous proto-agents. John von Neumann also proposed the concept of cellular automata to model self-replicating organisms (Sarkar 2000).

Cellular automata are important because they provide a basic tool to begin to bridge the micro-level behaviors with the macro-level simulation. John Conway's (1970) proposal of the "Game of Life" further developed the concept of cellular automata, which still continues today. This was one of the first recognitions of emergent behavior from the interaction of simple agents with simple rules (Sarkar 2000). Four simple rules determine an agent's behavior within its neighborhood. From these simple rules, striking patterns begin to emerge as each round, or clock tick, passes.

The combination of these concepts of proto-agents with simple rules interacting with their landscape gave way to the Epstein and Axtell (1996) publication on "Artificial Societies." The life in the world created by Epstein and Axtell resembled homogenous ants that did exhibit some emergent behaviors, but still did not effectively bridge the divide between micro and macro with interactions occurring at all levels (Hanappi 2017).

The final piece that helped create the fully functional agents we see in ABM today came from network theory. This insight helped to bring the concepts of Schrödinger, relating to particle physics, to bear on the problem of bridging the micro and macro interactions. Work in the area of network theories by Paul Erdos, and later in the 1990s by Laszlo Barabasi, helped link the concepts of game theory to that of networks whereby the network nodes behave as agents. Their insights and algorithms allowed the artificial agents to use their internal models of other agents to influence their decisions. They were also able to then adopt their internal models of the other agents by sensing (observing)—in other words, they could learn. When these agents have the capacity to learn, they are able to interact with their environment in a strategic way and thereby link the micro-level behaviors to the strategic (macro) environment (Hanappi 2017).

The Challenge of Learning

One of the continuing deficiencies in the field of ABM involves the relatively simplified approaches to populating the motivations of individual agents. While it is not possible to program learning into agents, the nature of how this learning should occur remains a continuing challenge. The totality of possible motivational sets within agents also remains a fundamental difficulty in ABM (Namatame and Chen 2016). Epstein again stepped in to this challenge with his interest in attempting to interject neurocognitive elements into the motivational and behavioral sets of agents. Epstein's *Agent_Zero* (2014) was the first comprehensive effort to suggest that more work was needed to detail and "complexify" the cognitive elements of agents. This approach began to provide at least a partial means for producing more complexity within individual agents and thus create more complexity within the experimental models. A new layer of complexity is now potentially added to ABM.

Can simulated agents be programmed to genuinely learn, and if so, how? These questions are now central to explorations in ABM. For the most part, the ability of autonomous agents to see, or otherwise sense (experience), the construct and changes of the simulated environments they inhabit is well documented. Autonomous agents require the ability to learn so they can engage in realistic and adaptive responses to both their environments and other agents. Learning enables the agents to adapt and handle unanticipated events as well as allowing them to discover emergent behaviors. While a great deal of the current research on learning deals with settings involving single agents, there is an increasing emphasis on multi-agent learning, which is an essential component to building intelligent systems (Macal and North 2007).

In its most basic form, an autonomous agent can take an action, receive feedback from the environment and then perform future actions. Simple proto-agents either live or die as a result of the feedback, as they lack the capacity to change their behavior. More complex autonomous agents do change their behaviors, which is the indication of learning. If an autonomous agent is programed with the capacity to observe the actions and feedback of other autonomous agents, then it can learn vicariously. In multi-agent systems, communities of autonomous agents can learn from the others' experiences and adapt their behaviors (Macal and North 2007). This enables us to model consumer and financial market behaviors, such as the "bandwagon" effect (Macal and North 2007). These types of autonomous agents can be truly "Bayesian" in their decision-making styles.

To enable new types and difficulties of complex tasks to be successfully learned, academic and industrial labs have pushed forward breakthroughs in deep learning (SIMSOC 2018). These breakthroughs, and others involving the application of deep reinforcement learning techniques in multi-agent systems, have inspired additional research into the development of even more capable deep-learning multi-agent systems. Breakthroughs in these areas will be particularly exciting from both theoretical and empirical perspectives because they will enable the investigation and understanding of many new and complex problems.

Recent calls for research papers (SIMSOC 2018) on the topic of "New Horizons in Multiagent Learning" in the journal *Autonomous Agents and Multi-Agent Systems* offer insights into the near-term direction of learning in ABM. Suggested topics of concern include learning in Markov games, imperfect information games, evolutionary methods and learning in the presence of other strategic agents. New knowledge is also needed in the realms of opponent modeling, inter-agent teaching and transfer and learning in heterogeneous multi-agent systems. As we develop further understandings of neural networks and integrate them into these deep-learning architectures for multi-agent systems, our efforts to accurately simulate complex social systems may gain greater fidelity. This in turn will hopefully allow us a greater understanding of the complex social phenomena we observe in the physical environment. These insights are the common goals across multiple disciplines, which is why ABM is becoming such an increasingly popular tool in both scholarly and applied domains.

One of the primary assumptions of ABM is the assumption of bounded rationality. Rather than assuming utility-maximizing individuals, we expect that agents engage in satisficing strategies consistent with the path-breaking work of Simon (1955, 1956), as opposed to utility-maximizing strategies—which has been historically the default assumption of microeconomic theory—where economic actors only have limited information regarding their immediate environment, although one of the important strengths of these simulations is that the extent of knowledge can be allowed to vary. Such assumptions also allow us to explore and build into our models the findings of Kahneman and Tversky (1979, 1996) and Gigerenzer (2008b; Gigerenzer and Brighton 2009), and to examine some of the important contours of that debate, whereby the former have viewed the mental shortcuts, or heuristics, used by boundedly rational individuals as being "second best" to more comprehensively rational approaches to problem-solving, and which lead to systematic errors in decision-making. Gigerenzer, in contrast, views heuristics as adaptive and superior to traditional utility-maximizing assumptions. Agent-based modeling may help in providing important insights into this debate.

Moreover, such simulations may shed new light on research placing the concept of bounded rationality within the computational complexity framework (Velupillai and Kao 2014). Complex environments are consistent with complex adaptive systems that make boundedly rational thinking adaptive, and can be considered as a solution to addressing problems that are computationally difficult. Indeed, one of the major areas of research in computational complexity has to do with distinguishing between problems that can be computed in polynomial or a tractable period of time

(P) and for which a general problem-solving algorithm exists, versus what are known as NP, or nondeterministic polynomial, problems that—while solutions to particular problems can be found—the computing time to develop a general solution or algorithm can be extremely long (see Cobham 1965; Ladner 1975). For a discussion of a related issue addressing what are known as NP-complete problems, see Garey and Johnson (1979). In short, ABM may provide important insights into the underlying dynamics of decision-making and computational complexity.

Critiques of Agent-Based Modeling

It is important to recognize that agent-based models are not without their critics. A fundamental criticism of ABM and simulation in general is that simulation model formulations and outcomes are not typically given in mathematical terms, making it difficult to bring the tools of mathematical analysis to bear. Epstein (2006) notes in an important contribution that the distinction between agent-based and equation-based models is illusory. Epstein observes that every ABM is a computer program and, as such, is Turing computable. Therefore, "for every Turing machine there is a unique corresponding and equivalent Partial Recursive Function" (Epstein 2006, 51; Rogers 1967); however, these functions are highly complex and difficult to interpret such that the analysis of them is seldom productive. Consequently, ABMs are indeed deductive, but deductive models are not necessarily generative in character (see Dean and Elliott 2017a).

A potentially important advantage to ABMs is that generative social science, or small-world simulation, makes no assumptions regarding a singular, correct worldview. There is no reality outside of the agents and the world that has been created, and within which agents and their world coevolve. ABM allows for the modeling of individual agents specifying the possible behavior of the agent in the presence of different environments and different agents (Dean and Elliott 2017b). It assumes that each agent maintains only a "local observer view" (LOV), in which agents respond to adjacent agents and the immediate environment. Moreover, agents are capable of using decision rules that relax traditional assumptions of classical logic (Borrill and Tesfatsion 2011, 230). In particular, it is not necessary in this world for the Law of the Excluded Middle to strictly apply. Agents can simultaneously believe A, not A, or they can be uncertain. Agents could possess contradictory beliefs about a topic, just as individuals in the real world can hold contradictory beliefs. As Borrill and Tesfatsion (2011) note,

> ABM agents can have uncomputable beliefs about their world that influence their interactions. These uncomputable beliefs can arise from inborn (initially configured) attributes, from communications received from other agents, and-or from the use of non-constructive methods. ... These uncomputable beliefs enable agents to make creative leaps, to come up with new ideas about their world.
> (203–231)

The fact that the social sciences are limited to an LOV of the world makes them a good candidate for the application of the tools of constructive mathematics. At a minimum, constructive mathematics can be viewed as an important supplement to classical logic and mathematics (Dean and Elliott 2017b, 193–195). At its heart, constructive mathematics and the nonstandard logics that flow from it allow for different observers to reach contradictory conclusions. Under those logics, statements that are not necessarily algorithmic, and are hence uncomputable, are not uncommon. Those approaches allow for belief revision and for the recognition that agents acting in complex environments are subject to beliefs that are logically contradictory without those beliefs being necessarily trivial. Those inconsistencies and contradictions can say something meaningful about the agent holding those beliefs, and about the world.

Verification and Validation Challenges

The challenge of verification and validation is not a novel dilemma in the social sciences. However, there are special challenges when working with simulation methodologies. For example, how can we convince others that our models are actually tools for decision-making and not mere toys posing as hard science? How do we generate sufficient trust in our models to have policymakers use them in addressing critical policy issues? The answer lies in the verification and validation of agent-based models.

To start, definitions of each are in order. Verification involves testing the model for adherence to design parameters. Does the model behave as it was designed to behave? For simple models, this process is relatively straightforward; for more complex models, the process can be cumbersome. The model is run with various parameter settings to ensure it behaves within design parameters. If it does not, the debugging process of the software begins, changes are made and tests are run again. The interesting thing to point out is that, as Macal and North (2007) note, "The end result of verification is technically not a verified model, but rather a model that has passed all the verification tests" (222). However, at least in principle, after verification testing, the model should behave in conformance with the design parameters.

Validation is the comparison of the model to the real-world system it is representing. The only way we truly learn is by creating mental models of our environment. By building agent-based models, we are attempting to understand the environment at the component level. Thus, if the models can accurately reproduce the system of interest in the real world within statistically valid parameters, then it is considered to be a valid model. But this process again is not as straightforward as one may hope. There is also a distinct difference between virtual models of physical systems and those of social systems.

When building virtual models of physical systems, many of the system attributes can be directly tested and validated. Consider a flight simulator. Test pilots can fly the physical aircraft under different conditions, and the behavior of the aircraft (the physical system if you will), once documented, can be programmed into the behavior of the simulator (the virtual system). For example, older-model F/A-18s had an interesting behavior when the flight control system was degraded. The mode was called MECH, and it ocurred when the flight control computers would stop providing inputs, causing the flight controls to behave as though they were directly connected to the control stick. In advanced fighter aircraft, the pilot acts as a voting member in which control surfaces move—the computers make the final decision. When this degraded mode is entered, the computers withdraw from participation and the pilot is the sole manipulator of the controls. The aircraft is designed to remain fully controllable, but there was one rather dangerous aspect to this mode of flight: if the flaps were set to "full down," as they would normally be for landing, the nose would pitch down so severely that there was not sufficient control authority with the control stick to counter it. The aircraft would literally nose over into the ground. The only way to recover from this condition was to set the flap position to "half."

Discovering this aspect of the system emerged from aerodynamic theories during design that were tested in the wind tunnel and confirmed by test pilots in the aircraft (at a safe altitude!). From this knowledge, the simulators were programmed to behave in a similar manner. Now pilots can experience the terror of having the nose of the aircraft pitch violently down while only a few hundred feet above the ground, but in the safety of the simulated virtual system, not in the physical system. This and a multitude of other horrific experiences are programmed into most of the high-fidelity simulators in which pilots routinely train. The lessons are firmly implanted in the mind without danger. There is no need to experience these types of abnormal conditions in the physical system where the penalty for error is usually death. This type of virtual system training is readily accepted because the verification and validation processes are extremely clear-cut. While the simulator may not be able to replicate the physical world exactly, it is close enough to provide the necessary lessons to keep aviators safe. The same cannot be said for social systems.

There are very few "safe modes" to conduct tests of theories on large complex social systems. Again, Macal and North (2007, 227) raise some of the following important issues:

- If the real-world system that is being modeled does not currently exist, how can the model be validated?
- If only one or two cases exist for the real-world system (for example, a single historical dataset), how can we know that the model will perform well for cases that are far away from the range of experience?
- If the model is not deterministic and has random or stochastic elements, that is, each run of the model produces a different result due to the modeled random effects, how can the model be validated?
- How can agent behaviors and interaction mechanisms be validated?

The last of these can be addressed directly. Do we have good theories of individual agent behaviors, and is there corresponding supporting empirical evidence? If so, then there is no issue with validation as long as the theory is valid and the model is making valid use of the theory. If not, then the last issue blends into the first.

The problems arise when facing the first three questions. Many of the complex social systems we are interested in modeling suffer from these difficulties. The problem can be circular in that it can be impractical or unethical to monitor individual activities for long periods of time to assess the impact of macro-level policy changes on individual behaviors. But without those monitoring data, how do we validate a model of this complex system?

An example of these types of problems encountered in agent-based model validation is a continuing topic of concern within the agent-based modeling community (SIMSOC 2018). For example, one concern involves how to validate a model that was built using a national survey to calibrate agent behaviors at the local level. The issue was that the researchers were attempting to simulate the behaviors at the local level because there were no data for behaviors at the local level—it was the reason for the research! Several interesting suggestions were offered to address this problem that should be kept in mind by agent-based model designers.

One suggestion that also is consistent with the ideas of Macal and North (2007) is the notion of using either high-level empirical data or the expertise of subject-matter experts to determine whether or not the model is producing sensible patterns. While this is not a direct validation of the model, it can build confidence in its fidelity to the real world. Another indirect method suggested was the use of an alternative case study to demonstrate the generalizability of the model. The third type of interest would be to examine "interesting events." These would be extraordinary events that, if predicted by the model and exhibited in the real world at a macro-level, would validate the model. This last suggestion, while valid, would be incredibly difficult to find and would be unlikely.

The most appropriate choice in this instance would be to use all three of the indirect methods to basically triangulate the validation. ABM scholars (SIMSOC 2018) have referred to this as a "pattern-oriented modeling approach." Alternatively, the purpose of the work could be reframed. It could be used to investigate what types of empirical research are needed to gain more insight regarding the system instead of attempting to use the model to explore a series of system case studies (SIMSOC 2018). In any case, to quote Macal and North (2007), "no model using ABMS or any other computational technique will ever be fully validated" (227). The goal is to provide enough confidence in the model design and outputs that decision-makers are comfortable using them as policy simulators.

More recently, Guerini and Moneta (2017, 4) have suggested that there may be serious methodological issues with ABMs, owing to their unclear relationship with the empirical evidence. While the flexibility of agent-based models has been a major virtue, the downside has been the issue of validation, a theme discussed above. They suggest that ABMs have been evaluated primarily on the basis of their "ex post ability" to reproduce certain stylized facts, which raises troubling issues of rigor. At least when applied to macroeconomic models, and keeping in mind there may well be some important applications outside of economics, Guerini and Moneta (2017) show this by comparing Structural Vector Autoregression models that are estimated from both artificial and real-world data using causal search algorithms where the idea is to find the causal structure in both sets of models. Their own approach worked well in an agent-based model that sought to bridge the gap between "Keynesian theories of demand generation and Schumpterian theories of technologically-fueled economic growth" (Guerini and Moneta 2017, 21).

Agent-based modeling may prove to be an especially useful tool given that one of the foundations of modern economic theory is being undermined by new research. Modern economic theory makes a fundamental assumption regarding the mathematical framework of an economic system, namely, its ergodicity. As such, these assumptions may conflict with empirical reality, a problem discussed in Guerin and Moneta's article discussed above regarding more general issues of verification and validation. As Kirstein (2015) notes, in spite of its foundational character and importance, the assumption of ergodicity is overlooked when discussing the development of the economics discipline. What is ergodicity? Ergodicity occurs when the time average of a system or process is equal to its ensemble average. Consider a set of gamblers in Las Vegas, where it is determined what they won or lost and the probabilities for those winnings and losses. Now assume that over some period of time those same distributions of winnings and losses are replicated. The time average is the same as the ensemble average. If the time average differs from the ensemble average, then a system is said to be non-ergodic.

All of modern economic theory assumes ergodicity. But is this actually true? Is it realistic to expect that economic phenomena are characterized by what some might view as a very naïve assumption? Recent research suggests that the assumption of ergodicity is fatally flawed. Peters and Gell-Mann (2016) present compelling evidence of just such an assumption concerning ergodicity and that the foundations of modern utility theory, assuming bounded utility, is wrong. Another contribution by Peters and Adamou (2018) demonstrates that cooperation evolves in systems where ergodicity is broken, contrary to what could be expected under traditional assumptions of ergodicity. Rosser (2015), a contributor to this volume and an economist who raises important epistemological and ontological issues regarding complex systems, has stressed the relationship between fundamental uncertainty and ergodic and non-ergodic behavior within the context of longstanding debates in economics over Keynesian and Knightian uncertainty.

If ergodicity is not a common feature of economic systems, then agent-based or other emergent approaches that avoid the flawed assumptions discussed above may be critical technologies in placing economics on a firmer footing. This would also be consistent with Velupillai's (2010) ambitious research agenda, which is to reconstruct the enterprise of economics and ground it more squarely in a more secure empirical reality that avoids some of the excessive mathematicization of the field that may, if Peters and Gell-Mann and Adamou are correct, be leading us down a profoundly unproductive path.

Public Policy and Agent-Based Modeling

While agent-based modeling has a rich history in various academic disciplines, it remains a challenge to leverage it as a basis for public policy decision-making. As Lempert (2002) notes, "prediction-based policy analysis has inhibited the full use of agent-based models as policy simulators because it diverts focus from the questions decision-makers are most prone to ask and agent-based simulators are best positioned to answer" (7196). Particularly, ABM's main strength is the ability to consider "multiscenario simulation" as a means to improve policymaking. With agent-based models, researchers can more fully employ sensitivity analysis using various what-if situations to produce results quickly, which is a marked improvement over traditional policy analysis.

One of the major policy arenas is obesity (see Chapter 7 in this volume). Obesity has been linked with many serious health conditions, including heart disease, Type II diabetes, arthritis, high cholesterol, respiratory problems and even cancer. To better grapple with this question, Hennessy et al. (2016) provided a step-by-step guide on how to develop an agent-based model to examine policies to address obesity. This would provide a robust perspective for policymakers to address obesity prevention from a multi-faceted perspective. The model leveraged various parameters, such as environment (where they live, gyms, grocery stores), agent behavior (activity, diet, sleep, movement), and various factors such as caloric intake and weight. Based on these models, scholars can model and determine the most effective policies. By conducting this analysis, policymakers can potentially create incentives to address these policy recommendations. There has been an array of research using ABM in this policy arena (Hammond 2009; Hennessy et al. 2016; Wang et al. 2014; Zhang et al. 2015).

Given agent-based models' ability to better address complexity, this approach provides an opportunity to examine various "what if" scenarios. While this will not completely replace traditional policy analysis, it can expand on it. Traditional policy analysis is particularly powerful for examining the effectiveness of a policy after it has been implemented. While we can leverage policy analysis from different settings and contexts to extrapolate the potential outcomes of a policy, it is clear that external validity becomes a major concern for traditional policy analysis (i.e., Location A may not work in Location B). Thus, agent-based models are better equipped to account for various parameters to better project future outcomes across contexts. This could be useful as we try to address pressing policy concerns, such as educational voucher programs, immigration, national security and healthcare. There is a greater effort being made by scholars in this area, yet these types of tools are still not robustly used in the field of public policy. But without a doubt, there will be growth in ABM as a means to capture dynamic public policy processes.

Emerging Prospects for Agent-Based Modeling

The future of agent-based modeling appears bright. Moreover, the fourth World Congress on computational social science offers insights into emerging developments in ABM (Chen et al. 2014). Moving toward agent-based models founded on empirical evidence, such as web-based questionnaires, may be used to validate ABMs. The use of experimental data may also be an effective means to develop agents with more complex navigational systems for adapting to a variety of landscapes. The notion of participatory modeling allowing multiple stakeholders and policy-like simulations to serve as drivers of agents may also help to produce more realistic simulations.

Emerging views of human behavior within social environments suggests that even more must be done to fully develop ABM. The growing recognition among social scientists that we are fundamentally biological and evolved creatures raises new concerns and new interests on how to think about human behavior in groups, but also on how we think about modeling such behavior (Collarelli and Arvey 2015; Somit and Peterson 2003) Social and behavioral scientists should now see humans as bio-psycho-social creatures interacting with other such beings on frequently shifting landscapes. Thus, we now have a means to consider an even more complex view of such simulated environments.

Agent-based modeling should now begin to consider biological factors, such as time-of-day effects, and what influence such effects have on psychological states and behavioral motivations. The bio-psycho-social approach to modeling begins to provide the complexity that may further add to both the challenges and benefits of ABM. While we are not close to developing models that reflect the totality of the dynamics of human social interactions—in particular contending with the changing dynamics of individual states, moods and related behaviors—we can begin to see that these new challenges may have real payoffs for further developing social science from the bottom up.

Current and emerging technologies present real potential for embedding more detailed bio-psycho-social information as drivers of agent behavior. For example, Pentland's (2008) work using sensing technologies, such as the sociometer, provide means to gather data from individuals that may serve as the bases for motivating agent behavior. The sociometer, a patented technology now available, captures detailed non-linguistic data from individuals ranging from who they are communicating with, the extent of their communication, the length of their communication and even the intonation suggesting increases and decreases in emotional resonance when interacting face-to-face with others (Kim et al. 2012).

Another array of bio sensing technologies, such as those that track heart rates and blood pressure, should allow modelers to use empirical data to interject levels of stress or calm into agents on a very discrete level. Bio monitors are now available that track everything from blood pressure to activity levels. These monitors again may serve as a basis for interjecting empirical data into the behavior of agents. These innovations offer genuine means for adding the biological component into the bio-psycho-social reality of human behavior. We may begin to develop models that, instead of simply producing massive iterations, may produce iterations in which time becomes a real factor. In this sense, the time-of-day effects of increased blood pressure or stress or activity can all be used to develop more discrete models of human behavior relevant to a wide variety of social situations.

Another emerging technology is the use of mobile electro encephalography (EEG) to examine mental states and individuals (de Vos and Debener 2014; Soto et al. 2018). These EEG markers could be used to interject more complexity into agents, not coming close to the reality of a human being, but perhaps producing avatars in our simulations that are much more realistic than the relatively simple algorithm-driven agents of the current paradigm. It is not difficult to imagine agent-based simulations that actually extract near-real-time data from actual human beings to simulate behavior and to predict outcomes within groups or large social system settings. There is already an emerging body of research examining EEG synchronization within human teams and the effects this may have on decision-making and the quality of decisions (see chapter 1 by Stephen Guastello in this volume).

To continue the advancement of agent-based modeling, there is a need for more advanced software that can provide a standardized interface yet remain easy to use (Macal 2016). Additionally, there needs to be more involvement with behavioral theories to facilitate more realistic models, particularly in areas such as behavioral economics (Kaheman and Egan 2011). Also, there needs to be more large-scale agent-based modelling using big data, cloud computing, social media, etc. As Macal (2016) argues:

A large-scale ABMS challenge is to engineer processes for efficiently developing synthetic populations of agents, whether agents represent actual people, which comes with the associated data access and privacy issues, or only surrogate agents that correspond to the population, but only in the aggregate to properly address anonymity requirements.

(153)

Conclusion

Agent-based modeling offers many prospects for enhancing our knowledge of social simulation and of the world around us. It represents the efforts of analysts across numerous social sciences to better understand the dynamic sociopolitical challenges in an era of rapid change. The characteristics of the current historical era, perhaps best described by Hartmut Rosa (2013) as a period of social acceleration, mean keeping up with social change is an increasingly challenging and problematic endeavor. Perhaps the fundamental lesson emerging from the study of the complexity sciences in the social and behavioral sciences over the last twenty-five years is that our first-order concern is humility.

The dynamism, the nonlinearity and the nonstationary nature of much of the human experience demands that we recognize the limits of human knowledge when it comes to understanding the very social realities that make the human experience so enthralling and uncertain. We appear to live in a world in which we can often define the parameters of change, but picking a definitive point within those parameters and defining its future location may be a reality that, although we hesitate to say it, may be a fixed component of the human experience. This understanding is not heavily pessimistic for it is uncertainty that drives evolution, and all of its vagaries appear to serve as a substrate in the social realm in which adaptation is necessary for the survival of our species.

CHAPTER 7

An Agent-Based Model of Obesity and Policy Implications

Saikou Y. Diallo, Christopher J. Lynch, Jose J. Padilla and Ross Gore[1]

Introduction

This chapter presents an exploratory study that examines policies for obesity prevention and reduction over the next thirty years using an agent-based model (ABM). Over the past two decades, the increase in the number of overweight and obese individuals has become a serious health issue in the United States and worldwide (Vainio and Bianchini 2002). Obesity is linked with increases in conditions such as type II diabetes, hypertension and cerebrovascular, respiratory and heart diseases (Malnick and Knobler 2006; Must et al. 1999), as well as shortening life expectancy (Wyatt, Winters, and Dubbert 2006). It has an estimated $147 billion economic impact on annual medical expenditures in the US alone (Finkelstein et al. 2009). Approximately 68.5% of adults (age > 20 years) in the US are overweight (25 ≤ Body Mass Index (BMI) < 30 kg/m^2) or obese (BMI ≥ 30; US Department of Health and Human Services 2012; Ogden et al. 2014). These levels are attributed to the imbalance of caloric intake and

---

1. We thank Dr. Sokolowski and Dr. Banks of the Virginia Modeling, Analysis and Simulation Center (VMASC) for their great support on this project. We also thank Dr. Rudatsikira for his insights on the clinical side of weight loss. We thank Dr. Douglas Eaton for his comments and insights.

the availability of food high in sugar and fat content (Bianchini, Kaaks, and Vainio 2002; Finkelstein et al. 2012; Van Cauwenberg et al. 2011).

The development and implementation of health policies provides one approach to reducing the percentage of overweight and obese individuals. Health policies have contributed to the establishment of cleaner food preparation facilities in restaurants, better sanitation and changes in attitudes and behaviors, such as washing hands (Schmid, Pratt, and Howze 1995). These policies have proven successful and have had a broad impact. Policies designed to fight overweight and obesity have been proposed to move from individual- to community-level efforts at both legislative and organizational levels to prevent cardiovascular diseases (Schmid, Pratt, and Howze 1995). Sallis, Bauman and Pratt (1998) propose interventions in four environmental categories to promote physical activity: (1) natural environment, such as providing shelter in areas with frequent snow or rain; (2) constructed environment, such as establishing walking and biking trails separated from roads; (3) policies related to incentives, like subsidizing health club memberships for workplace employees; and (4) policies related to resources and infrastructure, like changing building codes to place parking lots further from buildings. Others advocate for a combination of food policies, including tax policies on unhealthy products, and means to increase physical activity (Nestle and Jacobson 2000; Frieden, Dietz, and Collins 2010).

While these policies might be useful and helpful, it is challenging to objectively evaluate them before they are implemented in the real world. In some cases, it may be acceptable to assume that the world will retain the same or very similar assumptions into the future; however, this assumption does not apply when historical data are limited, internal feedback and nonlinear interactions are utilized and when dealing with processes of large-scale human intervention (Gross and Strand 2000). The uncertainty and non-linearities of the decisions and interactions (environmental and individual) made by people with respect to obesity can benefit from the use of complexity theory. Complexity theory emphasizes uncertainty, randomness and non-linear dynamic systems to provide new approaches for analyzing theories and understanding the world (Grobman 2005). Further complications for system evaluation can result from increasing system complexity due to individual system components; internal couplings of social, technical and socio-economic systems; and couplings across any combinations of these systems (Terra and Passador 2016).

The modeled system may enter into a new state in the future that changes the nature of feedback within the model or creates new types of feedback that do not currently exist in the model (Gross and Strand 2000). Predictions through extrapolations due to exponential growth within the simulation pose a risk to trusting the results because the model suffers from external uncertainties and intrinsic instabilities (Schuster 2015). Models may also rely on networks where the edges connect agents based on constraints within a social space (De Caux et al. 2014). These models can only simulate types of networks constructed or designed prior to the execution of the simulation. The model cannot predict a future technology that will alter or create new social networks unless such a contingency is specifically built into the model.

To address this challenge, we use an ABM to generate and quantitatively evaluate potential future policies toward reducing obesity and overweight levels. The model combines factors that contribute to energy intake and energy expenditure and allows us to identify and evaluate balanced health policies where both eating and physical activity can be considered. Furthermore, we are interested in what specific combination of factors results in policies that reduce obese and overweight percentages over the next thirty years. While an overweight and obese rate of zero is desirable, it may not be an achievable or feasible goal. Instead, we investigate what it would take over the next thirty years to bring all of the states to the 2010 level of Colorado (assuming that it stays constant), since Colorado has the lowest obesity and overweight rate at 57.6%.

We attempt to verify and validate a non-trivial model of obesity to (1) show how to perform verification and validation (VandV) on an ABM, (2) discuss the implication of each VandV technique on the usability of the model for exploratory or confirmatory purposes and (3) discuss the implications of modeling for future studies.

Background

We use ABM to conduct confirmatory and exploratory studies. Confirmatory studies test *a priori* hypotheses used to develop the model, while exploratory studies generate *a posteriori* hypotheses based on experience gained from the model (Jaeger and Halliday 1998). For ABMs, confirmatory studies utilize the interactions of agents to generate known or expected system-level behaviors. For instance, Bagni, Berchi and Cariello (2002) create an ABM to conduct a confirmatory study on the spread of infectious disease among bovines on dairy farms. The methods for spreading the disease, preventing the spread of disease and the expected recovery of the animals are all known, and the objective is to use these known values to recreate the historical data on the spread of the disease. Alternatively, exploratory studies seek to find out something new about a system by testing how combinations of agent behaviors and environmental changes can lead to certain outcomes. Axtell et al. (2002) conduct an exploratory study to determine if rules created based on the anthropological and archaeological evidence of the Anasazi in Long House Valley are sufficient to recreate the known settlement patterns and demographic behaviors. Diallo et al. (2015) conduct an exploratory study to identify emergent behaviors in an ABM of the Ballistic Missile Defense System based upon the interactions of the system's defensive components. These two studies qualify as exploratory because they search for combinations of rules and interactions that lead to the historical or expected outcomes that were not known in advance of running the models, instead of using known data to recreate historical outcomes based upon known agent behaviors.

Whether a model is used for confirmatory or exploratory research, the model needs to undergo VandV to ensure that (1) its implementation is correct (Sargent 1987; Whitner and Balci 1989; Sargent 2013), (2) that it represents its original purpose (Tanriover and Bilgen 2011) and (3) that it satisfies its specifications and requirements (Sokolowski and Banks 2010; Tolk 2012). A review of validation approaches for ABMs within the *Journal of Artificial Societies and Social Simulation* (JASSS) reveals twelve approaches. These techniques include empirical approaches for conducing sensitivity analysis to examine how model inputs affect the model outputs through: indirect calibration, the Werker-Brenner approach and the historic friendly approach (Windrum, Fagiolo, and Moneta 2007); internal verification and case-based calibration and validation to ensure that a model works for a specific case (Boero and Squazzoni 2005); statistical validation where different real-world datasets are used for comparing the results of calibration and validation activities (Kaye-Blake, Schilling, and Post 2014); validation of patterns to determine if the model replicates known or expected trends (Küppers and Lenhard 2005); a Markov Chain Monte Carlo approach for investigating the links and correlations between input parameters and output behaviors (Sallans et al. 2003); cross-element validation to determine if changes to elements within a model, such as agents with different properties, change the outputs (Takadama et al. 2003); textual traces of exchanged messages or final values of the simulation to allow for an in-depth examination of how the simulation outcomes are reached (Courdier et al. 2002); and cross-model validation to determine if the results of one model map to the results of a similar model (Takadama, Kawai, and Koyama 2008). Informal techniques are commonly utilized the most, given their lower learning curves and lower time requirements (Balci 1998; Padilla et al. 2018).

For our study, we focus on sensitivity analysis, statistical debugging and trace experiments for verification and calibration and cross-model validation for validation. The following sections provide background information specific to these techniques.

Verification

Comprehensive checks of an ABM's parameter space can identify errors that occur under specific input values (Galán et al. 2009). The data needed to accomplish this check can be generated as an evenly distributed and unbiased sample using Latin Hypercube Sampling (LHS) to determine if the ABM's outputs are sensitive to its input values (Collins et al. 2013; Thiele, Kurth, and Grimm 2014). Individual agents can be checked to see if they violate any specifications or produce suspicious behavior during execution (Gore, Reynolds, and Kamensky 2011). Statistical debugging applied to the input and output combinations of the LHS can identify if any input sets contribute to suspicious model behaviors (Diallo et al. 2015; Diallo and Lynch 2018).

Trace experiments track the behaviors of agents throughout their execution (Bharathy and Silverman 2010; Courdier et al. 2002; Gore, Lynch, and Kavak 2017) to check that the behaviors represent the real system and the specifications given for the model. Trace validation can be used to confirm that agent roles, message exchanges and system states are correct within the simulation as explored by Courdier et al. (2002). Trace experiments can follow the values of parameters within the agents over time (micro level), or they can obtain the input and output parameter combinations from multiple model executions (macro level). These experiments generate data files containing information, such as initial values of each agent, values of variables of interest for each agent throughout execution and system-level outputs. These files can be checked to ensure that constraints are not violated and to find conditions that produce expected or unexpected values using a technique such as statistical debugging (Gore, Lynch, and Kavak 2017), or through visual inspection techniques, such as heat mapping the environment with respect to various agent attributes (e.g., exploring the density of obese agents compared against the placement of fast food restaurants; Lynch et al. 2017).

Statistical debugging is a software engineering technique for finding faults in code (Gore, Reynolds, and Kamensky 2011) that can be applied to ABMs (Diallo et al. 2015; Diallo et al. 2016; Gore et al. 2015). Statistical debugging ensures that the ABM's boundary conditions and behaviors are as expected (useful in testing models for confirmatory studies). To create new *a posteriori* hypothesis from the simulation (exploratory studies), a great amount of *a priori* knowledge about how the interactions within the system should occur is required.

Sensitivity analysis tests the uncertainty of a model's outputs by varying its input parameters to determine the relationship between the input and output values (Windrum, Fagiolo, and Moneta 2007; Saltelli et al. 2010). Sensitivity analysis can increase understanding or quantification of a system and assist in model development (Pannell 1997). Determining which parameters are sensitive helps to address questions of scalability, since these parameters can be removed from the parameter space in the design of follow-on experiments. Sensitivity analysis identifies the dependent and independent parameters for an output of interest. For example, Putra, Zhang and Andrews (2015) conduct a confirmatory study on the response of the real estate market to coastal climate change and use sensitivity analysis to test the sensitivity of the model against its assumptions.

Validation

Many validation experiments determine validity by comparing historical data against the simulation outcomes. However, this can bias the model development toward using parameters for which known data already exist (Windrum, Fagiolo, and Moneta 2007). These tests are useful for confirmatory studies by utilizing correlation tests to compare trends, interval tests to compare actual values, and compound tests to compare the match between the combination of trends and actual values. Similarly, cross-model validation is useful for confirmatory studies by checking the trends (correlations) and actual values between the expected values from the other models and the values obtained from the simulation. This is less useful for exploratory purposes, but it can provide a general direction for what may be missing from the model or areas that may be over-specified by comparing the assumptions made between the models.

Gross and Strand (2000) present the concept of *validation through retrodiction*, which states that a model can be trusted for the future given that it sufficiently recreates historical data. Calibration is normally conducted by adjusting the inputs of the model to reflect the known outputs of the system (Hofmann 2005). This is a form of *micro-level validation* that requires creating "correspondence" between the parameters and the functions of the agent populations to determine if they result in similar outcomes to what is expected (Bharathy and Silverman 2010, 448). Calibration approaches, such as the history-friendly approach, attempt to align the model with observable empirical data to constrain the parameters, interactions and decisions available within the model and then to calibrate the model against the historical traces (Windrum, Fagiolo, and Moneta 2007); for instance, Bloomquist and Koehler (2015) use calibration to confirm that taxpayer reporting compliance matches historical values.

Cross-model validation determines if simulation data map onto or extend the data from similar models (Takadama, Kawai, and Koyama 2008) constructed using the same or different modeling paradigms (Rouchier et al. 2008). For ABMs, cross-model validation can provide additional insight by representing stochastic elements of the system that may not be present in other types of models (Izquirdo, Izquierdo, and Gotts 2008). However, cross-model validation requires generating simulation outputs in a format that can be directly compared to the outputs of the other simulation models (i.e., comparing yearly data against yearly data). Monte Carlo techniques provide a method for designing the experiments and generating the outcomes from the model, as they involve running the model numerous times by generating random samples of a population to statistically analyze patterns or behaviors (Carsey and Harden 2013; Mooney 1997).

Next, we present the design of the model of obesity. The VandV processes that we apply to deem the model suitable for creating future policy hypotheses for preventing and reducing obesity are described below and demonstrate the level of effort needed to get the model into a form that can be used for the generation of policy futures.

Model Description

We construct a model to examine how the combination of individual and environmental factors contributes to the spread of obesity within an area using the Modeling and Simulation—System Development Framework (MS-SDF) proposed by Tolk et al. (2013) and expanded by Diallo et al. (2014). The model builds upon the premise that the food we eat and our ability to exercise is a function of our individual choices as well as the environment in which we live (Handy et al. 2002; Reidpath et al. 2002; Frank, Andresen, and Schmid 2004). This premise is supported by the literature (Sallis, Bauman, and Pratt 1998; Powell, Chaloupka, and Bao 2007; Morland et al. 2002; Frank, Andresen, and Schmid 2004). The model assumes that food and means for physical activity are within the proximities of individuals' homes and workplaces. The model also considers that transport modality has an impact on physical activity and energy expenditure (Sallis et al. 2004; Ainsworth et al. 2000), as does the type of work that individuals perform (Brownson et al. 2009; Sallis et al. 2004). Other factors, such as susceptibility to social pressure and calorie conversion to fat, are also taken into account (Bouchard 1991; Norgan and Durnin 1980).

We use computational agents to create synthetic cohorts of 1,000 individuals in a representative environment for each state. Agents are used because they provide an established means to model complex behavior using simple rules to represent how agents interact with each other as well as with their environment (Axtell et al. 2002; Epstein et al. 2004; Lim, Metzler, and Bar-Yam 2007). In the cohort, we track each individual's daily weight based on their eating habits, exercising habits, and Basal Metabolic Rate (BMR) for thirty years and compute population-level statistics, including average BMI and activity levels.

The model represents people as agents and the behaviors and interactions of individuals situated within an environment containing restaurants, workplaces and recreational facilities. People gain and lose weight due to a tradeoff between the intake and expenditure of calories, and they share a set of physiological factors, including age, height, weight, BMI level, gender and life expectancy. The model assigns initial ages, heights and BMI classifications at random, and an individual's weight is a dependent variable based on these values, as shown in equations 1 and 2, with height remaining a constant value.

$$BMI = \frac{W}{H^2} * 703 \tag{1}$$

$$W = \frac{BMI * H^2}{703} \tag{2}$$

The BMR equations capture the calorie requirements of each individual for maintaining their current weight levels (Harris and Benedict 1918; Roza and Shizgal 1984), as shown in equations 3 and 4. The BMR equations determine the effect of metabolism on energy expenditure while at rest and vary based on gender.

$$\begin{aligned} \text{Males}: BMR &= 88.362 + (29.5353 * W) \\ &+ (1.8893 * Height) - (5.677 * Age) \end{aligned} \tag{3}$$

Females: $BMR = 447.593 + (20.3861*W) + (1.21969*Height) - (4.330*Age)$ (4)

where *W* is weight in pounds, *Height* is in inches and *Age* is in years.

We adjust the BMR requirement of each individual based on their weekly energy expenditure, as shown in equations 5–9. Individuals can be not active (less than 75 minutes of activity per week), lightly active (less than 150 minutes of activity per week), moderately active (151–300 minutes of activity per week), very active (301–450 minutes of activity per week) or extra active (over 450 minutes of activity per week).

Not Active: *Daily Calorie Need* = $BMR * 1.2$ (5)

Lightly Active: *Daily Calorie Need* = $BMR * 1.375$ (6)

Moderately Active: *Daily Calorie Need* = $BMR * 1.55$ (7)

Very Active: *Daily Calorie Need* = $BMR * 1.725$ (8)

Extra Active: *Daily Calorie Need* = $BMR * 1.9$ (9)

The US Department of Health and Human Services, National Institutes of Health, and National Heart, Lung, and Blood Institute (2005) suggest that people reduce their daily calorie intake by 500–1,000 calories to safely lose around 1–2 pounds per week. Therefore, we constrain weekly weight gain or loss at 2 pounds. We restrict daily eating opportunities to three meals and individuals' commute to work to five days per week. An individual's transportation method determines the maximum distance that the individual can travel (Ainsworth et al. 2000; Brownson et al. 2009; Sallis et al. 2004).

Calorie expenditure due to physical activity includes regular physical activity (i.e., exercise); workplace physical activity (i.e., on-the-job physical activity); and travel method (i.e., biking to work; Sallis, Bauman, and Pratt 1998; Ainsworth et al. 2000). Regular physical activity involves the conscious decision to exercise and is optional within the model. Workplace activity reflects normal job-related energy expenditure and is not optional.

Workplaces specify workplace activity levels for their employees, serve as central points from which employees select their lunch locations and specify the amount of time that employees have for lunch. Individuals eat at restaurants within 10 minutes of their workplace for a 30-minute lunch period, or within 20 minutes if they have 60 minutes to eat. The frequency of meals, including snacking, and the time between meals has not been shown to affect an individuals' propensity to becoming obese (Ma et al. 2003; Swinburn et al. 2004). However, the eating of snacks can be a significant source of calories throughout the day (Forslund et al. 2005) and is accounted for when examining expected calorie consumption among individuals. Studies show that the average conversion of excess calories into fat varies from person to person (Bouchard et al. 1990; Bouchard 1991); therefore, we use a parameter to represent the percentage of excess calories converted into fat each week. People eat (gain calories) at markets and restaurants (both fast food and otherwise; Powell, Chaloupka, and Bao 2007; Morland et al. 2002). However, their eating habits affect the calorie range they can obtain from each meal and they do not prevent them from eating at any specific restaurant. Table 7.1 provides a complete list of the model's parameters.

Following the implementation of the model of obesity, we conduct VandV to ensure that our model is capable of reproducing historical trends and generates projections that are consistent with those from other studies.

Table 7.1 Complete List of Parameters for the Model of Obesity

Index	Parameters	Index	Parameters
1	Population	20	PercentDriveToWork
2	WorkPlaces		PercentBikeToWork
3	HousingUnits		PercentWalkToWork
4	NumberOfRecreationalFacilities	21	AreaSize
5	AverageTravelTimeToWork	22	PercentWorkplaces_30MinLunch
6	AvgLifeExpectancy		PercentWorkplaces_60MinLunch
7	MaxTravelTimeToRecFacility	23	PercentPeerPressured_Yes
	RestaurantPercentMarket		PercentPeerPressured_No
8	RestaurantPercentFastFood	24	Market_highCal_min
	RestaurantPercentNonFastFood		Market_highCal_max
9	PercentMale		Market_highCal_mode
	PercentFemale	25	Market_medCal_min
10	PercentObese		Market_medCal_max
	PercentOverweight		Market_medCal_mode
	PercentNormal	26	Market_lowCal_min
	PercentUnderweight		Market_lowCal_max
11	Percent5andUnder		Market_lowCal_mode
	Percent5to18	27	FastFood_highCal_min
	Percent18to65		FastFood_highCal_max
	Percent65andOlder		FastFood_highCal_mode
12	Restaurants	28	FastFood_medCal_min
13	PercentEatingHabitsLowCalorie		FastFood_medCal_max
	PercentEatingHabitsMediumCalorie		FastFood_medCal_mode
	PercentEatingHabitsHighCalorie	29	FastFood_lowCal_min
14	PercentPhysicalActivityNotActive		FastFood_lowCal_max
	PercentPhysicalActivityLightlyActive		FastFood_lowCal_mode
	PercentPhysicalActivityModeratelyActive	30	NonFastFood_highCal_min
	PercentPhysicalActivityVeryActive		NonFastFood_highCal_max
	PercentPhysicalActivityExtraActive		NonFastFood_highCal_mode
15	PercentHealthConscious_Yes	31	NonFastFood_medCal_min
	PercentHealthConscious_No		NonFastFood_medCal_max
16	PercentWorkplaceActivityNone		NonFastFood_medCal_mode
	PercentWorkplaceActivityLight	32	NonFastFood_lowCal_min
	PercentWorkplaceActivityMod		NonFastFood_lowCal_max
	PercentWorkplaceActivityVery		NonFastFood_lowCal_mode
17	AverageDrivingVelocity	33	PercentCaloriesConvertedToFat_min
18	AverageBikingVelocity		PercentCaloriesConvertedToFat_max
19	AverageWalkingVelocity		PercentCaloriesConvertedToFat_mode

Note: Parameters that share an index value are dependent upon each other; for example, *PercentMale* and *PercentFemale* must sum to 100 at initialization.

Then, we conduct experiments to identify policies for obesity prevention and reduction.

Verification of the Model of Obesity

We conduct verification by (1) combining trace experiments with statistical debugging and (2) conducting sensitivity analysis. Our goal is to VandV the model with respect to its confirmatory purpose to ensure that it does not violate any specifications, and thereby increase confidence that its implementation is correct.

Trace Experiment with Statistical Debugging

The trace experiment starts with identifying the questions or specification to check within the model, including expected outcomes, the parameters associated with these outcomes or expected agent characteristics and behaviors. To conduct the trace experiment, we follow a sample set of individuals during runtime and collect several of their statistics. The sample is selected at random from the population of simulated individuals. The main objectives of the trace experiment include checking the following questions:

i) Can initial conditions of the individuals be violated?
ii) Can initial conditions of the restaurants be violated?
iii) Can individuals gain more than two pounds per week?
iv) Can individuals lose more than two pounds per week?
v) Are the weekly calorie needs of the individuals correct?
vi) Do BMI and BMR values correspond to weight and age values per individual?

Information from each individual necessary to address these questions includes: the individual's identification number; age; height; weight; BMI; BMR; weekly calorie need; weekly net calorie gain; life expectancy; and the total weekly time spent exercising. These parameters are necessary for testing the above conditions. We collect statistics every 90 days for multiple runs of the simulation using different initial conditions. The trace follows each restaurant's type, position and calorie distributions. To analyze the results, we check to see if the agent violates any of the seven conditions above. We use a combination of statistical debugging and time-series plots to check the individuals' behaviors.

Statistical debugging provides a more comprehensive check of the trace data in a quicker and more thorough manner than visually checking plots. The initial conditions for the traced individuals are found to be correct and properly represent the distributions used to assign the initial values (objective 1—success). The initial conditions for the restaurants are also found to correctly represent the distributions used to assign initial values (objective 2—success). None of the individuals are able to gain or lose more than two pounds per week (objectives 3 and 4—success). The BMI and BMR values for the individuals are found to accurately reflect their corresponding equations; therefore, we conclude that these functions execute the correct number of times and only at the correct times (objectives 5 and 6—success).

Additionally, we conduct an exploratory test to determine if there exist configurations of parameter values that are reliably predictive of model outcomes. Therefore, we use LHS to generate an aggregated, system-level trace of the model to search for potential input conditions that lead to suspicious outcomes using initial values for each US state. We run a set of experiments to evenly sample the parameter space for various inputs. Using statistical debugging (Gore, Reynolds, and Kamensky 2011; Gore et al. 2015), we identify the top five conditions that were *highly predictive of non-obesity*, as follows (with model parameter names in italics):

- Experiments with *Area Size* < 8.634 result in a population of 15% with BMI ≥ 30;
- Experiments with *Percent Workplace Activity—Very* > 27.067 result in a population of 10% with BMI ≥ 30;
- Experiments with *Percent Workplace Activity—None* < *Area Size* result in a population of 8% with BMI ≥ 30;
- Experiments with *Percent Normal (Initial)* > 29.180 result in a population of 7% with BMI ≥ 30; and
- Experiments with *Percent Eating Habits—Low Calorie* > 83.771 result in a population of 7% with BMI ≥ 30.

These conditions show that, if the percentage of people with a low calorie eating habit is greater than 83% (independent of all other parameters), only 7% of the state's population will have a BMI over 30. As expected, low-calorie eating habits and being very active while at work are good predictors of non-obesity, while lack of access to market restaurants and long travel times to workout facilities are good predictors of obesity.

Other interesting findings include that workplace activity produces a greater tendency toward non-obesity than an individual's activity level preference, since personal workouts are voluntary, while workplace activity is mandatory. None of these observed conditions suggest that the model behaves in a manner that contradicts its specifications.

Sensitivity Analysis Experiment

We conduct sensitivity analysis and apply Analysis of Variance (ANOVA) to determine if the level of overweight and obese in the population is sensitive to the input parameters in table 7.1. ANOVA assumes that data are collected independently of each other (Iversen and Norpoth 1987); therefore, we conduct multiple statistically independent runs until we reach a 95% confidence level. The ANOVA test determines whether there is a systematic difference between the group means or whether the difference is due to chance (Iversen and Norpoth 1987). We use the null hypothesis that the model is not sensitive to the parameter. Obtaining an F-value that is greater than the F-critical value shows that the model is sensitive to the parameter. Table 7.2 provides the results of the sensitivity analysis.

The model is not sensitive to parameters pertaining to the quantity of simulated elements, but it is sensitive to the distributions of the attributes across the population, such as gender, eating habits and activity levels. The model splits on parameters pertaining to the agents' ability to access food or exercise. The model is not sensitive to travel times to work or to recreational facilities. However, it is sensitive to the total size of the area, to average walking and driving speeds and to the calorie distributions of the restaurants. Additionally, it is not sensitive to whether or not individuals are health conscious. This reinforces the notion that the outcomes are driven by the physiological characteristics of the individuals, the influences that people have on each other and the food content of the environment.

The results of the trace experiment with statistical debugging and the sensitivity analysis increase our confidence that the implementation is correct under the boundaries of the experiment for both the agents and the model as a whole. These results also support that any suspicious behaviors

Table 7.2 Results of the Sensitivity Analysis Experiments Using One-Way ANOVA

Parameter	Experiment value			One-way ANOVA value		Result
	Min	Max	Step	F	F-Critical	Sensitive
Population	500	13,000	2,500	0.238	2.386	No
Workplaces	200	1,000	200	0.423	2.579	No
Housing units	200	1,200	200	1.455	2.386	No
Recreational facilities	0	100	20	2.184	2.386	No
Restaurants	50	3,050	500	0.842	2.246	No
Average travel time to work	10	110	20	0.445	2.386	No
Average life expectancy	10	100	20	0.811	2.386	No
Max travel time to rec facility	0	150	30	0.934	2.386	No
Percent health conscious—yes	0	100	20	1.322	2.386	No
Average biking velocity	2.5	15	2.5	1.197	2.386	No
Average walking velocity	1.5	8.5	1.5	1.533	2.386	No
Percent workplace lunch length—30 min	0	100	20	0.842	2.386	No
Market—high cal—max	750	1,250	100	2.244	2.386	No
Fast rood—med cal—max	1,100	1,400	60	3.123	2.386	Yes
Non fast food—low cal—min	400	650	50	2.602	2.386	Yes
Percent obese—initial	0	100	20	2,934.175	2.386	Yes
Percent male	0	100	20	149.000	2.386	Yes
Percent age—18 to 65	0	100	20	2.919	2.386	Yes
Percent markets	0	100	20	61.094	2.386	Yes
Percent eating habits—low calorie	0	100	20	124.153	2.386	Yes
Percent physical activity—none	0	100	20	9.328	2.386	Yes
Percent workplace activity—none	0	100	20	2.939	2.386	Yes
Average driving velocity	6	36	6	3.186	2.386	Yes
Percent of calories converted to fat—mode	50	86	9	3.372	2.578	Yes

Table 7.2 (Continued)

Parameter	Experiment value			One-way ANOVA value		Result
	Min	Max	Step	F	F-Critical	Sensitive
Percent travel method—drive	0	100	20	18.020	2.386	Yes
Area size	50	1,300	250	5.600	2.386	Yes
Percent peer pressured—yes	0	100	20	2.690	2.386	Yes

Note: The second, third and fourth columns display the minimum, maximum and step size values. Columns five and six display the F- and F-critical values from the output data. The final column displays whether or not the model is sensitive to the parameter.

identified during the validation process are not likely due to implementation errors. As expected, these tests confirm that the model is sensitive to the parameters that deal with calorie gain and loss among the individuals since these are dependent variables for the individuals. This test does not prove that the simulation is correct for all possible cases outside of the experimental boundaries. However, the use of statistical debugging strengthens the usability of the model by reducing the chance that seemingly correct results are generated through invalid means. Now that we have confidence that the implementation is correct, we conduct validation to determine if the model generates believable results.

Validation of the Model of Obesity

We investigate the model's validity by conducting calibration and cross-model validation with the non-sensitive parameters from the sensitivity analysis experiments removed from the experimental design. We conduct calibration using historical obesity data from the Centers for Disease Control and Prevention (CDC) to achieve validation through retrodiction. Next, we conduct cross-model validation using a Monte Carlo experiment to generate projections of obesity to compare our simulated projections against existing projections of obesity.

Calibration Experiment

We determine if the model can match historical data by conducting calibration to simulate the levels of obesity in each US state from 1995 to 2010. Experiments run with 10–30 replications until reaching a 95% confidence level, and we record the percent of the population with BMI ≥ 25 each year. The calibration attempts to minimize the average difference between the experimental and historical data points. The best run for each state is checked to see if the experimental data points fit within the bounds of the historical data's confidence interval and to see how well the output data correlate with the historical data, as shown in table 7.3.

Table 7.3 Percent of Experimental Data Points that Fall Within the Historical Confidence Interval of the CDC Data

State	Percent within confidence interval for BMI < 25	Percent within confidence interval for BMI ≥ 25	Correlation between experimental and historical data for BMI < 25	Correlation between experimental and historical data for BMI ≥ 25
Alabama	18.75	18.75	0.947	0.947
Alaska	12.5	12.5	0.931	0.930
Arizona	62.5	68.75	0.942	0.942
Arkansas	37.5	81.25	0.977	0.977
California	6.25	37.5	0.867	0.866
Colorado	0	0	0.936	0.956
Connecticut	0	25	0.943	0.941
Delaware	18.75	62.5	0.931	0.934
Florida	0	6.25	0.964	0.965
Georgia	62.5	93.75	0.944	0.943
Hawaii	0	18.75	0.933	0.932
Idaho	50	93.75	0.907	0.907
Illinois	18.75	75	0.970	0.970
Indiana	37.5	62.5	0.955	0.955
Iowa	0	18.75	0.960	0.960
Kansas	25	68.75	0.935	0.934
Kentucky	25	87.5	0.958	0.958
Louisiana	25	37.5	0.960	0.960
Maine	81.25	100	0.961	0.960
Maryland	6.25	25	0.979	0.978
Massachusetts	0	0	0.954	0.954
Michigan	31.25	87.5	0.936	0.933
Minnesota	56.25	93.75	0.911	0.911
Mississippi	18.75	25	0.953	0.953
Missouri	43.75	75	0.960	0.961
Montana	18.75	31.25	0.926	0.926
Nebraska	93.75	100	0.972	0.971
Nevada	43.75	68.75	0.882	0.881
New Hampshire	56.25	93.75	0.969	0.969
New Jersey	0	0	0.969	0.969
New Mexico	43.75	81.25	0.963	0.963
New York	37.5	93.75	0.927	0.929

Table 7.3 (Continued)

State	Percent within confidence interval for BMI < 25	Percent within confidence interval for BMI ≥ 25	Correlation between experimental and historical data for BMI < 25	Correlation between experimental and historical data for BMI ≥ 25
North Carolina	81.25	93.75	0.965	0.965
North Dakota	56.25	100	0.864	0.862
Ohio	37.5	56.25	0.960	0.960
Oklahoma	25	68.75	0.968	0.967
Oregon	50	100	0.947	0.947
Pennsylvania	6.25	68.75	0.968	0.968
Rhode Island	68.75	100	0.981	0.981
South Carolina	50	81.25	0.956	0.957
South Dakota	18.75	81.25	0.937	0.938
Tennessee	31.25	56.25	0.908	0.908
Texas	25	93.75	0.962	0.961
Utah	0	43.75	0.955	0.955
Vermont	0	25	0.927	0.927
Virginia	62.5	87.5	0.814	0.810
Washington	31.25	50	0.918	0.917
West Virginia	0	0	0.943	0.942
Wisconsin	68.75	93.75	0.965	0.965
Wyoming	0	31.25	0.971	0.970

Five states have a 100% match against the sixteen-year calibration for the BMI ≥ 25 category, and for thirty-two states, at least half of the data points fall within the historic confidence interval. For BMI < 25, fourteen states contain at least a 50% match with the historic confidence interval. However, no state produces a 100% match for this category. Therefore, we conclude that the model is a decent predictor of obesity outcomes.

The calibration experiments show that there are input parameter sets resulting in a 100% match to historical data over the period 1995–2010. Correlations are high across all fifty states for both BMI classifications, with forty-six states having positive correlations greater than 90%. Only four states' correlations are under 90%. Nebraska shows the best match to the historical data, with a 100% match on the BMI ≥ 25 side and a 93.75% match on the BMI < 25 side. Overall, the model is not biased toward states with higher or lower levels of obesity. Correlation results show that the model is highly correlated to the historical levels. Based on these findings, we conclude that the model is a good predictor of obesity trends. Next, we validate the model against other models' predictions of obesity.

Cross-Model Validation

We use the best calibration result to serve as the starting point to create projections of BMI levels from 2010 to 2040. We use the CDC's Behavioral Risk Factor Surveillance System (BRFSS) data to provide the starting percentages of obese, normal, overweight and underweight populations for the year 2010. We compare the projections against other obesity projections at the national and state levels using projections based on NHANES (Finkelstein et al. 2012; Wang et al. 2008) and BRFSS (Trust for America's Health and Robert Wood Johnson Foundation 2012) data. Table 7.4 provides the experimental values.

Next, we conduct a comparison of our experimental data against Wang et al.'s (2008) 2020 and 2030 projections. Wang et al.'s (2008) 2020

Table 7.4 Monte Carlo Results for Percentage of BMI ≥ 25 Populations over Thirty Years

State	Historic value	Projected values (experimental)		
	2010	2020	2030	2040
Alabama	70.00	48.631	49.324	54.128
Alaska	65.90	46.729	47.412	52.232
Arizona	64.90	46.749	47.283	52.010
Arkansas	67.20	47.103	47.641	52.767
California	61.60	47.512	48.173	53.299
Colorado	57.60	46.737	47.314	52.130
Connecticut	60.50	46.239	46.708	51.609
Delaware	64.00	46.884	47.617	52.469
Florida	65.00	46.173	47.012	51.926
Georgia	65.70	46.427	47.078	52.242
Hawaii	57.20	47.265	47.996	53.078
Idaho	62.90	46.240	46.942	52.162
Illinois	63.20	47.072	47.742	52.238
Indiana	66.40	46.493	47.230	52.254
Iowa	66.20	46.909	47.318	52.456
Kansas	64.50	46.154	46.750	51.533
Kentucky	67.50	46.822	47.397	51.943
Louisiana	66.40	46.983	47.573	52.583
Maine	63.70	46.604	47.336	52.166
Maryland	66.10	47.184	47.882	52.809
Massachusetts	60.10	47.280	47.879	53.057
Michigan	66.80	46.775	47.616	52.520
Minnesota	63.10	45.936	46.682	51.927

Table 7.4 (Continued)

	Historic value	Projected values (experimental)		
State	2010	2020	2030	2040
Mississippi	68.80	47.145	47.845	52.660
Missouri	65.80	46.697	47.355	52.386
Montana	61.30	46.341	46.895	52.024
Nebraska	64.90	47.210	47.853	53.069
Nevada	60.20	46.506	47.294	52.112
New Hampshire	63.10	46.084	46.827	51.782
New Jersey	61.60	46.877	47.602	52.500
New Mexico	60.70	47.242	48.060	52.778
New York	61.40	47.143	47.757	52.694
North Carolina	65.30	47.308	47.957	52.693
North Dakota	64.70	46.917	47.577	52.486
Ohio	65.70	46.612	47.057	51.764
Oklahoma	67.30	46.965	47.623	52.567
Oregon	60.90	47.061	47.798	52.514
Pennsylvania	65.80	47.183	47.812	53.078
Rhode Island	63.50	46.601	47.260	52.550
South Carolina	67.40	46.360	46.979	51.870
South Dakota	65.70	46.854	47.505	52.481
Tennessee	67.80	46.608	47.348	52.042
Texas	66.50	46.890	47.709	52.579
Utah	57.70	47.330	47.758	52.715
Vermont	58.50	46.556	46.949	52.125
Virginia	61.20	46.968	47.675	52.736
Washington	61.80	47.311	47.854	52.929
West Virginia	67.90	46.399	47.176	51.995
Wisconsin	63.60	47.228	47.857	52.917
Wyoming	63.80	47.128	47.729	52.656
National average	63.99	46.849	47.500	52.445

projection expects 78.5% (with a confidence interval between 75.6 and 81.4) of the national population to be overweight and obese (BMI ≥ 25). For 2030, the expected percentange of overweight and obese rises to 86.3 (with a confidence interval between 82.9 and 89.8). Our experimentally projected values follow:

- 78.22% of the population as obese and overweight in 2020; and
- 80.5% of the population as obese and overweight in 2030.

Our projection for 2020 is close to their projection values and falls within their calculated confidence interval. However, our experimental data for 2030 fell 2.4% below the lower confidence interval of their projection.

Table 7.5 Comparison of Experimental Data to Finkelstein et al. (2012) at the National Level for Adult Populations with BMI ≥ 30

Year	National Percentage of Obese Adults (BMI ≥ 30): Expected Value Obtained from (Finkelstein et al. 2012)	National Percentage of Obese Adults (BMI ≥ 30): VMASC Experimental Outputs Expected Value	Difference: VMASC Experimental Value—(Finkelstein et al. 2012)'s Expected Value
2015	34.5	36.57597	2.07597
2020	37.4	38.0239	0.6239
2025	39.9	40.26772	0.36772
2030	42.2	43.4805	1.2805

A possible cause of the difference between outputs is that we initialize our model with the CDC's BRFSS data, and Wang et al. (2008) initialize with NHANES's data. The BRFSS data show an average of 27.5% obesity in 2010, and the NHANES data show 35.7% for 2010 nationally (Trust for America's Health and Robert Wood Johnson Foundation 2012). Another difference involves the assumptions that comprise the models. Wang et al.'s (2008) model assumes that everyone is susceptible to obesity in the same way and that there is a linear increase over time. Our projection accounts for the stochastic behavior of individuals, and at the national level we see a much smaller increase in the level of obesity from 2020 to 2030.

We then compare the Monte Carlo projections against projections made by Finkelstein et al. (2012). Our projections are within 0.368 and 2.075% of their projected values. Table 7.5 provides the comparison of our projections with Finkelstein et al. (2012).

We compare the experimental data for state-level projections in the year 2020 against the projections made by Trust for America's Health and the Robert Wood Johnson Foundation (2012). Table 7.6 provides the comparison of values between these projections and our experimental data. All of our experimental results are lower than the other model's projections by 1.6–22.75%.

Overall, our projections are less pessimistic at the state and national levels than those obtained from the statistical models due to methodological and data differences. However, we are in line with the other models' projections. The results of this experiment and the calibration experiments give us confidence that we can use the model as an acceptable proxy to study the spread of obesity with respect to trends. Therefore, we are

Table 7.6 Comparison of Experimental Outputs to Trust for America's Health and Robert Wood Johnson Foundation (2012) Projections for BMI ≥ 30

State	VMASC experimental data for 2020: state-level percentage of obese adults (BMI ≥ 30)	Trust for America's Health and Robert Wood Johnson Foundation (2012) projection for 2020: state-level percentage of obese adults (BMI ≥ 30)	Difference
Alabama	42.991	62.6	19.609
Alaska	43.983	45.6	1.617
Arizona	43.289	58.8	15.511
Arkansas	44.225	60.6	16.375
California	43.973	46.6	2.627
Colorado	42.973	44.8	1.827
Connecticut	43.371	46.5	3.129
Delaware	44.266	64.7	20.434
Florida	43.938	58.6	14.662
Georgia	43.289	53.6	10.311
Hawaii	43.628	51.8	8.172
Idaho	43.448	53	9.552
Illinois	44.244	53.7	9.456
Indiana	43.484	56	12.516
Iowa	43.511	54.4	10.889
Kansas	43.034	62.1	19.066
Kentucky	42.527	60.1	17.573
Louisiana	44.253	62.1	17.847
Maine	44.835	55.2	10.365
Maryland	43.692	58.8	15.108
Massachusetts	43.910	48.7	4.790
Michigan	44.453	59.4	14.947
Minnesota	43.481	54.7	11.219
Mississippi	43.944	66.7	22.756
Missouri	43.528	61.9	18.372
Montana	43.929	53.6	9.671
Nebraska	43.389	56.9	13.511
Nevada	43.042	49.6	6.558
New Hampshire	45.096	57.7	12.604
New Jersey	43.264	48.6	5.336
New Mexico	42.487	54.2	11.713
New York	43.392	50.9	7.508
North Carolina	42.183	58	15.817
North Dakota	43.608	57.1	13.492
Ohio	43.675	59.8	16.125
Oklahoma	43.852	66.4	22.548
Oregon	42.817	48.8	5.983
Pennsylvania	42.582	56.7	14.118
Rhode Island	43.019	53.8	10.781
South Carolina	43.322	62.9	19.578
South Dakota	44.239	60.4	16.161
Tennessee	43.125	63.4	20.275

(*Continued*)

Table 7.6 (Continued)

State	VMASC experimental data for 2020: state-level percentage of obese adults (BMI ≥ 30)	Trust for America's Health and Robert Wood Johnson Foundation (2012) projection for 2020: state-level percentage of obese adults (BMI ≥ 30)	Difference
Texas	44.098	57.2	13.102
Utah	43.377	46.4	3.023
Vermont	43.505	47.7	4.195
Virginia	44.319	49.7	5.381
Washington	43.670	55.5	11.830
West Virginia	43.420	60.2	16.780
Wisconsin	44.246	56.3	12.054
Wyoming	43.741	56.6	12.859

confident that the model is valid based on its ability to match historical data and to corroborate predictions made by other models of obesity and that the model can be reasonably used to generate hypotheses for preventing or reducing the levels of obesity into the future.

Future Policies in Obesity Prevention and Reduction

To generate future policies for obesity prevention and reduction, we use 2010 data to initialize individuals and their environment. For each state, we look for the optimal combination of variables that consistently (with a 95% confidence level) result in the closest obese and overweight levels to those of contemporary Colorado (57.6%). Figure 7.1 shows the individual- and environmental-level conditions of each state when run for thirty years that produce the closest match to Colorado's 2010 levels in the form of a heat map.

The heat map uses the equations shown below to generate a single value for each policy; the values shown in the heat maps deal directly with the gain of calories or the expenditure of energy among the individuals. Calorie gain for the area is calculated as the combination of the types or restaurants available, the food preference of the individuals (i.e., their eating behaviors), and the amount of calories that the individuals convert to fat (the value used here is the *mode* of the distribution used across the population). Energy expended from commuting is calculated based on the percentages of the population that drives, walks and bikes multiplied by the level of benefit, with driving being the least beneficial and biking being the most beneficial. Energy expended from workplace activity is converted to the amount of time that is attributed to spending energy within the workplace daily. Energy expended from physical activity is calculated by taking the percentage of the population within each activity level and multiplying it by the extra percentage of calories required to maintain their weight at each of the activity levels.

Calories gained is calculated by:

- *VenueCalsIn = (Percent_Market*700 + Percent_NonMarket*1100 + Percent_FastFood*1250)*
- *CalsInPref = (Low + Medium + High)* where:
  - *Low = (Percent_Market*400) + (Percent_NonMarket*650) + (Percent_FastFood*700)*
  - *Medium = (Percent_Market*600) + (Percent_NonMarket*950) + (Percent_FastFood*1100)*
  - *High = (Percent_Market*800) + (Percent_NonMarket*1100) + (Percent_FastFood*1325)*
- *FatConversionCalsIn* = A single value provided by the simulation (i.e., *Alabama—87.936*)

Energy Expended—Commuting is calculated by:

- *CommuteCalsOut = (Percent_Drive*170 + Percent_Walk*350 + Percent_Bike*480)*

Energy Expended—Workplace Activity is calculated by:

- *WorkActCalsOut = (Percent_Not_Active *0 + Percent_Light_ Activity *5 + Percent_Moderate_Activity *15 + Percent_Very_ Active *30)*

Energy Expended—Physical Activity (outside of the workplace) is calculated by:

- *PhysActCalsOut* = (*Percent_Not_Active**1.2 + *Percent_Light_Activity**1.375 + *Percent_Moderate_Activity**1.55 + *Percent_Very_Active**1.725 Percent_Extra_Active**1.9)

The scales of these policies are very different, so the heat map normalizes the data for each policy (x) to a 0–1 scale (z-scale) using the following formula:

$$z(i) = \frac{x_i - min(x)}{max(x) - min(x)}$$

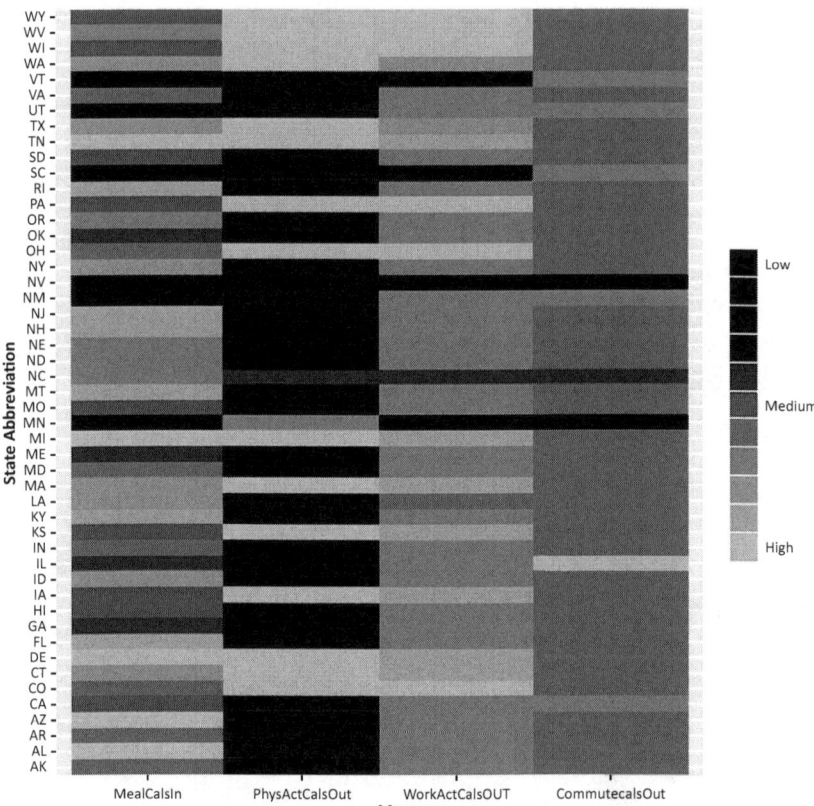

Fig. 7.1. Heat Map of Experimental Results Examining Calories in and Energy Expenditure

Values for each policy in the range of 0 to .5 are given increasingly lighter shades of grey until they appear as white. Values for each policy in the range .5 to 1.0 are given increasingly darker shades of grey until they appear dark black.

The heat map consolidates parameters related to caloric intake and energy expenditure and ranks the states by energy expenditure at work (WorkActCalsOut). For each state, the map shows total caloric intake (MealsCalsIn), energy expenditure due to exercising outside of work (PhysActCalsOut), energy expenditure due to exercising while at work or due to the work itself (WorkActCalsOut), and energy expenditure due to commuting (CommuteCalsOut). Taken individually or collectively, each category can be seen as a potential subject for policy or can be used to inform policy debates.

At the national level, the results show that there is no overwhelming evidence of a single policy that would reduce obesity and overweight levels across all fifty states (a national policy would have appeared if each state within a single column of figure 7.1 had the same shade of color). However, we observe that the most impactful opportunities for calorie expenditure occur through (1) physical activity while at work (i.e., the physical activity required in the normal workday or by exercising while at work) or (2) physical activity associated with commuting to and from work without a motor vehicle (i.e., via walking or biking). This means that, while individual preferences for exercising are important, we have to focus on policies that engage active travel methods and an active workplace if we want to curb the levels of overweight and obese populations. Results of the statistical debugging show that, independent of all other parameters in year 30, if the percentage of people who are very active at work (individuals who exert more than 5 hours of physical activity at work per week) is greater than 27%, then only 10% of the state's population has a BMI over 30. Yet, we are becoming an increasingly service-oriented economy with a majority of people living a sedentary lifestyle. In short, at the national level, we have to fundamentally reexamine the way we live, travel and work to reduce obesity.

At the state level, figure 7.2 shows the potential impact of reducing obesity and overweight to Colorado's levels for states with high (Alabama and West Virginia), medium (Minnesota) and low (Colorado) obesity and overweight levels. The results show that, regardless of the starting point

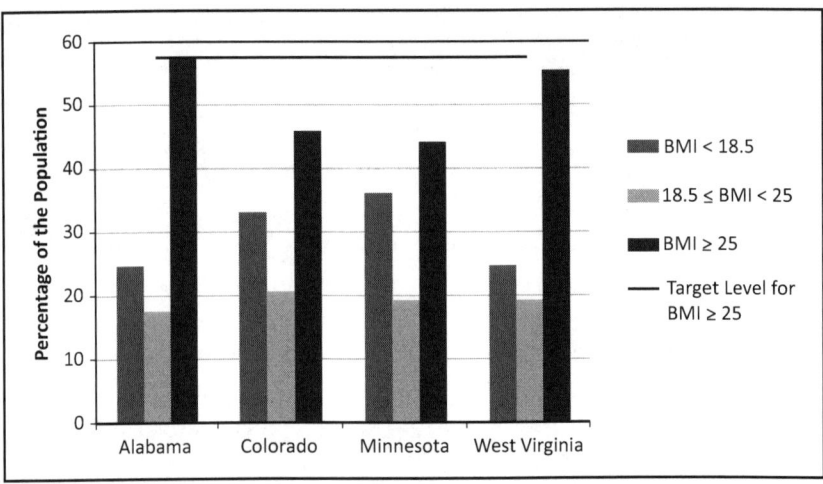

Fig. 7.2. The Results of Thirty-Year Projections for States with High (Alabama and West Virginia), Medium (Minnesota), and Low (Colorado) Levels of Overweight and Obese Populations

Note: The flat line (black) represents the percentage of overweight and obesity that each state is trying to achieve. This target line is the level of overweight and obesity of Colorado from 2010. Over the thirty-year projection, the states show a tendency to overshoot the target level and have a lower percentage of people with BMI ≥ 25. However, a tendency also emerges where the percentage of people with BMI < 18.5 exceeds the percentage of people that have a healthy BMI level.

and the policy chosen, we can achieve and exceed the target goal. The sharp decline will vary in real life as it depends on how compliant the population is with respect to any policy. In this case, we assume that the population is 100% compliant. However, in every state, the successful reduction of obese and overweight levels consistently leads to large numbers of underweight in the population, which could be worse than obesity in terms of mortality (Jerant and Franks 2012; Cao et al. 2014). For instance, Alabama has a 24.7% underweight and severely underweight rate, West Virginia a 25% rate, Minnesota a 36.3% rate and Colorado a 33.2% rate.

At the state level, the issue is not so much whether a policy can be successful; rather, we need to contemplate effects that can arise if everyone complies with every policy. Table 7.7 provides the projected percentage of obese and overweight populations in 2040 when trying to get the simulation to match Colorado's percentages, and table 7.8 provides the corresponding percentages of normal and underweight populations.

Table 7.7 Experimental Results for Overweight and Obese Classifications when Conducting Experiments to Attempt and Match Each State's Thirty-Year Projection against Colorado's Projected Obesity Percentage

State	Objective value	2010 historic value of BMI ≥ 25	2040 projected value of BMI ≥ 25 (experimental)	BMI ≥ 25 percent decrease from 2010 to 2040
Alabama	2.153	70	57.8	12.2
Alaska	8.161	65.9	49.2	16.7
Arizona	1.691	64.9	58.2	6.7
Arkansas	4.458	67.2	54.6	12.6
California	13.598	61.6	44.9	16.7
Colorado	12.078	57.6	46.2	11.4
Connecticut	8.653	60.5	49.9	10.6
Delaware	1.535	64	56.4	7.6
Florida	3.704	65	56.5	8.5
Georgia	3.840	65.7	55	10.7
Hawaii	8.556	57.2	50.2	7
Idaho	5.670	62.9	51.9	11
Illinois	5.653	63.2	53.1	10.1
Indiana	4.279	66.4	53.2	13.2
Iowa	3.059	66.2	55.7	10.5
Kansas	2.953	64.5	52.3	12.2
Kentucky	2.344	67.5	62.2	5.3
Louisiana	2.262	66.4	55.9	10.5
Maine	2.027	63.7	60.2	3.5
Maryland	5.460	66.1	54.4	11.7
Massachusetts	8.985	60.1	47.7	12.4
Michigan	2.674	66.8	59.9	6.9
Minnesota	14.574	63.1	44.2	18.9
Mississippi	2.226	68.8	58.5	10.3
Missouri	3.133	65.8	54.7	11.1
Montana	3.022	61.3	54.4	6.9
Nebraska	4.530	64.9	56.2	8.7
Nevada	9.692	60.2	49.5	10.7
New Hampshire	5.004	63.1	55.2	7.9
New Jersey	3.149	61.6	55.3	6.3
New Mexico	14.032	60.7	41.9	18.8
New York	2.858	61.4	54	7.4
North Carolina	13.194	65.3	48.6	16.7
North Dakota	4.225	64.7	55.8	8.9
Ohio	6.035	65.7	50.8	14.9
Oklahoma	4.371	67.3	54.2	13.1
Oregon	4.305	60.9	52.7	8.2
Pennsylvania	7.009	65.8	51.3	14.5
Rhode Island	2.458	63.5	57.6	5.9
South Carolina	11.278	67.4	48.5	18.9
South Dakota	6.350	65.7	51.4	14.3
Tennessee	3.953	67.8	55.3	12.5
Texas	1.779	66.5	59.6	6.9
Utah	16.666	57.7	44.3	13.4

(*Continued*)

Table 7.7 (Continued)

State	Objective value	2010 historic value of BMI ≥ 25	2040 projected value of BMI ≥ 25 (experimental)	BMI ≥ 25 percent decrease from 2010 to 2040
Vermont	17.060	58.5	39.3	19.2
Virginia	6.783	61.2	50.6	10.6
Washington	2.924	61.8	57.2	4.6
West Virginia	2.865	67.9	55.6	12.3
Wisconsin	8.251	63.6	51.8	11.8
Wyoming	8.801	63.8	49.7	14.1

Note: An objective function determines how well each projection matches the desired level of 57.6% BMI ≥ 25 for each run. Per year, the objective function takes the value of the percent BMI ≥ 25 (30 points), takes the absolute value of the difference from 57.6% and averages the difference of the 30 data points.

Table 7.8 Experimental Results for Severely Underweight, Underweight, and Normal BMI Classifications in 2040

State	Percent severely underweight (BMI < 16)	Percent underweight (16 ≤ BMI < 18.5)	Normal (18.5 ≤ BMI < 25)
Alabama	16.9	7.8	17.5
Alaska	20.9	10.4	19.5
Arizona	14	8.1	19.7
Arkansas	18.1	8.5	18.8
California	28	9.5	17.6
Colorado	22.2	11	20.6
Connecticut	23.8	7.8	18.5
Delaware	16.5	8.5	18.6
Florida	17.3	9	17.2
Georgia	17	8.8	19.2
Hawaii	21.5	8.1	20.2
Idaho	20	8	20.1
Illinois	19.1	10.1	17.7
Indiana	20.9	8.8	17.1
Iowa	17.5	7.9	18.9
Kansas	19.8	8.6	19.3
Kentucky	14.3	7.6	15.9
Louisiana	16.9	8.4	18.8
Maine	14.1	8.8	16.9
Maryland	16.3	9.3	20
Massachusetts	22.5	9.2	20.6
Michigan	17.7	7.5	14.9
Minnesota	26.9	9.4	19.5
Mississippi	17	7.2	17.3
Missouri	21.1	7.7	16.5
Montana	18.4	7.6	19.6

Table 7.8 (Continued)

State	Percent severely underweight (BMI < 16)	Percent underweight (16 ≤ BMI < 18.5)	Normal (18.5 ≤ BMI < 25)
Nebraska	18.6	6.5	18.7
Nevada	19.4	10.1	21
New Hampshire	17.5	8.3	19
New Jersey	17.8	6.5	20.4
New Mexico	27.4	10.5	20.2
New York	17.6	7.1	21.3
North Carolina	28.3	7.1	16
North Dakota	17.6	8.5	18.1
Ohio	22.5	8.8	17.9
Oklahoma	20.1	7.9	17.8
Oregon	18	8.9	20.4
Pennsylvania	20.5	9.8	18.4
Rhode Island	14	8.6	19.8
South Carolina	25.9	8.7	16.9
South Dakota	21.2	9	18.4
Tennessee	20.7	7.4	16.6
Texas	16.3	8.2	15.9
Utah	27.4	10.5	17.8
Vermont	29.9	11.1	19.7
Virginia	19.6	9.9	19.9
Washington	16.7	8.3	17.8
West Virginia	18	7	19.4
Wisconsin	22.2	8.6	17.4
Wyoming	21.1	9	20.2

Note: This provides the sub-categorizations of the BMI < 25 data as an extension of the perspective provided in table 7.7.

Figure 7.1 conveys that the number of calories expended needs to exceed the number of calories gained to see consistent weight loss. However, the gap between the calories available and calories expended should not be too large, otherwise people tend to overshoot their target goal of a healthy weight. This observation is important because it implies that calorie-capping policies and exercise-increasing policies should not be simultaneously put in place for a given population for a long period of time (more than five years). The goal should be to reduce the gap between the difference of individuals' calorie expenditures and calorie intakes with respect to their calorie needs for maintaining their current weight levels.

The difficulty involved with generating policies to do this is that, as people's weights change, their calorie needs for maintaining their current

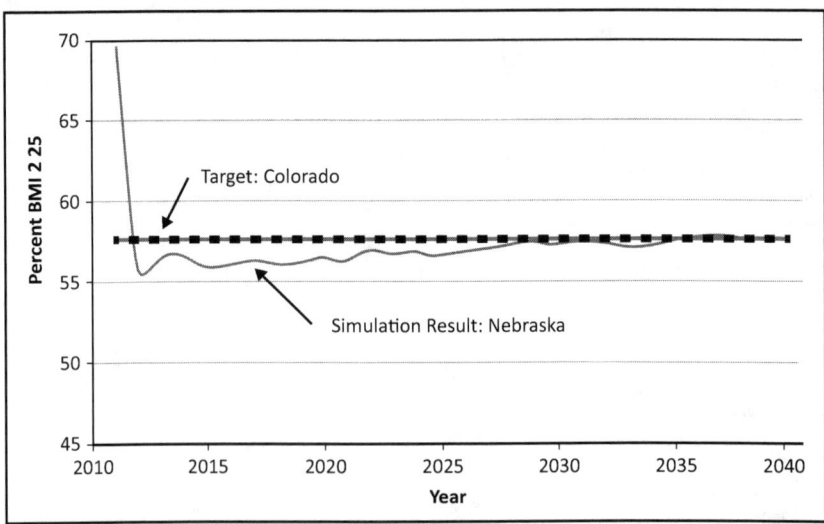

Fig. 7.3. A Thirty-Year Projection of the Percentage of Nebraska Residents that are Overweight and Obese

Note: The projection uses a policy of high-calorie food combined with high workplace activity and high commuting activity requirements to bring Nebraska to the level of Colorado.

weights adjust and they must further adjust their intake and expenditure accordingly. For instance, consider the state of Nebraska where a policy suggests that to move obesity and overweight levels to Colorado's level (figure 7.3), 100% of the population needs to be physically active at a level consistent with:

- walking to and from work,
- being moderately active while at work, and
- having little (38%) to a majority (62%) of the population be physically active outside of work.

However, the policy also suggests that everyone should have access to places that serve high-calorie meals with 92% of people having a high-calorie eating habit. This is not to say that Nebraska should promote eating high-calorie meals; rather, it means that by emphasizing energy expenditure, they have to ensure that individuals have access to the level of calories commensurate with their increased activity levels to facilitate gradual, healthy weight loss (see table 7.9).

Table 7.9 Nebraska Experimental Outputs

Parameter	Policy 1						Policy 2			Policy 3		Policy 4	Policy 5
	Run 1	Run 10	Run 9	Run 6	Run 2	Run 4	Run 7	Run 8	Run 3	Run 5
Restaurant—percent market	0	0	0	0	0	0	0	0	0	0
Restaurant—percent fast food	91.086	91.086	91.086	91.086	100	100	100	100	100	100
Restaurant—percent non fast food	8.914	8.914	8.914	8.914	0	0	0	0	0	0
Percent eating habits—low calorie	0	0	0	0	0	0	0	0	0	0
Percent eating habits—medium calorie	11.2	11.2	11.2	11.2	42.919	42.919	59.85	59.85	0	8.173
Percent eating habits—high calorie	88.8	88.8	88.8	88.8	57.081	57.081	40.15	40.15	100	91.827
Percent physical activity—not active	42.536	42.536	42.536	42.536	0	0	41.248	41.248	56.699	62.301
Percent physical activity—lightly active	53.827	53.827	53.827	53.827	0	0	58.752	58.752	43.301	37.699
Percent physical activity—moderately active	3.637	3.637	.637	3.637	0	0	0	0	0	0
Percent physical activity—very active	0	0	0	0	100	100	0	0	0	0
Percent physical activity—extra active	0	0	0	0	0	0	0	0	0	0
Percent peer pressured—yes	2.607	2.607	2.607	2.607	0	0	0.678	0.678	0	0
Percent peer pressured—no	97.393	97.393	97.393	97.393	100	100	99.322	99.322	100	100
Percent workplace activity—none	0	0	0	0	0	0	0	0	0	0
Percent workplace activity—light	11.225	11.225	11.225	11.225	0	0	0	0	8.042	0
Percent workplace activity—moderate	70.956	70.956	70.956	70.956	32.177	32.177	100	100	67.405	100
Percent workplace activity—very	17.819	17.819	17.819	17.819	67.823	67.823	0	0	24.553	0
Percent travel method to work—drive	0	0	0	0	0	0	0	0	0	0
Percent travel method to work—bike	0.334	0.334	0.334	0.334	0	0	0.681	0.681	0	0
Percent travel method to work—walk	99.666	99.666	99.666	99.666	100	100	99.319	99.319	100	100
Percent calories converted to fat—mode	65.911	65.911	78.621	90	60.269	90	90	79.315	72.91	73.787
Objective function value	4.529	3.822	4.137	5.243	4.516	4.961	5.544	5.999	2.128	1.746

Note: Five distinct policy sets are identified from the ten iterations. The final row of the table provides the value of the objective function for each policy and represents how close Nebraska got to Colorado's values for each experiment.

Finally, we note that changing the target goal of the simulation results in different policies but the same overall behavior. For instance, we were unable to achieve a 1% percent annual reduction of obese and overweight numbers over the next thirty years for Alabama, Colorado, West Virginia and Minnesota, and we had a 10% average increase in underweight to severely underweight population when compared to the previous target goal of maintaining Colorado's 2010 levels across all states for thirty years into the future. In short, we were not able to achieve the 1% annual reduction goal and obtained adverse results, which confirms our assertion that goal selection is a big challenge for obesity policy.

Discussion

Agent-based models designed for both exploratory and confirmatory studies for the system that they represent provide a significant benefit to future studies. Ensuring that the confirmatory components of a simulation are correct increases confidence and credibility in the model for its use for exploratory purposes. Our combination of sensitivity analysis, calibration, cross-model validation and statistical debugging with trace validation show that the model (1) is sensitive to parameters that contribute to the calorie gain or loss for the individuals and (2) is able to recreate historic trends and match expected outcomes from other models of obesity. Statistical debugging and trace validation contribute to the ability for the modeler to form these hypotheses by analyzing the model's outputs to determine if any suspicious conditions or behaviors arise. The application of statistical debugging and trace validation shows that a large amount of effort may be required to generate the data needed to conduct an analysis for suspiciousness.

While it seems desirable for future studies' models to always be both confirmatory and exploratory to increase confidence in their results, this is not always possible as there may not be existing historical information that allows for a confirmatory study to occur. In these cases, the modelers still need to conduct verification to ensure that their model is implemented correctly, along with some form of validation to increase confidence in the results. They also need to convey in their research findings that the study is intended only for exploratory purposes and state any limitations that the model faces.

For VandV purposes, calibration and sensitivity analysis serve as techniques for analyzing confirmatory studies by affirming that certain model behaviors are dependent upon specific model inputs; however, these techniques can also be used to create hypotheses about how to combine inputs to produce a new output from the system. Cross-model validation also serves as a confirmatory approach by determining if a model's outputs match the expected outputs from a similar model. Statistical debugging and trace validation fill a unique role in the VandV process because they can test ABMs that are confirmatory or exploratory. Statistical debugging and trace validation can (1) confirm that hypotheses are supported or not supported based on the model's execution and the created outputs and (2) determine new hypotheses based on the interactions and outcomes observed from the model runs. If the model appears to be programmed correctly with respect to its specifications, then examining what is contained within or what is missing from the model can lead to the formulation of new hypotheses.

We identify several limitations of this study with respect to future research. First, after the initialization of each simulation, the environment remains static. Second, after the initialization of each simulation, we assume unchanging assumptions about agent behaviors into the future (i.e., static agent structure). Third, policies apply to every individual, regardless of their starting obesity status. Fourth, individuals cannot choose to disregard policies.

A challenge to the future study of policies for reducing and preventing obesity is that the factors that contribute to an individual's weight gain or loss are dependent upon combinations of behavioral components that take place over time at various locations (i.e., temporal and spatial dependencies), which increases the difficulty involved with explaining the model's behavior. Agent-based models are ideally suited to model problems that deal with temporal and spatial dependencies while also serving as a modeling platform that conducts both confirmatory and exploratory research. On the confirmatory side, this allows for validation that the behavioral and environmental hypotheses for weight change used to construct the model are sufficient to recreate historical data. On the exploratory side, following the analysis of the confirmatory study, this allows for the identification of future policies pertaining to obesity at the state and national levels.

Conclusion

The model shows that state-level policies might not be the best options to reduce the levels of overweight and obesity because they lead to a large overweight and severely underweight population. We need to investigate whether we can achieve better results by (1) targeting areas within the state that have a high prevalence of overweight and obesity, or (2) using a policy set that changes over time to counteract the tendencies of people to move underweight or overweight and try to hold the population within the normal BMI range, or (3) targeting specific groups of individuals directly. Overall, the results suggest that each policy has to be considered carefully in terms of its formulation, the feasibility of its goals and its intended implementation.

Agent-based models for conducting future studies must be examined with respect to their ability to recreate known historical circumstances and to create plausible hypotheses for future policies. The VandV process provides the ability to check agent behaviors and environmental components for errors or suspicious behaviors, which increases confidence that the ABM is programmatically correct and that it generates valid outputs. The VandV process is not limited to analyzing only the system-level behaviors or the individual agents; it can also check the behaviors of various groups of agents within the overall agent population. The stochastic nature of agents drives the need to conduct VandV of an ABM in both an execution-driven manner as well as with respect to the input and output combinations for the model.

Future work involves exploring whether or not policies can be identified that target certain sub-populations within the overall population to more effectively reduce obesity while not increasing the underweight population. Future work also includes expanding the hypotheses underlying the model to exploring the effects of relaxing the limitations identified in the "Discussion" section with respect to future policies in obesity prevention and reduction. For example, we can explore the expected success of a policy while accounting for the expected compliance rate of the population.

PART 4

Scaling and Self-Organization

CHAPTER 8

It's About Time

Bruce J. West

Introduction

The fundamental question addressed in this chapter is whether the physical time determined by the clock on the wall is the same quantity as that determined by biological processes in living systems. This is not a metaphysical query, but is actually an empirical one that can be answered by experiment. Phrased in a somewhat different way, we can ask whether time for a lumbering elephant is the same as that for a scurrying mouse. Apparently the time shared by the two animals is the same when referenced to an external mechanical clock, but it is not the same when referenced to their individual physiological clocks. It is noteworthy that the lifespans of an elephant and a mouse are essentially equal when the two lifetimes are measured using the product of the number of heartbeats and the average time interval between beats. However, their separate lifespans vary significantly when measured in years, that is, when they are referenced to physical time. This change of reference for time quantification, from the ticking of a clock to the beating of a heart, suggests that an interval of physiologic time may be a monotonic function of an interval of physical time (West and West 2013).

This difference in the meaning of time has led to such concepts as biological time (Winfree 1987), physiologic time (Brody 1945) and metabolic time (Schmidt-Nielsen 1997), all in an effort to highlight the distinction between time in living and in inanimate systems. The intrinsic time in a living process was first called biological time by Hill (1950), who reasoned that since so many properties of an organism change with size that time itself may scale with the organism's total body mass (TBM). Natural scientists have subsequently hypothesized that physiologic time differs from the ticking of a mechanical clock in that the former changes with the size of the animal (Calder 1984; Schmidt-Nielsen 1984), whereas the latter does not. On the other hand, physical time is related to the entropy of a physical system and proceeds irreversibly in the direction of increasing entropy (Prigogine and Stengers [1984] 2018), a property of which we can make use.

Piccinini et al. (2016) recently observed that in the middle of the last century, the mathematician Norbert Wiener (1948b) speculated that a system high in energy can be controlled by one that is low in energy. This controlling force is produced by the low-energy system being high in information content, and the high-energy system being low in information content. Consequently, there is an information gradient between the two networks that produces a force by which the low-energy system controls the high-energy system through the flow of information against the traditional energy gradient. Quantifying the information flow from a more complex system, high in information, to a less complex system, low in information, was the first articulation of a universal principle of network science, which subsequently became the Principle of Complexity Management (PCM; West, Geneston, and Grigolini 2008). The PCM was proposed as a quantitative statement of Wiener's qualitative proposition and was proven for ergodic networks (Aquino et al. 2010; Aquino et al. 2011) as well as for non-ergodic networks (Piccinini et al. 2016). Both proofs used non-equilibrium statistical physics to determine that the PCM entails an information flow, from networks of high complexity to those of low complexity, consequently exerting a force of one network on the other.

One definition of complexity, the one adopted in this chapter, is that of a balance between regularity and randomness (West, Geneston, and Grigolini 2008). Consequently, complexity can be enhanced by increasing the number of degrees of freedom and/or the level of nonlinearity describing a system's dynamics. Both the nonlinearity and the size of the system increase the level of uncertainty in the Newtonian dynamics, resulting in an accompanying increase in the system's complexity as measured by its information content. Large systems are invariably heterogeneous, having patchy regions of varying complexity that give rise to information transport to reduce the disparity in complexity and minimize the information imbalance.

Historically the disciplines of statistical physics and thermodynamics were thought to be sufficient for describing complex physical phenomena solely through the use of analytic functions. The recognition of the importance of scaling and fractals in the last half of the twentieth century established that, to understand complexity, science must go beyond the analysis of analytic functions, not just in physics, but in the social, ecological and life sciences, as well. This is the approach we take to understanding time and its quantification (West 2016b).

Time and Allometry

Lindstedt and Calder (1976) developed the concept of biological time further and determined experimentally that biological time, such as species longevity, satisfies an allometry relation (AR) of the form

$$Y = aX^b \quad (1)$$

with Y being the functionality of the system and X the measure of system size. Lindstedt, Miller and Buskirk (1986) clarify that biological time, $Y = \tau$, is an internal mass-dependent $X = M$ time scale:

$$\tau = aM^b \quad (2)$$

to which the duration of biological events are entrained. In this temporal AR, the allometry coefficient a and the allometry exponent b are empirical constants.

In figure 8.1 we record the average heart rate for sixteen animals (Al-dabaan n.d.) as a function of TBM covering six orders of magnitude. The solid line segment is the fit to the data given by

$$R = 205 M^{-.248} \quad (3)$$

so that the average heart rate R is consistent with $b = 1/4$, given that the physiologic time increases as $1/R$. It is worth noting that Mathematica was used to directly fit the nonlinear AR equation, with a quality of fit given by $r^2 = 0.96$ (West and West 2013). Other, more exhaustive fits to larger data sets, made by other investigators supporting the notion of physiologic time is extensive and may be found in many other places (Calder 1984; Schmidt-Nielsen 1984), but the results are equivalent.

Subsequently, Lindstedt and Calder (1976) presented a partial list of such temporal ARs that includes breath time, time between heartbeats, blood circulation time, and time to reach sexual maturity. In these phenomenological examples and many others, the empirical allometry exponents cluster around the value $b = 1/4$, leading some to the sophisticated speculation that there is a universal allometry exponent in physiological systems (West and Brown 2004; West, Brown, and Enquist 1997). But others (West and West 2013; Glazier 2010) have established that the allometry parameters a and b co-vary and, therefore, neither of them can have a single universal value.

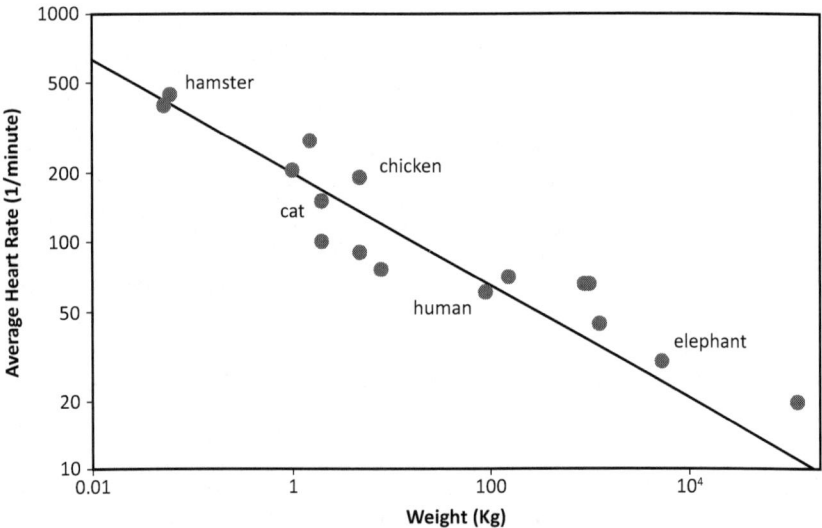

Fig. 8.1. The Average Heart Rate in Beats per Minute for 16 Animals: From the Fastest—Hamsters—to the Slowest—Large Whales—with Humans in the Center of a Logarithmic Scale

Source: The data were obtained from Al-dabaan (n.d.). Used from West (2013) with permission.
Note: The solid line segment is the AR given by Eq. 2 with $r^2 = 0.96$.

The term physiologic time was used by Brody (1945), over a half-century ago, in recognition of the fact that small animals do not live as long as large animals (Speakman 2005). A maximum efficiency argument, in support of physiologic time, was advanced by Andresen et al. (2002) in which a constant rate of entropy production defined an intrinsic time, or "eigen time," for the system. This constant rate of entropy production is a consequence of the principle of minimum entropy production, and the eigen time was identified with physiologic time. This suggests that a natural measure of these complex systems may be the probability density function (PDF) from which to construct the system's information entropy, rather than relying on individual mass trajectories to determine system behavior.

This increase in the rate of entropy, together with an assumption regarding the statistics of the spontaneous fluctuations in living systems, is used to establish the AR for physiologic time. In this respect, time itself becomes a measure of the system's complexity.

Allometry/Information Hypothesis

At the turn of the nineteenth century, the statistical uncertainty in experimental data was explained by two mathematicians, Gauss (1809) in Germany and Adrian (1808) in the United States, and revolutionized how scientists thought about error in measurement. In the same period, the zoologist Cuvier (1812) was measuring the weight (mass) of animal brains as a measure of size and observing that brain mass does not increase linearly with total body mass. Nearly a century passed before this empirical observation was expressed mathematically as an AR given by Eq. 1. Note that the schematic AR given by Eq. 1 is typically interpreted as being independent of time so that, in practice, the variables are replaced by their average values. Denoting an average by a bracket yields (West 2017)

$$\langle Y \rangle = a \langle X \rangle^b \qquad (4)$$

which is the heuristic AR found in applications. Focusing on the statistical nature of allometry, we emphasize that ARs ought to be strictly a relation between average quantities (West and West 2013; Calder 1984; Schmidt-Nielsen 1984; West and West 2012).

The recognition that ARs are given in terms of average values immediately brings to the forefront one of the major problems in constructing a theoretical understanding of time using allometry. The fact is that the empirical AR cannot be derived from the theoretical AR by averaging over a PDF due to Jensen's inequality (Jensen 1906), $\langle X \rangle^b \neq \langle X^b \rangle$ when $b \neq 1$. A derivation of the empirical AR given by Eq. 4 requires use of the probability calculus and other mathematics not often required in physics or engineering curricula.

Given the variety of disciplines in which ARs have been found (West and West 2012), any fundamental principle on which to base AR behavior must be independent of any particular discipline. We hypothesize that the empirical AR given by Eq. 4 is a consequence of the imbalance between the complexity associated with the system functionality and the complexity associated with the system size, both being measured by the Wiener/Shannon information. We refer to this as the allometry/information hypothesis and postulate that, in a complex system composed of two interacting subsystems, one subsystem is the functionality and the other is the system size, and the flow of information is driven by an information gradient from the subsystem having greater complexity to the one with lesser complexity. Thus, this imbalance produces an information force (West 2016b) that entails an AR within the complex system.

Implicit in the allometry/information hypothesis is the assumed existence of dependencies of both system size and system functionality on complexity. Such dependencies have been observed in: the positive feedback between social complexity and the size of human social groups (Collard et al. 2013), as well as in ant colony size (Ferguson-Gow et al. 2014), and in the increase in biological complexity with size of ecosystem (Cadenasso, Pickett, and Grove 2006). Other relations have been observed: the increase of prey refuge from predators with habitat complexity (Gotceitas and Colgan 1989); computational complexity increasing with program size (Joosten, Soler-Toscano, and Zenil 2011); and gene functionality depending on system complexity (Jain, Rivera, and Lake 1999). We abstract from these observations that the complexity of a system increases with system size and subsequently that the system functionality increases with system complexity.

The principle of entropy maximization has recently been used to suggest a general thermodynamic model of adaptive behavior as a non-equilibrium process in open systems (Wissner-Gross and Freer 2013) based on entropic forces. Thermodynamic entropic forces drive a physical system toward higher entropy macrostates, which can even overcome mechanical forces generated by energy gradients under well-defined conditions (Wiener 1948b; West 2016b). Herein we measure a system's complexity in terms of its PDF and its information content by the Wiener/Shannon information entropy. Consequently, the familiar entropic force evident in physical systems also acts in non-physical systems, in a somewhat less familiar way, to produce an information force (West 2016b).

Outline

In the next section, the fractional probability calculus is introduced and related to scaling. In particular, the fractional Fokker-Planck equation (FFPE) is solved in the absence of a potential using renormalization group arguments. The scaled PDF is used to determine the general form of the relation between physiologic time and the average TBM in the third section. Next, the growth of the system entropy in time is determined using the scaled PDF, as well as the sensitivity of the average TBM to the information difference generated by the growth of the system. In the final section, we draw some conclusions.

Fractional Probability Calculus

Historically, complex physical systems were modeled by replacing individual particle trajectories with ensembles of such trajectories using PDFs. Eventually the particle dynamics given by the solution to differential equations were replaced with phase space equations for the PDF, such as the Fokker-Planck equation (FPE). However, as the dynamics became ever more complex—for example, single particle trajectories becoming chaotic—the dynamic description required the inclusion of scaling effects. Consequently, Zaslavsky (2002) applied renormalization group theory to the dynamics of chaotic trajectories and replaced the FPE by a fractional kinetic equation (FKE) in which broad spectra of space and time scales are tightly coupled.

A dynamic variable $Z(t)$ scales if, for a constant λ, it satisfies the homogeneous relation

$$Z(\lambda t) = \lambda^\mu Z(t) \tag{5}$$

where μ is the scaling exponent. Modifying the units of the independent variable t therefore changes the overall observable by a multiplicative factor. A review of allometry in physiology/biology from the scaling perspective was made by Gayon (2000), but scaling alone is not sufficient to prove that a mathematical function is fractal; but if such a function is fractal, it does scale in this way. Fractal statistics are heterogeneous in "space" and/or intermittent in time and it is the statistical scaling that is evident at increasing levels of resolution (Mandelbrot 1977). Note that here we interpret space to be a dynamic observable, which is almost never physical space in any discipline outside physics. In a phase space description of the system dynamics, the dynamic variable $Z(t)$ is replaced with the phase space variables (z,t). Moreover, it is the PDF $P(z,t)$ that satisfies the scaling relation

$$P(\lambda^\mu z, \lambda t) = \lambda^{-\mu} P(z,t), \tag{6}$$

and the homogeneous scaling relation is interpreted in the sense of the PDF and not the dynamic variable.

The phase space equation for the PDF is given by

$$\frac{\partial P(z,t)}{\partial t} = \mathcal{L}_z P(z,t), \tag{7}$$

where the operator $\mathcal{L}_z$ determines the evolution of the phase space variable. In simple physical systems, this operator is typically that given in a FPE and consists of a diffusive piece, as well as a piece dependent on the potential gradient. However, our interest here is not in simple physical systems, but rather in the more complex scaling dynamics of social, economic and biological systems.

Time series with the scaling statistical properties given by Eq. 6, which are solutions phase space equations having the schematic form of Eq. 7, are found in multiple disciplines, including finance (Mandelbrot 1997; Mantegna and Stanley 2000), neuroscience (Allegrini et al. 2010; Werner 2010), geophysics (Turcotte 1992), physiology (West 2010) and general complex networks (West 2010). An extensive discussion of PDFs with such scaling behavior is given by Beran (1994) in terms of the long-term memory captured by the scaling exponent. In these non-physical contexts, the time appearing in Eq. 7 is not the physical time. In Appendix A we present a brief discussion of subordination theory, which explains how the operational time within a system of interest can be related to physical time.

Alternatively, Zaslavsky (2002) demonstrated how to relate the limit of a PDF defined on a fractal set of points $P(z,t)$ to the fractional derivative

$$\partial_t^\alpha \left[P(z,t) \right] \equiv \lim_{\Delta t \to 0} \frac{P(z, t+\Delta t) - P(z,t)}{\Delta t^\alpha} \qquad (8)$$

using renormalization group arguments. This situation arises when the single particle trajectory is chaotic and the PDF is defined over an ensemble of such chaotic trajectories. The parameter α is the critical exponent that characterizes the fractal structure of the trajectory in time t and determines the order of the fractional derivative. In this case, the phase space equations are called FKEs.

In an allometry context, one version of the FKE would be (West 2017)

$$\partial_\tau^\alpha \left[P(m,\tau) \right] = K \partial_{[m]}^\alpha \left[P(m,\tau) \right] \qquad (9)$$

where $P(m,\tau)dm$ is the probability that the dynamic mass variable $M(\tau)$ lies in the interval $(m, m+dm)$ at time τ. The dynamic variable $M(\tau)$ represents the TBM of a mature individual species member, within an ensemble of realizations, at the physiologic time τ. The properties of the chaotic trajectories are captured by $\partial_\tau^\alpha [\cdot]$, the Caputo fractional derivative in time, and $\partial_m^\alpha [\cdot]$, the Reisz-Feller fractional derivative in "mass space," and K is the fractional "diffusion" coefficient. A derivation of the FKE based on the continuous time random walk (CTRW), rather than chaotic trajectories, has also been constructed, with inverse power-law waiting-time distributions, having index α, and inverse power-law step-size distributions, having index β (see, for example, the discussions in West 2016a; Zaslavsky 2002; Metzler and Klafter 2000).

The method for solving the fractional partial differential equation for the PDF requires some details from the fractional calculus and is outside the scope of the present discussion. However, for completeness, the solution to Eq. 9 is given in Appendix B. The exact form of the solution is given by the scaling equation Eq. 41:

$$P(m,\tau) = \frac{1}{\tau^\mu} F\left(\frac{m}{\tau^\mu}\right),$$

where the scaling exponent is determined by the ratio of the fractional derivatives

$$\mu \equiv \frac{\alpha}{\beta}.$$

This PDF is trivially shown to satisfy the scaling relation given by Eq. 6.

Note that for classical diffusion, $M(\tau)$ would be the displacement of the diffusing particle from its initial position at time τ, $\alpha_z = 1/2$, since $\alpha = 1$ and $\beta = 2$, and the functional form of $F(m/\sqrt{\tau})$ would be a Gaussian distribution. However, for general complex phenomena, there is a broad class of PDFs for which the functional form of $F(\cdot)$ satisfies the generalized central limit theorem and the scaling index $\mu_z \neq 1/2$. An example of the latter PDF would be a stable Lévy distribution (Samorodnitsky and Taqqu 1994; Zolotarev 1986).

Temporal Allometry Relations

One can use the scaled PDF to write the average TBM in terms of the physiological time as

$$\langle m \rangle = \int m P(m,\tau) dm = \bar{m}\tau^\mu \qquad (10)$$

where the constant coefficient in front of the power law in time is defined by

$$\overline{m} = \int qF(q)dq; q \equiv \frac{m}{\tau^{\mu}} \qquad (11)$$

Consequently, inverting Eq. 19, we obtain the theoretical temporal AR

$$\tau = a\langle m \rangle^{b} \qquad (12)$$

where the allometry coefficient in this expression has a theoretical value expressed in terms of the average scaled variable

$$a = \frac{1}{\overline{m}^{b}} \qquad (13)$$

and the allometry exponent is expressed as the ratio of the fractional derivative indices

$$b = \frac{1}{\mu} = \frac{\beta}{\alpha}. \qquad (14)$$

Consequently, the physiological complexity of an animal, as determined by its size, entails the physiologic time through the scaling statistics. It should also be mentioned that this is the first theory providing a relation between the two allometry parameters (West and West 2013; West 2017).

It is noteworthy that the temporal ARs denoted in Eqs. 2 and 12 are not the same; the latter is expressed explicitly in terms of an average TBM, in agreement with the empirical AR, whereas the former is not. Moreover, since each of the periodic physiological systems that qualify as time-pieces are described by the temporal AR, they each have statistics described by the scaled PDF. Such a PDF, in turn, implies that the complexity of physiological processes manifests itself through the renormalization group behavior of the statistics. Just as the Gauss distribution is a manifestation of the linear additive nature of simple stochastic processes, the scaling PDF is entailed by the general scaling nature of nonlinear dynamic processes, resulting in the temporal AR.

Information Stability

The dependence of the temporal AR on the overall state of the organism is captured by the information. It is worth emphasizing that we could just as easily be talking about an organization within a society, rather than an organism within an ecosystem, where m would be the size of the organization. It is the scaling behavior of the system's dynamics, not the details of the units making up the system, that are important. The Wiener/Shannon information entropy associated with the organism (organization) manifesting temporal AR is

$$S(\tau) = -\int P(m,\tau) \ln P(m,\tau) dm. \quad (15)$$

Inserting the scaled PDF given by Eq. 41 into the integral results in

$$\Delta S(\tau) \equiv S(\tau) - S_0 = \mu \ln[\tau], \quad (16)$$

where S_0 is the reference entropy:

$$S_0 = -\int F(q) \ln F(q) dq. \quad (17)$$

Thus, on a log-linear graph, the entropy increases linearly along a straight line of slope μ.

Consequently, as we mentioned earlier, given a monotonic function relating physical to physiologic time $t = g(\tau)$ such that

$$\frac{dg(\tau)}{d\tau} = g' \geq 0,$$

we have for the physical time derivative of Eq. 16:

$$\frac{d\Delta S(\tau)}{dt} = \frac{\mu}{\tau g'} \geq 0. \quad (18)$$

Therefore, the entropy generation in physical time for the physiologic process entailing the temporal AR is positive semi-definite according to Eq. 18. Thus, the rate of entropy generation asymptotically approaches zero as an inverse power law, leaving the system, with its temporal AR, in a state of maximum entropy.

Inserting Eq. 16 into the equation for the average TBM, Eq. 10, yields

$$\langle m \rangle = \bar{m} e^{\Delta S(\tau)}, \qquad (19)$$

with the constant coefficient given by Eq. 11. This equation indicates that the average TBM responds exponentially to changes in the organism's information. During the growth process, Eq. 15 indicates a sensitive dependence of the average response of an organism to changes in the organism's complexity. An expression similar to Eq. 15 was constructed by Demetrius et al. (2009) where, in that case, $\Delta S(t)$ was related individually to the evolutionary entropy for both size and functionality. Here the functionality of the organism has been its time-keeping function and the relation of that function to the organism's complexity, but the functionality could have been the organism's basal metabolic rate or any of a number of other functions (West 2017). Consequently, the functionality and the size variables would have the same form of scaling PDF, with suitably indexed parameters, and consequently would have the same formal dependence of their averages on the information change.

Conclusions

The more the fractional time index α deviates downward from 1, the greater influence the history of the mass ensemble has on its present behavior. The more the fractional mass index β deviates downward from 2, the greater is the nonlocal coupling of the masses across scales. But these two mechanisms do not independently determine the scaled PDF. It is their ratio that determines the balancing of effects through the scaled variable $q = m/\tau^{\mu}$, with $\mu = \alpha/\beta > 1$ in living systems. It is this coupling of the scales in mass and physiologic time that entails the temporal AR with $b < 1$, as well as the positive growth of entropy in approaching the steady state asymptotically.

The results of these brief arguments are encapsulated in the Principle of Complexity Management (PCM), which establishes that, in the interaction between two complex networks, information flows from the more complex network to the less complex network. Information transfer is at its maximum when the complexities of the two networks are matched (West 2017). In the time-size application of this chapter, the PCM takes the form: *The origin of natural patterns manifest by temporal ARs is the imbalance between the complexity associated with a system's measure of time and the complexity associated with a system's size.* The network's complexity is measured by the Wiener/Shannon entropy.

We emphasize that temporal ARs are not restricted to living systems, but arise in social and ecological systems, as well. This is not entirely unexpected since the average TBM in the temporal AR discussed here is a surrogate for the living system's complexity. We experience time as a unidirectional flow of conscious experience from the fixed past, through the malleable present, into the unknowable future. But Newton's law of motion (1668) predicts future behavior, with time moving in both the positive and negative directions without contradiction. The direction of time we humans experience did not enter into physical theory until complexity was identified and modeled by thermodynamics (Callender 2010). The significance of the direction of time was emphasized in Ilya Prigogine's 1978 Nobel Lecture in which the source of order in non-equilibrium physical/chemical/ biological systems was traced to a new type of dynamic state produced by irreversible processes. This irreversibility is captured here in the phase space equations for the PDF and in the scaling behavior of the exact solution to these equations.

Consequently, we expect that temporal ARs ought to appear in social and ecological contexts, as well, where the average TBM is replaced with the average population density. This does, in fact, occur in the form of ARs for rates, rather than time. An exemplar is Farr's Law, which dates back to the nineteenth century and quantifies the "evil effects of crowding," relating a population's mortality rate to an institution's population density in the form of a rate AR (West 2017; Farr 1885). Other examples of social temporal ARs include an increasing urban crime rate, the more rapid spread of infectious diseases and a speedup in pedestrian walking, all with increasing city size, as quantitatively confirmed by Bettencourt et al. (2007, 2010). Unlike the biologic case, in the social rate ARs the allometry index has a value greater than one, $b > 1$, confirming that cities have, at all times and in all places, throughout history, entailed increased rates in human activity, for both good and ill.

Appendix

A. Subordination of Time

Due to the recent availability of time-resolved data, researchers in the biological and social sciences have started adopting the notion of multiple clocks, distinguishing between cell-specific and organ-specific clocks in biology and person-specific and group-specific clocks in sociology. Of course, the notion of subjective and objective time dates to the middle of the nineteenth century with the introduction of the empirical Weber-Fechner Law (Fechner 1860).

While the global activity of an organ, such as the brain or heart might be characterized by regular, often periodic, fluctuations, the activity of single neurons demonstrate burstiness and noisiness. Similarly, in a society, people operate according to their individual schedules, not always being able to perform particular actions in the same global time frame. Thus, due to the stochastic behavior of one or both clocks, a probabilistic transformation between times is necessary. An example of such transformation is the subordination procedure.

Let us define two clocks, the first of which records a discrete operational time n measuring the time $T(n)$ of an individual and the second of which records the continuous chronological time t, measuring the time $T(t)$ of a system of individuals. If each tick of the discrete clock n is thought of as an event, then the relation between the operational time and chronological time can be given by a waiting-time PDF of those events in chronological time $\psi(t)$. Assuming a renewal property for events, as given by chain condition from renewal theory, one can relate operational time to chronological time by

$$\langle T(t) \rangle = \sum_{n=1}^{\infty} \int_0^t \Psi(t-t')\psi_n(t')T(n)dt' \qquad (20)$$

Every tick of the operational clock is an event, which in the chronological time occurs at time intervals drawn from the renewal PDF. Because of this randomness, one needs to sum over all events, and the result is an average over many realizations of the transformation.

As an example, consider the behavior of a two-state operational clock whose evolution is shown in figure 8.2. In operational time, the clock switches back and forth between its two states at equal-unit time intervals. In the chronological time, however, this regular behavior is significantly distorted. In the figure, the time transformation was taken to be an inverse power law (IPL) PDF of waiting times. Thus, a single time-step in the operational time corresponds to a time interval being a random number drawn from $\psi(t)$ in chronological time. The long tail of the IPL PDF leads to especially strong distortions of the operational time trajectory, since there exists a non-zero probability of drawing very large time intervals between events. However, since the transformation between the operational and chronological time scales involves a random process, one needs to consider infinitely many trajectories in the chronological time, which leads to the average behavior of the clock in the chronological time denoted in Eq. 2 by the bracket.

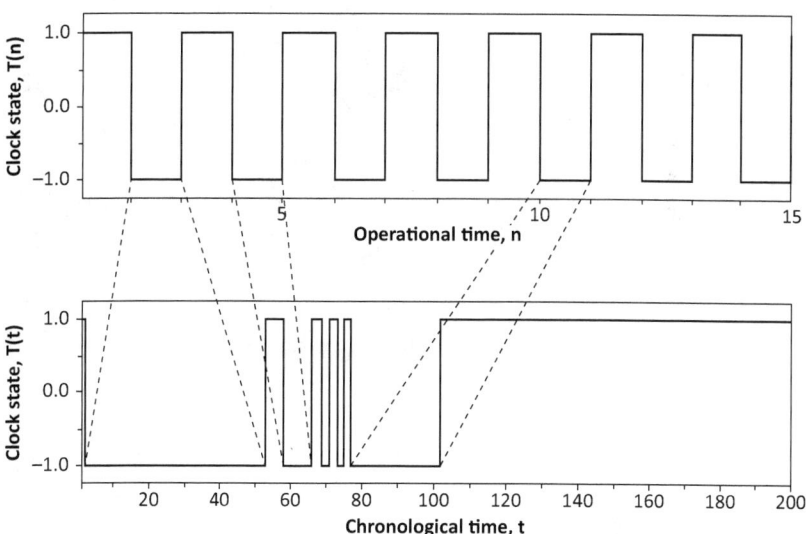

Fig. 8.2. Regular Transition between the Two States of the Individual in Operational Time (Upper Curve) and the Subordination of the Transition Times to an IPL PDF to Obtain Chronological Time (Lower Curve)

To determine the network's influence on the dynamics of the individual, we adapt the subordination argument and relate the time scale of the mean field $\xi(t)$ to the time scale of the individual. The PDF for a single isolated individual making transitions in discrete time n in steps of $\Delta\tau$ is

$$\varphi(n+1) - \varphi(n) = -g\Delta\tau\varphi(n), \qquad (21)$$

in the notation $\varphi(n) = \varphi(n\Delta\tau)$, and g is the rate of transition. The solution to this discrete equation is

$$\varphi(n) = (1 - g\Delta\tau)^n \varphi(0) \qquad (22)$$

which, in the limit $g\Delta\tau \ll 1\, g\Delta\tau \to 0$ Eq(22) becomes an exponential. However, when the individual is a part of a group with which they interact, the dynamics are not so simple.

Adopting the subordination interpretation, we define the discrete index n as an individual's operational time that is stochastically connected to the chronological time t, in which the global behavior is observed. We assume that the chronological time lies in the interval $(n-1)\Delta\tau \leq t \leq n\Delta\tau$ and, consequently, the equation for the average dynamics of the individual PDF is given by (West 2017):

$$P(t) = \langle \varphi(t) \rangle = \sum_{n=1}^{\infty} \int_0^t \Psi(t-t')\psi_n(t')\varphi(n)dt'. \qquad (23)$$

Here, the time t in the waiting-time PDF $\psi(t)$ determined from the derivative of the survival probability, which is taken to be

$$\Psi(t) = \left(\frac{T}{T+t}\right)^{\mu-1}. \qquad (24)$$

The dominant behavior of the survival probability is IPL, however, at early times the probability of not making a transition approaches the constant value of 1.

Using a renewal theory argument, Pramukkul et al. (2013) show that Eq. 23, expressed in terms of Laplace transform variables indicated by $\hat{f}(u)$ for the time-dependent function $f(t)$, has the form

$$\hat{P}(u) = \frac{P(0)}{u + \lambda_0 \hat{\Phi}(u)} \qquad (25)$$

where $\lambda_0 \equiv g\Delta\tau$ and $\hat{\Phi}(u)$ is the Laplace transform of the Montroll-Weiss memory kernel (Pramukkul et al. 2013):

$$\hat{\Phi}(u) = \frac{u\hat{\psi}(u)}{1 - \hat{\psi}(u)} \qquad (26)$$

The asymptotic behavior of an individual in time is determined by considering the waiting-time PDF as $u \to 0$,

$$\hat{\psi}(u) \approx 1 - \Gamma(1-\alpha)T^\alpha u^\alpha; 0 < \alpha = \mu - 1 < 1 \qquad (27)$$

so that Eq. 25 reduces to

$$\hat{P}(u) = \frac{P(0)}{u + \lambda_0 u^{1-\alpha}}. \qquad (28)$$

The inverse Laplace transform of Eq. 28 yields the fractional rate equation

$$\partial_t^\alpha [P(t)] = -\lambda^\alpha P(t), \qquad (29)$$

where the operator $\partial_t^\alpha [\cdot]$ is the Caputo fractional derivative for $0 < \alpha < 1$ (West 2016a) and

$$\lambda T = \left(\frac{g\Delta\tau}{\Gamma(2-\mu)} \right)^{\frac{1}{\mu-1}}. \qquad (30)$$

B. Solution to FKE

For the fractional operator in Eq. 9 we use the Caputo fractional derivative in time, which we define by the inverse of its Laplace transform (West and Grigolini 2011):

$$\mathcal{LT}\left\{\partial_t^\alpha [G(z,t)]; u\right\} = u^\alpha \hat{G}(z,t) - u^{\alpha-1} G(z,0); 0 < \alpha \leq 1, \quad (31)$$

and $\hat{G}(z,u)$ is the Laplace transform of $G(z,t)$. However, we use the Feller-Reisz fractional derivative in "space," which we define by the inverse of its Fourier transform (West and Grigolini 2011)

$$\mathcal{FT}\left\{\partial_{\lceil z \rceil}^\beta [G(z,t)]; k\right\} = -\lceil k \rceil^\beta \tilde{G}(k,t) \quad (32)$$

wherever there is $\lceil \cdot \rceil$ in a equation replace with $|\cdot|$ and $\tilde{G}(k,t)$ is the Fourier transform of $G(z,t)$.

The Fourier transform of Eq. 9 yields, for the right-hand side,

$$\mathcal{FT}\left\{\partial_{\lceil m \rceil}^\beta [P(m,\tau)]; k\right\} = -\lceil k \rceil^\beta \tilde{P}(k,\tau), \quad (33)$$

resulting in the fractional rate equation in terms of the Fourier transform of the PDF, also known as the characteristic function

$$\partial_\tau^\alpha \left[\tilde{P}(k,\tau)\right] = -\lceil k \rceil^\beta K \tilde{P}(k,\tau), \quad (34)$$

whose solution is the Mittag-Leffler function (MLF; West and Grigolini 2011)

$$\tilde{P}(k,\tau) = E_\alpha\left(-K\lceil k \rceil^\beta \tau^\alpha\right), \quad (35)$$

where the MLF is defined by the series

$$E_\alpha(x) = \sum_{n=0}^{\infty} \frac{x^n}{\Gamma(n\alpha + 1)} \quad (36)$$

The solution to the FFPE, in a potential-free region, can then be expressed as the inverse Fourier transform of the MLF

$$P(m,\tau) = \mathcal{FT}^{-1}\left\{E_\alpha\left(-K\lceil k\rceil^\beta \tau^\alpha\right); m\right\}. \tag{37}$$

A discussion of the properties of the PDF so defined can be found in a number of places (West 2016a; Metzler and Klafter 2000), in particular the fact that $\alpha = 1$ produces the Lévy distribution.

Inserting the series expansion for the MLF given by Eq. 36 into Eq. 37 allows us to write the scaling relation

$$P(\lambda m, \gamma\tau) = \sum_{n=0}^{\infty} \frac{(-K[\gamma\tau]^\alpha)^n}{\Gamma(n\alpha+1)} \frac{\Gamma(n\beta+1)}{\lceil \lambda m\rceil^{n\beta+1}}, \tag{38}$$

where the second factor in the summation is the result of applying a Tauberian theorem to the inverse Fourier transform of $\lceil k\rceil^\beta$. The coupling between the TBM and the physiologic time is determined by the simultaneous measurements of the two variables, and a renormalization group scaling equation emerges when the parameters satisfy the equality

$$\lambda^\beta = \gamma^\alpha. \tag{39}$$

This relation among the parameters is the condition to achieve the lowest rank fixed-point solution for Eq. 9 (Zaslavsky 2002). Inserting the parameter $\lambda = \gamma^{\alpha/\beta}$ into series solution Eq. 38 yields, after some simplification:

$$P(\gamma^{\alpha/\beta} m, \gamma\tau) = \frac{1}{\gamma^{\alpha/\beta}} P(m,\tau). \tag{40}$$

If we now select the time scaling parameter to be $\gamma = 1/\tau$, the scaled variable $m/\tau^{\alpha/\beta}$ becomes the new dynamic variable. The PDF solution to the FFPE then has the general form (West and Grigolini 2011):

$$P(m,\tau) = \frac{1}{\tau^\mu} F\left(\frac{m}{\tau^\mu}\right). \tag{41}$$

We have introduced the new function

$$F\left(\frac{m}{\tau^\mu}\right) \equiv P\left(\frac{m}{\tau^\mu}, 1\right),$$

and the new power law index is given by the ratio of fractional indices $\mu = \dfrac{\alpha}{\beta}$.

CHAPTER 9

Lessons from Collective Intelligence

William Sulis

The Social Insect Colony

Social insects, particularly ants, are among the most ubiquitous of all organisms. Ants comprise a large percentage of the world's biomass. They are one of the principal movers of earth and play a fundamental role in the ecology of soil. The social insects are ancient, tracing their ancestry back 200 million years. They are superlative examples of successful adaptation and survival. They are also the paradigmatic example of collective decision-making in absence of a central authority (Wheeler 1911; Wilson 1971).

Social insect colonies are exclusively female. They consist of a queen who resides in the nest producing eggs. She produces only female offspring until the time when the colony must reproduce, at which point she begins producing a small number of males and potential queens. These males will join with the nascent queen offspring and travel elsewhere to establish new colonies. Once they mate, the males die, leaving a female-only colony. The workers of the colony divide into various castes, distinguished by morphology and task. The main roles are brood carers, midden workers, foragers and soldiers (Wilson 1971; Holldobler and Wilson 1990). Task allocation and transitions between tasks are fascinating studies in their own right but will not be discussed here. They were discussed in some detail in Sulis (2009).

Each colony creates a nest where the production and rearing of the brood is carried out. These nests vary enormously in form and scale and are well adapted to whatever environment within which they exist. They may be underground, on the surface, in mounds or in vegetation. They may be formed of tunnels in soil, in mounds of soil, of processed leaves, of bodily secretions or of bodies themselves (Wilson 1971; Holldobler and Wilson 1990). They may be static or mobile. They may migrate according to an internal mechanism, the seasons or only following disruption to the nest. Foraging may be structured, as in the case of the army ants, or more or less random, as in the case of many desert or temperate species. Communication between workers may be tactile, chemical (pheromones) or visual (waggle dance of honeybees). The sheer diversity is staggering.

This chapter focuses almost exclusively on one species of ant, *Temnothorax albipennis* (also known as *Leptothorax albipennis* in some old papers), a nest-dwelling temperate species found commonly in Dorset, UK. The individual workers are themselves tiny, being around 1 mm in length. They live in small colonies consisting of up to 500 workers and a queen. These colonies reside in tiny nests formed in rock crevices in cliffs, and are subject to frequent emigrations as their surroundings are unstable. Colonies appear able to discriminate among various nest sites based on factors such as the degree of light, heat, humidity, exposure to threat, spatial expanse, elevation and so on. They are easy to cultivate in the laboratory where a nest consists of some pieces of cardboard placed between glass slides. They are just a few centimeters in size.

When emigration begins, scouts leave to seek out new sites, assessing each by several criteria and integrating these into a quality measure expressed as a wait time before recruitment that varies inversely with quality. Recruitment initially occurs through tandem running. This gradually increases the number of workers within the new site. When a threshold in numbers is achieved or exceeded (quorum threshold) the scouts shift strategy and initiate social carrying, which brings large numbers of nest mates to the new site. Research into nest emigration prior to 2009 was discussed in detail in Sulis (2009) and will be described only briefly here.

A low quorum threshold implies that a scout initiates social carrying earlier, suggesting more individualistic decision-making. A high quorum threshold requires more recruitment to the site, which allows for greater scouting and more collective contributions to the final decision

(Moglich, Maschwitz, and Holldobler 1974; Moglich 1978; Sendova-Franks and Franks 1995; Mallon, Pratt, and Franks 2001).

Mallon, Pratt and Franks (2001) showed that colonies of *Leptothorax albipennis*, when given a choice of two nest sites, mediocre and superior, were able to preferentially choose the superior site. A superior site, based upon naturalistic observations, had a floor area of 825 mm^2, a height of 1.6 mm and an entrance width of 2mm. A mediocre site had either less height, floor area or a wider entrance.

Franks et al. (2003) explored decision-making in *Leptothorax albipennis* in detail. These ants appear to select nest sites based upon three main features: darkness of the nest, internal height of the cavity and width of the entrance. Colonies were allowed to choose between two and five possible sites that varied in their attributes. A decision was marked by a majority of workers moving to the site. Preference was marked by a majority of colonies choosing that particular set of attributes. The colonies were fairly consistent, preferring dark over bright, thick over thin, narrow over wide.

Franks et al. (2006) showed small and large colonies were equally adept at nest selection. Large colonies were faster and appeared to use higher quorum thresholds. Both small and large colonies preferred nest sites that could accommodate a fully grown colony, apparently anticipating future needs.

Franks et al. (2003) showed that, under harsh conditions (the presence of wind or predators), colonies of *Leptothorax albipennis* exhibited sub-optimal decision-making. They often chose a nest site more quickly and with less discrimination even though they discovered all of the potential sites.

Langridge, Franks and Sendova-Franks (2004) demonstrated a form of learning in that colonies of *Leptothorax albipennis*, given repeated emigration trials separated by 1–6 days could improve their performance, as shown by decreased emigration times and increased efficiency using fewer workers to transport nest mates. This effect did not occur if the separation between trials was greater than 6 days, suggesting the possibility of a form of forgetting.

In subsequent sections, more recent research will be presented that expands upon and refines these earlier results and that makes extensive use of methods derived from complex systems theory. These examples illustrate the usefulness of combining observation and experiment with analysis and modeling using concepts and methods from complex adaptive systems theory.

Adaptive Complex Systems

The Newtonian "clockwork universe" model of physical reality was based upon idealizations derived from observations of the motions of isolated single objects, the ballistic interactions between two (or a few) objects and the mechanical properties of simple machines, such as the lever or pulley. From these, Newton discovered his three laws of motion, leading to a deterministic world view in which the future follows inexorably and predictably from any given set of initial conditions. Most importantly, Newton based his idea upon the behavior of inanimate matter—matter that was only capable of reaction, never action. Such matter could react to its environment but could not, freely and of its own accord, initiate action upon its environment.

Physicists may have created theories and understanding, but it was engineers who first cleared the path for them. Engineers built the first simple machines and structures upon which Newton and other early physicists based their theories. In the eighteenth century, they began to build steam engines, paving the way for a paradigm shift toward stochasticity. Heat engines involve interactions between vast numbers of entities forming gases and fluids under extreme conditions. Their study forced the acceptance of new concepts and laws, such as turbulence and the laws of thermodynamics. These new phenomena and their laws were the earliest examples of emergence—examples of wholes that are not merely sums of their parts. Concepts such as temperature and pressure apply to large collections of particles but not to individual particles. Their understanding required the introduction of ideas, such as randomness, probability, statistics, noise and heat, and required that physics move beyond the traditional deterministic world view.

The formal study of emergence, however, did not begin until the twentieth century and mostly in the early 1980s as a result of the interplay between mathematics, physics and computer science. Indeed, the study of emergence and complex systems would be almost impossible if not for the examples provided by computer simulations. Of course, the history of these ideas might have been very different if only physicists had started with biology rather than engineering. Biologists had not only been studying complex systems—that is, systems that not only interact with their environment but require such interaction for their survival—but had been studying complex adaptive systems, or agents. Unlike inanimate matter, which can only *react* to their environment, agents have the ability to *initiate* actions upon their environment. Physicists, unfortunately, were influenced by the idea of reductionism, that the search for understanding should lead downward toward smaller and smaller collections of entities and ultimately to the fundamental constituents of all matter. From knowledge of the behavior of these fundamental atoms or particles, one could derive the universal laws governing all matter and, from these, predict everything above. Physicists avoided biology precisely because it was too complex, too messy.

The famed biophysicist Robert Rosen (1987) wrote:

> the basis on which theoretical physics has developed for the past three centuries is, *in several crucial respects*, too narrow and that, far from being universal, the conceptual foundation of what we presently call theoretical physics is still very special; indeed, far too much to accommodate organic phenomena (and much else besides). That is, I will argue that it is physics, and not biology, which is special; that, far from contemporary physics swallowing biology as the reductionists believe, biology forces physics to transform itself, perhaps ultimately out of all present recognition.
>
> (315, emphasis in original)

Rosen's pessimism arises due to the process nature of biological phenomena and the presence of emergence, features that were mostly ignored by physicists until recent times. Whitehead emphasized the importance of the concept of process in understanding biological phenomena in his Process Theory, described as a theory of organisms (Whitehead 1978). Mostly ignored by physics, it was ahead of its time in giving importance to the role of information in the determination of events in the physical world.

Although the study of emergence is still in its infancy, several key aspects have been discovered (Cohen and Stewart 1994; Lumsden,

Brandts and Trainor 1997; Laughlin 2005). Most books on emergence will mention social insect colonies, the prototypical examples of complex adaptive systems known as collective intelligence. The manifestation of complex adaptive behaviors at the colony level, none of which are able to be expressed by the individual agents that form the colony, provides one of the most striking and widely studied examples of emergence in the natural world.

Several important features of the complex dynamics of collective intelligence (Sulis 1997, 1999) have been identified:

a) *Self Organization* (Bonabeau et al. 1997; Camazine et al. 2001) is the idea that the stable behavior of a complex system arises from positive and negative feedback and the amplification of fluctuations in the absence of leaders, blueprints, templates or recipes.
b) Stochastic determinism, the determination of a property through stochastic processes, underlies mass action. Wilson (1971) described this in *Eciton burchelli* "As workers stream outward carrying eggs, larvae, and pupae in their mandibles, other workers are busy carrying them back again. Still other workers run back and forth carrying nothing. Individuals are guided by the odor trail, if one exists, and each inspects the nest site on its own. There is no sign of decision-making at a higher level. On the contrary, the choice of nest site is decided by a sort of plebiscite, in which the will of the majority of workers finally comes to prevail by virtue of their superior combined effort."
c) Interactive determinism is the determination of a property of a system as a result of interactions occurring among the constituent components of the system (Sulis 1995b) such as occurs in task allocation in *Pogonomyrmex barbatus*.
d) Nonrepresentational contextual dependence refers to the fact that knowledge within a collective intelligence is nonrepresentational. The environment carries the information that a collective intelligence requires, and this information is most often expressed either as pheromones or as stigmergic artifacts. Pheromone responses are often highly tuned. The same pheromone, for example, results in the rapid assembly of workers of *Acanthomyops claviger*, while in *Lasius alienus*, workers scatter widely (Wilson 1971).

e) Nondispersive temporal evolution refers to the fact that the probability measures that describe the possible behaviors arising from exposure to environmental contexts do not disperse over time. Colonies, for example, tend to generate similar task distributions in similar environments in spite of intervening experience.

f) Phase transitions, critical, and control parameters describe situations in which a system is able to exhibit a range of different patterns of behavior that correlate with the values of some variable parameter, a control parameter, and which are stable over some range of this parameter. This is in analogy to the phases of matter, solid, liquid, gas, that are stable over a range of the control parameter, temperature. The critical parameter describes the phase itself. For example, in an *Eciton burchelli* colony, the number of workers serves as a control parameter for the distinct phases of collective motor behavior, from endless milling to ecologically salient foraging.

g) Broken ergodicity, a term coined by Palmer (1982), is a typical feature of complex systems in which the dynamics of the system are frustrated and certain regions of the phase space are avoided. This feature is also expected due to coupling to environmental contexts. One consequence is that averages lose meaning and the classical statistical approaches to modeling, such as through statistical mechanics, break down and lose applicability.

h) Broken symmetry is closely related to broken ergodicity and refers to situations in which the dynamical symmetries observed in the behavior of individual agents of the collective are not preserved in the collective, complicating theoretical analysis. This symmetry breaking often occurs through the amplification of fluctuations. For example, given a choice of two equal paths from colony to food source, the majority of workers will, over time, tend to utilize just one of the paths, and this occurs through amplification of fluctuations of pheromone levels on the paths. Millonas (1993) studied this using a statistical mechanical model which showed just such feedback amplification of the pheromone signals. Some recent work (L'Anson et al. 2016) examined symmetry breaking in *Monomorium pharaonis*, a mass recruiting ant. They showed that when a colony was presented with a choice of two paths, one leading to a high quality food and the other to a lower quality food (in equal quantities), the symmetry in traffic along the paths broke, with the greater number of ants using the path to the higher quality food. When the colony was presented with equal quantities of food of identical quality, symmetry breaking still occurred but only when the food was of low quality. As the quality of the food increased the degree of symmetry declined until it disappeared for the highest quality food. They suggested that Weber's Law, which states that the perceived difference between two stimuli depends on the proportional size of the two stimuli may explain this. When the food quality is highest, large numbers of ants appear along both paths, so that the difference in the quantity of pheromone is proportionately small. When food quality is low, far fewer ants lie along each path, so that any difference in the amount of pheromone between the two paths appears proportionately greater. This adds a subtlety to the pheromone hypothesis, suggesting that perceived rather than absolutely differences influence subsequent recruitment of ants to a path.

i) Pattern isolation and reconfiguration refers to the appearance of dynamical regularities among the dynamical transients exhibited by a system such that these transients can be identified as entities or as states of entities in their own right, having their own temporal evolution and patterns of action and interaction. The original description of the system goes over to a new description in terms of these new entities and their dynamics. Such pattern isolation and reconfiguration is in general, non-generic and dependent upon initial conditions and context. Different descriptions and criteria are required for colony level behavior compared to that of individual workers, and these are derived through pattern isolation and reconfiguration (Sulis 2002).

j) Salience refers to the identification of dynamical stimuli that are capable of influencing the dynamical behavior of a system in a meaningful and consistent manner (Sulis 2002) such as occurs in TIGoRS. Salient stimuli produce dynamically robust and stable effects. Conversely, irrelevance (Laughlin 2005) refers to the situation in which specific features of the dynamical behavior of a system at one level, say for example the functional form of a phase transition curve, do not depend in any meaningful manner upon knowledge of the dynamical behavior at lower levels, such as the specific nature of microscopic interactions. Saliency and irrelevance play opposite roles in understanding the relationships between the dynamics of individuals and the dynamics of the collective. Salience can be observed in the differential responses of different species to the same pheromone. For example, both *Acanthomyops claviger* and *Lasius alienus* utilize undecane as an alarm trigger, but in response to its release, *A. claviger* workers aggregate in a truculent manner while workers of *L. alienus* disperse (Wilson 1971, 237). On the other hand, irrelevance underlies the ability of researchers to examine behaviors such as nest selection in laboratory as opposed to naturalistic settings (Mallon, Pratt and Franks 2001).

k) Compatibility and the Mutual Agreement Principle refers to the notion that interactions between the individuals of a collective are not always random but frequently involve a choice to interact or not which depends upon extrinsic factors salient to the individuals and an interaction does not occur unless both parties agree (Trofimova 2002). This may play a role in task selection. By contrast, interactions during foraging appear to be random.

(Sulis 2009, 47–48)

Decision-Making: Rational, Non-Rational and Irrational

The study of human thought and decision-making is ancient, going back at least to the time of Aristotle. He is credited with being the first to explicitly describe the principles of logic. Logic is a particular form of thinking that starts with statements known to be true and proceeds to derive new statements, previously unknown, but whose truth can be guaranteed so long as each successive statement is derived from previous statements according to the rules of logic.

Logic, however, does not necessarily inform as to which statements are true, especially when they reference some aspect of the natural world. Moreover, the natural, and especially the economic and political worlds, frequently present us with several choices, different paths of reasoning leading to different outcomes. Logic alone does not specify which path to follow. Even in logic *per se*, a given set of statements can give rise to multiple chains of deduction, but which chain is important depends upon non-logical considerations.

Two such considerations have become important over time. The first comes from economics, which introduced the concept of utility. Utility has no formal definition. It is an abstract idea that captures the value, usefulness or importance of discrete options to an individual. Economics posits that each individual assigns a utility to each possible option from which to make a choice and, moreover, posits that each individual will chose in such a manner as to maximize their utility. Utility captures ideas of costs and benefits, suggesting that individuals will attempt to maximize benefits (profits) over costs. A decision-making strategy that enables the individual to consistently maximize their utility is said to be rational.

The second consideration comes from evolutionary biology. This is the concept of fitness. As for utility, fitness does not have a specific formal definition. There are many kinds of fitness: metabolic fitness, reproductive fitness, mating fitness, foraging fitness, defensive fitness and so on. Regardless of the specifics, a fundamental idea of biological decision-making is that individual organisms will act to maximize their fitness. An organism acts rationally if it possesses a strategy that enables it to consistently maximize its fitness. As an example, one feature of rationality is transitivity—if a subject prefers option A over option B, and option B over option C, then they will prefer option A over option C.

Both utility and fitness require that the individual possesses complete knowledge of all possible options, their outcomes, their possible costs and benefits. This is an assumption that works when building formal theories and models, and is particularly useful for mathematical modeling, which is always more difficult whenever restrictions must be made to the possible cases to be considered. However, in the real world, individuals do not have such knowledge, either in principle or in practice.

Acceptance of these limitations was remarkably late in coming (Newell and Simon 1972) as was the introduction of knowledge from psychology into economic theory. Simon introduced the concept of bounded rationality to describe decision-making under conditions of limited information. The term non-rationality might be used to describe those forms of decision-making that occur in the presence of limited information and that lead to locally optimal outcomes. Such a notion has a counterpart in the theory of local minima and fitness landscapes in complex systems theory (Cohen and Stewart 1994). There, a physical system attempts to minimize its energy, but if the energy landscape possesses multiple local minima, it may get stuck in one of these and be unable to find the absolute minimum. It is under such a circumstance that noise becomes of value, as it may enable the system to leave one local minimum and discover another local minimum that is lower in absolute value than that in which it had previously been. In the presence of limited information, some features of rationality break down. For example, if only allowed to make pair-wise comparisons, a subject might prefer a chocolate over potato chips, and potato chips over a mango, yet prefer a mango over chocolate (author's experience).

Generally, all forms of non-rational decision-making are termed irrational (Sutherland 1992). This seems to cast too wide a net since the forms of decision-making described above do still follow the goal of optimizing something, and do achieve that goal, at least in a local sense. In the absence of complete information, it is not possible *a priori* to know which local extremum is in fact the absolute extremum, but this is not for a lack of trying. Psychiatry generally judges impairments of thinking based on the concept of reality testing. If an individual demonstrates an inability to correctly obtain information about their circumstances and to interpret that information correctly, and then to adopt strategies of thinking that consistently lead to locally sub-optimal or even harmful choices, then they are viewed as having a thought disorder. The use of the term irrational would seem better spent on those decision-making strategies that consistently lead to locally sub-optimal or harmful outcomes. Nevertheless, common parlance will be followed here, and the term irrational will be used to describe all forms of decision-making that are not rational.

Decision-making also includes a component of probabilistic processing, a feature that was considered to be an essential aspect of intelligence and an orientation-related trait of temperament (Trofimova 2019). Irrational decision strategies frequently involve heuristics, strategies that can be effective for certain situations but that may break down and become ineffective in other situations. Several such heuristics have been identified

(Newell and Simon 1972; Tversky 1972; Tversky and Kahneman 1973) and studied in the context of social insect colonies and collective intelligence. These include a) *satisficing* (the first which is good enough); b) *elimination by aspects* (attributes are ranked, the alternatives are ranked by the first ranked attribute and all lower ranking alternatives are eliminated, then repeated for the subsequent attributes in rank order); c) *the lexicographic heuristic* (attributes are ranked, each alternative is ranked for each attribute, the highest ranked for the highest attribute are selected, then if there are ties the procedure is repeated for the next ranked attribute, etc.); d) *the equal weight heuristic* (no ranking of attributes, each attribute of each alternative is scored and multiplied by the same weight, the subscores for each alternative are then pooled to give each a grand total); and e) *the weighted additive strategy* (each attribute of each alternative is given a score according to its importance, and individual choices are ranked according to their total score). The weighted additive strategy is the most thorough but also the most computationally expensive.

Decision-Making by Social Insect Colonies

Franks et al. (2003), in their study of nest selection in *Leptothorax albipennis*, showed a) the ants were fairly consistent in their preferences; b) the ants appeared to rank different attributes, with light level ranking higher than cavity height and cavity height ranking higher than entrance size; c) the preferences appeared to exhibit transitivity; and d) the ants appeared to weight the different attributes, for example, preferring bright, thick, narrow over dark, thin, wide. They concluded that the colony was utilizing the most computationally expensive and time-consuming strategy, the weighted additive strategy. This shows remarkable sophistication in their decision-making.

Edwards and Pratt (2009) examined the decision-making of colonies of *Temnothorax curvispinosus* for evidence of irrational decision-making. Specifically, they looked for evidence of the *decoy effect*. Subjects, when presented with two alternatives, neither of which is clearly superior, generally choose randomly. However, when a decoy option is present that is asymmetrically dominated—meaning that it is inferior to (dominated by) one option but not to the other—then the subject will show a preference for the dominating option. This violates the principle of regularity, which asserts that a preference should not change merely through the introduction of additional (non-preferred) options (Edwards and Pratt 2009; Sasaki and Pratt 2011). Edwards and Pratt presented colonies of *Temnothorax curvispinosus* with two nest options: A (low light, mid-sized entrance) and B (mid-level light, small entrance). Two decoys were also established: DA (low light, large entrance) and DB (bright light, small entrance). When the colonies were presented with a choice between A and B, no preference for either option occurred. When presented with either decoy, no preference for the dominating option occurred. This showed that colonies behaved in a rational manner, or at least did not display irrationality in the form of the decoy effect, or violations of regularity.

Sasaki and Pratt (2011) examined the decision-making of individual workers and compared this against that of the colony as a whole. They subjected colonies of *Temnothorax rugatulus* to two alternative nest sites constructed with attributes that forced a trade-off decision to be made. Nest site A had a small entrance (preferred) but was well lit (non-preferred). Nest site B had a large entrance (not-preferred) but was dark (preferred). The choice was identified as being the nest to which either the colony or individual workers gathered the greater number of brood. When presented with these alternatives alone, colonies and individual workers chose either site equally. Next, two decoy sites were created. DA had an entrance identical to A but was more brightly lit. DB was lit similarly to B but had a larger entrance. In terms of preference, the decoys were asymmetrically dominated, DA by A (but not by B) and DB by B (but not by A). Individual workers were next tested separately. First, they were exposed to one decoy alone and observed to be certain that they actually explored this site. Then sites A and B were introduced and their decision identified as the site to which they moved a collection of brood. In neither case did the worker choose the decoy. Following exposure to DA, the majority of workers chose site A. Following exposure to DB, the majority of workers chose B. Thus the workers appeared to manifest the decoy effect.

The colonies were then tested with the decoy. In this case, the decoy was presented first and the colony was forced to emigrate to it. Once there, the alternatives A and B were presented. The decoy had to be damaged to force emigration, following which the colonies generally chose either site A or B. Interestingly, the preference was slightly and non-significantly biased but in a trend opposite to that shown by the individual workers, that is, for site B following DA and site A following DB. This showed that, contrary to common opinion, the collective decision-making of the group compensated for the non-rational decision-making of its constituent members. Group rationality won out over individual irrationality.

Several early papers showed that individual ants appeared to be capable of making comparison judgments (see Sulis 2009). Robinson et al. (2009), however, showed that the behavior of individual ants, when presented with good and poor site alternatives, was not consistent with the use of a comparison strategy. They presented colonies of *Temnothorax albipennis* with two nest alternatives, a near poor nest and a far good nest. As a control, they presented the same colonies with near and far nests of equal, good quality. In this case, the vast majority of the colonies (93%) chose the near site. In the test situation, 4/9 colonies chose the far, good site, 3/9 chose the near, poor site and 2/9 split between them. This showed that an active decision was taken by the colony. When the behavior of individual workers was examined, it was found that workers that first visited the near, poor site made frequent emigrations and 44% went on to visit the far good site. However, those workers that visited the far, good site first were much less inclined to emigrate and only 3% visited the near, poor site. It was clear that the individual ants were not making comparisons prior to deciding in which site to remain.

Robinson, Feinerman and Franks (2014) tested whether at the colony level, comparisons or individual thresholds matter most. They did this by presenting *Temnothorax albipennis* colonies with a choice between two nests—one good, one poor. Individual workers were RFID tagged and doors were placed at the entrance to each site, which could be remotely opened or closed by computer. Two experimental conditions were studied. In the first condition (control), ants were allowed to visit either nest site, which permitted comparisons to be made. In the second condition, once an ant had visited one site, it was barred from visiting the other site, the door closing if it tried to enter the other site. The same colonies were tested under both experimental conditions, with a sufficient time delay to eliminate any learning that might have taken place. Remarkably, the colonies behaved almost the same in both conditions in terms of the proportion of times that the good nest was selected and in the time taken to arrive at the decision.

If the collective decision depended upon the ability of the individual ants to make comparisons between the alternatives, then the performance of the colonies in the no-comparison group should have declined. This was not the case. This suggested that individual ants were more likely using some form of threshold rule. This could also be observed in the behavior of the individual ants. The ants that were able to visit the good site first showed fewer emigrations from that site, and much fewer visits to the region near the poor site. On the other hand, those ants that chose the poor site made frequent emigrations from that site and made repeated visits to the region near the good site. This would be expected if a threshold was used since exposure to the site that did not exceed the threshold would leave the ant free to continue exploring for better sites. One should note that distance to the sites plays a role in the effectiveness of the choice because, when the site alternatives are far from the home nest, the colonies choose the good site, whereas when the site alternatives are nearby to the home nest, split decisions become more prevalent.

A useful window into decision-making strategies is to examine the relationship between different parameters for the decision process. The most common are parameters such as time, accuracy and resource use (such as space, energy). Another parameter is cohesion, defined as the degree to which the group acts as a single entity. Franks et al. (2013) studied speed-cohesion tradeoffs in *Temnothorax albipennis* and were the first to report their existence. In this study, accuracy was held constant but the time urgency varied. In conditions of time pressure, colonies made decisions at the expense of group cohesion, whereas when the decision could be made slowly, group cohesion could be maintained.

The choice of a decision strategy may depend upon the costs associated with implementing the strategy and the value of the outcome. For example, in conditions in which time and energetic resources are not significant factors, so that search and sampling costs are low, more detailed and accurate strategies may be implemented. This is particularly important when the implications of the outcome for the survival of the searcher are high, such as when selecting a home range. Clearly choosing a site with a rich supply of food and water compared to one with minimal such resources is critically important. There are situations, on the other hand, where costs are high but being able to select the optimal choice is less imperative. This might occur when foraging, or when choosing a mate or a specific nest site.

In such a case, a "good enough" strategy might suffice. A simple example of such a strategy is sequential search with threshold, in which an individual searches until a choice is encountered that meets or exceeds a fixed threshold, at which point the decision is made regardless of whether or not this choice is optimal. Several examples of these strategies have been observed in nature (Robinson et al. 2011). Thus social insect colonies appear capable of utilizing a number of different search and decision-making strategies depending upon the local conditions present in the environment during the time that the decision is carried out.

Much of the previous research has used the same basic strategy for testing—expose colonies and/or individual workers to fixed choices of possible nest sites. This leaves open the question of whether the strategies employed by either the workers of the colonies are fixed, or whether they are capable of modification as a result of experience. More recent studies have focused upon the role that experience and learning might play in decision-making. Stroeymeyt et al. (2011), following upon earlier research, carried out series of experiments in which colonies of *Temnothorax albipennis* were given a choice between a mediocre or a poor nest. If the colonies had never been exposed previously to the mediocre nest so that the exposure to both nests was novel, then they universally chose the mediocre nest over the poor nest. If, however, the colony was exposed to the mediocre site for 6 days and, upon forced emigration, was made to choose between the same mediocre nest and a poor nest, a substantial fraction (25%) of colonies chose the poor nest. In a second series of experiments, colonies were raised in either a mediocre or a good nest, and then exposed to a new but mediocre nest for 6 days. Following that, another mediocre nest was introduced and emigration was forced. The colonies raised in the mediocre nest showed no preference to either of the new mediocre nests, and choose between them randomly. Colonies raised in the good nest avoided the familiar mediocre nest and chose the unfamiliar nest instead. Interestingly, the colonies raised in the mediocre nest were more active with more spontaneous exploration compared to those raised in the good nest (this observation was reproduced in Doran et al. 2013). This suggests that prior experience, whether in the nest itself or of nearby nests prior to emigration, has an influence on the subsequent decision-making of the colony.

The decision-making here appears to be irrational. Previously, though, it was suggested that collective decision-making provided some protection against irrationality. However, in that previous work, the colonies had more or less similar histories vis-à-vis nest sites, and the decision-making involved a pair of unfamiliar choices. Here the colonies experienced different histories, and some of the choices were familiar to them. This suggests that a form of learning occurs, which results in irrational decision-making. This appeared to be a colony-level effect as the situation was simulated using a Markov model in which the individual workers used fixed acceptance thresholds that were heterogeneously distributed. The resulting distribution of active scouts was determined by the quality of the original home nest, with lower quality nests encouraging more workers to scout for new sites, thus changing the distribution of the pool of scouts. This in turn affected the outcome at the colony level.

Healy and Pratt (2008) showed that colonies of *Temnothorax curvispinosus*, when raised in a good nest, were more willing to accept a move to a mediocre nest compared to those raised in a poor nest. They suggested that this might be due to the greater perceived loss of quality from a good nest which led to a greater sense of urgency among the workers, thus leading to an earlier decision of acceptance of even a mediocre site.

Sasaki and Pratt (2013) also explored the role of experience on site selection. Their arrangement was rather ingenious. First they exposed the colonies to a pair of sites that differed in entrance size and light with one site small and bright, the other large and dark, creating a tradeoff situation. The colonies were then exposed over four repetitions to either a standard nest or a nest in which just one attribute (either entrance size or light level) was varied to create a poor site differing in only one attribute. At the end of each trial, the colonies all chose the standard nest so that the initial nest site remained the same for each trial. At the end, the colonies were presented with the original pair of nest sites to consider. There was a systematic shift in preference biased along the single modified attribute. Of the twenty-six colonies given the entrance treatment, ten chose the entrance prior to treatment, seventeen afterwards. Of the twenty-eight colonies given the light treatment, sixteen chose light prior to while nineteen chose light afterwards. Prior experience with an attribute thus seemed to sensitize the colony to prioritize this attribute in its decision-making.

Experience may expedite decision-making as well. Stroeymeyt, Franks and Giurfa (2011) showed that if some scouts are exposed to a good nest option prior to emigration being initiated, then when emigration does occur they are able to find this good nest site more quickly and provide a greater share of recruitment and transport compared to workers naïve to this good option. Thus, there are situations in which prior experience may enable certain workers to exert greater influence over the colony's decision-making process and thus its ultimate outcome. This is important because it suggests that collective colonies are able to exploit different strategies under different circumstances and thus improve their overall success across a variety of conditions.

O'Shea-Wheller et al. (2017) further studied individual assessments by workers. In particular, they sought evidence concerning the acceptance thresholds of *Temnothorax albipennis* workers. To do so, they selected individual workers from a colony and placed them within each of three nests: poor, good and excellent. Some workers were then exposed to them in increasing rank order, others in the reverse order. They noted that the duration that a worker spent in a nest varied directly with nest quality. Moreover, there appeared to be a learning aspect because, if the poor nest was presented first, the durations progressively lengthened, but if the excellent nest was presented first, then the difference between durations in the poor and good nests became essentially identical. Furthermore, the individual durations appeared to be non-normally distributed across several orders of magnitude, indicative of considerable heterogeneity in acceptance thresholds. Interestingly, the durations for individual workers still followed the average pattern. Markov simulations were then carried out under assumptions of heterogeneity and homogeneity. The assumption of heterogeneity appeared to confer a speed advantage to the simulated colony even though a quorum was reached in both cases. If two sites were offered, each having different qualities below the acceptance threshold, then those colonies with the heterogeneous condition produced more accurate choices. The homogeneous condition resulted in more optimal choices when the excellent site was close to or above the acceptance threshold.

Franks et al. (2015) further explored quorum sensing in varying environments. In many situations a choice must be made when information about the various options is noisy or inconsistent. For example, one wants to see a movie and, before choosing, refers to online reviews. Ten reviewers rate the film as excellent whereas another ten rate it as poor. Does this mean that the film is simply average? Perhaps the film is offensive to a certain segment of the population, in which case the potential viewer faces some risk in choosing to see it, and disappointment if they do not. The question is whether social insect colonies that base their decisions on quorum thresholds might be more adept at making decisions in the face of such varying information.

In their experiment, colonies were forced to choose between an average nest and a nest that varied between good and poor. The latter was achieved by changing the lighting of the nest using a removable filter. Three variation schedules were considered: 75% good and 25% poor, 50% good and 50% poor, or 75% poor and 25% good. Three quarters of the colonies achieved a quorum threshold. Colonies chose the fluctuating nest over the mediocre nest with a probability that varied directly with average quality of the nest: 0.809 (75% good, 25% poor); 0.484 (50% good, 50% poor); 0.327 (25% good, 75% poor).

Robinson, Feinerman and Franks (2012) examined whether the propensity to forage by individual ants was determined by factors intrinsic to the ant itself or by extrinsic factors related to the environment, nest mates or experience. They focused on two factors, corpulence and recent experience. Corpulence had previously been shown to be a factor driving foraging behavior. In an ingenious experiment, they were able to negatively pair corpulence and experience. They tagged individual workers with RFID tags and could then select which ants were allowed to leave the nest to forage based upon their corpulence and their recent experience. They could thus negatively correlate these factors. They found that corpulence remained the major factor driving the propensity to forage so that lean ants tended to forage more often than more corpulent ants, regardless of prior foraging success. Among already lean ants, those who had recent foraging success did tend to forage more often than their less successful counterparts; thus, experience does appear to have some influence over foraging behavior, but only in those ants already disposed to forage.

Stroeymeyt et al. (2014) explored the effect that seasonality has on decision-making. They first induced a colony to be averse to their home nest (dark) by allowing them to familiarize themselves with a bright nest over several days. Then they were forced to emigrate and choose between the familiar nest or an identical unfamiliar nest in one of three conditions: 1) control, in which the familiar nest was picked up, then exactly replaced; 2) exchange, in which the positions of the familiar and unfamiliar nests were exchanged; and 3) removal, in which an identical but clean nest replaced the familiar nest.

In summer, the control colonies preferred the unfamiliar nest, while in winter they preferred the familiar nest. In the exchange group, in both summer and winter, they preferred the unfamiliar nest. In the removal condition, neither summer nor winter colonies showed any significant preference. This suggested that summer colonies were influenced by factors associated with the nest itself, and indeed the loss of this influence under the removal condition suggested the presence of some pheromone, local to the familiar nest, that influenced the aversion response. On the other hand, winter colonies appeared to be influenced more so by positional factors, choosing whichever nest occupied the same position as the original familiar nest. Thus, dispositional factors appeared to be involved, which altered the collective decision-making of the colony depending upon the season.

The Utility of Complex Systems Methods

The process of experimentation and theory building in the physical sciences has been based on three central goals: 1) a search for generic properties observable across many classes of phenomena, 2) a search for quantitative relationships among such properties in both isolated entities and among entities in interaction with one another and 3) a search for general or universal principles underlying these quantitative relationships. Generic properties that have been discovered include mass, charge, energy, parity, polarization, temperature, pressure, volume, density, specific heat and so on. Quantitative relationships include phase diagrams, the distribution of black body radiation and laws of reflection and refraction, among others. General principles include the laws of conservation of momentum and energy, the second law of thermodynamics, the principle of least action and the principle of least time.

The success of the physical sciences is due in large measure to the fact that the entities that they study are inanimate. They are not agents, as are all biological entities. They react but do not act. Such systems can generally be studied in isolation from their environment, which is mostly treated as a heat source or sink. They can easily be reproduced, as different copies possessing the same set of properties will generally behave in exactly the same manner. Any variations can be attributed to noise and dismissed.

The assumptions that have enabled the physical sciences to progress do not hold in either biology or psychology. Different individuals are not merely Gaussian variations of a single archetypal entity. The study of individual differences (Trofimova 2016a) has revealed systematic differences between individuals that range from the physiological (hepatic isoenzymes) and neurobiological (temperament) to the psychological (personality). These differences have a significant impact in medicine, where the search for individualized medicine is growing. One reason for the replication crisis in psychology may be the failure to take individual psychological differences (temperament and personality) into account when designing studies and analyzing data. These systematic differences are simply treated as noisy variation around some mean. This is false, and it falls upon the researcher to demonstrate that such variation has no influence over the outcome.

Moreover, outside of psychophysics, theory building in psychology tends to be based upon the analysis of correlations, more often called the analysis of variance just to confuse the matter. The most prominent methods for analyzing such correlations are factor analysis and its variants, and structural equation modeling. Such methods are ill suited to the study of complex systems such as occur in psychology (Sulis 2017). The fundamental assumptions underlying those methods do not hold in general for complex adaptive systems, which involve large numbers of heterogeneous agents interacting with one another across multiple spatio-temporal scales, both top-down and bottom-up, interacting with an equally complex environment involving nonlinear dynamics and intrinsic randomness. Variation is a fundamental expression of the internal dynamics of complex systems and not simply a reflection of error or independent variability. Factor analysis and structural equation modeling seek to eliminate variance, subsuming it into various "factors," whereas in complex systems theory the analysis of the nature and form of variance leads to insights into the nature of the underlying dynamics.

Over the past thirty years, a host of sophisticated mathematical tools have been developed to analyze variation in complex systems. These include fluctuation spectra, entropy spectra, information spectra, spectral analysis, identification of power law relationships and time series analysis, to mention a few (Sulis 2017). The study of fluctuations has proven to be particularly fruitful as has the discovery of universality, which has demonstrated that certain quantitative relationships retain a fixed form across multiple complex systems. Universality has been identified in phase transitions and in complex systems exhibiting power law fluctuations.

The trend toward "Big Data" as a solution to these problems is particularly troubling. The mere accumulation of ever-increasing amounts of data in the absence of a concept-driven approach to their selection and analysis is unlikely to yield much of depth. Tools such as factor analysis and structural equation modeling allow virtually any data as inputs and are guaranteed to yield results. In the absence of controlled experimentation to examine falsifiable predictions, the theories so obtained are of limited value and may even be misleading. At best, such techniques might lead to useful organizational depictions of data but they do not substitute for formal theory.

The study of collective intelligence, particularly the dynamics of the social insects, provides many examples illustrating the power of complex systems methods. Here there has been a very fruitful interplay between observation and experiment, followed by simulations to test hypotheses, often using parameter values derived directly from observations of actual colonies and workers, and a theory-driven analysis of behavioral statistics. To illustrate this interplay, two examples are presented. First, the nature of variability in nest emigrations is analyzed from the perspective of power law fluctuations. Second, an example of universality is given involving the relationship between event duration and activity speed.

The Use of Complex Systems Methods: Nest Emigrations

The most progress to date in applying complex systems methods to the study of collective intelligence has been made by Nigel Franks and his collaborators. In two papers they studied dynamical features of emigrations from the nest (Richardson et al. 2010; Richardson et al. 2011). One of the most fundamental divisions of labor is between those workers that remain in the nest and those workers that leave the nest to forage, search for new nest sites or provide defense. Workers that have left the nest face a far greater set of perils than do those within the nest, and the long-term viability and integrity of the colony depend upon effectively balancing between safety and risk. Too much emphasis on safety imperils the food supply, while too much emphasis on risk imperils the workers themselves. Regulation of this division is thus an important task for the colony.

Workers leave and re-enter the nest throughout the day. This is a complex process with many interacting variables, thus general results are difficult to obtain. From a theoretical and modeling standpoint it is easier to study systems in which some resource is being consumed over time, such as in the case of radioactive decay. The problem of nest emigration was converted into a problem of resource decay by the simple, but rather brilliant, expedient of removing every ant that emigrated from the nest. Thus, over time, the number of workers remaining in the nest steadily declined. In the first study (Richardson et al. 2010), several nests were established and the individual workers tagged with RFID devices so that they could be identified. In the control state, an exit was noted only when an ant left the nest for the very first time. In the experimental states, workers, once they had exited the nest, were removed for lengths of time varying from two hours to five days, following which they were returned to their original colony.

If individual ants made their decision to leave the nest at random, independently from whatever other ants were doing, then it would be reasonable to expect that the number of exits over a given time period would follow a Poisson probability distribution. Recall that a Poisson probability distribution is a discrete probability distribution in which the probability of k events occurring in a time interval t, given that they occur at a rate r, is

$$P(k,r,t) = e^{-rt} (rt)^k/k!$$

The presence of interactions between workers, either locally between individual workers or globally between individual workers and some proxy for a collective effect (pheromone density, population density, stigmergic products, etc.), would result in a departure from Poisson statistics. One possibility that these researchers considered was that emigration by individual workers could be triggered by the appearance of record events—that is, events that exceed some previously established limit. The statistics of records has been studied in complex systems theory (Sibani 1993;

Anderson et al. 2004). It has been shown that the number of records (a record is an event that exceeds in magnitude all previously recorded events) follows a Poisson distribution, but in logarithmic time (unlike the usual Poisson distribution, which is in normal time). In other words, the probability of k records occurring in a time interval t is given by

$$P(k,t) = (\ln t)^{(n-1)}/t(n-1)!$$

The waiting time between successive events is exponentially distributed in normal time for the Poisson distribution but exponentially distributed in log time for the record dynamics. Likewise, the average number of events grows linearly in normal time for the Poisson process and linearly in log time for the record dynamics. A null model was simulated in which exits were modeled as a heterogeneous Poisson process with individual exit rates determined by gaster size (a measure of corpulence). Corpulence has been shown to influence the exit rates of ants (Robinson, Feinerman, and Franks 2012). The model was used to simulate the behavior of each colony, with the exit rates determined by actual measurements of gaster sizes for all of the workers. The model thus provided a reasonable set of null statistics based on the premise of there being no collective effects.

Data for waiting times, average numbers of events and event rate were collected and analyzed. In every case, the resulting distributions were incompatible with the assumption of Poisson dynamics and compatible with the assumption of record dynamics. Moreover, estimates of foraging rates in the non-removal and removal cases showed that the foraging rates decreased in the presence of removal of ants from the colony. This suggests that the colony is able to regulate the exit rate according to the size of its population, thus protecting labor resources against losses to the environment.

The fact that the statistics match those of record dynamics suggests that the decision to leave the nest is influenced by interactions with other ants and by fluctuating record signals. While this does not specify what those interactions might be, it does suggest the presence of long range correlations in ant behavior similar to those that appear in many complex systems.

The authors point to several factors that have been conjectured to influence exit probability: age, caste, genetics, physiological state (corpulence), reproductive state, dominance interactions and previous experience. In this study, they found that corpulence indeed was inversely correlated with exit probability, with most of the exiting ants being the least corpulent. Previous experience was not a factor in general, but did seem to increase the exit probability among the least corpulent ants, pointing to a subtle interaction between physiology and experience.

In the second study (Richardson et al. 2011), the authors further examined some of the factors involved in determining the record dynamics of the exit rates. They took colonies of the ants and examined them under two conditions. In the first case, the brood was removed. In the second case, the brood was left intact but only young (callow) workers were allowed to remain. Previous work (Robinson et al. 2011) had shown that there is a non-random distribution of both brood and workers within the nest. The brood acquires an angular distribution with workers arrayed concentrically around the brood, youngest closest to the brood and oldest toward the periphery. Thus, the presence of the brood appears to provide an organizing factor, while callow workers are less likely to exit and appear to be influenced by the brood.

In the present study, both the control and no-brood colonies showed that the proportion of ants remaining in the nest, relative to the original population size, declined in log-time as a log-Poisson process, while in the callow colonies, this proportion declined in linear time as a simple Poisson process. The no-brood colonies showed a weaker log-Poisson pattern than did the controls. The striking difference between the control and callow colonies showed that the presence of interactions between young, callow, inexperienced workers and older, lean, experienced workers plays an important role in generating the record dynamics. That the no-brood colonies showed behavior that was somewhat interposed between that of the control and callow colonies shows that the presence of the brood is also important for the development of record dynamics. The precise mechanisms underlying these influences are still to be determined, but the use of complex systems dynamics tools and concepts provides a window into more subtle aspects of colony dynamics.

The Use of Complex Systems Methods: Universality

An important concept in the physical sciences is that of universality. The idea arose initially in condensed matter physics, particularly in the study of phase transitions. The two most familiar types of phase transitions, first order (sublimation) and second order (melting), have been supplemented by an ever-increasing catalogue of novel transitions. It has been discovered that for many different types of phase transition, there are universal relationships that hold between certain parameters of the system regardless of the nature of the dynamics underlying the transitional behavior. For example, phases are generally described by an order parameter, a, such as magnetization. The phase transition is associated with some critical parameter, β, such as temperature, and occurs at some critical value of β, say β_c. Nearby this critical value, the order parameter varies as

$$a = a_0 |\beta - \beta_c|^\alpha$$

where the critical exponent α is fixed for all systems exhibiting the specific phase transition irrespective of the specific dynamics giving rise to the transition. Universality is a very powerful phenomenon since it provides positive evidence for situations in which the underlying dynamics of a system may be ignored and only generic features need be considered.

Another example of universality comes from dynamical systems theory. An iterated function system consists of a function, f, defined on some set of points, X. Starting with some point x in X, a trajectory is constructed by successively applying f to the previous point—that is, x, f(x), f(f(x)), f(f(f(x))), … . Iterated function systems may be defined using functions having an independent parameter in their definition, for example, the logistic map, $f(x) = ax(1-x)$. As the parameter a is varied, the resulting trajectories may change form, from fixed point, to periodic, to periodic but with a different period, to chaotic. In particular, as a varies, the periods may change in a specific manner—p, 2p, 4p, 8p, …—called period doubling. Mitchell Feigenbaum (1978) discovered that if the points at which these period doublings occur are placed in order—$a_1, a_2, a_3, \ldots$—then the ratio $|a_{n-1} - a_{n-2}|/|a_n - a_{n-1}|$ tends to a limit as n tends to infinity:

$$\Delta = \lim_{n \to \infty} |a_{n-1} - a_{n-2}|/|a_n - a_{n-1}| \to 4.669201 \ldots$$

This limit holds true for a large class of functions. For example, all functions f that have just a single local maximum (like the logistic map) all yield the same limiting value, which is called the Feigenbaum constant.

Universality has been studied in the context of social insect colonies (Christensen et al. 2014). Activity speed versus activity duration was studied in colonies of *Temnothorax albipennis*. Intuitively, one might expect that the duration of activity would either be independent of speed (if the ants acted at a constant speed) or inversely related (greater speed resulting in less time). Instead they found that speed was directly related to duration. They studied three colonies in two nest sizes and recorded all activity within the nest for 100 minutes at roughly 0.1-second time intervals. Individual ants were tracked using video tracking software and, to reduce errors due to the discrete nature of the sampling procedure, the data were coarse grained corresponding to a sampling duration of 0.8 seconds.

The duration T of an event was measured and the average speed v(t,T) at time t ≤ T was calculated across all events of duration T. The average speed across the event was then calculated by averaging over t for every duration T. The relationship between average speed v(T) and event duration T was found to follow the following rule:

$$v(T) = aT^\beta$$

The value of a appeared to be similar for both large and small nest sizes, but the value of the exponent β was significantly larger for the larger nest (0.60) than for the smaller nest (0.47). Both exponents being less than 1 implies a sub-linear growth relationship.

They then rescaled the results, redefining average local speed in terms of average speed—v(t,T)/v(T)—and local time in terms of event duration—t/T. They then plotted these rescaled local speeds as a function of the rescaled local time. This function begins and ends at 0 speed, climbs and descends rapidly at the end points and is more or less constant throughout the duration of the event. Comparing this function between all colonies and all nest sizes, they discovered that the resulting functions were virtually identical for all conditions. They thus found an apparently universal relationship between event speed and event duration.

To show that the result was non-trivial, they examined a null model constructed by reassigning local speeds among all events of duration T, which effectively eliminates any possible correlations between local speeds, and repeated the calculations. The resulting function was more or less a constant 1 for all times and all durations.

Hunt et al. (2015) extended this work by studying speed–duration relationships among ants moving outside of their nest. They considered two scenarios. In the first, single ants were removed from their colony and permitted to move in an open field for 45 minutes. Their activity was tracked for the duration and then they were removed. In one condition, the ants were introduced successively into the same open field so that any pheromones that might have been excreted remained undisturbed. In the other condition, the open field was thoroughly cleaned to remove any possible pheromones. Compared to event durations within the nest (3.53 sec), durations in the open field were significantly longer, with event durations in the no-cleaning condition being the longest (10.52 sec) and intermediate in the cleaning condition (8.43 sec.). This suggested that subtle socialization influences, mediated presumably by pheromones, resulted in the variations in event durations. The authors suggested that unfamiliarity represented by the cleaning condition resulted in caution and, as a result, shorter activity durations. The average event speed-duration relation was determined and found to follow the same power law as in the previous study of activity, namely, $v(T) = aT^{\beta}$. Interestingly, they found that the parameters varied with different conditions. The values of β were 0.22 (open field, cleaning or no-cleaning), 0.47 (small nest) and 0.60 (large nest). The values of a were 0.12 (small and large nest), 2.45 (cleaning) and 2.82 (no-cleaning). The relationship among the β values suggested that its value was determined by spatial factors, since the main difference between the conditions was the area of the physical space that the ants explored. The a values, on the other hand, did not admit a simple interpretation. The difference between the no-cleaning and cleaning conditions suggested a role for socialization factors, likely mediated by the presence of pheromones.

Modeling Collective Intelligence

Franks and colleagues have been particularly adept at using models in several ways to further their research. One approach has been to verify various hypothetical mechanisms for decision-making. They have made careful, painstaking observations of the behavior of ant colonies by either marking or RFID-tagging all of the workers in a colony and then precisely tracking the behavior of each worker over time. They have also measured the values of various physiological parameters which were thought to play some role in modulating the dynamics. Computer simulations were then developed based on the hypotheses to be tested, and the parameters in these simulations were fitted with the values obtained through experimental observation. The simulations were then run for a time corresponding to that of naturalistic observations, and the statistics obtained from the simulation were compared to those obtained by direct observations. A second use of models is to examine in finer detail the dynamical properties, symmetries, transitional phenomena, attractor types and statistical properties of a system, which might lead to the elucidation of general principles or universal behavior.

Several models of the first type were described in Sulis (2009). Pratt et al. (2005) studied the emigration behavior of *Temnothorax albipennis* through a detailed stochastic agent-based simulation which modeled each stage in the decision-making process of each individual ant when evaluating a site. The simulation parameters were estimated from actual observations of emigrations. The model reproduced many of the features of the observed emigrations. It also predicted the emergence of variation in individual behavior.

In a subsequent paper, Pratt and Sumpter (2006) introduced the Ant House-Hunting Algorithm, an agent-based, stochastic model that represented each individual ant in the colony. The authors measured the assessment of nest quality by the wait time for recruitment. The choice of recruitment (tandem running versus social carrying) was based on a context-dependent quorum threshold. This model qualitatively matched with empirical observations. Marshall, Dornhaus, Franks and Kovacs (2006) showed that this decision process was Pareto optimal since a willingness on the part of individual workers to change their decisions could only improve accuracy at the expense of speed.

Sendova-Franks, Franks and Britton (2002) also developed a model of colony emigration in *Leptothorax albipennis*, this time as a set of coupled ordinary differential equations. Based on empirical observations of emigration, they determined that three main tasks needed to be carried out sequentially in spite of the fact that the stimuli for these three tasks all increase simultaneously. The tasks are nest mate transport, brood sorting and nest building. Their equations described the amount of each task and the number of assigned workers and included thirty-four tunable parameters that were estimated directly from observations. The model reproduced the temporal structure of the observations including the proper sequence of colony-level task switching, which appeared in spite of the fact that the sequence of tasks carried out by individual workers was not specified in advance and could follow any ordering. This is typical of a colony-level emergent phenomenon.

Several models have been developed examining nest selection and the role of quorum thresholds (Sulis 2009). Earlier models assumed that workers used more or less similar thresholds for nest site selection in deciding whether or not to emigrate. Detailed research has shown that individual workers actually differ in their responses to different nest site characteristics. Some workers may refuse to move to a lower value nest site even if no other options are presented to them. Other workers will more readily explore both low- as well as high-value sites. This heterogeneity in acceptance thresholds must therefore be taken into account in models of nest selection. Robinson et al. (2011) examined a Markov chain model of nest selection with acceptance based on individual thresholds. Their model was simple, involving just four states: assessing poor site, assessing good site, committed to poor site, committed to good site. There are three relevant probabilities: p—the average per-visit probability of accepting a poor site; g—the average per-visit probability of accepting a good site; and r—the probability that an ant rediscovers the site it has just been in. From this it is possible to calculate E, the expected time to accept any site:

$$E = 4(1-r) + 2r(p+g) - p - g/2((2r-1)pg + (1-r)(p+g))$$

This served as a proxy for recruitment latencies, which are difficult to calculate formally in a Markov model. The probabilities in the model were derived from studies of actual *Temnothorax albipennis* nests, in which the individual workers were RFID tagged, and their individual characteristics determined from direct observation. The model was simulated repeatedly and data were collected. In one experiment, the two nest alternatives were equidistant from the colony. The observations and the simulation data showed the same patterns for the number of ants staying in a potential nest site versus switching to the other site. The numbers that stayed or switched depended on the quality of the nest site, with little to no switching from the good site. In a second experiment, the two sites were at different distances from the nest, the further site being the good site. Again, the actual colonies and the simulations produced similar results.

It has been suggested that decisions regarding alternatives could be made either by best-of-n comparisons, through selection of recruitment latency, or through sequential search. This study showed that the observed behavior could be reproduced using the simplest "good enough" strategy, namely, sequential search. To further examine this, both colonies and simulations were subjected to three alternatives. They argued that if best-of-n comparison were the mechanism, then the number of sites sampled prior to recruitment should not depend on the quality of the first nest sampled. If recruitment latency were the mechanism, then quality-dependent recruitment latencies should be observed in both two and three alternative situations. However, in both direct observation and in simulation, there are no quality-dependent differences in recruitment latencies. Moreover, in the two alternative spatially distinct situations, a successful choice can be made even when the time taken to reach the good nest is greater than the duration of the greatest recruitment latency, so that such latencies could have no effect on the resulting decision.

The above model allowed for spatial factors. In a subsequent study, Masuda et al. (2015) examined a pair of simplified models (a differential equation model and a related agent-based model) in which spatial factors were removed, only two sites were considered and ants had either high or low thresholds. Two parameters were found to be important: H, the fraction of high threshold ants, and α_s, the rate of switching to the good site. They studied the relationship between speed and accuracy as H varies. For large values of α_s, speed and accuracy are positively correlated, so both increase as H increases. However, as the value of α_s decreases, this correlation turns negative, meaning that there is now a speed–accuracy trade off. They also examined the relationship between speed and cohesion and found evidence for a speed–cohesion tradeoff, exactly as has been observed in actual colonies. This provides additional evidence for the power of the simple sequential search strategy and its associated heterogeneous thresholds.

Dussutour et al. (2009) utilized a stochastic differential equation to study foraging in *Pheidole megacephala*. Many foraging ant species show a limited ability to change their decision regarding which food source to forage from, even when a new, better site is offered. They first studied the behavior of *Pheidole megacephala* colonies directly. The colonies were either allowed continuous access to two identical food sources, one near and one far, or given a varying environment. In the latter, they were allowed access to both sites for one hour, following which access to the near site was blocked. After a second hour, access to the near site was restored. In both conditions, ants preferred to access the nearer nest. This remained true throughout the three hours in the static condition. In the dynamic condition, after the first hour, most ants switched to the far nest. After the second hour, when access to the near nest was restored, 9 of 21 ants switched to the near nest, 6 of 21 remained with the far nest and 6 of 21 accessed either site. However, 30 minutes into this final stage, 16 of 21 preferred the near nest.

The experiment was then simulated using both a deterministic differential equation model and a stochastic version in which the numbers of foraging ants were allowed to fluctuate according to a Gaussian distribution. In the deterministic model, the ants did not switch their preference in the dynamic environment whereas they were able to do so in the stochastic model. This suggested that the ants were able to exploit the presence of noise in the level of foraging activity to enable a more rational decision-making strategy. Such noise-induced transitions have been observed in a variety of complex dynamical systems.

As a final example, consideration is given to emigration in another social insect, the honeybee. Pais et al. (2013) used a dynamical systems framework to study decision-making in house-hunting honeybee swarms. In particular, they focused on the role of cross inhibition in mediating an ability to influence decision-making based on the difference in value and mean value of alternatives. The model consists of a set of coupled stochastic differential equations

$$dy_A = (y_U \gamma_A - y_A(\alpha_A - y_U \rho_A + y_B \sigma_B))dt + fdW$$

$$dy_B = (y_U \gamma_B - y_B(\alpha_B - y_U \rho_B + y_A \sigma_A))dt + gdW$$

where y_A is the proportion of workers committed to selection A, y_B is the proportion of workers committed to selection B, y_U is the proportion of uncommitted workers, $y_U = 1 - y_A - y_B$, α_A is the rate at which workers committed to A abandon their commitment, γ_A is the rate at which uncommitted workers spontaneously commit to and begin recruiting to A, ρ_A is the rate at which workers committed to A recruit uncommitted workers to A, and σ_B is the rate at which workers committed to B induce workers committed to A to un-commit (and vice-versa for the remaining parameters). In the model, they set $\sigma = \sigma_A = \sigma_B$, called the *cross inhibition*. These parameters depend on the values of the two selections, v_A and v_B. The mean value v is defined as $v = (v_A + v_B)/2$, while the value difference Δv is defined as $\Delta v = v_A - v_B$. The variables f, g and dW are the stochastic terms. These will not figure in this discussion.

In the case in which v is large (so high average value of resources) and $(\Delta v)/v$ is small (thus a small difference between alternatives), a technique called singular perturbation analysis shows that there is a separation of timescales, with fast convergence governed by y_U to a one-dimensional decision manifold, followed by slow evolution along this manifold governed by y_A, y_B.

This one-dimensional decision manifold is given by

$$y_A y_B = (2v/\sigma) y_U (1 + y_A)(1 + y_B)/(3 - y_U)$$

It clearly depends on v and σ, while the dynamics on the manifold depends on v, σ and Δv.

They further showed that the dynamics resembles a drift-diffusion model, which is significant because this model represents a statistically optimal tradeoff between speed and accuracy and closely approximates the reaction time and error rate distributions of subjects taking psychological tests. This relatively simple model of collective decision-making thus closely resembles the decision-making of human test subjects.

When the alternatives have the same value ($\Delta v = 0$), the dynamics depends on the degree of cross-inhibition. For low values of cross inhibition, the colony remains deadlocked, choosing equally between the two alternatives. However, when the cross-inhibition reaches a critical value σ^*, the dynamics undergoes a pitchfork bifurcation, meaning that the symmetry between the alternatives is broken and the colony will then preferentially go to one or the other of the alternatives, the choice being made randomly. This critical value depends on the mean value of the alternatives and is given as

$$\sigma^* = 4v^3/(v^2 - 1)^2$$

This is an explicit prediction that can be tested experimentally.

When the alternatives are of low value, the colony remains deadlocked with a large pool of uncommitted workers able to continue to search for alternative resources. Should a higher value alternative be found, the deadlock breaks and the colony shifts to this better choice. This value sensitivity introduces significant subtlety into the decision-making process.

If there is a difference in value between alternatives, the dynamics becomes even more interesting. Repeating the analysis shows that there again exists a pitchfork bifurcation. Prior to the bifurcation in which there is only a single attractor, this attractor favors the higher-value alternative. However, it is possible that the numbers of workers recruited to the higher-value alternative do not reach the quorum threshold level, so a definite decision does not occur. For given values of v and σ, there will be a minimum value of Δv, which ensures that a decision is reached. It turns out that the relationship between v, Δv and σ takes the form

$$(\Delta v)/v = K(\sigma)$$

for some function K. The authors remark that this relationship bears a striking similarity to Weber's Law, which states that the minimal perceptual difference between two stimuli varies linearly as their mean intensity. This relatively simple model predicts a basic psycho-physiological result, without the presence of any conscious agent making the decision. The model exhibits much greater dynamical complexity, but these details suffice to illustrate the usefulness of a dynamical approach to modeling.

Conclusions

Collective intelligence systems provide one of the prototypical examples of adaptive complex systems in which emergent processes figure prominently in their dynamics. They are important for the study of emergence in all of its ramifications, as well as the study of adaptive complex systems generally. The archetypal examples of collective intelligence are provided by social insect colonies, which are capable of decision-making and adaptive behavior that exceeds the capacity of any one of their members, and which are possible in the absence of any central authority.

Collective intelligence systems provide insights into human decision-making, which is also emergent from the activities of billions of neurons, again in the absence of a central authority. They also provide insight into human collectives, whether they be small groups, crowds, mobs, organizations, communities or whole populations. Social psychology takes as its focus these various forms of collective behavior. Traditionally it has relied on observation, some direct experimentation and questionnaire data, and has focused on building qualitative models of observed correlations.

The examples of research into the behavior of social insect colonies presented in this chapter, particularly the study of nest selection by colonies of *Temnothorax albipennis*, illustrate the various ways in which highly detailed observations, analyzed through the lens of concepts derived from the theory of complex systems, and systematically modeled through the use of complex-systems-inspired simulations, rigorously incorporating empirically derived parameters, can produce profound insights into the nature of collective intelligence. It is hoped that social psychology, inspired by the kinds of results described herein, will take up the challenge and begin to incorporate rigorous, painstaking and time-consuming methodologies and the use of analytical tools and models derived from complex systems theory to further research collective behavior among humans. Some first tentative steps toward this are already being taken, such as the Weighted Calculus of Communicating Systems (Tofts 1993), the Process Algebra language (Sulis 2017) and the Functional Differentiation/Fractal Functionality approach (Trofimova 2016b, 2017). Each of these is an attempt to move beyond the standard ordinary differential equation and stochastic differential equation approaches and to incorporate ideas of process with all that entails, front and center.

The study of collective intelligence has afforded entomologists, mathematicians and physicists a wonderful opportunity for collaboration. The examples presented here provide striking evidence of this. The opportunity is ripe for an equally productive interplay among social psychologists, mathematicians and physicists. The language, concepts and methods of complex systems theory can provide a critical bridge linking these disciplines. Time will tell if this proves to be the case.

PART 5

Philosophy of Science and Epistemology

CHAPTER 10

Philosophy of Science, Network Theory and Conceptual Change

Paradigm Shifts as Information Cascades

Patrick Grim, Joshua Kavner, Lloyd Shatkin and Manjari Trivedi

Introduction

The attempt to understand science, its dynamics, and how it changes might call for any of various levels of analysis—and must ultimately include them all. A psychologist might approach the issue with an eye to creativity and conformity. An economist might approach the topic in terms of incentives for research, for innovation or exploitation of existing resources. A sociologist might think of the task as primarily a social study, concentrating on research communities, structures of journal communication and academic procedures for advancement and funding.

Philosophers have typically thought of particular areas of scientific research as characterized by "theoretical frameworks," "disciplinary matrices," "scientific paradigms," or "conceptual schemes" at a particular time, with scientific change to be understood as changes in those conceptual structures. It is presumed that such schemes exist psychologically in some individual head, that they are shared and changed through the social dynamics of science and that change may follow a form of both individual and social incentive. The philosopher's level of analysis, however, is the "theoretical framework," "disciplinary matrix," "scientific paradigm," or "conceptual scheme" itself, envisaged as something like an abstract object. The philosopher's presumption is that at least major aspects of scientific change will be understandable as broadly logical and boundedly rational changes in the scheme itself, though those changes play out in epistemic economics, through psychological mechanisms and in a social dynamic. Under pressure of new evidence, theoretical frameworks and scientific paradigms can be expected to change. The philosopher's goal, at that level of analysis, is to better understand how.

The work we offer here triangulates from familiar work by the two most influential and familiar philosophers of science of the twentieth century: Karl Popper and Thomas S. Kuhn (Popper 1959, 1963; Kuhn 1962, 1969, 1970). If the influence of an academic discipline is measured by the extent to which its concepts are incorporated within the wider culture, twentieth-century philosophy of science can boast of only two such successes. The influence of logical positivism, logical empiricism, Carnap, Hempel, Goodman, Quine and Bayesian epistemology has been largely *intra*-discipline (Carnap 1966, 1969; Hempel 1966; Goodman 1955; Quine 1951, 1953; Bovens and Hartmann 2003). Only two conceptual configurations have crossed disciplines to enter wider scientific discourse and the discourse of society at large. Both of those influential philosophical achievements are theories of scientific change.

Popper (1963) speaks of hypothesis and observation as always presupposing "a frame of reference: a frame of expectations: a frame of theories ... a theoretical framework" (62). Kuhn (1969) is speaking at the same level of analysis when he refers to a "'disciplinary matrix' ... a set of 'shared beliefs, values, instruments, and techniques'" (174). His other term for a "disciplinary matrix," of course, is a "scientific paradigm." Popper and Kuhn clearly agree that to understand the dynamics of science we need to understand change within theoretical frameworks or disciplinary matrices: the structure and change of scientific paradigms.

The basic idea of paradigms has a long and distinguished history. The idea that science and cognition in general operate not in terms of isolated elements but a system is as old as Plato's *logos* in the Theatetus, Aristotle's *scientia* in the *Posterior Analytics*, the Medieval *summa*, and explicit attention to system in Descartes, Malebranche, Spinoza, Newton and Leibniz. The concept continues beyond Kuhn in Imre Lakatos's research programs (Lakatos 1968), Larry Laudan's research traditions (Laudan 1978), Willard van Orman Quine's "webs of belief" (Quine and Ullian 1978) and widespread contemporary references to "conceptual schemes," "conceptual frameworks," and "scientific worldviews."

Despite this long philosophical tradition, thinking in terms of paradigms, theoretical frameworks and conceptual schemes, however, no one in the philosophical tradition has attempted to model a conceptual scheme or track its dynamics. How precisely might one model a paradigm? How might one track, even theoretically, the dynamics of paradigm shift?

Our attempt here is to take some first steps by putting the tools of complex systems and network theory, in particular, to use in philosophy of science. The science of complexity, we argue, carries important philosophical lessons regarding the complexity of science.

Scientific Paradigms: A First Model

How might one model a paradigm? As a first step, consider a set of claims—the claims of a scientific theory, or of linked scientific theories within a discipline. Those claims together compose the theoretical framework or scientific paradigm operative at a particular time. But of course, those parts of a paradigm do not float independently: the claims of such a framework are linked by broadly logical connections. Some claims follow from others. Some are read as evidential instantiations of others. Some are read as theoretical generalizations. It is a set of claims bound by connections of mutual support that constitute a scientific paradigm. It is the intuition that we can model scientific paradigms as networks that guides our work throughout.

We start with a model of mutual support within elements of a paradigm using the simplest possible model: an undirected graph. With even that simple picture, however, we can model two clear aspects of scientific dynamics. Science grows. And science changes.

Consider a set of nodes with no connections. Those are disparate observations, perhaps hypotheses and conjectures, but they have not yet been integrated into a systematic body of theory. As a science develops, those claims become further integrated. They start to form a larger whole—something that begins to deserve the name of science—the conceptual system that constitutes a paradigm. That process of progressive integration, long observed in historical episodes of science, can be modelled by

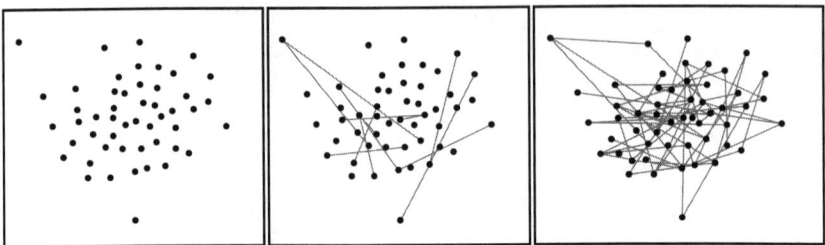

Fig. 10.1. Modeling Progressive Integration within a Network

progressively adding links within our model. As a discipline matures, its integration increases: the network grows new links (figure 10.1).

But of course, there are other aspects of scientific change. Theories not only rise but fall. Paradigms form but are also liable to collapse: the phenomenon of paradigm shift.

Modeling Popperian Falsification

How does science change? On the Popperian picture, science is a matter of conjectures in search of refutations. Targeting advocates of Freud and Marx, Popper argues that finding apparent confirmations or verifications of a set of beliefs is all too easy. With Einstein and the Eddington expeditions as a favored example, Popper argues that the mark of genuine science is not safety in vagueness but risk in precision. The fundamental mechanism of scientific changes is crucial experimentation in which conceptual systems are falsified (Popper 1959, 1963).

In a Popperian model, we let all nodes of our modeled conceptual system start with an "established" value: 1, for convenience. But falsifications happen. For modeling purposes, we suppose falsifications occur at random, somewhere in the conceptual structure. Because a Popperian "theoretical structure" is a structure of linked nodes, those falsifications may well spread. If an observational consequence of a given claim is falsified, it is not merely that claim but any claim that entails it—any higher elements of theory—that are falsified as well. Falsification can be expected to spread through the conceptual structure (figure 10.2).

What can we expect scientific change to look like on the Popperian picture? That is a question within the philosophy of science. A model allows

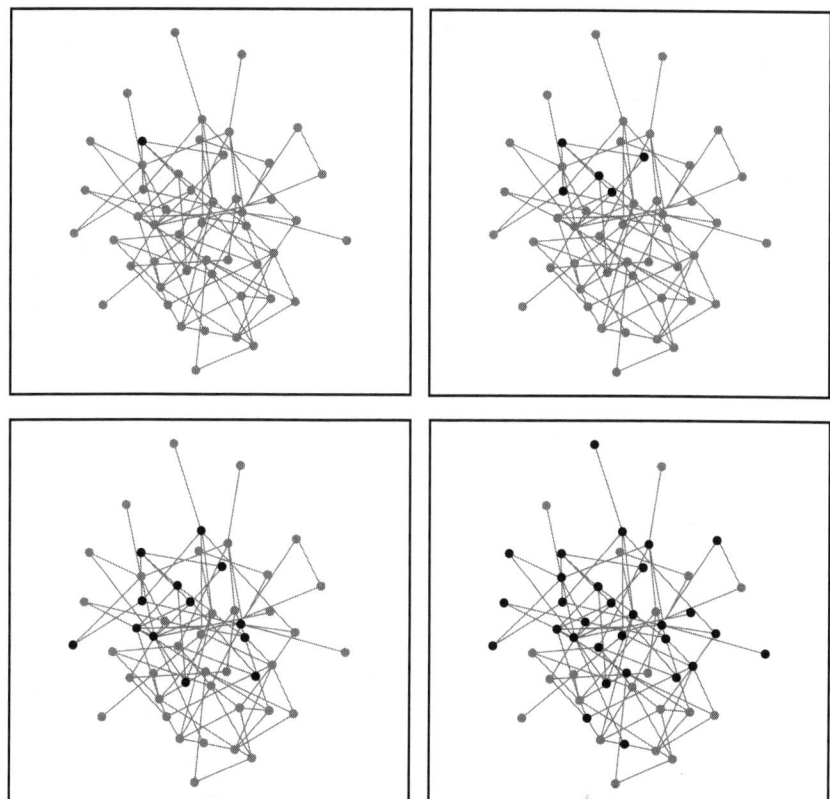

Fig. 10.2. Spreading Falsification within a Popperian Model

us to make it more specific. With a theoretical framework or conceptual system modeled as an undirected network, how much of that network can we expect to be affected by a random falsification? How often and how large can we expect falsification cascades to be?

The basic question is one in philosophy of science. But with a model in hand, it is complex systems, and specifically network theory, that offers us an answer. The sizes of falsifiability cascades in a Popperian network will depend on the connectivity of the network—its characteristic degree or average number of links per node—and will depend on characteristic degree in very interesting ways. We start with data from simulation, turning to the analytic background for explanation.

Beginning with a Popperian network of fifty nodes in which the average degree of our conceptual nodes is less than 1. We consider 1,000 random networks, each with characteristic degree—average node degree—of 0.5. Within each of those networks, we drop a falsification at a random point in the structure. We then track the sizes of "cascades": the number of points out of fifty that must fall by Popperian falsification spreading from that initial spot (figure 10.3).

Falsification cascades on networks with a characteristic degree of 1 or less show something like a power law distribution. That pattern changes dramatically for Popperian networks that have greater integration, marked

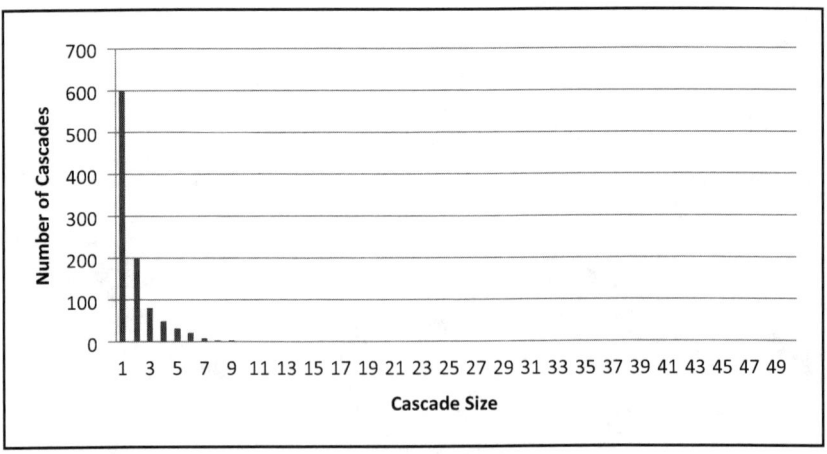

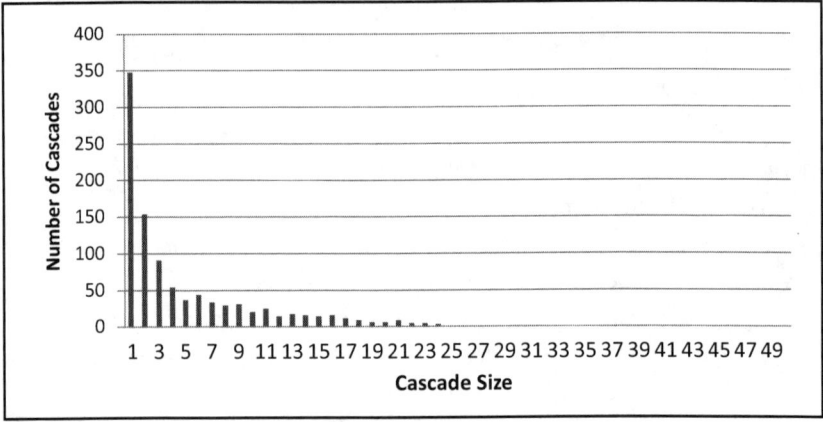

Fig. 10.3. Distribution of Cascade Sizes in Popperian Networks of Characteristic Degree 0.5 (Top) and 1 (Bottom)

Note: The scale on the y-axis is different for each graph.

by higher characteristic degrees. At a characteristic degree of 1.5, far fewer drops are isolated, with a distribution that clearly becomes bimodal. At characteristic degree 2, the pattern is even more noticeable. Here the cascade sizes that are most frequent are cascades of 41 or 42 nodes, with the bimodal distribution clearly dominated by large cascades at the right. At that degree of integration and above, the characteristic result of a single falsification is a widespread cascade throughout a major part of the network (figure 10.4).

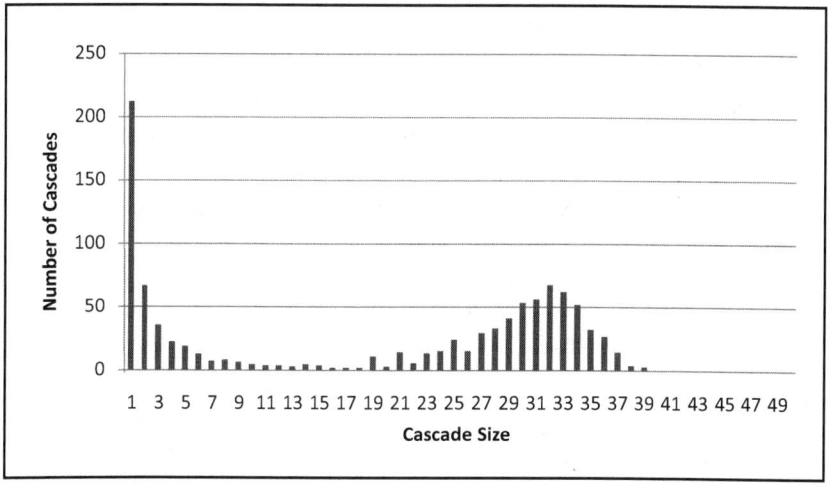

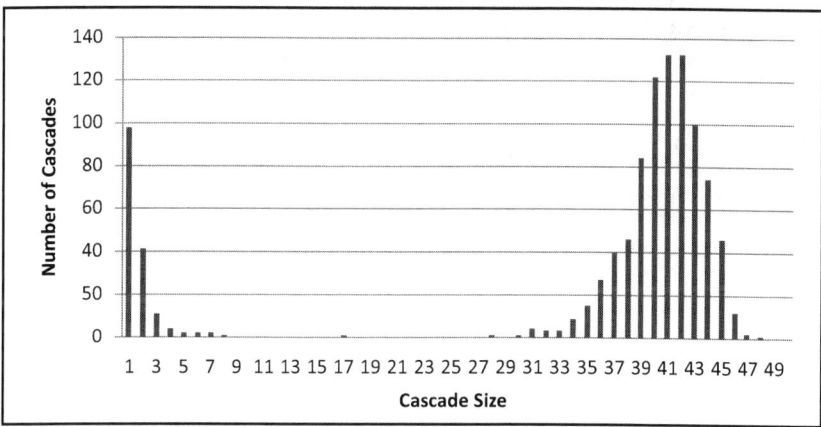

Fig. 10.4. Distribution of Cascade Sizes in Popperian Networks of Characteristic Degree 1.5 (Top) and 2 (Bottom)

Note: The scale on the y-axis is different for each graph.

Although the specific application of these results lies within philosophy of science, the formal basis lies within classic network theory. The formal basis for these results is the phenomenon of giant components, outlined in Erdös and Rényi's classic work on random graphs (1959; see also Newman 2010). Figure 10.5 shows the familiar graph of a phase transition to a giant component at a characteristic degree 1, with rapid increase in proportion of the network as characteristic degree increases.

The crucial fact in application to philosophy of science is that a falsification in a Popperian network will affect all of the nodes to which it is connected. If a "giant component" occupies a certain proportion of the network, the probability that a single falsification will cascade through that proportion of the network will be the probability that an arbitrary node is within the giant component. That probability, of course, will correspond to the proportion of the network occupied by the giant component.

To gauge the potential size of falsification cascades on Popperian conceptual networks, in other words, all we really need to know is the

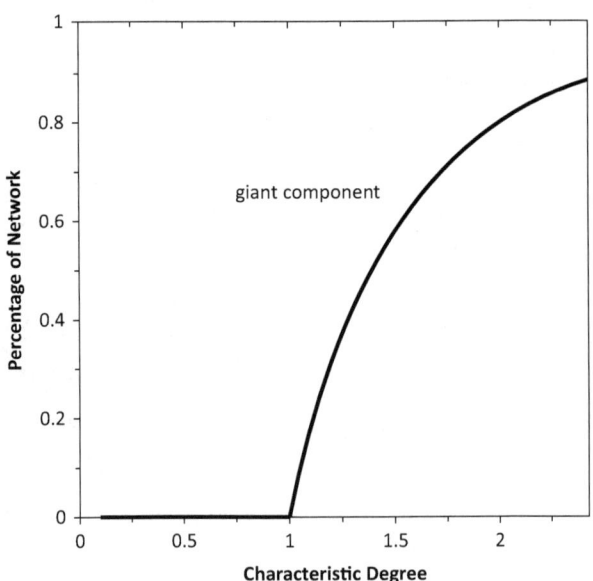

Fig. 10.5. Formation of a Giant Component as a Percentage of a Network at Different Degrees within an Undirected Random Network

Source: Modeled after Erdös and Rényi (1959).

characteristic degree of the network in question. Results correspond directly to the graphs of cascade sizes we've shown you. Another aspect of this analysis, to which we will return below, is that the proportion of the network occupied by a giant component is scale free, independent of network size n.

Modeling Kuhnian Dynamics

Despite the fact that Kuhn and Popper are often portrayed as antagonists, Kuhn writes explicitly of all that they have in common (Kuhn 1970). But he emphasizes that scientific change is rarely if ever a matter of decisive falsification on the basis of a single crucial experiment. A single anomaly— an unexplained phenomenon or apparent piece of counter-evidence—is never fatal. In 1827, Robert Brown noticed through a microscope that grains of pollen dance on the surface of water. But Brownian motion remained simply an unexplained curiosity until incorporated into theories of molecular motion (Perrin 2005). Copernican theory predicts stellar parallax: two closely separated stars ought to appear closer to each other at some times than at other times. But from Copernicus's time well into the nineteenth century no stellar parallax was observed—an anomaly that was shrugged off using an auxiliary hypothesis regarding the limits of available telescopes (Curd 1982).

Established paradigms resist change, maintained by explaining away apparent counter-evidence, impugning the expertise of critics, building ad hoc supplementary hypotheses. But anomalies build up. No single anomaly is fatal. But anomalies can accumulate in such a way as to weaken confidence in one part of a theory, or one aspect of a paradigm. That in turn can weaken confidence in another part of the theory or paradigm. The build-up of anomalies across different areas of a paradigm can lead to crisis, signaling an imminent paradigm shift.

We can model the Kuhnian picture of scientific change by replacing simple values of 1 and 0 for our nodes with thresholds: the number of accumulated anomalies at which a specific component of the network will be abandoned. The failure of one portion of a paradigm—a node or set of nodes—will pass the pressure of anomaly to other portions. Often, as Kuhn notes, an anomaly may remain localized, without affecting the structure as a whole. But in some contexts, there will be a cascade of anomalies across the structure: the mark of a paradigm shift.

We assign random node thresholds between 1 and 5, and then begin dropping "anomalies" at random. In Kuhnian fashion, anomalies accumulate, so we retain the same network throughout a consecutive sequence of drops. When a node reaches its threshold, it drops anomalies to each of the other nodes to which it is connected. The result may be simply a small number of anomalies distributed locally. But under some conditions node after node may reach anomaly threshold, producing a cascade of anomaly-forced change across the network.

It should be emphasized that the Kuhnian model differs in major ways from the Popperian. There, we dropped a single falsification on 1,000 networks. Here, we drop 1,000 cumulative anomalies on a single network, though we then average results over 100 such networks.

There are a number of variations possible in a Kuhnian model. Here we offer two. In a first case, when a node reaches its full threshold value it passes a single anomaly to the nodes to which it is connected (one anomaly passed). In this form of the model, we measure a cascade in terms of the number of nodes that reach full threshold from an anomaly drop on a random node (a full-tipping cascade). We zero-out a node's anomalies when it has "discharged" an anomaly down the line. It becomes a new node, as it were, in a new paradigm.

Paradigm-shift cascades on a Kuhnian network, like falsification cascades on a Popperian network, will depend on the integration of the network. Results for a random network of characteristic degree 1 are shown in figure 10.6. Most single anomalies will fail to tip even that node

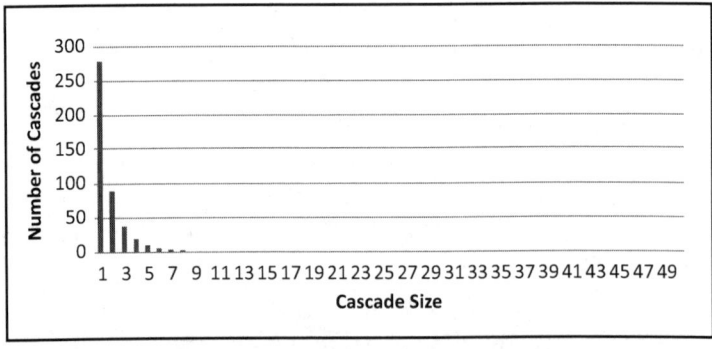

Fig. 10.6. Cascades of Fully Tipped Nodes in a Kuhnian Network of Characteristic Degree 1, with One Anomaly Passed to Neighboring Nodes at Threshold

on which they drop. The highest number of drops will result in a single tip, with fewer that result in a cascade that tips two nodes, fewer still that tip three. The result is a power law distribution at low node degree very much like that for Popperian networks.

Results with the same mechanism for Kuhnian networks of higher degree are shown in figure 10.7. Despite the fact that the Kuhnian model uses a very different mechanism than the Popperian—1,000 successive anomalies dropped on single networks, rather than single falsifications dropped on 1,000 networks—the qualitative character of cascade distributions is very similar. At low degree, the pattern shows a power law. At higher degree, a clear bimodal pattern emerges, with global cascades across a large portion of the network.

Patterns of global cascade in threshold networks roughly analogous to the Kuhnian model remain a topic of continuing research (Watts 2002). As Watts notes,

> Global cascades in social and economic systems, as well as cascading failures in engineering networks, display two striking qualitative features: they occur rarely, but by definition are large when they do. This general observation, however, presents an empirical mystery. Both power-law and bimodal distributions of cascades would satisfy the claim of infrequent, large events, but these distributions are otherwise quite different, and might require quite different explanations.
>
> (5771)

It is clear both here and in the continuing research that the clue to large cascades in threshold networks is not simply the formation of a giant component, as in the case of Popperian networks, but the formation of a giant *vulnerable* component: a connected set of nodes, all of which are a small component shy of threshold and thus ready to tip. A clue to the qualitative similarity between Popperian and Kuhnian networks is the fact that the Popperian can be seen as a limiting case of the Kuhnian: a Kuhnian model in which node thresholds are set uniformly to 1.

As noted, there are a range of variations possible in a Kuhnian model. In a second variation we have nodes pass their full threshold values on saturation, rather than a single anomaly. Here we measure a cascade as the number of nodes beyond the drop spot, the contents of which are changed, whether or not those nodes reach full threshold. With that different concept of cascades, an intriguingly different pattern appears (figure 10.8).

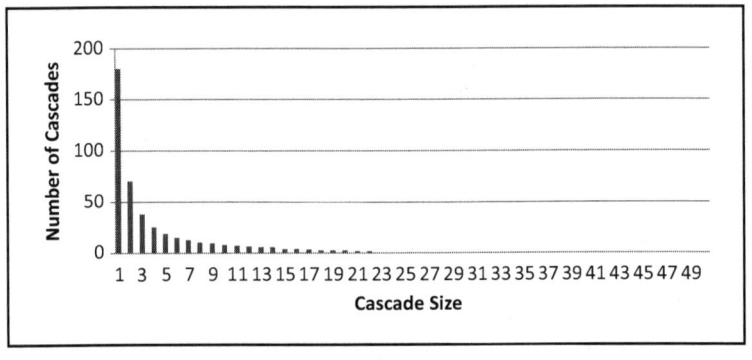

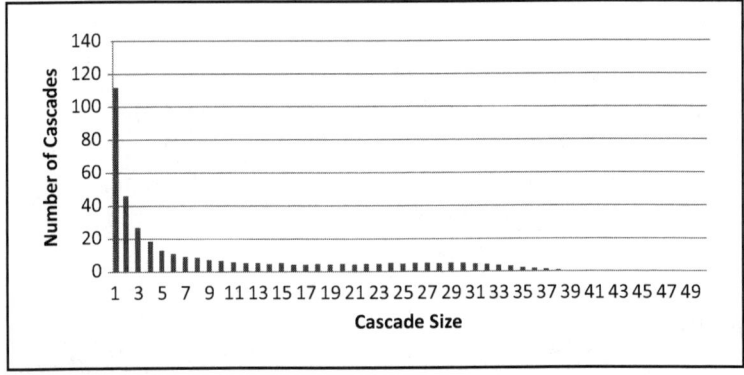

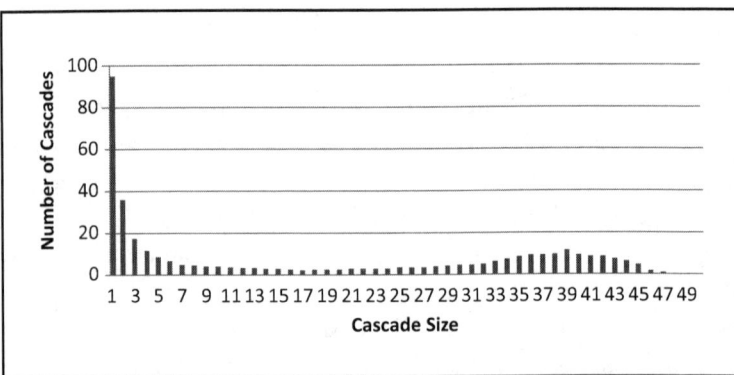

Fig. 10.7. Cascades of Fully Tipped Nodes in Kuhnian Networks of Characteristic Degree 2 (Top), 3 (Middle) and 4 (Bottom), with One Anomaly Passed to Neighboring Nodes at Threshold

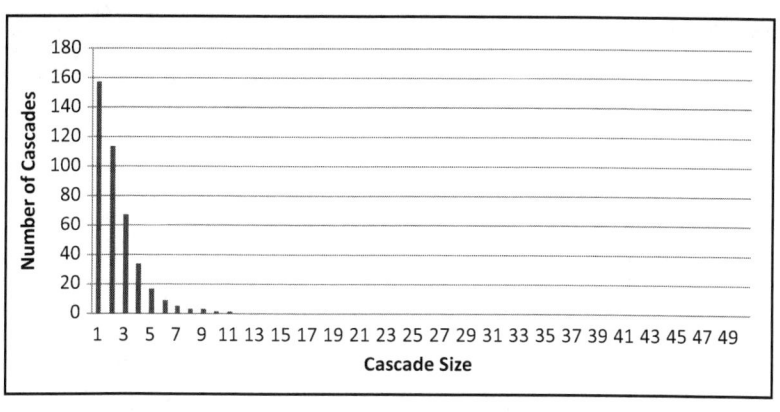
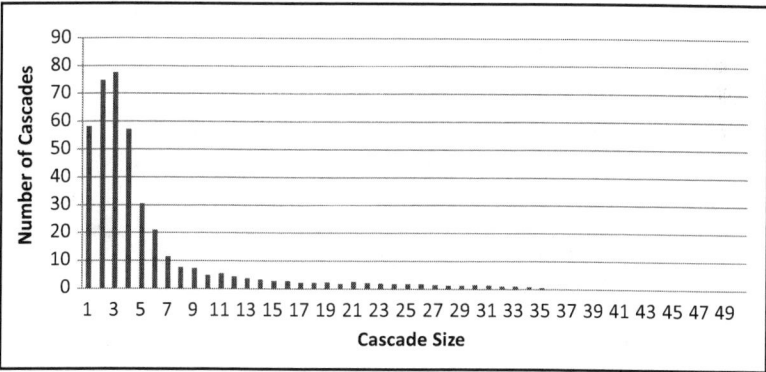
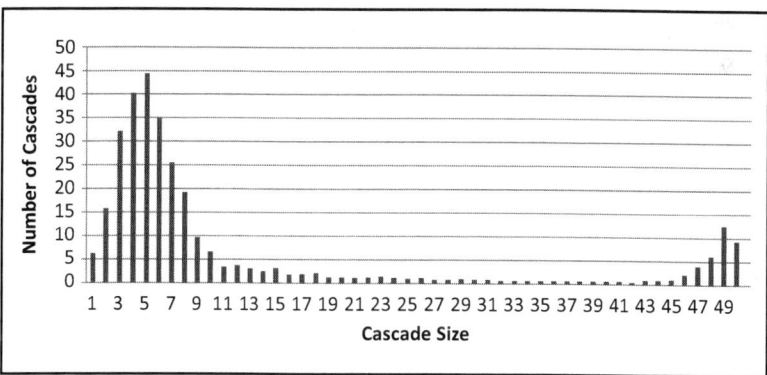

Fig. 10.8. Cascades of Affected Nodes in Kuhnian Networks of Characteristic Degree 1, 2, 4 and 6 (from top to bottom), with Full Anomaly Thresholds Passed to Neighboring Nodes

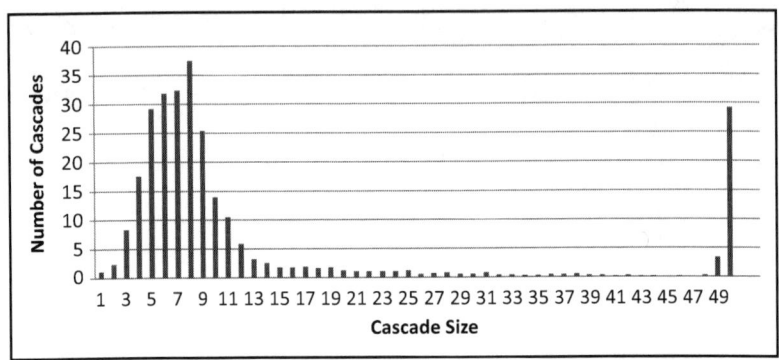

Fig. 10.8. (*Continued*)

In this form of the model, distributions again start with a power law at low degree, with a cluster that moves slowly right in the pattern of a giant component. At a characteristic degree of 4 and above, however, something importantly different occurs: a significant number of total or nearly total cascades at the extreme upper end. These are cases in which virtually *every* node in the network is affected by a single drop. At a characteristic degree of 6, moreover, those genuinely global cascades of change are among the most common.

Modeling the History of Scientific Change: Popper and Kuhn

We began by noting two aspects of scientific dynamics: science grows and science changes. The first element is an increasing integration of theory over time, modellable as an increasing characteristic degree of a conceptual network as links are added. The second element is a dynamic of scientific change that we have seen to be dependent on degree of integration over time: Popperian falsification cascades or Kuhnian paradigm shifts. By bringing these two aspects together we can create models of science developing, crashing and rebuilding over time.

Here we take falsification for what it is: the failure of an entire set of links within a sub-network. On the advent of a cascade, we will treat all links involved in the cascade as broken. As the process of scientific development proceeds, however, *new* links will be added.

We start with a Popperian network of fifty nodes with characteristic degree 1, dropping a single falsification somewhere in the network at each iteration. Links from "falsified" elements are eliminated. But at each iteration an additional random link is added somewhere in the network, representing the force of increased scientific integration. We track the size of integrated scientific theory at a time by simply tracking the number of links in our model of a conceptual structure. The development of science on that Popperian dynamics is shown in figure 10.9.

Science builds and crashes. On the Popperian picture the crashes are frequent. The integrative links in our model only once peak above twenty.

In a similar model for Kuhnian dynamics, starting with the same degree and number of nodes, we treat a build-up of anomalies beyond its threshold as "discrediting" a node. Links from that node disappear. We replace it with a new node, with a new threshold, and again build up links. Figure 10.10 shows a Kuhnian picture of the development of science.

The first thing to note in these two images is the difference in scale on the y axis; the first goes to 25, while the second extends to 60. The crashes are both less frequent and more drastic. One might have thought that it would be the Popperian picture of scientific development as conjectures and refutations that would be more rugged, but in fact, it is the Kuhnian process that paints a more dramatic picture of progressive accumulations and dramatic crashes—the revolutionary collapses of massive paradigm shifts.

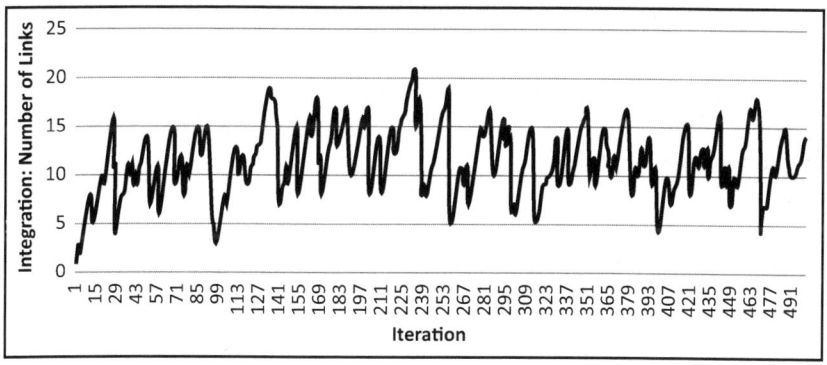

Fig. 10.9. Scientific Change within a Popperian Model over Time

Note: All links within a falsification cascade are broken, with new links added at each iteration.

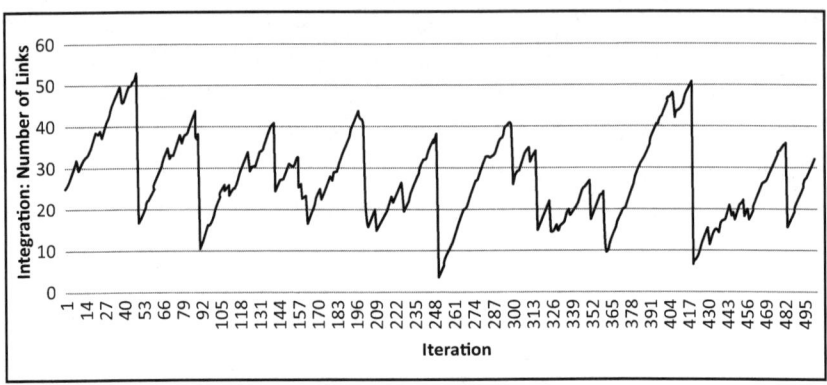

Fig. 10.10. Scientific Change within a Kuhnian Model over Time, Using Transfer of a Single Anomaly

Note: All links from a node that reaches anomaly threshold are broken, with new links added at each iteration.

Directed Networks: A Second Model of Scientific Paradigms

To this point we have envisaged conceptual systems and scientific paradigms as networks of mutual support between elements, hence the use of undirected graphs. It can be argued, however, that a more realistic portrayal would use directed graphs instead. We might think of a scientific theory, for example, as a complex of "if … then" statements between observational phenomena and other conceptual elements. In such a picture, our links should be directed: if this holds, then this follows; if this law applies, then this phenomenon is to be expected; given this as a cause, this can be an expected effect.

Directed network models for conceptual systems have precedent in the long but varied history of conceptual maps. In 1913, John Henry Wigmore developed a "chart method" for analyzing evidence in a legal case (Wigmore 1913). Wigmore's "chart method" uses a directed graph (figure 10.11). In the 1970s, Robert Axelrod sketched cognitive maps as signed digraphs (Axelrod 1976); generalizations employing continuous values appear in the fuzzy cognitive maps of Bart Kosko (1986). Cognitive maps as directed graphs have been used extensively as heuristics for group discussion regarding complex issues (Hobbs et al. 2002; van Vliet, Kok, and Veldkamp 2010; Soler et al. 2012; Cakmak et al. 2013; Jetter and Sperry 2013).

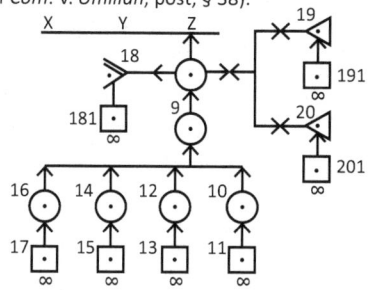

Fig. 10.11. Wigmore's (1913) Outline of Legal Reasoning in Terms of a Directed Graph

How do the modeling phenomena we've noted play out when our picture of scientific paradigms or conceptual systems in general takes the form of directed as opposed to undirected graphs? Here again the key will be integration of a network measured in terms of characteristic degree. We'll count in-links and out-links together as node degree: average degree is the average of both.

Figure 10.12 shows cascade sizes from falsification for directed Popperian networks of increasing degree, with results averaged over 1,000 networks. The basic Popperian pattern remains the same as in the undirected case: a power-law-like distribution at low degree, with the appearance of a clearly bimodal distribution as the integration of a conceptual network increases.

Figure 10.13 shows the results for a Kuhnian model employing a directed network. We drop 1,000 "anomalies" consecutively on nodes with random thresholds between 0 and 5, passing a single anomaly to neighboring

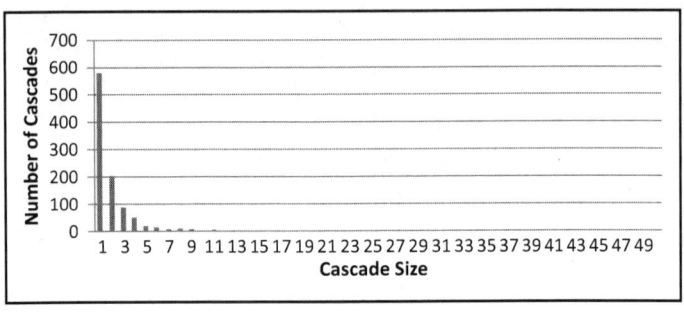
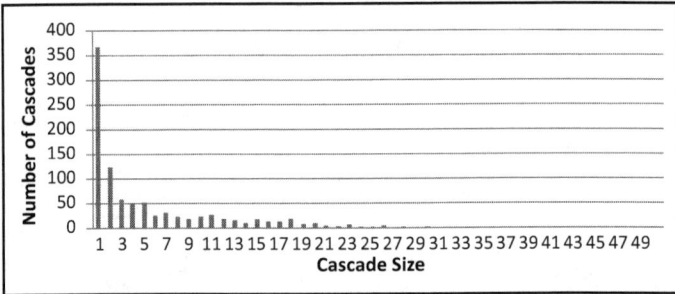
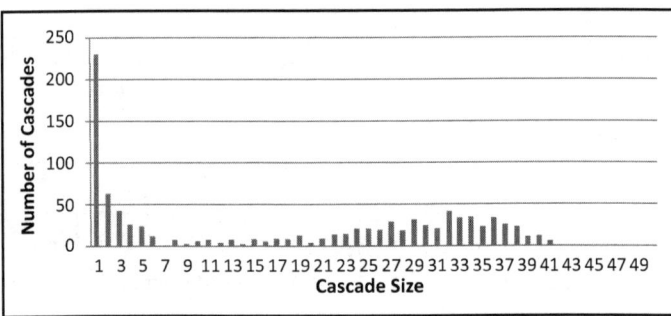
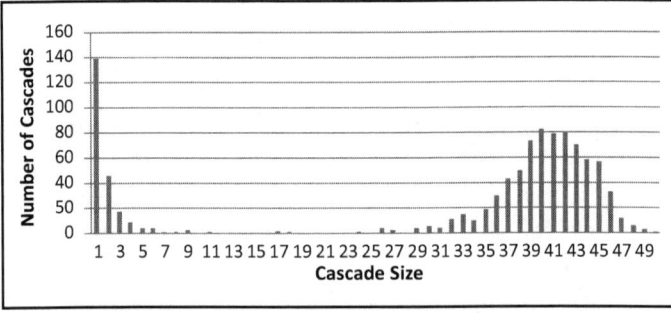

Fig. 10.12. Distribution of Cascade Sizes in Directed Popperian Networks of Increasing Degree

Note: The scale on the y-axis is different for each graph. The network degrees for each graph are, from top to bottom: 1, 2, 3, 4.

Philosophy of Science, Network Theory and Conceptual Change 319

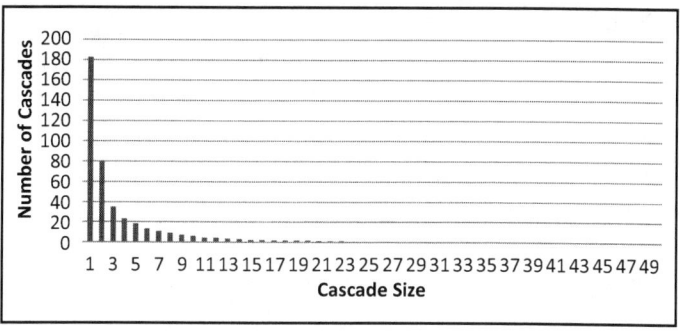

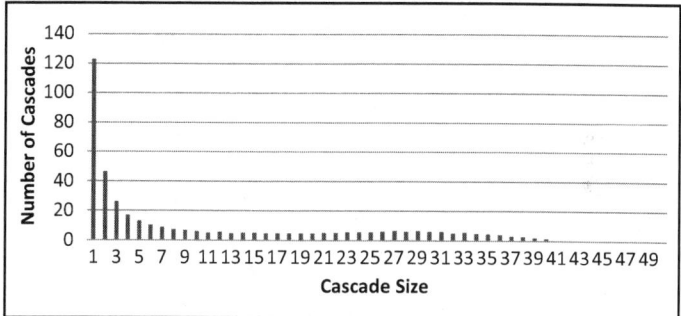

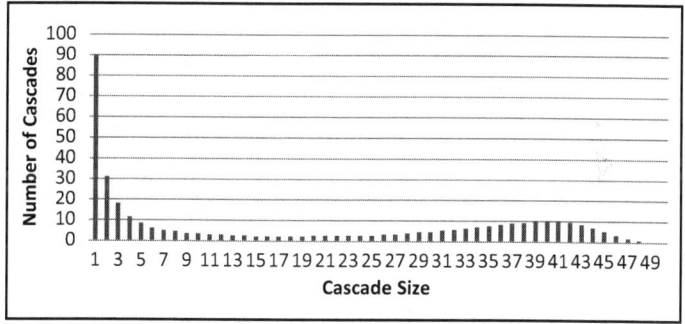

Fig. 10.13. Distribution of Cascade Sizes in Directed Kuhnian Networks of Increasing Degree

Note: The scale on the y-axis is different for each graph. The degrees for each graph are, from top to bottom: 4, 6, 8.

nodes when a node reaches its threshold. Cascades are measured as the number of nodes fully tipped by a single dropped anomaly. For Popper and Kuhn we see the same patterns on both network types: Popperian and Kuhnian dynamics are robust across representations of conceptual networks as either undirected or directed networks.

A formal network analysis in terms of giant components is available for the case of directed networks as it was for the case of undirected, though for directed networks one needs to consider not a single giant component but three elements of a "bow-tie" diagram. The core is a "strongly connected component" in which any node has a directed path to every other node in the component. In the case of directed graphs, however, we also need to track in-links and out-links (see figure 10.14).

Despite the fact that we've gone from undirected to directed graphs, the path to a giant component—here a strongly connected component abetted by in- and out- links—is remarkably similar (see figure 10.15).

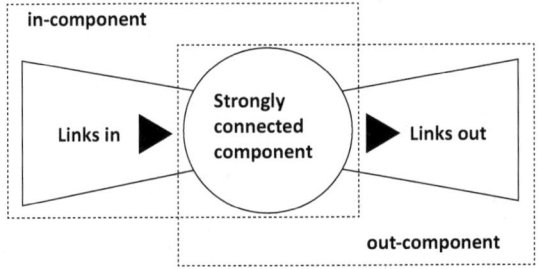

Fig. 10.14. The Bow-Tie Diagram of Components in a Directed Graph

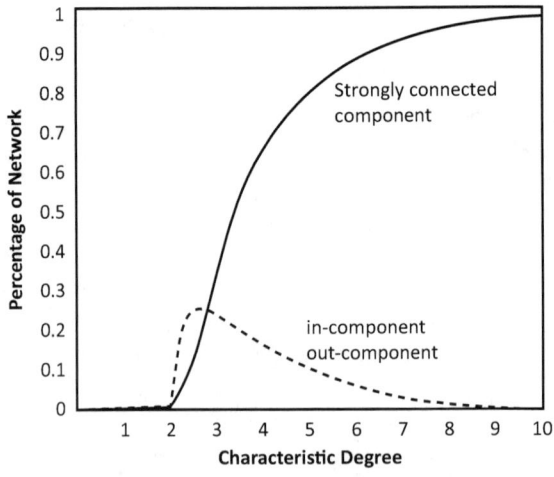

Fig. 10.15. Formation of Strongly Connected Components, In-Component and Out-Components as a Percentage of a Network at Different Degrees within a Directed Random Network

Source: Adapted from James B. Glattfelder (2013).

Philosophy of Science, Network Theory and Conceptual Change 321

The simple message is that, here again, it is the sudden and dramatic growth of that central component that explains much of the cascade distributions we see in our graphs. Another aspect of this analysis, to which we will return below, is that the proportion of the network occupied by strongly connected components in directed graphs is scale free, independent of network size.

We can also model the developmental history of science within Popperian and Kuhnian models of scientific change (figure 10.16). One might have thought that we would see a smoother development of models of history in the directed than in the undirected case, since in the latter case cascades must percolate through a more elaborate pattern of directed links. It turns out, however, that the history of science as a series of paradigm shifts is at least as dramatic when conceptual systems are envisaged as

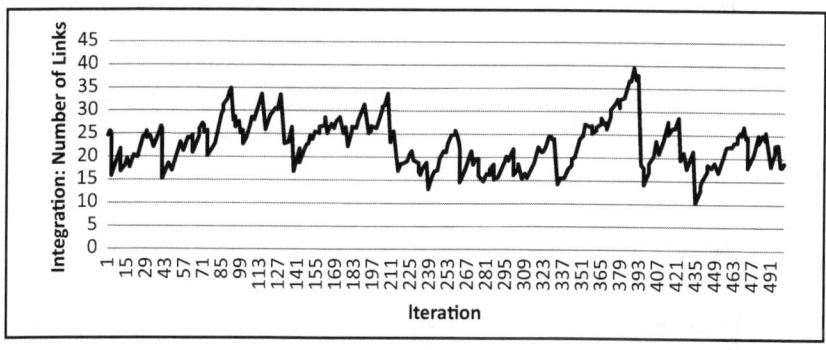

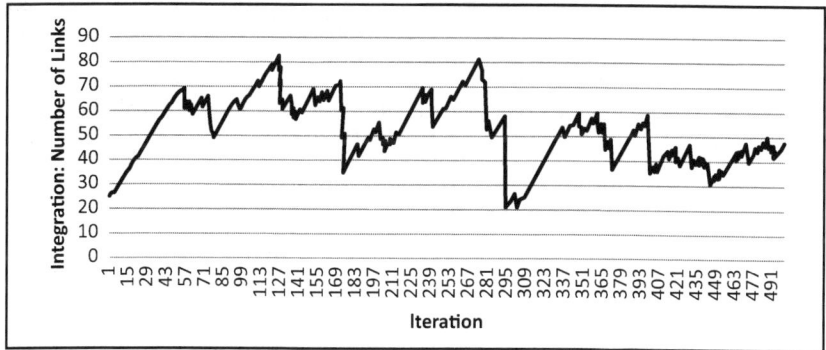

Fig. 10.16. The History of Science in Popperian (Top) and Kuhnian (Bottom) Models Using Directed Conceptual Networks

Note: Beyond the use of directed in place of undirected graphs, all parameters are the same as in Figures 10.9 and 10.10.

directed networks. Here again our results prove robust across this variation in basic modeling of conceptual systems.

Science and Self-Organized Criticality

We have one final concept from complex systems to add to the mix: that of self-organized criticality, which finds a new application here.

Self-organized criticality first appears in Bak, Tang and Wiesenfeld (1988). In Bak's words, "many composite systems naturally evolve to a critical state in which a minor event starts a chain reaction that can affect any number of elements in the system." "Large iterative systems perpetually organize themselves to a critical state in which a minor event starts a chain reaction that can lead to a catastrophe" (Bak and Chen 1991, 46).

Avalanches in a sand pile constitute the primary model in Bak's original presentation. Drop a single grain on a sandpile and little or nothing may happen ... until something does. Drop a further grain, and a further ... and one will have avalanches both small and large. The core idea is that the pile will "self-organize" toward criticality: without any outside tuning of parameters, the system itself evolves to the point that it's "ready" for a major avalanche. And it does so again and again.

Self-organized criticality has found wide application both within its original home in physics—with applications in solar, magnetospheric and fusion plasma instabilities—and well beyond. It has emerged as a strong explanatory candidate for patterns of earthquakes, solar flares and forest fires. It has been proposed as an element of explanation for fluctuations in economic models and for punctuated equilibria in biological evolution (Watkins et al. 2016). Most tantalizing with an eye to conceptual networks and philosophy of science, perhaps, self-organized criticality has both been proposed within the computer sciences as an efficient mechanism of search and within the brain sciences as a crucial mechanism in the functioning brain (Levina, Herrmann, and Geisel 2007, 2009; Brochini et al. 2016; Hoffman and Payton 2018).

What our results seem to hint is that the process of science may be self-organizing as well. Science itself may be an informational instantiation of self-organizing criticality. It must be admitted that the concept of self-organized criticality has yet no established mathematical formalism or generally accepted definition. Even in Bak's original presentations, the concept is outlined not by strict definition but in terms of "marks" of self-organized criticality

One of those marks is "flicker noise" or 1/f noise. White or random noise shows no correlation from point to point. In flicker noise, ubiquitous in natural systems, there *is* a strong correlation between points and their predecessors—a clear indication of a path-dependent dynamics. Correlation of that type is clear throughout the phenomena we've tracked in both Popperian and Kuhnian networks.

Bak's other major mark of self-organized criticality is the fractal characteristic of scale-invariance. In theory, the relative size of cascades should be the same in sand piles regardless of size. That characteristic is also clear here.

Our model results throughout have used networks of fifty nodes. But they didn't have to. Beyond a critical point, our results scale up regardless of the size of the network. Figure 10.17 compares cascades on Popperian networks of fifty and one hundred nodes. Although more finely tuned in the second case, with results across more options for cascade sizes, the same clear pattern appears.

As we've indicated, a core explanation for the cascade patterns tracked here is in the emergence of giant components in networks, both undirected and directed. It is because giant components of a particular size appear—tied directly to the characteristic degree of a network—that cascades of that size dominate our graphs. What is of importance here is the proportion of a network occupied by a giant or strongly connected component, in the case of either undirected or directed graphs, is scale-invariant. Beyond a surprisingly low phase transition, the proportion of a network occupied by such a component is independent of the size of the network. To the extent that our cascade distributions are tied to the presence of such components, precisely because the network proportion of those components is scale invariant, our cascade distributions will be as well (see figure 10.18).

A clearer example of self-organization than the Kuhnian dynamics of scientific change that we've modeled would indeed be difficult to find. The system self-organizes toward that point at which a major cascade across much of the network—a revolutionary paradigm shift—is well-nigh inevitable.

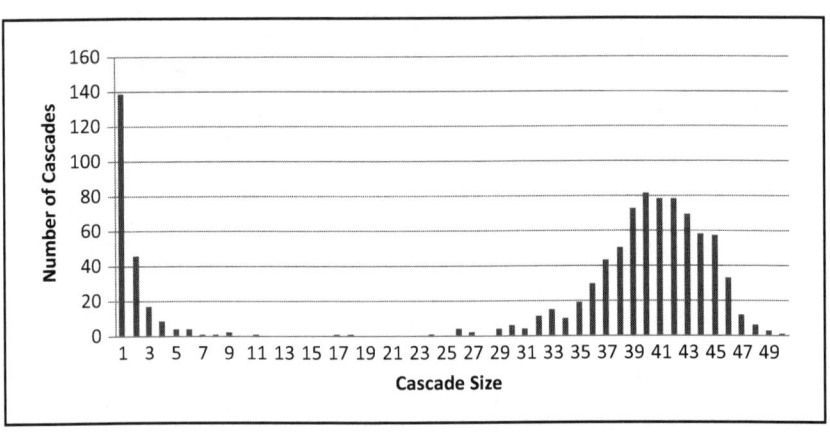
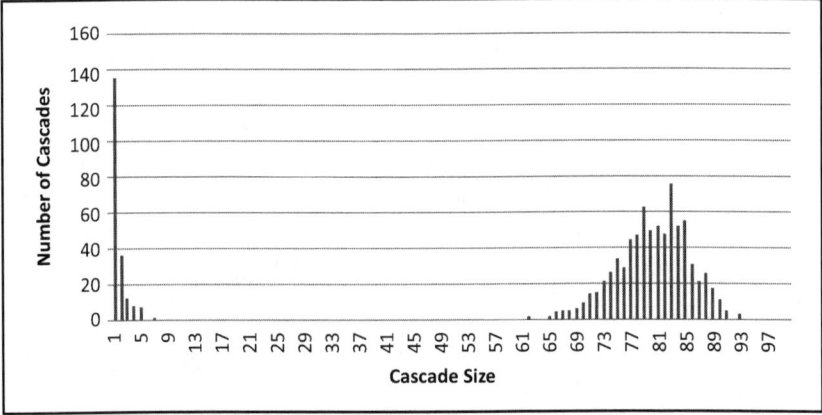

Fig. 10.17. Comparative Cascade Sizes in Popperian Networks of Fifty (Top) and One Hundred (Bottom) Nodes

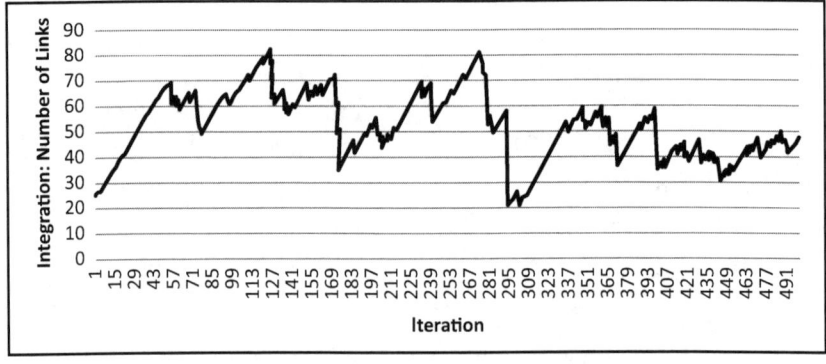

Fig. 10.18. The History of Science on a Kuhnian Directed Model

Conclusion: Prospects for Expanding the Models

It must be admitted that this remains a work in progress. There are three clear directions for future development.

The models for conceptual networks used here have been the simplest: undirected and directed random graphs. One clear direction for future work is to investigate cascade phenomena using other network types as representations of conceptual systems. One prime candidate is Boolean networks. Do dynamics change when we make explicit a structure developed in terms of logical connectives? Another clear candidate is Bayesian networks. What are the characteristics under which conceptual cascades occur in networks within which nodes update priors on input from other nodes? Those remain unanswered questions.

There is another natural expansion of the model that is clearly called for. Here we have followed Kuhn and Popper in treating a conceptual system as a shared paradigm, a single possession of a scientific community. But of course different individuals have different conceptual systems. Given specific patterns of communication, certain changes in one may effect certain changes in others. Cascades can be expected to happen on the social level as well. What is called for in expansion is a two-level model embedding individual conceptual networks within a second level of social communication.

A third direction called for—here and in agent-based modeling in general—is a closer link to empirical data. One aspect of our results has been a picture of the history of science on Popperian and Kuhnian models. The work offered here remains very much on the abstract end, the theoretical rather than the empirical, philosophy of science rather than history of science. The question of whether the history of science has something like the topography of our graphs remains an open question, empirical and hard.

CHAPTER 11

Complexity and Knowledge

J. Barkley Rosser, Jr.

Introduction

Knowledge is hard to obtain regarding complicated reality and complicated systems. However, complex systems lead to even greater problems of knowledge than complicated ones, even when in important ways complex systems may appear simpler than complicated ones. A complicated system will have many parts that are interconnected in a variety of ways that may not be obvious and may be hard to discern or untangle. However, merely complicated systems will "add up" in a reasonably straightforward way. Once one figures out these interconnections and their nature, one can understand the whole relatively easily as it will ultimately be the sum of those parts, which may nevertheless be hard to understand on their own. However, in the case of complex systems, by their nature they usually manifest the phenomenon first identified by Aristotle that the whole may be greater than the sum of the parts. This greater degree of wholeness will often be due to nonlinear relations within the system, such as increasing returns to scale or tangled non-monotonic relations. Even though there may be fewer variables and relations, the complex nature of the relations makes knowledge and understanding of the system more difficult (Israel 2005).

The knowledge problem is more formally known as the epistemological problem, and this author has previously addressed it in this context (Rosser 2004). However, while drawing on discussion in that paper, this chapter will not only update arguments made there but will also consider additional topics, such as the complexity foundations of Herbert Simon's "bounded rationality" concept (Simon 1957, 1962) as well as how complexity can underlie non-ergodicity and related phenomena to generate fundamental uncertainty (Davidson 1982, 2015; O'Donnell 2014–15; Rosser 2016; Alvarez and Ehnts 2016). In this case, the epistemological problem may well arise from the underlying complex ontology (Davidson 1996; Rosser 1998, 2001).

How nonlinear dynamical systems manifest problems of knowledge is easily seen for chaotic systems, which are characterized by the problem of sensitive dependence on initial conditions, known popularly as the "butterfly effect." If minute changes in initial conditions, either of parameter values controlling a system or of initial starting values, can lead to very large changes in subsequent outcomes of a system, then it may essentially require an infinite precision of knowledge to completely know the system, which undermines the possibility for rational expectations for such systems (Rosser 1996). Also, fractality of dynamic attractor basin boundaries in systems with multiple such basins can behave similarly such that even the slightest amount of stochastic noise in the dynamical system can lead to very different outcomes (Rosser 1991).

The problem of logic or computation arises in complex systems of multiple interacting heterogeneous agents thinking about each other's thinking. Although game theoretic solutions, such as Nash equilibria, may present themselves, these may involve a certain element of ignorance, a refusal to fully know the system. Efforts to fully know the system may prove to be impossible due to problems of infinite regress or self referencing that lead to non-computability (Binmore 1987; Albin 1998; Koppl and Rosser 2002; Mirowski 2002; Landini et al. 2020). This becomes entangled with deeper problems in the foundations of mathematics involving constructivist logic and its link to computability (Velupillai 2000; Zambelli 2004; Rosser 2010, 2012).

We consider the role of Herbert Simon in understanding the deep relations between complexity and the limits of knowledge. As a founding figure in the study of artificial intelligence, he was fully aware of the computational complexity issues arising from the logical paradoxes of self-referencing and related matters. He was also of the limits of computational capabilities of humans as well as the high cost of obtaining information.

From these ideas he developed the concept of *bounded rationality* (Simon 1957) and basically invented modern behavioral economics based on this. He also dug more deeply into complexity issues, as he largely developed the idea of hierarchical complexity (Simon 1962), which adds further layers to the epistemological difficulties associated with understanding complex systems. The influence of these ideas of Simon has been both deep and wide (Rosser and Rosser 2015).

Finally we will consider the question of the ergodic/nonergodic approach to understanding fundamental Keynesian uncertainty (Davidson 1982). This approach has come under criticism by O'Donnell (2014–15) who argues that Davidson has misinterpreted the nature of ergodicity and calls for a behavioral approach to understanding uncertainty, with Davidson (2015) replying. Rosser (2016) offers an analysis that reconsiders the foundations of ergodicity and shows that both have made arguments based on misunderstandings, with some crucial exceptions to widely repeated views arising in chaotic and other complex systems (Shinkai and Aizawa 2006), once again finding a deep role of complexity in understanding the limits of knowledge.

Forms of Complexity?

In *The End of Science*, John Horgan (1997, 303) reports on forty-five definitions of complexity that have been gathered by the physicist Seth Lloyd. Some of the more widely used conceptualizations include *informational entropy* (Shannon 1950), *algorithmic complexity* (Chaitin 1987), *stochastic complexity* (Rissanen 1989), and *hierarchical complexity* (Simon 1962). Three other definitions have been more frequently used in economics that do not appear on Lloyd's list, namely, simple complicatedness in the sense of many different sectors with many different interconnections (Pryor 1995; Stodder 1995), dynamic complexity (Day, 1994) and computational complexity (Lewis 1985; Velupillai 2000). We will not consider the knowledge problems associated with mere complicatedness, which are simpler than those associated with true complexity (Israel 2005).

According to Day (1994), dynamic complexity can be defined as arising from dynamical systems that endogenously fail to converge to either a point, a limit cycle or a smooth explosion or implosion. Nonlinearity is a necessary but not sufficient condition for such complexity. Rosser (1999) identifies this definition with a *big tent* view of dynamic complexity that can be subdivided into four sub-categories: *cybernetics, catastrophe theory, chaos theory,* and *small-tent complexity* (now more commonly called *agent-based complexity*). The last of the four does not possess a definite definition; however, Arthur, Durlauf and Lane (1997) argue that such complexity exhibits six characteristics: 1) dispersed interaction among locally interacting heterogeneous agents in some space, 2) no global controller that can exploit opportunities arising from these dispersed interactions, 3) cross-cutting hierarchical organization with many tangled interactions, 4) continual learning and adaptation by agents, 5) perpetual novelty in the system as mutations lead it to evolve new ecological niches, and 6) out-of-equilibrium dynamics with either no or many equilibria and little likelihood of a global optimum state emerging. Certainly such systems offer considerable scope for problems of how to know what is going on in them.

Computational complexity essentially amounts to a system being noncomputable. Ultimately this depends on a logical foundation, that of non-recursiveness due to incompleteness in the Gödel sense (Church 1936; Turing 1937a). In actual computer problems, this problem manifests itself most clearly in the form of the halting problem (Blum et al. 1998)—that the halting time of a program is infinite. Ultimately, this form of complexity has deep links with several of the others listed above, such as Chaitin's algorithmic complexity. These last two approaches are the ones we consider in more detail in the next two sections.

Dynamic Complexity and Knowledge

In dynamically complex systems, the knowledge problem becomes the general epistemological problem. Consider the specific problem of being able to know the consequences of an action taken in such a system. Let $G(\mathbf{x}_t)$ be the dynamical system in an n-dimensional space. Let an agent possess an action set **A**. Let a given action by the agent at a particular time be given by $\mathbf{a}_{it}$. For the moment, let us not specify any actions by any other agents, each of whom also possesses their own action set. We can identify a relation whereby $\mathbf{x}_t = f(\mathbf{a}_{it})$. The knowledge problem for the agent in question thus becomes, "Can the agent know the reduced system $G(f(\mathbf{a}_{it}))$ when this system possesses complex dynamics due to nonlinearity?"

First, it may be possible for the agent to be able to understand the system and to know that he or she understands it, at least to some extent. One reason why this can happen is that many complex nonlinear dynamical systems do not always behave in erratic or discontinuous ways. Many fundamentally chaotic systems exhibit *transiency* (Lorenz 1992). A system can move in and out of behaving chaotically, with long periods passing during which the system will effectively behave in a non-complex manner, either tracking a simple equilibrium or following an easily predictable limit cycle. While the system remains in this pattern, actions by the agent may have easily predicted outcomes, and the agent may even be able to become confident regarding his or her ability to manipulate the system systematically. However, this essentially avoids the question.

Let us consider four forms of complexity: chaotic dynamics, fractal basin boundaries, discontinuous phase transitions in heterogeneous agent situations, and catastrophe theoretic models related to this third form. For the first of these there is a clear problem for the agent, the existence of sensitive dependence on initial conditions. If an agent moves from action $\mathbf{a}_{it}$ to action $\mathbf{a}_{jt}$, where $|\mathbf{a}_{it} - \mathbf{a}_{jt}| < \varepsilon < 1$, then no matter how small ε is, there exists an m such that $|G(f(\mathbf{a}_{it+t'})) - G(f(\mathbf{a}_{jt+t'}))| > m$ for some t' for each ε. As ε approaches zero, m/ε will approach infinity. It will be very hard for the agent to be confident in predicting the outcome of changing his or her action. This is the problem of the butterfly effect, or sensitive dependence on initial conditions. More particularly, if the agent has an imperfectly precise awareness of their actions, with the zone of fuzziness exceeding ε, the agent faces a potentially large range of uncertainty regarding the outcome of his or her actions. In Edward Lorenz's (1963) original study of this matter in which he "discovered chaos," when he restarted his simulation of a three-equation system of fluid dynamics partway through, the roundoff error that triggered a subsequent dramatic divergence was too small for his computer to "perceive" (at the fourth decimal place).

There are two offsetting elements for chaotic dynamics. Although an exact knowledge is effectively impossible, requiring essentially infinitely precise knowledge (and knowledge of that knowledge), a broader approximate knowledge over time may be possible. Thus, chaotic systems are generally bounded and often ergodic (although not always). While short-run relative trajectories for two slightly different actions may sharply diverge, the trajectories will, at some later time, return toward each other, becoming arbitrarily close before once again diverging. Not only may the bounds of the system be knowable, but the long-run average of the system may be knowable. There are still limits, as one can never be sure that one is not dealing with a long transient of the system, with it possibly moving into a substantially different mode of behavior later. But the possibility of a substantial degree of knowledge, with even some degree of confidence regarding that knowledge is not out of the question for chaotically dynamic systems.

Regarding fractal basin boundaries—first identified for economic models by Hans-Walter Lorenz (1992) in the same paper in which he discussed the problem of chaotic transience—whereas in a chaotic system there may be only one basin of attraction, albeit with the attractor being fractal and strange and thus generating erratic fluctuations, the fractal basin boundary case involves multiple basins of attraction whose boundaries with each other take fractal shapes. The attractor for each basin may well be as simple as being a single point. However, the boundaries between the basins may lie arbitrarily close to each other in certain zones.

In such a case, although it may be difficult to be certain, for the purely deterministic case once one is able to determine which basin of attraction one is in, a substantial degree of predictability may ensue, although again there may be the problem of transient dynamics, with the system taking a long and circuitous route before it begins to get anywhere close to the attractor, even if the attractor is merely a point in the end. The problem arises if the system is not strictly deterministic, if G includes a stochastic element, however small. In this case one may be easily pushed across a basin boundary, especially if one is in a zone where the boundaries lie very close to one another. Thus, there may be a sudden and very-difficult-to-predict discontinuous change in the dynamic path as the system begins to move toward a very different attractor in a different basin. The effect is very similar to that of sensitive dependence on initial conditions in epistemological terms, even if the two cases are mathematically distinct.

Nevertheless, in this case, as well, there may be something similar to the kind of dispensation over the longer run we noted for the case of chaotic dynamics. Even if exact prediction in the chaotic case is all but impossible, it may be possible to discern broader patterns, bounds and averages.

Likewise, in the case of fractal basin boundaries with a stochastic element, over time one should observe a jumping from one basin to another. Somewhat like the pattern of long-run evolutionary game dynamics studied by Binmore and Samuelson (1999), one can imagine an observer keeping track of how long the system remains in each basin and eventually develop a probability profile of the pattern, with the percentage of time the system spends in each basin possibly approaching asymptotic values. However, this is contingent on the nature of the stochastic process as well as the degree of complexity of the fractal pattern of the basin boundaries. A non-ergodic stochastic process may render it very difficult, even impossible, to observe convergence on a stable set of probabilities for being in the respective basins, even if those are themselves few in number with simple attractors.

For the case of phase transitions in systems of heterogeneous locally interacting agents, the world of the so-called "small-tent complexity," Brock and Hommes (1997) have developed a useful model for understanding such phase transitions based on statistical mechanics. This is a stochastic system driven fundamentally by two key parameters: a strength of interactions or relationships between neighboring agents and a degree of willingness to switch behavioral patterns by the agents. For their model, the product of these two parameters is crucial, with a bifurcation occurring for their product. If the product is below a certain critical value, then there will be a single equilibrium state. However, once this product exceeds a particular critical value, two distinct equilibria will emerge. Effectively the agents will jump back and forth between these equilibria in herding patterns. For financial market models (Brock and Hommes 1998) this can resemble oscillations between optimistic bull markets and pessimistic bear markets, whereas below the critical value the market will have much less volatility as it tracks something that may be a rational expectations equilibrium.

For this kind of a setup there are essentially two serious problems. One is determining the value of the critical threshold. The other is understanding how the agents jump from one equilibrium to the other in the multiple equilibrium zone. Certainly the second problem resembles somewhat the discussion from the previous case, if not involving as dramatic a set of possible discontinuous shifts.

Of course once a threshold of discontinuity is passed, it may be recognizable when it is approached again. But prior to doing so, it may be essentially impossible to determine its location. The problem of determining a discontinuity threshold is a much broader one that vexes policymakers in many situations, such as attempting to avoid catastrophic thresholds that can bring about the collapse of a species population or of an entire ecosystem. One does not want to cross the threshold, but without doing so, one does not know where it is. However, for less dangerous situations involving irreversibilities, it may be possible to determine the location of the threshold as one moves back and forth across it.

On the other hand, in such systems it is quite likely that the location of such thresholds may not remain fixed. Often such systems exhibit an evolutionary self-organizing pattern in which the parameters of the system themselves become subject to evolutionary change as the system moves from zone to zone. Such non-ergodicity is consistent not only with Keynesian-style uncertainty, but may also come to resemble the complexity identified by Hayek (1948, 1967) in his discussions of self-organization within complex systems. Of course for market economies, Hayek evinced an optimism regarding the outcomes of such processes. Even if market participants may not be able to predict outcomes of such processes, the pattern of self-organization will ultimately be largely beneficial if left on its own. Although Keynesians and Hayekian Austrians are often seen as in deep disagreement, some observers have noted the similarities of viewpoints regarding these underpinnings of uncertainty (Shackle 1972; Loasby 1976; Rosser 2001). Furthermore, this approach leads to the idea of the openness of systems that becomes consistent with the critical realist approach to economic epistemology (Lawson 1997).

Considering this problem of important thresholds brings us to the final of our forms of dynamic complexity to consider here—catastrophe theory interpretations. The knowledge problem is essentially that previously noted, but is more clearly writ large, as the discontinuities involved are more likely to be large as the crashes of major speculative bubbles. The Brock-Hommes model and its descendants can be seen as a form of what is involved, but returning to earlier formulations brings out underlying issues more clearly.

The very first application of catastrophe theory in economics by Zeeman (1974) indeed considered financial market crashes in a simplified two-agent formulation: fundamentalists who stabilized the system by buying low and selling high and "chartists" who chase trends in a destabilizing manner by buying when markets rise and selling when they fall. As in the

Brock-Hommes formulation, he allows for agents to change their roles in response to market dynamics so that as the market rises fundamentalists become chartists, accelerating the bubble, and when the crash comes they revert to being fundamentalists, accelerating the crash. Rosser (1991) provides an extended formalization of this in catastrophe theory terms that links it to the analysis of Minsky (1972) and Kindleberger (1978), further taken up in Rosser et al. (2012) and Rosser (2020a). This formulation involves a cusp catastrophic formulation with the two control variables being the demands by the two categories of agents, with the chartists' demand determining the position of the cusp that allows for market crashes.

The knowledge problem here involves something not specifically modeled in Brock and Hommes, although they have a version of it. It is the matter of the expectations of agents about the expectations of the other agents. This is effectively the "beauty contest" issue discussed by Keynes in chapter 12 of this *General Theory* (1936). The winner of the beauty contest in a newspaper competition is not who guesses the prettiest girl, but who guesses best the guesses of the other participants. Keynes famously noted that one could start playing this about, guessing the expectations of others in their guesses of others' guesses, and that this could go to higher levels, in principle, an infinite regress leading to an impossible knowledge problem. In contrast, the Brock and Hommes approach simply has agents shifting strategies after watching what others do. These potentially higher-level problems do not enter in. These sorts of problems reappear in the problems associated with computational complexity.

Knowledge Problems of Computational Complexity

Regarding computational complexity, Velupillai (2000) provides definitions and general discussion, and Koppl and Rosser (2002) provide a more precise formulation of the problem, drawing on arguments of Kleene (1967), Binmore (1987), Lipman (1991) and Canning (1992). Velupillai defines computational complexity straightforwardly as "intractability" or insolvability. Halting problems, such as those studied by Blume et al. (1998), provide excellent examples of how such complexity can arise, with this problem first studied for recursive systems by Church (1936) and Turing (1937a).

In particular, Koppl and Rosser reexamined the famous "Holmes-Moriarty" problem of game theory, in which two players who behave as Turing machines contemplate a game between each other involving an infinite regress of thinking about what the other one is thinking about. This has a Nash equilibrium, but "hyper-rational" Turing machines cannot arrive at knowing it has that solution or not due to the halting problem. That the best reply functions are not computable arises from the self-referencing problem involved fundamentally similar to those underlying the Gödel Incompleteness Theorem (Rosser 1936; Kleene 1967, 246). Such problems extend to general equilibrium theory as well (Richter and Wong 1999; Landini et al. 2020).

Binmore's (1987, 209–212) response to such undecidability in self-referencing systems invokes a "sophisticated" form of Bayesian updating involving a degree of greater ignorance. Koppl and Rosser agree that agents can operate in such an environment by accepting limits on knowledge and operate accordingly, perhaps on the basis of intuition or "Keynesian animal spirits" (Keynes 1936). Hyper-rational agents cannot have complete knowledge, essentially for the same reason that Gödel showed that no logical system can be complete within itself.

However, even for Binmore's proposed solution there are also limits. Thus, Diaconis and Freedman (1986) have shown that Bayes' Theorem fails to hold in an infinite dimensional space. There may be a failure to converge on the correct solution through Bayesian updating, notably when the basis is discontinuous. There can be convergence on a cycle in which agents are jumping back and forth from one probability to another, neither of which is correct. In the simple example of coin tossing, they might be jumping back and forth between assuming priors of 1/3 and 2/3 without ever being able to converge on the correct probability of 1/2. Nyarko (1991) has studied such kinds of cyclical dynamics in learning situations in generalized economic models.

Koppl and Rosser compare this issue to that of the Keynes's problem (1936, chapter 12) of the beauty contest in which the participants are supposed to win if they most accurately guess the guesses of the other participants, potentially involving an infinite regress problem with the participants trying to guess how the other participants are going to be guessing about their guessing and so forth. This can also be seen as a problem of reflexivity (Rosser 2020b). A solution comes by, in effect, choosing to be somewhat ignorant or boundedly rational and operating at a particular level of analysis. However, as there is no way to determine rationally the degree of boundedness, which itself involves an infinite regress problem (Lipman 1991), this decision also ultimately involves an arbitrary act, based on animal spirits or whatever, a decision ultimately made without full knowledge.

A curiously related point here is the newer literature (Gode and Sunder 1993; Mirowski 2002) on the behavior of zero intelligence traders. Gode and Sunder (1993) have shown that in many artificial market setups, zero intelligence traders following very simple rules can converge on market equilibria that may even be efficient. Not only may it be necessary to limit one's knowledge to behave in a rational manner, but one may be able to be rational in some sense while being completely without knowledge whatsoever. Mirowski and Nik-Kah (2017) argue that this completes a transformation of the treatment of knowledge in economics in the post-World War II era from assuming that all agents have full knowledge to all agents having zero knowledge.

A further point on this is that there are degrees of computational complexity (Velipillai 2000; Markose 2005), with Kolmogorov (1965) providing a widely accepted definition that the degree of computational complexity is given by the minimum length of a program that will halt on a Turing machine. We have been considering the extreme cases of no halting, but there is indeed an accepted hierarchy among levels of computational complexity, with the knowledge difficulties experiencing qualitative shifts across them. At the lowest level are linear systems, easily solved, with such a low level of computational complexity we can view them as not complex. Above that level are polynomial (P) problems that are substantially more computationally complex, but still generally solvable. Above that are exponential and other non-polynomial (NP) problems that are very difficult to solve, although it remains as yet unproven that these two levels are fundamentally distinct, one of the most important unsolved problems in computer science. Above this level is that of full computational complexity associated where the minimum length is infinite, where the programs do not halt, the sort we have discussed in most of this section. Here the knowledge problems can only be solved by becoming effectively less intelligent.

Complexity Foundations of Bounded Rationality and Limited Knowledge

Herbert A. Simon was a polymath who published over 900 papers in numerous disciplines and is generally considered to be the "father of modern behavioral economics" (Rosser and Rosser 2015). He certainly coined the term (Simon 1955), although earlier economists certainly accepted many ideas of behavioral economics going at least as far back as Adam Smith (1759). Central to his conception of behavioral economics was the concept of *bounded rationality*. His concern with this idea and his search for its ultimate foundations would lead him to consider the "thinking" of computers as a way of studying human thinking, with this making him a founder of the field of artificial intelligence (Simon 1969).

What is not widely recognized is how complexity ideas underlie this fundamental idea of Simon's. He was fully aware of the debates in logic regarding the solvability of recursive systems (Church 1936; Rosser 1936; Turing 1937a) and indeed the deeply underlying problems of incompleteness and inconsistency that hold for any computational system, whether one in a fully rational person's head or inside a computer. The limits imposed by computational complexity were for him profound and ultimate. However, even before these limits were reached he doubted the computational capabilities of humans at more basic levels, especially in the face of a reality full of complex systems. And Simon was aware of the unusual probability distributions that nonlinear dynamical systems can generate (Ijiri and Simon 1964). In addition, his awareness of hierarchical complexity simply added to his understanding of the limits of knowledge by the many forms of complexity (Simon 1962), with Simon one of the few figures so early on to be attuned to the multiple varieties of complexity.

Simon's awareness of the limits to knowledge and the importance of bounded rationality led to him emphasizing various important concepts. Thus, he distinguished *substantive* from *procedural* rationality (Simon 1976), with the latter being what boundedly rational agents due in the face of the limits to their knowledge. They adopt heuristic rules of thumb, and knowing that they will be unable to fully optimize, they seek to achieve set goals, *satisficing*, with Simon's followers developing this into a whole theory of management (Cyert and March 1963). Simon never declared agents to be irrational or crazy, simply unavoidably bounded by limits that they must face and operate within.

A curious matter here has been the occasional effort by more standard neoclassical economists to try to subsume Simon and his view into their worldview. Thus, Stigler (1961) argued that Simon's view simply amounted to adding another variable to be optimized in the standard model, namely minimizing the costs of information. If full information is impossible due to infinite cost, then one estimates just the right amount of information to obtain. This sounds good on the surface, but it ignores the problem that people do not know what the full costs of information are. They may need to pursue a higher-level activity: determining the costs of information. But that then implies yet another round of this: determining the costs of determining the costs of information, yet another ineluctable infinite regress as ultimately appears in Keynes's beauty contest (Conlisk 1996), yet another example of complexity undermining the ability to obtain knowledge.

Just as Stigler attempted to put Simon's ideas into a narrow box, so others since have attempted to do so as well, including many behavioral economists. But drawing on multiple approaches to complexity, Simon's understanding of the nature of the relationship between knowledge and complexity stands on its own as special and worthy of its continuing influence (Velupillai 2019).

Knowledge and Ergodicity

Finally, a controversial issue involving knowledge and complexity involves the deep sources of the Keynes-Knight idea of fundamental uncertainty (Keynes 1921; Knight 1921). Both of them made it clear that for uncertainty there is no underlying probability distribution determining important events that agents must make decisions about. Keynes's formulation of this has triggered much discussion and debate as to why he saw this lack of a probability distribution arising.

One theory that has received much attention, due to Davidson (1982–83), is that while neither Keynes nor Knight ever mentioned it, what can bring about such uncertainty, especially for Keynes's understanding of it, is the appearance of nonergodicity in the dynamic processes underlying economic reality. In making this argument, Davidson specifically cited arguments made by Paul Samuelson (1969, 184) to the effect that "economics as a science assumes the ergodic axiom." Davidson relied on this to assert that failure of this axiom is an ontological matter that is central to understanding Keynesian uncertainty, when knowledge breaks down, with many since repeating this argument, although Alvarez and Ehnts (2016) argue that Davidson misinterpreted Samuelson who actually dismissed this ergodic view as being tied to an older classical view that he did not accept.

Davidson's argument has more recently come under criticism by various observers, perhaps most vigorously recently by O'Donnell (2014–15), who argues that Davidson has misrepresented the ergodic hypothesis, that Keynes never considered it, and that Keynesian uncertainty is more a matter of short-run instabilities to be understood using behavioral economics rather than the asymptotic elements that are tied up with ergodicity. An important argument by O'Donnell is that, even in an ergodic system that is going to go to a long-run stationary state, it may be out of that state for a period of time so long that one will be unable to determine if it is ergodic or not. This is a strong argument to which Davidson (2015) has not succeeded in fully replying.

Central to this is to understand the ergodic hypothesis itself and its development and limits, as well as its relationship to Keynes's own arguments, which turns out to be somewhat complicated, but indeed linked to central concerns of Keynes in an indirect way, especially given that he never directly mentioned it. Most economists discussing this matter, including both Davidson and O'Donnell, have accepted as the definition of an ergodic system that over time (asymptotically) its "space averages equal its time averages." This formulation was due to Paul and Tatiana Ehrenfest (1912), with Paul Ehrenfest a student of Ludwig Boltzmann (1884), who initiated the study of ergodicity (and coined the term) as part of his long study of statistical mechanics, particularly how a long-term aggregate average (such as temperature) could emerge from a set of dynamically stochastic parts (particle movements). It turns out that, for all its widespread influence, the precise formulation by the Ehrenfests was inaccurate (Uffink 2006). Nevertheless, this reflected that there were multiple strands in the meaning of "ergodicity."

In fact, there is ongoing debate about how Boltzmann coined the term in the first place. His student, Ehrenfest, claimed it was from combining the Greek *ergos* ("work") with *hodos* ("path"), while it has been argued by

Gallavotti (1999) that it came from him using his own neologism, *monode*, meaning a stationary distribution, instead of *hodos*. This fits with most of the early formulations of ergodicity that analyzed it within the context of stationary distributions.

Later discussions of ergodicity would draw on two complementary theorems proven by Birkhoff (1931) and von Neumann (1932), although the latter was proven first and influenced the proof of the former, with von Neumann's approach more algebraic and emphasizing measure preservation, while Birkhoff's variation was more geometric and related to recurrence properties in dynamical systems. Both involve long-run convergence, and Birkhoff's formulation showed not only measure preservation but that for a stationary ergodic system a *metric indecomposability* such that not only is the space properly filled, but that it is impossible to break the system into two that will also fully fill the space and preserve measure.

The link between stationarity and ergodicity would come to weaken in later study, with Malinvaud (1966) positing that a stationary system might not be ergodic—one example is a limit cycle—and with Davidson aware of this case from the beginning of his discussions. However, it continued to be believed that ergodic systems must be stationary, and this remained a key for Davidson as well as being accepted by most of his critics, including O'Donnell. However, it turns out that this may break down in ergodic chaotic systems of infinite dimension, which may not be stationary (Shinkai and Aizawa 2006), which brings back the role of chaotic dynamics in undermining the ability to achieve knowledge of a dynamical system, even one that is ergodic.

Given these complications, it is worthwhile to return to Keynes to understand what his concerns were, which came out most clearly in his debates with Tinbergen (1937, 1940; Keynes 1938) over how to econometrically estimate models for forecasting macroeconomic dynamics. A deep irony here is that Tinbergen was a student of Paul Ehrenfest and was indeed influenced by his ideas on ergodicity, even as Keynes did not directly address this matter. In any case, what Keynes objected to was the apparent absence of *homogeneity*, essentially a concern that the model itself changes over time. Keynes's solution to this was to break a time series down into sub-samples to see if one gets the same parameter estimates as one does for the whole time series. Homogeneity is not strictly identical to either stationarity or ergodicity, but it is probably the case that, at the time, Tinbergen, following Ehrenfest, probably assumed all three holding for the models he estimated. Thus, indeed, the ergodic hypothesis was assumed to hold for these early econometric models, whereas Keynes was skeptical of there being a sufficient homogeneity for one to assume one knew what the system was doing over time.

Conclusions

We have reviewed issues related to the problem of knowledge in complex systems. While there are many competing definitions of complexity, we have identified two that have been most frequently used in economics: dynamic complexity and computational complexity. Each has its own sort of epistemological problems. Dynamic complexity is subject to such issues as the sensitive dependence on initial conditions of chaos theory, or the uncertainty due to fractal basin boundaries in stochastic nonlinear systems, or the pattern of phase transitions and self-organizing transformations that can occur in systems with interacting heterogeneous agents. Such problems imply that, in effect, only an infinite degree of precision of knowledge will allow one to fully understand the system, which is impossible.

In computationally complex systems, the problem is more related to logic, the problems of infinite regress and undecidability associated with self-referencing in systems of Turing machines. This can manifest itself as the halting problem, something that can arise even for a computer attempting to precisely calculate a dynamically complex system, such as, for example, the exact shape of the Mandelbrot set (Blum et al. 1998). A Turing machine cannot understand fully a system in which its own decision-making is too crucially a part. However, knowledge of such systems may be gained by other means.

These computational problems as well as those arising in nonlinear dynamical systems were key to Herbert Simon formulating his concept of bounded rationality. This was reinforced by his initiation of the idea of hierarchical complexity as well.

In dynamical systems, debates have long arisen regarding how fundamental uncertainty of the Keynes-Knight type can arise. Davidson and others have argued that this is deeply linked to nonergodicity of such systems, but in fact such elements as homogeneity and stationarity may be more important. The realization that a chaotic ergodic system might be nonstationary makes clear that the problems of knowledge in such systems go well beyond just nonergodicity.

In the end, the serious epistemological problems associated with complex economic systems do imply that there exist serious bounds on the rationality of economic agents. These bounds take many forms—inability to understand the internal relations of a system, inability to fully know crucial parameter values, inability to identify critical thresholds or bifurcation points and inability to understand the interactions of agents, especially when these agents are thinking about how each other are thinking about each other's thinking. Infinite regress problems imply non-decidability and non-computability for hyper-rational Turing machine agents. Thus, economic agents must ultimately rely on arbitrary acts and decisions, even if those simply involve deciding what will be the bounds beyond which the agent will no longer attempt to solve the epistemological problem.

CHAPTER 12

Biological Hypercomputation

Social and Political Implications

Carlos Eduardo Maldonado

Introduction

A technical, and in this case, computational idea has been recently posited that has clear social and political implications. This concept, entitled biological hypercomputation (BH), represents a new paradigm within the framework of the sciences of complexity. BH claims that living beings do not process information like a Turing Machine (TM), under any circumstances. Moreover, living beings cannot be considered in any sense as machines, in the sense of the Church–Turing Thesis. The emerging approach argues that living beings process information in a very singular way that can be labeled as non-algorithmic. In the language of computation, such a characteristic is generally known as unconventional computation.

This chapter explores the social and political implications of non-algorithmic information processing. Traditionally, human culture has been founded on laws, norms, commandments, tactic and strategy—in one word precisely, algorithm. That has been the story of the past. Non-algorithmic information processing must be made explicit. This is the foundational tenet of this chapter. Accordingly, a number of features, consequences and problems are explored that radically challenge the history of mankind as it has been viewed to date. Complexity science now stands at the precipice of a true civilizatory shift in human history.

Our world is complex and characterized by turbulence, instabilities, fluctuations, randomness and unpredictability. In this highly networked world, strongly defined by non-linearity, our best efforts are required to produce explanation and understanding. As a result, sincere efforts to coin new terms, to bring out new conceptual tools, to develop creativity and insight are necessary to help people and societies, nations and states, to fully grasp global events and circumstances. One such effort involves the sciences of complexity, a group of sciences, hence also disciplines, methodologies, methods, techniques, languages and approaches aimed at understanding the role of randomness in the world. These sciences provide important insights into the importance of non-causal phenomena and processes, the meaning of non-linearity, and the emergence and self-organization pervading society and nature at large.

Our current historical era is often defined by the three labels of the information society, the knowledge society and the network society, all supporting the same socio-cultural momentum. Yet, in such a world, there seems to be a strong asymmetry of information, particularly between the foundations of society and the big corporations and superpowers, such as China, the US and Russia. Such an asymmetry can also be witnessed when confronting small states and superpowers.

To be sure, one the most conspicuous conceptual paths developed already is complexity science, or by its alternative moniker, complexity theory. Rightly understood, it should be named as the sciences of complexity, meaning by this a set of sciences for which disciplines, approaches, tools and languages are aimed at understanding and explaining increasingly complex systems. Far beyond an adverb or an adjective, we are currently living in a complex world. It is a world where synergies and small changes have as consequences unpredictable outcomes that cannot be fully anticipated by the data and processes that work as inputs. It is a highly sensitive world in many respects, highly interconnected, hence, where one stance, level, layer or region cannot adequately be explained without, simultaneously taking into considerations many other levels, layers or regions. Most significantly, it is a world that does not obey a singular center, be it Rome, Washington, Beijing or Moscow, simply because we now live in a multi-centric world. These and other features can be summarized in the single expression—a non-zero-sum world. Multi-disciplinary and cross-disciplinary approaches become necessary as one single science or discipline cannot cope with the dynamics and processes that are currently underway. The sciences of complexity in general, and BH in particular, exhibit a sort of *Zeitgeist* that both demands and allows for transversal and synthetic explanations and endeavors.

This chapter explores the social and political implications of a very radical idea, namely, that understanding, explaining and living in a complex world means thinking and living in a non-algorithmic way. To adequately grasp this idea, four arguments are presented. First, it is necessary to correctly understand what the sciences of complexity are and what they entail. The claim is made that complexity science is primarily concerned with gaining degrees of freedom. The argument is justified and explained. The second argument consists of an introduction, particularly for newcomers, to the concept of BH. The radical argument here is that thinking in terms of BH means thinking without categories. Accordingly, the third argument digs deeper into the concept of BH and argues that a computational understanding of BH is necessary. The justifications of such a need are defined and the consequences are considered in detail. The fourth argument presents the core of this chapter and details the social and political implications of BH. A number of consequences are sketched out and discussed ranging from sociology to politics, from economics to military studies, from anthropology to cultural and historical frameworks.

Along the lines of this text, a most fundamental conclusion can be drawn, namely, that the spine, so to speak, of complexity science is computational theory in the sense that it is the foundation around which other members and organs hang and that trigger several functions, actions and movements (Arora and Barak 2009; Goldreich 2008; Rosenberg 2010).

Nonetheless, from the outset it should be clear that the sciences of complexity are sciences of life in the sense that the most complex system ever is life, meaning life as we know it. Thus, the entire enterprise is about understanding, explaining life, making it possible as much as we can imagine, but also about enhancing, caring and dignifying life in every sense and concern. The sciences of complexity are not anthropology in any sense of the word, and its frame and basis is not, at least not any longer, an anthropological, an anthropomorphic or an anthropocentric view of the world and nature. Instead, life in general is placed at the focus and all endeavors are devoted to grasp it and make it possible, as much as it is imaginable. I shall broaden and justify this idea throughout the chapter.

Complexity Science is Ultimately About Gaining Degrees of Freedom

There is a generalized confusion when discussing complex systems. This confusion is clarified in table 12.1.

straightforward expression, complexity science is to be separated and not necessarily opposed to systems science, revealing an issue that is often taken for granted. The question that arises here consists in working out a sort of demarcation criterion very much in the spirit of the Vienna Circle's[1] efforts to develop a worldview that unified the sciences.

The core concern, here, is that complexity science consists of: a) studying how a system gains degrees of freedom, or else also b) in working out how, or creating, a system that can gain degrees of freedom. The difference between a) and b) arises from the role of the agent, say, the scientist or researcher.

Thus, the complexity of a deterministic system, phenomenon or behavior consists exactly in the degrees of freedom the system exhibits or has (Maldonado 2018a). The concept of "degrees of freedom" arises originally from physics and mathematics, but when it is placed within the framework of the social and human sciences, it becomes highly suggestive. This is the main subject of this first section of this chapter.

There are numerous definitions of "complexity" (Horgan 1995). As a consequence, complex systems are usually explained not in terms of what they are, but by their properties or characteristics. Complex systems exhibit numerous features, such as nonlinearity, self-organization, emergence, percolation, turbulence, instability and many others. Here a most salient feature will be pointed out, namely, a complex system exhibits a large number

Table 12.1 Two Ways of Understanding Complexity

Systems Thinking	Complexity Science
A *holistic* or *systemic* view in which all the parts of a system are closely interrelated, and yet the whole is more than the sum of the parts.	An understanding of how ruptures, discontinuities and inflections happen and, if possible, how to gain *degrees of freedom*.

---

1. For comparison, see Stadler (1997).

of degrees of freedom; representing possibilities and independent variables affecting the range of states of a determined system of phenomenon.

Technically, the concept of degrees of freedom comes from both statistics and physics, but it has been widened to a number of fields and disciplines. It means the possible movements a given system has or can have so that the higher the degrees of freedom, literally, the more complex it becomes. Complexity, I shall claim, can be adequately grasped in a twofold sense, namely:

- Complexity is about studying and explaining the degrees of freedom any given system has—or can have—or once had, all depending on the interests of the researcher. As a consequence, complexity science consists in understanding how a system has degrees of freedom, or also, more radically, how it can gain (or has gained) more degrees of freedom. If the latter is the case, the study of complexity precisely consists in working with possibility spaces, mathematically called Hilbert space.
- Complexity science consists in introducing degrees of freedom in any given system at stake. In this case, the researcher has a variety of ways by which a system can gain degrees of freedom, for instance, via modeling and simulation—more adequately called Agent-Based Modeling (ABM). Modeling and simulation is one of the methods for working on complex systems at large. There are other methods and techniques that will be mentioned within this chapter, although this is not the main contention of this text.

In other words, complexity science is about understanding and explaining if and how any linear system becomes a nonlinear one, or else also, if and how any linear system can be converted or transformed into a nonlinear one (Maldonado 2016a). As it is well known, a nonlinear system is the one that gains information, although not necessarily memory. Thus, gaining information is another way to state the fact that a system gains degrees of freedom.

More directly, complexologists either introduce into the world what the world does not have as yet, namely degrees of freedom, or also help increase the degrees of freedom that a system already has. It goes without saying that there is no upper limit to the degrees of freedom. The idea literally means increasing the degrees of freedom as much as possible. A principle of indeterminacy and openness serves here as a gate that points toward the entire history of the human spirit. In other words, there is no limit of the degrees of freedom for a system to be under one proviso, namely, the open and direct acknowledgement that the sciences of complexity are sciences of life. Indeed, the most complex system imaginable is life, that is, living beings, and the sciences of life are ultimately about increasing the degrees of freedom of life.

Among the various tools and methods in complexity science is BH (Maldonado and Gómez 2014). It is the problem consisting in acknowledging that living beings do process information, albeit in a non-algorithmic way. In other words, living beings cannot and should not be considered in any sense as machines, and most notably, as Turing machines (TM). Not even considering that there are a variety of TMs, such as the deterministic TM, the nondeterministic TM, the oracle TM, the uncertain TM, and several others—an issue that is mainly of interest for computing scientists—living beings cannot by any means be considered as machines in any sense of a TM. Moreover, information processing for living beings is a matter of life or death, for bad or incorrect processing can bring a living being, or species, into danger and occasionally to extinction.

That living beings are not machines and hence do not process information algorithmically can be stated in two equivalent versions. On the one hand, it is the classical explanation provided originally by Schrödinger ([1944] 2012) according to which life consists in an unceasing negation of physics (i.e., of the laws of classical physics). The expression coined by Schrödinger was "negentropy," an ugly expression (openly acknowledged by Schrödinger himself) but that pointed in the right direction. Briefly said, life continuously negates the second law or principle of thermodynamics.

In this sense, life is an everlasting process of negation—that is, a rejection or avoidance of physics. It is physics that speaks of laws, space, time, state, power, mass, inertia, action and reaction, free fall, force and many other similar concepts, processes and states. Briefly said, physics is about dead objects, non-living entities subject therefore to physical explanations. Life in general cannot by any means be explained and understood in such terms, hence the concept of negentropy, meaning that living beings reject, refuse, negate entropy—the second law of thermodynamics. So far so good, for this is nonetheless a negative explanation of life. Yet, positively or affirmatively, what is life? Schrödinger left the question unanswered even though he provided fundamental insights toward the right answer.

Later in his life, Schrödinger repeatedly said that he was not satisfied with the concept of negentropy. A more positive answer to the question raised was provided by I. Prigogine (1980) who noted that living beings exist far from equilibrium. This can be translated as saying that life consists in dynamic or punctuated equilibriums (Gould 2007). On the other hand, the other more straightforward explanation claims that living beings— most conspicuously, human beings—cannot be understood or explained only or mainly on the basis of laws, commandments, rules, recipes and the like. Computationally speaking, this means algorithms. Voilà, a most disturbing statement when seen through the eyes of tradition, or when seen from the standpoint of institutionalism, in any sense of the word— institutionalism or status quo.

Rules and laws certainly have played a most important role in the history of humankind. Some of the most conspicuous cases are Hammurabi's Code, the Ten Commandments, the rise of Roman Law and the Napoleon Law, up until today. The list could be large and rich, as is indeed the case. As it is said, laws in any sense of the word are computationally conceived as algorithms. Since the origins of computation and information, algorithms too have played an important role in regard to technology. Technology has been friendly to society precisely thanks to algorithms that make it easy to use it, ranging from elevators to computers, to mobile phones to the internet, from search engines to TV cable, for instance. The point, however, is the recent discovery that claims that life and living beings cannot be *reduced* to algorithms, in any sense of the word. BH is the term coined for such a discovery. Here, I unfold its consequences. Before that, nonetheless, a clear-cut understanding of the concept and problem is necessary.

Biological Hypercomputation: A First-Hand Approach

As it happens, BH has a history that can be summarized as follows. Nine landmarks paved the road toward BH. These are (Maldonado and Gómez 2014):

- Classical computation,
- Unconventional computation,

- Bioinspired models of computation,
- Biology as implementation substrate,
- Classical hypercomputation,
- Bioinspired hypercomputation,
- Nonclassical computation, and
- Biological hypercomputation.

The framework, as it can be seen, is computational science. The reason is that computational science widely allows us to overcome any mechanistic view of the world and nature. In this sense, the nine landmarks mentioned can be summarized as thus: physical machines compute. Indeed, the best machine ever developed and conceived is logically, mathematically, computationally and philosophically called a TM. Well, TMs compute; that is, they compute functions and numbers. A sophisticated development of a TM can even be said that it hypercomputes; this is the concept introduced for an all-purpose machine, namely, a computer. Yet, living beings can compute in the sense that they are physical objects, although not only and not mainly physical objects. Anatomy and physiology largely still conceive of human beings as "perfect machines." The explanation of the brain—neurons, mainly, in terms of *on* and *off* mechanisms—can also be mentioned along the same wave-length. However, ultimately, living beings are not machines and they hypercompute—that is, they solve very complex problems as if they were simple or elementary problems. In biology, such is the case of protein folding, antigen production and many others.

Surely, living beings also compute dynamics, phenomena and processes. Rather than algorithms, interaction and emergence serve to help us better understand why and how living beings compute. Computing properly means metabolizing or transforming one thing, A, into another, B. Computing, thus, does not mean only analyzing or "thinking" in a wide and undefined way. Metabolism is for living beings what computing is for a TM. In other words, time is incorporated within computation, it is just that computation takes place in a given time lapse.

That said, living beings are not compressible in terms of TM. Consequently, the computations carried out by living beings are not compressible either. Most importantly, BH entails that the difference between the environment and the living being cannot by any means be traced.

Certainly, interaction is much more expressive than what can be an algorithm or a TM. Briefly said, for life, computation means living, and bad computing brings living systems to the edge of peril, danger or extinction (Maldonado and Gómez 2014).

The nine landmarks mentioned above can be stated in a timeline. Table 12.2 presents the timeline that results in BH. As a consequence, BH belongs to a recent tradition that seeks to understand living beings by means of computational approaches, widening or deepening other traditions based mainly in physics, chemistry, biology and even the very social and human sciences.

Three main obstacles can be identified resulting from the origins of modern science and continuing through the present. These are determinism, reductionism and dualism. Science was born after the Renaissance with a spirit of determinism. The past determines the present, and the timeline that leads from the past to the present determines the future. No one jumps over one's own shadow, as Hegel noted. Modern science is characterized by reductionism. Reductionism can be taken among many other variants as the belief that there is a fundamental science, method or view that prevails over all others. Classical mechanics plays this role from Galileo and, until very recently, even among the social and human sciences. It can be safely said that both determinism and reductionism have already been solidly criticized and recognized as wanting. The trouble remains with dualism.

Table 12.2 Timeline toward Biological Hypercomputation

Line of Complexification	Years
Classical Computation	1930s–1940s
Unconventional Computation	1980s–present
Bio-inspired Models of Computation	1900s
Biology as Implementation Substrate	1994
Classical Hypercomputation	1999
Bio-inspired Hypercomputation	2004–2005
Non-classical Hypercomputation	2009
Biological Computation	2012
Biological Hypercomputation	2014–2015
Biological Hypercomputation as a Complex Problem	2014–present

Source: Table modified and enlarged after Maldonado and Gómez (2014).

The most recent version of dualism finds its root in Descartes's philosophy and extends its influence even today. Dualism can be overcome via a different approach, not so much via physics or the humanities by themselves. A correct understanding of what computation means allows for finally overcoming dualism, too. This, however, should by no means be taken as if computation would then arise as a fundamental science, just like physics was during the eighteenth century, or statistics during the second half of the nineteenth century. From a computational point of view, there is no distinction between the hardware and the software in the cell—and from there on to the entire organism. Interactive computation most notably allows reckoning that the distinction between a living being and the environment is merely artificial (Goldin et al. 2006).

Certainly, BH firmly sets the ground for overcoming dualism in that living beings are certainly physical entities that nonetheless cannot be reduced to physics, very much as they cannot be rightly understood or explained in terms of algorithms, in any sense or translation of the word. By processing information, living beings make their environment their own surroundings (*ur-welt*), and they create the world with all of their continuous processing.

More radically, information does not exist before it is processed, or after it is processed. Information only exists insofar as it is being processed. The processing of information is just the technical expression for saying "living."[2] Computationally speaking, the most salient feature of a language or logic is its expressiveness. The more expressive a language is, the better the information is processed. Living beings are not just machines or sheer physical objects. Quite to the contrary, living beings unceasingly create a world according to the very avatars of their life. Evolution, said one important biologist, occurs as a tinkering (*bricolage*, in French; Jacob 1981). Thus, BH does not take place according to plans, programs, strategies and the like. Biological hypercomputation is computing freely, non-teleologically. Whereas computation in a TM happens as a program that is somehow sketched and sets the rules, for living beings the rules are at

---

2. This explains the difference between *Erfahrung* and *Erlebnis*, in German. Living beings do not just have experiences of the world (*Erfahrungen*), but they create and re-create continuously the world around them (*Erlebnis*).

their best when they do not determine the course of a life. BH is computing for free.[3]

Accordingly, BH sheds brand new light on complexity science. That evolution expresses itself as tinkering rather than as an *a priori* program entails an important distinction vis-à-vis complexity theory. Indeed, we can distinguish thinking in terms of systems where the whole is more than the sum of the parts, conceiving of the world in terms of holism, of closely interrelated parts. This is what exactly comprises systems science.

On the other hand, however, we can also take thinking in terms of disruptions, turbulence, discontinuities, fluctuations, instabilities, ruptures and discrete systems and behaviors.[4] By and large, the most "popular" take of complexity is the former, that is, the systemic one. It is my contention, though, that the distinction—not necessarily the opposition—must be made between systems science and complexity science. The discussion herein of the social and political implications of BH helps us step forward in the direction of such a distinction.

It is my contention that complexity theory becomes much more helpful and valuable when it is interpreted as the study of ruptures, inflections and disclosures. BH then means that living beings process information non-locally, in parallel, in distributed ways, non-sequentially, non-hierarchically, in and as interaction with their environment as well as with other individuals and species, as emergent processing, and definitely non-algorithmically—entailing then that the entire story is about gaining degrees of freedom, not just matching or integrating within larger frameworks.

Thus, this leads to the consideration of how living beings, in general, process information. BH opens the door to aspects such as challenging, betting and defiance, which point toward autonomy, enacting, freedom or autarchy, four ways to name of and the same behavior. I shall return later to these characteristics.

---

3. This is very much related to the free-lunch theorem (you are reading this correctly: not with the non-free-lunch theorem). In the world, we encounter order-for-free (Kauffman 1995). Well, the correlation for the order-for-free is precisely BH.
4. For a comparison, see Maldonado (forthcoming).

Biological Hypercomputation: A Computational Understanding

The scope of this chapter is computational. Rather than taking it as a reductionist point of view, thinking computationally means thinking about transformations, such as changing A into B. Roughly speaking, computers are processors, and computing really consists in processing. The two most basic ways of processing appear, then, as classical processing and non-classical or unconventional processing. Quantum information processing is one example of what unconventional processing means. In terms of cryptography, for instance, there is already some work that examines post-quantum cryptography (Bernstein et al. 2009). The term used to express such a process here was metabolizing. To be sure, metabolizing is a fundamental process for life—certainly not the only one, a trivial statement, but the one that best sheds light on what life is all about.

Living beings make themselves possible and always more and more possible. Complexity appears already complex at the outset of the universe or reality. More meaningfully, the best understanding of complex systems is that they become increasingly complex. We speak, then, about increasingly complex systems. Computationally speaking, this idea means that living beings process increasing information, or that living beings increasingly process information. Either way, it should be clear that this idea goes hand in hand with the very evolution and history of life writ large. Life, as defined by development and evolution, is about increases in information processing. Death occurs when no further information can be processed, and we are literally stuck with information. More exactly, no new information can be adequately processed. Aging and death occur then (Vedral 2010; Maldonado 2018b).

Certainly, the very idea that living beings—or more radically, living—entails thinking and living non-algorithmically, is a most crucial idea with consequences that have not been seen, as yet. It is time we draw some consequences. Algorithms stand at the antipode of freedom, autonomy, enaction or autarchy. These are four names for one and the same behavior, namely, one without constraints or restrictions. Before justifying this claim, it is necessary to shed some light on the four kinds of life just mentioned. I proceed initially with a historical argument.

Autarchy is a most fundamental kind of life characterized by the fact that human beings have or find the ground for their own life within themselves. *Arché* means both *ground* and *principle*, fundament and soil, whereas *autos* refers to the self. Historically speaking, this was the way life was characterized during the Archaic Period of Ancient Greece. With the arrival of the Classical Period, and more particularly the rise of the Hellenic Period, autonomy became more important, and autarchy disappeared. Moreover, during the rest of the history of Western civilization, autarchy was rarely mentioned again. This prior focus was displaced by autonomy and freedom.

Enaction is a beautiful concept originally introduced by Varela (1992), and it has been deepened and enlarged. Enaction is the concept that describes the interactions between an organism and its environment in a way that maintains a dynamic balance between both. The organism is capable of autonomy. Ultimately, the concept has been developed within the frame of the philosophy of mind. Varela (1989) had a broader view about enaction. He openly introduced the concept and developed it in close relation to the idea that what most radically characterizes a living being is its autonomy. Thus, in the development of his thought, autonomy led to enaction and the very frame was originally not so much the mind, but the entire living being. Put differently, it is the recognition that the mind is embodied, and the embodiment of the mind—that is, the unity of the living being—can adequately be grasped as enaction.

We have thus four ways to name one and the same problem: autarchy, autonomy, freedom and enaction that can computationally rightly be interpreted as non-algorithmicity. Living beings are under no conditions machines. Living beings are not just ruled by physics, and they do not think and live like the other physical entities in spite of being themselves physical beings. There is a very radical interpretation of this perspective. From the outset, the Western world assumed that there are categories, and that thinking means thinking with and about categories. The whole story was wrong. Categorizations, such as labeling, tagging and pigeon-holing, are ways to follow programs, yet they impede our ability to truly see the world around us as it emerges.

When we view the world through categories we do not really see the world, but rather we see our own categories, such as those inherited from culture, those transmitted via education, those uncritically used every day. Categories are the first hurdle to freedom, to having and developing one's own criteria. As Kant once said it—yes, the very same Kant who believed in categories just like Aristotle—as the *sapere aude*! All in all, categories are algorithms that freeze the world and nature. Algorithms freeze thought and life, as they make life and thought mechanistic. It is well understood that Kant's emphasis stands not so much in the *sapere*, but in the *aude—dare* to know by yourself. Do not follow previously established rules, laws, recipes and commandments.

As it is well known, an algorithm is basically a way to solve a problem. An algorithm is a program set out under the proviso of a protocol in computing science. The way in which algorithms are developed and implemented in the world is via writing code. Programming languages are but codes developed with an aim in mind. The better the solution to the problem, the stronger the algorithm. The epidermis, or the most popular expression of this entire process, is known under three names, namely, artificial intelligence, artificial life and robotics. This is, so to speak, one side of the token; the other side is composed of expert systems, machine learning and deep learning. The name of the token is the internet, but the name of the game with the token has received various labels and levels, thus we experience the web 1.0, the web 2.0, the current paradigm of web 3.0. We now foresee the upcoming web 4.0, and the already envisioned web 5.0, known as the emotional web.

It is not just a metaphor or a fancy expression: we are currently entering an age in which the biological, the physical and the digital dimensions of life are being synthesized. The emerging horizon has just been sketched and the truth is that no one truly knows what its consequences are. It appears to be true that human beings make their own history, but they never make it in the way they want it or plan it. Society at large is being programmed and, hence, ruled by algorithms of various kinds. Computer scientists have even developed programs that program themselves without the need for a programmer, resulting in a most wonderful contradiction (Nagel and Newman 1958).

We can, for the sake of brevity, abbreviate artificial intelligence, artificial life and robotics with one single name—artificial life—simply because it has become popular, and it has largely advanced the other two in the realm of culture, at large. To be sure, the issue has produced two main camps, the ones who fear artificial intelligence and its consequences and, on the other side, those who trust artificial life and believe it can enhance the evolution of life. Perhaps the most conspicuous representative of the first camp was Hawking (2015), whereas the most prestigious spokesperson of the second camp is Kurzweil (2005).

The core of the discussion has to do with the role human beings can play as starring in evolution, or as becoming supporting actors of evolution. Being as it is, the question has a fundamental essence. This essence is what technically has been named as the technological singularity. The singularity has two expressions, either as the interface between chip and cell, or as the moment in which artificial intelligence will clearly, even not surprisingly, overcome human intelligence, at least for mechanical tasks.

Computationally speaking, the problem concerns whether machines can learn by themselves and consequently act and make choices by themselves, or whether human beings can still maintain control of evolution, as most believe we can. The problem pervades philosophy and science, culture and the arts, the so-called hard sciences, the social and human sciences and raises basic questions about the destiny or fate of life on Earth.

Algorithms are but the most recent translation and expression of a most sensitive issue, namely, that of control. Within the frame of a manifold of Turing machines all around us, that are increasingly running business and security, data and society, well, politics and economics at large, the truth is that an algorithmic and, if allowed, an "algorithmized" world is a world almost entirely pervaded by control and manipulation (Zuboff 2019).

The ingenuity of science and technology nowadays entirely relies on Turing machines. Numerous fields have benefitted from it, including medicine, telecommunications, transportation, banking and finance, research in numerous domains, informatics and even entertainment. Always more sophisticated algorithms rule everyday life from the backstage, and it seems that people are increasingly subject to the wonders of artificial intelligence, artificial life and robotics at large. Not ultimately, enormous databases have arrived to control life and rule society. The ongoing discussions and debates around the web 3.0 and the upcoming 4.0 are excellent examples of this. Vis-à-vis such a framework, the call for BH and what it means and entails appear as a single voice in the midst of a crowd. It can be easily appreciated, as the need for reflection on and about BH becomes necessary, if not inevitable.

Social and Political Implications

There is a fascinating story going on around, previous to, and before algorithms and from them on to BH. That story roughly coincides with the whole history of modernity. After the end of the Middle Ages, and the transition through the Renaissance, modernity begins with a tremendous effort to really think. Beyond Descartes's search for an apodictic truth, his effort can be historically and sociologically seen as the striving to find own's one guide. That guide consists exactly in the Cartesian *ergo cogito* that will end with Kant's (2017) reflection about how to orient oneself in thought. Reasoning appears both as condition and as a consequence, and the modern age starts with an authentic call or invitation to think, period.

The dominant story of modernity is to be found in Newton's work, classical mechanics. Hand in hand with the development or reaching of classical mechanics is the development or invention of calculus, by Newton-Leibniz. Calculus is the brand-new language that allows express dynamics, that is, movement. Movement is captured via differentiation and integration in calculus. From then until the present, the world seems to have stopped thinking or reasoning and has turned to calculate. As it is often said within the framework of physics: "Shut up and calculate!"

It is such a success of calculus that it entirely permeated the bodies of knowledge, from physics to engineering, from economics to political science. Reasoning was literally displaced by calculus (Dowek 2011). Yet, in the course of the twentieth century, the shift from thinking to calculus has been radicalized. This is precisely the story of programming. With the development and triumph of computing science and computation and information at large, the emphasis has been placed on programming rather than, and instead of, reasoning and calculating. Conceiving of nature and society in terms of a program became a standard metaphor or explanation, from biology (Watson and Crick), to chemistry, from sociology to social engineering, from policies to the information technologies.

Without much ado, our world has been programmed and is being increasingly programmed. Computation is nowadays not just a metaphor, but the very atmosphere of our times, to say the least. There are, as it happens, numerous algorithms, and the number of programming languages is limitless. From applications in mobile phones, to languages, coding appears as a common knowledge *and* practice at nearly infinite levels, layers, fields and dimensions of society at large. In mass-society, human beings are reduced to physical entities, machines, indeed. It is my claim that BH offers a liberation from that frame.

I am not arguing here against algorithms. BH does not reject algorithms or any TM; instead it points in a different direction, namely, how living beings process information. The argument here is that living beings— humans, too—do not process information in terms of numbers and functions. They process information non-algorithmically. Let us delve into this argument.

The expression "having criteria of one's own" was introduced above to point out to either one, namely autarchy, autonomy, freedom or enaction. The main argument is that it is possible to think and live non-algorithmically. Basically, it is about not following algorithms, which means the capacity of deciding and thinking for yourself, without affiliations. Corporations, armies and churches, for example, strongly argue in favor of developing a sense of belonging, of membership. Numerous rewards and penalties precede and follow according to the case. A mafia-like atmosphere seems to be reigning all around us.

Not following algorithms has different basic translations—which are, to say the least, very much politically incorrect. Disobedience is one of them. Over against membership and a sense of belonging to "something bigger than oneself" (as it has been often said nearly everywhere), disobedience is a most sound way of living. After all, for instance, Jesus of Nazareth was firmly disobedient against the Roman Empire and the Sanhedrim. No rebellion, no revolution is possible without people who can be disobedient, that is, people who cease to follow the normal and standard algorithms of the time. A huge set of examples of courageous people who dared to be disobedient can be brought to the fore. Disobedience, disrespect, rebelliousness, insubordination—these are rare words in the usual vocabulary of the social and human sciences, among others similar and close.

In this age in which Google and Facebook, Amazon and IBM, Apple and Huawei, to name the most relevant, store enormous data bases about the citizens, and those immense data bases are of "national interest," the question about Turing machines becomes a little bit more than an academic concern. The independence vis-à-vis social media and the control they have over people, a control that is being overlapped to economic, political and security domains, is literally a matter of freedom, autonomy.

In one word, it is life. Life is being denied in its greatness and is being reduced to machinery and an object of interest; that, it is my contention, is what truly is bringing the planet to danger. Global warming is just a consequence of the denial and reductionism of life.

Biological hypercomputation has been introduced as a new problem in complexity science. Complexity science can now be seen as a theory that encompasses a huge liberationist philosophy that has very rarely been highlighted. It is namely the call for leaving behind the anthropomorphic, anthropocentric, the anthropologic standpoint of reality. More exactly, it focuses on a bio-centric view of the world and nature.[5]

It is the merit of BH to bring to light very directly that other forms of thinking—that is, processing information—and living are possible. Some reviews of BH are negative, and are critical of the claims concerning the importance and meaningfulness of non-algorithmic information processing. Yet, a positive affirmation of non-algorithmicity must be possible. Some recent hints have been outlined in this direction (Maldonado 2017). Some of the terms introduced for a positive affirmation of non-algorithmic information processing are computationally and physics-inspired, such as processing in parallel, distributed processing, multi-level processing, non-local, fuzzy and other approaches. I have the conviction that several other translations, explanations and understandings must be possible. The crux, here, however, concerns the social and political implication of BH.

Rules are only necessary if no other possibilities have been explored. Rules serve to contain excesses and limitless actions; yet, evolution is made out of organisms and species that defy nature and explore the unexplored. In terms of research, it is primarily about thinking the unthinkable, discovering what has not yet been discovered, inventing what is not invented. Novelty and creativity are, just like life itself, about daring and challenging, betting and breaking limits and frontiers. Algorithms are really helpful with making the world work, not, albeit, about changing the world and making it better. Algorithms have made our world work for good and for bad. This is extremely evident when considering the framework of the

---

5. I am aware that the suffix, "center," plays a clumsy role here. However, it points in the right direction. Such a direction can be differently named as pantheism, hylozoism, bio-centrism or panpsychism. I have worked in this direction in Maldonado (2018c).

information society, the knowledge society or the networks society. The literature on this topic is voluminous and increasing.

Looking toward the future, much better and insightful possibilities are being imagined. To be sure, BH is one of them. We must cease thinking like human beings and start thinking like nature. Wisdom, not just science, education and research, arises when the reference of life and thought is nature, not just society and mankind. Nature, as does life and the body itself, processes information in ways unlike the classic machine.

BH thus consists in showing how it is possible to think and live with independence from rules, laws, commandments, acts, foundational papers, constitutions, holy books and the like, when those pretend to rule and control human life. The story of evolution is exactly the story against constructions and restrictions and in favor of open degrees of freedom. However, it is a nonlinear story, never a sequential, hierarchical, linear one.

Computationally speaking, and also in terms of engineering, history and evolution, we can witness the transition from central and hierarchical control, on to fuzzy control, to distributed control and finally to the absence of control. Systems science is fundamentally about control, with variances and degrees. On the contrary, complexity science concerns degrees of freedom; hence, it involves the search for a lack of control represented by life, autarchy and enaction.

Now, is it possible for life as we know it to exist with a total absence of control? Skepticism, if not cynicism, may pervade such discussions. Without any further reflection, the human body appears, as such, a system or phenomenon. A healthy human being is a system of systems, which means that there is not a center, and certainly not an *a priori* center. When reading or thinking, the brain and the central nervous system are manifest; however, when eating, the center is displaced by the digestive system and when jogging or exercising, the center becomes the musculoskeletal system, and so on across human anatomical-physiological systems. The center depends in every case on every case. A healthy human being, healthy in a largely, unprepared or unsuspected sense, is not aware of hierarchies or control. Life runs sometimes with upheavals, sometimes smoothly just like a river has rapids of varying intensities. And those rapids may change in intensity, from rapids rated 3 to rapids rated 5, and reverse their intensities in unexpected ways.

In other words, complexity science is not so much about states, but about processes, dynamics, flow. This explains the technical interest about first-order transitions and second-order transitions. The complexity of a given system or phenomenon is directly proportional to the degrees of freedom a system has or exhibits, so much so that the higher the degrees of freedom, the more complex it is. This is where mathematics and physics becomes suggestive for the social and human sciences, and cross-disciplinary approaches become potentially explosive.

Nature does not know of hierarchies, in any sense of the word. Reading hierarchies in nature such as the queen bee, or the king lion, or the queen ant is a cultural disability, vis-à-vis nature, that truly impedes our ability to see cooperation, learning, co-dependence, symbiosis, holobionts and many other horizontal or networked dynamics. Biomimicry, bio-inspired intelligence, cooperation and symbiosis have ceased to be one-discipline approaches, and have come to enrich and enlarge the vocabulary of the vanguard of science, in our current era that is complexity science (Benyus 2011; Nowak 2011; Wilson 2012).

A social and political structuring of society, hence of the economy and the world, is possible. More radically, another form of democracy is possible (see Seeley 2010).

Drawing Conclusions

The sciences of complexity strongly entail a philosophy of life in the sense that it is life—life in general, life as we know it as well as life as it could be possible—that is at stake within the framework of complexity theory. The primary concern with human beings certainly does not vanish, but it is included within a larger and richer frame. The sciences of complexity are sciences of life, even though the opposite cannot be said.

Biological hypercomputation is a broader concept that concerns how living beings process information. Here, the consequences of the concept have been examined with regards to human beings, from which the interest has been on the social and political consequences.

Some authors have even exposed that complexity theory goes hand in hand with anarchism under one proviso: anarchy is and must be taken in its ancient Greek or philosophical sense, namely, as *an-arché*—that is, the absence of a foundation that then allows, if not claims for, the search for a foundation (Maldonado and Mezza-García 2016). Nonetheless, it should be noted that the social and political consequences studied here pertain to other living beings as well, yet the time and space to prove that assertion remains, however, for another moment.[6]

We are living in an age of an enormous vitality in knowledge and research, probably the most compelling and thrilling of all recent discoveries is life (i.e., living beings). It all originated with E. Schrödinger's marvelous book, *What is Life?* ([1944] 2012), but the seed has grown, enlarged and amply extended. Understanding life, explaining it, caring for it, making it possible as much as possible is by and large the most compelling problem ever. It admits many arrays, a manifold of developments, a variety of forms, expressions and dynamics. Thinking about life means thinking about possibilities and a manifold, it is namely a manifold that cannot be reduced to a single form or expression, under any circumstance.

BH consists in pointing out that it makes sense to think not any longer like a machine, and hence that it is possible to stop being a machine. Living beings hypercompute and do so non-conventionally. As a consequence, we can start thinking and living not just as sheer human beings, but as natural entities. The array that has been recently explored is suggestive and amicable. Computing science appears as a key to a grandiose door in which the social and political consequences must be openly brought to light and discussed.

At the end of the day, the interplay between a TM and algorithms on the one side, and human beings and nature on the other side, leaves no further alternatives: we must be able to think together—human beings and computers, human beings and robots, human beings and algorithms. Thinking together nonetheless means for human beings thinking and living differently than what we have done so far. Complexity science offers a toolbox, if you wish, to such a radical change.

What is at stake is the meaning and destiny of life. Human beings are just an example of momentum in the larger story of life. This momentum can be extended, certainly, under the proviso that its agents change. That is what the social and human sciences at large are all about, namely, about making the world a better place.

---

6. I have worked in this direction. For comparison, see Maldonado (2016b). In addition, see De Waals (1996), Kohn (2013), Wholleben (2016), Groos and Valle̋y (2012), Mancuso and Viola (2015), Mancuso (2017), and Chamovitz (2013).

References

Abbott, A. 2001. *Chaos of Disciplines*. Chicago: University of Chicago Press.

Abney, D.H., A. Paxton, R. Dale, and C.T. Kello. 2015. "Movement Dynamics Reflect a Functional Role for Weak Coupling and Role Structure in Dyadic Problem-Solving." *Cognitive Processing* 16(4): 325–332.

Accard, P. 2018. "Criticality: How Changes Preserve Stability in Self-organizing Systems." *Organization Studies* 1(1): 1–17. https://doi.org/10.1177/0170840618783342

Adrian, R. 1808. "Research Concerning the Probabilities of the Errors which Happen in Making Observations, etc." *The Analyst or Mathematical Museum* 1(4): 93–109.

Ainsworth, B.E., W.L. Haskell, M.C. Whitt, M.L. Irwin, A.M. Swartz, S.J. Strath, W.L. O'Brien, D.R. Bassett, Jr., K.H. Schmitz, and P.O. Emplaincourt. 2000. "Compendium of Physical Activities: An Update of Activity Codes and MET Intensities." *Medicine and Science in Sports and Exercise* 32 (SUPP/1): S498–S504.

Albert, M., R. Nowakowski, and D. Wolfe. 2007. *Lessons in Play: An Introduction to Combinatorial Game Theory*. Wellesley, MA: A.K. Peters.

Albin, P. 1998. *Barriers and Bounds to Rationality: Essays on Economic Complexity and Dynamics in Interactive Systems,* edited by D. Foley, Princeton, NJ: Princeton University Press.

Al-dabaan, B. n.d. "Scaling Laws in Biology." Accessed November 6, 2018. http://www.scribd.com/document/61695353/bader2

Allegrini, P., P. Paradisi, D. Menicucci, and A. Gemignani. 2010. "Fractal Complexity in Spontaneous EEG Metastable-State Transitions: New Vistas on Integrated Neural Dynamics." *Frontiers in Physiology* 1: 128.

Allen, P. 2009. "Complexity, Evolution, and Organizational Behavior." In *Chaos and Complexity in Psychology: The Theory of Nonlinear Dynamical Systems,* edited by S.J. Guastello, M. Koopmans, and D. Pincus, 452–474. New York: Cambridge University Press.

Alvarez, M., and D. Ehnts. 2016. "Samuelson and Davidson on Ergodicity: A Reformulation." *Journal of Post Keynesian Economics* 39(1): 1–16.

Amaral, P.P., M.E. Dinger, T.R. Mercer, and J.S. Mattick. 2008. "The Eukaryote Genome as an RNA Machine." *Science* 319: 1787–1789.

Anderson, P. 1999. "Complexity Theory and Organization Science." *Organization Science* 10: 216–232.

Anderson, P., H. Jensen, L. Oliveira, and S. Sibani. 2004. "Evolution in Complex Systems." *Complexity* 10(1): 49–56.

Anderton, C.H. 1989. "Arms Race Modeling: Problems and Prospects." *Journal of Conflict Resolution* 332: 346–367.

Andresen, B., J.S. Shiner, and D.E. Uehlinger. 2002. "Allometric Scaling and Maximum Efficiency in Physiological Eigen Time." *Proceedings of the National Academy of Sciences* 99(9): 5822–5824.

Aquino, G., M. Bologna, P. Grigolini, and B.J. West. 2010. "Beyond the Death of Linear Response: 1/F Optimal Information Transport." *Physical Review Letters* 105(4): 040601.

Aquino, G., M. Bologna, B.J. West, and P. Grigolini. 2011. "Transmission of Information Between Complex Systems: 1/F Resonance." *Physical Review. E: Covering Statistical, Nonlinear, and Soft Matter Physics* 83(5): 051130.

Aragones, E., I. Gilboa, A. Postlewaite, and D. Schmeidler. 2005. "Fact-free Learning." *The American Economic Review*, 95 (5): 1355–1368.

Arbib, M., and A. Fagg. 1998. "Modelling Parietal-Premotor Interactions in Primate Control of Grasping." *Neural Networks* 11: 1277–1303.

Arora, S., and B. Barak. 2009. *Computational Complexity. A Modern Approach*. Cambridge: Cambridge University Press.

Arthur, W.B. 1994. "Inductive Behavior and Bounded Rationality." *American Economic Review* 84: 406–411.

Arthur, W.B., S. Durlauf, and D. Lane. 1997. "Introduction." In *The Economy as an Evolving Complex System II*, edited by W.B. Arthur, S.N. Durlauf, and D.A. Lane, 1–14. Boca Raton, FL: CRC Press.

Arthur, W.B., J.H. Holland, B. LeBaron, R. Palmer, and P. Tayler. 1997. "Asset Pricing Under Endogenous Expectations in an Artificial Stock Market." In *The Economy as an Evolving Complex System II*, edited by W.B. Arthur, S.N. Durlauf, and D.A. Lane, 15–45. Boca Raton, FL: CRC Press.

Asal, V., M. Findley, J.A. Piazza, and J.I. Walsh. 2016. "Political Exclusion, Oil, and Ethnic Armed Conflict." *Journal of Conflict Resolution* 608: 1343–1367.

Ashby, W.R. 1956. *Introduction to Cybernetics*. New York: Wiley.

Ashmos, D., D. Duchon, R. McDaniel, and J. Huonker. 2002. "What a Mess! Participation as a Simple Managerial Rule to 'Complexify' Organizations." *Journal of Management Studies* 39: 189–206.

Axelrod, R. 1976. "The Analysis of Cognitive Maps." In *Structure of Decision: The Cognitive Maps of Political Elites*, edited by R. Axelrod, 55–73. Princeton, NJ: Princeton University Press.

Axelrod, R. 1981. "The Emergence of Cooperation among Egoists." *American Political Science Review* 75: 306–318.

Axelrod, R. 1984. *The Evolution of Cooperation*. New York: Basic Books.

Axelrod, R. 1987. "The Evolution of Strategies in the Iterated Prisoner's Dilemma." In *The Dynamics of Norms,* edited by C. Bicchieri, B. Skyrms, and R. Jeffrey, 1–16. Cambridge: Cambridge University Press.

Axelrod, R. 1997. *The Complexity of Cooperation: Agent-Based Models of Competition and Collaboration*. Princeton, NJ: Princeton University Press.

Axelrod, R. 2003 "Risk in Networked Information Systems." Report sponsored by the Office of the Assistant Secretary of Defense for Networks and Information Integration. http://www-personal.umich.edu/%7Eaxe/risk.pdf

Axtell, R. 2005. "The Complexity of Exchange." *The Economic Journal* 115(504): F193–F210.

Axtell, R.L., J.M. Epstein, J.S. Dean, G.J. Gumerman, A.C. Swedlund, J. Harburger, S. Chakravarty, R. Hammond, J. Parker, and M. Parker. 2002. "Population Growth and Collapse in a Multi-Agent Model of the Kayenta Anasazi in Long House Valley." *Proceedings of the National Academy of Sciences* 99 (3): 7275–7279.

Back, I., and A. Flache. 2006. "The Viability of Cooperation Based on Interpersonal Commitment." *Journal of Artificial Societies and Social Simulation* 9(1): 1–23.

Bagni, R., R. Berchi, and P. Cariello. 2002. "A Comparison of Simulation Models Applied to Epidemics." *Journal of Artificial Societies and Social Simulation* 5(3): 1–18.

Bak, P. 1996. *How Nature Works*. New York: Springer.

Bak, P., and K. Chen. 1991. "Self-Organized Criticality." *Scientific American* 264(1): 46–53.

Bak, P., K. Chen, and C. Tang. 1990. "A Forest-Fire Model and Some Thoughts on Turbulence." *Physics Letters A* 147(5–6): 297–300.

Bak, P., C. Tang, and K. Wiesenfeld. 1988. "Self-Organized Criticality." *Physical Review A* 38(1): 364.

Baker, J.S., and P.W. Frey. 1980. "A Cusp Catastrophe, Hysteresis, Bimodality, and Inaccessibility in Rabbit Eyelid Conditioning." *Learning and Motivation* 10: 520–535.

Balci, O. 1998. "Verification, Calibration, and Testing." In *Handbook of Simulation: Principles, Methodology, Advances, Applications, and Practice*. 1st ed., edited by J. Banks, 335–393. New York: John Wiley and Sons, Inc.

Ball, D. 1981. *Can Nuclear War Be Controlled?* London: International Institute for Strategic Studies.

Bandura, A. 2001. "Social Cognitive Theory. An Agentic Perspective." *Annual Review of Psychology* 52: 1–26.

Bandura, A., and E.A. Locke. 2003. "Negative Self-Efficacy and Goal Effects Revisited." *Journal of Applied Psychology* 88: 87–99.

Barbati, M., G. Bruno, and A. Genovese. 2012." Applications of Agent-Based Models for Optimization Problems: A Literature Review." *Expert Systems with Applications* 39(5): 6020–6028.

Barker, J. 1992. *Future Edge*. New York: William Morrow.

Baron-Cohen, S. 1995. *Learning, Development, and Conceptual Change. Mindblindness: An Essay on Autism and Theory of Mind*. Cambridge: MIT Press.

Barro, R., and D. Gordon. 1983. "Rules, Discretion and Reputation in a Model of Monetary Policy." *Journal of Monetary Economics* 12: 101–121.

Bartholo, R.S., C.A.N. Cosenza, C.T.R. de Lessa, and F.A. Doria. 2009. "Can Economic Systems Be Seen as Computing Devices?" *Journal of Economic Behavior and Organization* 70: 72–80.

Bateson, G. 1972. *Steps to an Ecology of Mind: Collected Essays in Anthropology, Psychiatry, Evolution, and Epistemology*. Chicago: University of Chicago Press.

Baumann, O., and N. Siggelkow. 2013. "Dealing With Complexity: Integrated vs. Chunky Search Processes." *Organization Science* 24(1): 116–132.

Baumol, W. 2002. *The Free Market Innovation Machine*. Princeton, NJ: Princeton University Press.

Baumol, W. 2004. "Red Queen Games: Arms Races, Rule of Law and Market Economies." *Journal of Evolutionary Economics* 14(2): 237–47.

Bearce, D.H., and E.O. Fischer. 2002. "Economic Geography, Trade, and War." *Journal of Conflict Resolution* 463: 365–393.

Beck, T., and D. Plowman. 2014. "Temporary, Emergent Interorganizational Collaboration in Unexpected Circumstances: A Study of the Columbia Space Shuttle Response Effort." *Organization Science* 25(4): 1234–1252.

Becker, G.S. 1976. *The Economic Approach to Human Behavior*. Chicago: University of Chicago Press.

Beinhocker, E. 2011. "Evolution as Computation: Integrating Self-Organization with Generalized Darwinism." *Journal of Institutional Economics* 7(3): 393–423.

Ben-Jacob, E. 1998. "Bacterial Wisdom, Gödel's Theorem and Creative Genomic Webs." *Physica A: Statistical Mechanics and Its Applications* 248(1): 57–76.

Benyus, J.M. 2011. *Biomimicry: Innovation Inspired by Nature*. New York: Harper Perennial.

Beran, J. 1994. *Statistics for Long-Memory Processes*. New York: Chapman and Hall.

Bernheim, D. 2008. "On the Potential of Neuroeconomics: A Critical (but Hopeful) Appraisal." *American Economic Journal: Microeconomics* 1(2): 1–41.

Bernstein, D.J., J. Buchmann, and E. Dahmen, eds. 2009. *Post-Quantum Cryptography*. Berlin: Springer Verlag.

Bettencourt, L.M.A., J. Lobo, D. Helbing, C. Kühnert, and G. B. West. 2007. "Growth, Innovation, Scaling and the Pace of Life in Cities." *Proceedings of the National Academy of Sciences* 104(17): 7301–7306.

Bettencourt, L.M.A., J. Lobo, D. Strumsky, and G.B. West. 2010. "Urban Scaling and its Deviations: Revealing the Structure of Wealth, Innovation and Crime across Cities." *PloS One* 5(11): e13541.

Beyerchen, A. 1992. "Clausewitz, Nonlinearity and the Unpredictability of War." *International Security* 173: 59–90.

Bharathy, G.K., and B. Silverman, 2010. "Validating Agent Based Social Systems Models." In *Proceedings of the Winter Simulation Conference*, edited by B. Johansson, 441–453. Baltimore, MD: IEEE.

Bhatt, M., and C. Camerer. 2005. "Self-Referential Thinking and Equilibrium as States of Mind in Games: FMRI Evidence." *Games and Economic Behavior* 52: 424–459.

Bhavnani, R., and H.J. Choi 2012. "Modeling Civil Violence in Afghanistan: Ethnic Geography, Control and Collaboration." *Complexity* 176: 42–51.

Bhavnani, R., K. Donnay, D. Miodownik, M. Mor, and D. Helbing. 2014. "Group Segregation and Urban Violence." *American Journal of Political Science* 581: 226–245.

Bhavnani, R., K. Donnay, and M. Reul. 2019. "Evidence-Driven Computational Modelling Projects." In *Sage Handbook of Research Methods in Political Science and International Relations*, edited by R. Franzese and L. Curini, 60–78. Thousand Oaks, CA: Sage Publications.

Bianchi, F., and F. Squazzoni. 2015. "Agent-Based Models in Sociology." *Wiley Interdisciplinary Reviews: Computational Statistics* 7(4): 284–306.

Bianchini, F., R. Kaaks, and H. Vainio. 2002. "Weight Control and Physical Activity in Cancer Prevention." *Obesity Reviews* 3(1): 5–8.

Bigelow, J. 1982. "A Catastrophe Model of Organizational Change." *Behavioral Science* 27: 26–42.

Billinger, S., N. Stieglitz, and T. Schumacher. 2014. "Search on Rugged Landscapes: An Experimental Study." *Organization Science* 25(1): 93–108.

Binmore, K. 1987. "Modeling Rational Players: Part I." *Economics and Philosophy* 3(2): 179–214.

Binmore, K., and L. Samuelson. 1999. "Equilibrium Selection and Evolutionary Drift." *Review of Economic Studies* 66: 363–394.

Birkhoff, G.D. 1931. "Proof of the Ergodic Theorem." *Proceedings of the National Academy of Sciences* 17: 656–660.

Birnir, J.K., J. Wilkenfeld, J.D. Fearon, D.D. Laitin, T.R. Gurr, D. Brancati, S.M. Saideman, A. Pate, and A.S. Hultquist. 2015. "Socially Relevant Ethnic Groups, Ethnic Structure, and AMAR." *Journal of Peace Research* 521: 110–115.

Bloomquist, K.M., and M. Koehler. 2015. "A Large-Scale Agent-Based Model of Taxpayer Reporting Compliance." *Journal of Artificial Societies and Social Simulation* 18(2): 1–7.

Blume, L., F. Cucker, M. Shub, and S. Smale. 1998. *Complexity and Real Computation*. New York: Springer-Verlag.

Boero, R., and F. Squazzoni. 2005. "Does Empirical Embeddedness Matter? Methodological Issues on Agent-Based Models for Analytical Social Science." *Journal of Artificial Societies and Social Simulation* 8(4): 1–31.

Bohorquez, J.C., S. Gourley, A.R. Dixon, M. Spagat, and N.F. Johnson. 2009. "Common Ecology Quantifies Human Insurgency." *Nature* 462(7275): 911.

Boisot, M., and J. Child. 1999. "Organizations as Adaptive Systems in Complex Environments: The Case of China." *Organization Science* 10(3): 237–252.

Boisot, M., and B. McKelvey. 2010. "Integrating Modernist and Postmodernist Perspectives on Organizations: A Complexity Science Bridge." *The Academy of Management Review* 35(3): 415–433.

Boisot, M., and B. McKelvey. 2011. "Complexity in Organization-Environment Relations: Revisiting Ashby's Law of Requisite Variety." In *The Sage Handbook of Complexity and Management*, edited by P. Allen, S. Maguire, and B. McKelvey, 279–298. Thousand Oaks, CA: Sage.

Bonabeau, E. 2002. "Agent-Based Modeling: Methods and Techniques for Simulating Human Systems." *Proceedings of the National Academy of Sciences* 99: 7280–7287.

Bonabeau, E., G. Theraulaz, J. Deneubourg, S. Aron, and S. Camazine. 1997. "Self-Organization in Social Insects." *Trends in Ecology and Evolution* 12: 188–193.

Bondy, J.A., and U.S. Murty. 2008. *Graph Theory*. New York: Springer.

Borill, P.L., and L. Tesfatsion. 2011. "Agent-Based Modeling: The Right Mathematics for the Social Sciences." In *The Elgar Companion to Recent Economic Methodology*, edited by J.B. Davis and D.W. Hands, 228–258. Cheltenham, UK: Edward Elgar.

Bouchard, C. 1991. "Current Understanding of the Etiology of Obesity: Genetic and Nongenetic Factors." *The American Journal of Clinical Nutrition* 53: 1561S-1565S.

Bouchard, C., A. Tremblay, J.-P. Després, A. Nadeau, P.J. Lupien, G. Thériault, J. Dussault, S. Moorjani, S. Pinault, and G. Fournier. 1990. "The Response to Long-Term Overfeeding in Identical Twins." *New England Journal of Medicine* 322: 1477–1482.

Bouzy, B., and T. Cazenave. 2001. "Computer Go: An AI Oriented Survey." *Artificial Intelligence* 132: 39–103.

Bovens, L., and S. Hartmann. 2003. *Bayesian Epistemology*. Clarendon: Oxford University Press.

Brannick, M.T., R.M. Roach, and E. Salas. 1993. "Understanding Team Performance: A Multimethod Study." *Human Performance* 6: 287–308.

Brehmer, B., and D. Dörner. 1993. "Experiments with Computer-Simulated Microworlds: Escaping Both the Narrow Straits of the Laboratory and the Deep Blue Sea of the Field Study." *Computers in Human Behavior* 9: 171–184.

Bremer, S.A., and M. Mihalka. 1977. "Machiavelli in Machina: Or Politics among Hexagons." In *Problems of World Modeling*, edited by K.W. Deutsch, 303–338. Cambridge: Ballinger Pub. Co.

Bremmer, I., and P. Keat. 2009. *The Fat Tail: The Power of Political Knowledge for Strategic Investing*. New York: Oxford University Press.

Brito, D.L., and M.D. Intriligator. 1982. "Arms Races: Behavioral and Economic Dimensions." In *Missing Elements in Political Inquiry: Logic and Levels of Analysis*, edited by J.A. Gillespie and D.A. Zinnes, 307–327. Thousand Oaks, CA: Sage Publications.

Brochini, L., A. De Andrade, M. Abadi, A. Roque, J. Stolfi, and O. Kinouchi. 2016. "Phase Transitions and Self-Organized Criticality in Networks of Stochastic Spiking Neurons." *Scientific Reports* 6(1): 35831.

Brock, W.A., and C. Hommes. 1997. "A Rational Route to Randomness." *Econometrica* 65: 1059–1095.

Brock, W.A., and C. Hommes. 1998. "Heterogeneous Beliefs and Routes to Chaos in a Simple Asset Pricing Model." *Journal of Economic Dynamics and Control* 22: 1235–1274.

Brody, S. 1945. *Bioenergetics and Growth*. New York: Reinhold Publishing Corporation.

Brouwer, L.E.J. 1913. "Intuitionism and Formalism." Translated by A. Dresden. *Bulletin of American Mathematical Society* 20(2): 81–96.

Brown, D.G., S. Page, R. Riolo, M. Zellner, and W. Rand. 2005. "Path Dependence and the Validation of Agent-Based Spatial Models of Land Use." *International Journal of Geographical Information Science* 19(2): 153–174.

Brown, S., and K. Eisenhardt. 1998. *Competing on the Edge*. Boston: Harvard Business

Brownson, R., C. Hoehner, K. Day, A. Forsyth, and J. Sallis. 2009. "Measuring the Built Environment for Physical Activity: State of the Science." *American Journal of Preventive Medicine* 36(4): S99–S123.

Burgelman, R., and A. Grove. 2007. "Let Chaos Reign, then Rein in Chaos—Repeatedly: Managing Strategic Dynamics for Corporate Longevity." *Strategic Management Journal* 28: 965–979.

Burgess, A.P. 2013. "On the Interpretation of Synchronization in EEG Hyperscanning Studies: A Cautionary Note." *Frontiers in Human Neuroscience* 7: 881. https://doi.org/10.3389/fnhum.2013.00881

Burke, S., K.C. Stagl, E. Salas, and L. Pierce. 2006. "Understanding Team Adaptation: A Conceptual Analysis and Model." *Journal of Applied Psychology* 91(6): 1189–1207.

Byrne, R., and A. Whiten. 1988. *Machiavellian Intelligence: Social Expertise and the Evolution of Intellect in Monkeys, Apes, and Humans*. Oxford: Oxford University Press.

Cadenasso, M., S. Pickett, and J. Grove. 2006. "Dimensions of Ecosystem Complexity: Heterogeneity, Connectivity, and History." *Ecological Complexity* 3(1): 1–12.

Cakmak, E., H. Dudu, O. Eruygur, M. Ger, S. Onurlu, and O. Tonguç. 2013. "Participatory Fuzzy Cognitive Mapping Analysis to Evaluate the Future of Water in the Seyhan Basin." *Journal of Water and Climate Change* 4(2): 131–145.

Calder, W.A. 1984. *Size, Function, and Life History*. Cambridge: Harvard University Press.

Callender, C. 2010. "Is Time an Illusion?" *Scientific American* 302(6): 58. https://doi.org/10.1038/scientificamerican0610-58

Camazine, S., J. Deneubourg, N. Franks, J. Sneyd, G. Theraulaz, and E. Bonabeau. 2001. *Self Organization in Biological Systems*. Princeton, NJ: Princeton University Press.

Camerer, C., and M. Knez. 1997. "Coordination in Organizations: A Game-Theoretic Perspective." In *Organizational Decision Making*, edited by Z. Shapira, 158–188. Cambridge: Cambridge University Press.

Camerer, C., G. Loewenstein, and D. Prelec. 2005. "Neuroeconomics: How Neuroscience Can Inform Economics." *Journal of Economic Literature* 43(1): 9–64.

Canning, D. 1992. "Rationality, Computability, and Nash Equilibrium," *Econometrica* 60: 877–888.

Cannon-Bowers, J., E. Salas, and S. Converse. 1993. "Shared Mental Models in Expert Team Decision Making." In *Individual and Group Decision Making: Current Issues*, edited by N.J. Castellan, 221–246. Hillsdale, NJ: Lawrence Erlbaum Associates.

Cao, S., R. Moineddin, M.L. Urquia, F. Razak, and J. G. Ray. 2014. "J-Shapedness: An Often Missed, Often Miscalculated Relation: The Example of Weight and Mortality." *Journal of Epidemiology and Community Health* 68(7): 683–690.

Caplow, T. 1956. "A Theory of Coalitions in the Triad." *American Sociological Review* 21: 489–493.

Capra, B.A., dir. 1990. *Mindwalk*. Hollywood: Atlas.

Carley, K.M., D.B. Fridsma, E. Casman, A. Yahja, N. Altman, L.-C. Chen, B. Kaminsky, and D. Nave. 2006. "BioWar: Scalable Agent-Based Model of Bioattacks." *IEEE Transactions on Systems, Man, and Cybernetics-Part A: Systems and Humans* 362: 252–265.

Carnap, R. 1966. *Philosophical Foundations of Physics: An Introduction to the Philosophy of Science*. New York: Basic Books.

Carnap, R. 1969. *The Logical Structure of the World*. Berkeley: University of California Press.

Carsey, T., and J. Harden. 2013. *Monte Carlo Simulation and Resampling Methods for Social Science*. Thousand Oaks, CA: Sage.

Casti, J. 1994. *Complexification: Explaining a Paradoxical World through the Science of Surprises*. London: Harper Collins.

Cederman, L.-E. 1997. *Emergent Actors in World Politics: How States and Nations Develop and Dissolve*. Princeton, NJ: Princeton University Press.

Cederman, L.E. 2003. "Modeling the Size of Wars: From Billiard Balls to Sandpiles." *American Political Science Review* 971: 135–150.

Cederman, L.E., and L. Girardin 2007. "Toward Realistic Computational Models of Civil Wars." Paper presented at the Annual Meeting of the American Political Science Association, Chicago, IL.

Center for International Earth Science Information Network (CIESIN). 2005. "Gridded Population of the World Version 3 (GPWv3): Land and Geographic Unit Area Grids." New York: Columbia University Press. https://catalog.data.gov/dataset/gridded-population-of-the-world-version-3-gpwv3-land-and- geographic-unit-area-grids

Chaitin, G. 1987. *Algorithmic Information Theory*. Cambridge: Cambridge University Press.

Chaitin, G. 2012. *Proving Darwin: Making Biology Mathematical*. New York: Pantheon Books.

Chaitin, G. 2013. "Life as Evolving Software." In *A Computable Universe: Understanding and Exploring Nature as Computation*, edited by H. Zenil, 277–302. Hackensack, NJ: World Scientific.

Chaitin, G., F.A. Doria, and N.C. da Costa. 2012. *Gödel's Way: Exploits into an Undecidable World*. Boca Raton, FL: CRC Press.

Chamovitz, D. 2013. *What a Plant Knows. A Field Guide to the Senses*. New York: Scientific American/Rrrar, Straus and Giroux.

Chen, S.-H., T. Terano, R. Yamamoto, and C.-C. Tai (Eds.) 2014. *Advances in Computational Social Science: The Fourth World Congress*. Berlin: Springer-Verlag.

Cheng, Y., and A. Van de Ven. 1996. "Learning the Innovation Journey: Order Out of Chaos?" *Organization Science* 7: 593–614.

Chenoweth, E., and O.A. Lewis. 2013. "Unpacking Nonviolent Campaigns: Introducing the NAVCO 2.0 Dataset." *Journal of Peace Research* 503: 415–423.

Chiles, T., A. Meyer, and T. Hench. 2004. "Organizational Emergence: The Origin and Transformation of Branson, Missouri's Musical Theaters." *Organization Science* 15: 499–519.

Chiles, T., C. Tuggle, J. McMullen, L. Bierman, and D. Greening. 2010. "Dynamic Creation: Extending the Radical Austrian Approach to Entrepreneurship." *Organization Studies* 31(1): 7–46.

Choi, T., K. Dooley, and M. Rungtusanatham. 2001. "Supply Networks and Complex Adaptive Systems: Control versus Emergence." *Journal of Operations Management* 19: 351–366.

Christensen, K., D. Papavassiliou, A. de Figueiredo, N. Franks, and A. Sendova-Franks. 2014. "Universality in Ant behavior." *The Royal Society Interface* 12(102). https://doi.org/10.1098/rsif.2014.0985

Church, A. 1936. "A Note on the Entscheidungsproblem." *Journal of Symbolic Logic* 1: 40–41. Correction published in *Journal of Symbolic Logic* 1(3): 101–102.

Cioffi-Revilla, C. 2017. "Agent-Based Computational Modeling and International Relations Theory: Quo Vadis?" In *Oxford Research Encyclopedia: Politics*, edited by William R. Thompson. Oxford: Oxford University Press. https://doi.org/10.1093/acrefore/9780190228637.013.535

Clauset, A., and K.S. Gleditsch. 2012. "The Developmental Dynamics of Terrorist Organizations." *PloS One* 71(1): e48633.

Clauset, A., M. Young, and K.S. Gleditsch. 2007. "On the Frequency of Severe Terrorist Events." *Journal of Conflict Resolution* 51(1): 58–87.

Cobham, A. 1965. "The Intrinsic Computational Difficulty of Functions." In *Proceedings of Logic, Methodology and Philosophy of Science II*, edited by Y. Bar-Hillel, 24–30. New York: North Holland.

Cohen, B., and J. Kietzmann. 2014. "Ride on! Mobility Business Models for the Sharing Economy." *Organization and Environment* 27(3): 279–296.

Cohen, I.R. 1992. "The Cognitive Paradigm and the Immunological Homunculus." *Immunology Today* 13(12): 490–494.

Cohen, J., and I. Stewart. 1994. *The Collapse of Chaos: Discovering Simplicity in a Complex World*. New York: Viking Press.

Cohen, M.D., R.L. Riolo, and R. Axelrod. 2001. "The Role of Social Structure in the Maintenance of Cooperative Regimes." *Rationality and Society* 13(1): 5–32.

Colander, D., ed. 2000. *The Complexity Vision and the Teaching of Economics*. Cheltenham, UK: Edward Elgar.

Colander, D., M. Goldberg, A. Haas, K. Juselius, T. Lux, H. Föllmer, A. Kirman, and B. Sloth. 2009. "The Financial Crisis and the Systemic Failure of the Economics Profession." *Critical Review* 21(2–3): 249–267

Colbert, B. 2004. "The Complex Resource-Based View: Implications for Theory and Practice in Strategic Human Resource Management." *Academy of Management Review* 29(3): 341–358.

Collard, M., A. Ruttle, B. Buchanan, and M.J. O'Brien. 2013. "Population Size and Cultural Evolution in Nonindustrial Food-Producing Societies." *PloS One* 8(9): e72628.

Collins, J., A.J. Seiler, G. Gangel, and M. Croll. 2013. "Applying Latin Hypercube Sampling to Agent-Based Models: Understanding Foreclosure Contagion Effects." *International Journal of Housing Markets and Analysis* 6(4): 422–437.

Comer, D.R. 1995. "A Model of Social Loafing in Real Work Groups." *Human Relations* 48: 647–667.

Conlisk, J. 1996. "Why Bounded Rationality?" *Journal of Economic Literature* 34: 1–64.

Conte, R., and M. Paolucci. 2002. *Reputation in Artificial Societies: Social Beliefs for Social Order, vol. 6*. New York: Springer Science and Business Media.

Conte, R., N. Gilbert, G. Bonelli, C. Cioffi-Revilla, G. Deffuant, J. Kertesz, V. Loreto, S. Moat, J.-P. Nadal, and A. Sanchez. 2012. "Manifesto of Computational Social Science." *The European Physical Journal Special Topics* 2141: 325–346.

Conway, J. 1970. "The Game of Life." *Scientific American* 223(4): 4.

Conway, J.H. 2000. *On Numbers and Games*. Wellesley, MA: A.K. Peters.

Coricelli, G., and R. Nagel. 2009. "Neural Correlates of Depth of Strategic Reasoning in Medial Prefrontal Cortex." *Proceedings of the National Academy of Sciences* 106(23): 9163–9168.

Courdier, R., F. Guerrin, F.H. Andriamasinoro, and J.M. Paillat. 2002. "Agent-Based Simulation of Complex Systems: Application to Collective Management of Animal Wastes." *Journal of Artificial Societies and Social Simulation* 5(3): 1–17.

Crawford, V. 2003. "Lying for Strategic Advantage: Rational and Boundedly Rational Misrepresentation of Intentions." *American Economic Review* 93(1): 133–149.

Crawford, V.P. 1991. "An 'Evolutionary Interpretation' of Van Huyk, Battalio, and Beil's Experimental Results on Coordination." *Games and Economic Behavior* 3: 25–59.

Cukierman, A. 1992. *Central Bank Strategy, Credibility and Independence: Theory and Evidence*. Cambridge: MIT Press.

Cunningham, D.E., K.S. Gleditsch, and I. Salehyan. 2013. "Non-State Actors in Civil Wars: A New Dataset." *Conflict Management and Peace Science* 305: 516–531.

Curd, M. 1982. "The Rationality of the Copernican Revolution." *PSA: Proceedings of the Biennial Meeting of the Philosophy of Science Association* 1982(1): 3–13.

Cusack, T.R., and R.J. Stoll. 1990. *Exploring Realpolitik: Probing International Relations Theory with Computer Simulation*. Boulder, CO: Lynne Rienner Pub.

Cutland, N.J. 1980. *Computability: An Introduction to Recursive Function Theory*. Cambridge: Cambridge University Press.

Cuvier, G. 1812. *Recherches sur les Ossemens Fossiles De Quadrupèdes où l'on Rétablit les Caractères de Plusieurs Espèces D'animaux que les Révolutions du Globe Paroissent Avoir Détruites*. Paris: Deterville.

Cyert, R., and J. March. 1963. *A Behavioral Theory of the Firm*. Englewood Cliffs, NJ: Prentice-Hall.

da Costa, N.C.A., and F.A. Doria. 2005. "Computing the Future." In *Computability, Complexity and Constructivity in Economic Analysis*, edited by K.V. Velupillai, 15–50. Hoboken, NJ: Wiley-Blackwell.

da Costa, N.C.A., F.A. Doria, and E. Bir. 2007. "On the Metamathematics of the P vs. NP Question." *Applied Mathematics and Computation* 189: 1223–1240.

Daily, R.C. 1980. "A Path Analysis of R and D Team Coordination and Performance." *Decision Sciences* 11: 357–369.

Danan-Gotthold, M., C. Guyon, M. Giraud, E. Levanon, and J. Abramson. 2016. "Extensive RNA Editing and Splicing Increase Immune Self-Representation Diversity in Medullary Thymic Epithelial Cells." *Genome Biology* 17: 219.

Davidson, P. 1982. "Rational Expectations: A Fallacious Foundation for Studying Crucial Economic Decision-Making Processes." *Journal of Post Keynesian Economics* 5: 182–198.

Davidson, P. 1996. "Reality and Economic Theory." *Journal of Post Keynesian Economics* 18: 479–508.

Davidson, P. 2015. "A Rejoinder to O'Donnell's Critique of the Ergodic/Nonergodic Approach to Keynes's Concept of Uncertainty." *Journal of Post Keynesian Economics* 38: 1–18.

Davidsson, P. 2002. "Agent Based Social Simulation: A Computer Science View." *Journal of Artificial Societies and Social Simulation* 5(1). http://jasss.soc.surrey.ac.uk/5/1/7.html

Dawid, H., and M. Neugart. 2011. "Agent-Based Models for Economic Policy Design." *Eastern Economic Journal* 37(1): 44–50.

Dawkins, R. 1989. *The Extended Phenotype*. Oxford: Oxford University Press.
Dawson, J. 1997. *Logical Dilemmas: The Life and Work of Kurt Gödel*. Wellesley, MA: A.K. Peters.
Day, R. 1994. *Complex Economic Dynamics*. Vol. 1 of *An Introduction to Dynamical Systems and Market Mechanisms*. Cambridge: MIT Press.
Deakin, S. 2015. "Juridical Ontology: The Evolution of Legal Form." *Historical Social Research /HistorischeSozialforschung* 40(1): 170–184.
Dean, D., and E. Elliott. 2017a. "Complex Systems, Decision-Making and Computability: A Social Science Perspective." In *The Limits of Mathematical Modeling in the Social Sciences*, edited by F.A. Doria, 159–181. Hackensack, NJ: World-Scientific.
Dean, D., and E. Elliott. 2017b. "Is Classical Logic Enough? Applications of Nonstandard Logic to the Social Sciences." In *The Limits of Mathematical Modeling in the Social Sciences*, edited by F.A. Doria, 183–205. Hackensack, NJ: World Scientific.
De Caux, R., C. Smith, D. Kniveton, R. Black, and A. Philippides. 2014. "Dynamic, Small-World Social Network Generation through Local Agent Interactions." *Complexity* 19(6): 44–53.
Deffuant, G., S. Huet, and F. Amblard. 2005. "An Individual-Based Model of Innovation Diffusion Mixing Social Value and Individual Benefit." *American Journal of Sociology* 110(4): 1041–1069.
DeGreene, K. 1991. "Emergent Complexity in Person-Machine Systems." *International Journal of Man-Machine Studies* 35: 219–234.
Delaherche, E., M. Chetouani, A. Mahdhaoui, C. Saint-Georges, S. Viaux, and D. Cohen. 2012. "Interpersonal synchrony: A survey of evaluation methods across disciplines." *IEEE Transactions on Affective Computing* 3: 1–20.
Demetrius, L., S. Legendre, and P. Harremöes. 2009. "Evolutionary Entropy: A Predictor of Body Size, Metabolic Rate and Maximal Life Span." *Bulletin of Mathematical Biology* 71(4): 800–818.
Dennis, A.R., and J.S. Valacich. 1993. "Computer Brainstorms: More Heads are Better than One." *Journal of Applied Psychology* 78: 531–537.
Denton, F.H. 1966. "Some Regularities in International Conflict, 1820–1949." *Background* 94: 283–296.
Derbinski, J., A. Schulte, B. Kyewski, and L. Klein. 2001. "Promiscuous Gene Expression in Medullary Thymic Epithelial Cells Mirrors: The Peripheral Self." *Nature Immunology* 2: 1032–1039.
DeRouen, Jr., K., M.J. Ferguson, S. Norton, Y.H. Park, J. Lea, and A. Streat-Bartlett 2010. "Civil War Peace Agreement Implementation and State Capacity." *Journal of Peace Research* 473: 333–346.
De Vos, M., and S. Debener. 2014. "Mobile EEG: Toward Brain Activity Monitoring During Natural Action and Cognition." *International Journal of Psychophysiology* 91(1): 1–2.
De Waals, F. 1996. *Good Natured. The Origins of Right and Wrong in Humans and Other Animals*. Cambridge: Harvard University Press.
Dhami, S. 2016. *The Foundations of Behavioral Economic Analysis*. Oxford: Oxford University Press.

Diaconis, P., and D. Freedman. 1986. "On the Consistency of Bayes Estimates." *Annals of Statistics* 14: 1–26.

Diallo, S.Y., R. Gore, and C.J. Lynch. 2018. "Examination of Emergent Behavior in the Ballistic Missile Defense System: A Modeling and Simulation Approach." In *Engineering Emergence: A Modeling and Simulation Approach*, edited by L. Rainey and M. Jamshidi, 319–328. Boca Raton, FL: CRC Press.

Diallo, S.Y., R. Gore, C.J. Lynch, and J.J. Padilla. 2016. "Formal Methods, Statistical Debugging and Exploratory Analysis in Support of System Development: Toward a Verification and Validation Calculator Tool." *International Journal of Modeling, Simulation, and Scientific Computing* 7(1): 1–22. https://doi.org/10.1142/S1793962316410014.

Diallo, S., C. Lynch, R. Gore, and J. Padilla, 2015. "Emergent Behavior Identification Within an Agent-Based Model of the Ballistic Missile Defense System Using Statistical Debugging." *The Journal of Defense Modeling and Simulation: Applications, Methodology, Technology* 13(3): 275–289. https://doi.org/10.1177/1548512915621973.

Diallo, S.Y., J.J. Padilla, R. Gore, H. Herencia-Zapana, and A. Tolk. 2014. "Toward a Formalism of Modeling and Simulation Using Model Theory." *Complexity* 19(3): 56–63.

Diehl, P.F. 1983. "Arms Races and Escalation: A Closer Look." *Journal of Peace Research* 203: 205–212.

Dobson, M.W., M. Pengelly, J.-A. Sime, S.A. Albaladejo, E.V. Garcia., F. Gonzales, and J.M. Maseda. 2001. "Situated Learning with Co-Operative Agent Simulations in Team Training." *Computers in Human Behavior* 17: 547–573.

Dobzhansky, T. 1973. "Nothing in Biology Makes Sense Except in the Light of Evolution." *American Biology Teacher* 35(3): 125–129.

Donaldson, L. 1990. "A Rational Basis for Criticisms of Organizational Economics: A Reply to Barney." *Academy of Management Review* 15(3): 394–401.

Donnay, K., and R. Bhavnani 2016. "The Cutting Edge of Research on Peace and Conflict." In *Peace and Conflict 2016*, 20–34. New York: Routledge.

Donnay, K., E. Gadjanova, and R. Bhavnani 2014. "Disaggregating Conflict by Actors, Time, and Location." In *Peace and Conflict 2014*, edited by David A. Backer, Ravi Bhavnani, and Paul K. Huth, 44–56. New York: Routledge.

Dooley, K. 1997. "A Complex Adaptive Systems Model of Organization Change." *Nonlinear Dynamics, Psychology, and Life Sciences* 1(1): 69–97.

Dooley, K. 2009a. "Organizational Psychology." In *Chaos and Complexity in Psychology: The Theory of Nonlinear Dynamical Systems*, edited by S.J. Guastello, M. Koopmans, and D. Pincus, 434–451. New York: Cambridge University Press.

Dooley, K. 2009b. "The Empiricism-Modeling Dichotomy in Operations and Supply Management." *Journal of Supply Chain Management* 45(1): 38–43.

Dooley, K., T. Johnson, and D. Bush. 1995. "TQM, Chaos, and Complexity." *Human Systems Management* 14(4): 1–16.

Dooley, K., and A. Van de Ven. 1999. "Explaining Complex Organizational Dynamics." *Organization Science* 10(3): 358–372.

Doran, C., T. Pearce, A. Connor, T. Schlegel, E. Franklin, A. Sendova-Franks, and N. Franks. 2013. "Economic Investment by Ant Colonies in Searches for Better Homes." *Biology Letters* 9(5). https://doi.org/10.1098/rsbl.2013.0685

Doria, F.A. 2017. "Axiomatics, the Social Sciences, and the Gödel Phenomenon: A Toolkit." In *The Limits of Mathematical Modeling in the Social Sciences*, edited by F.A. Doria, 1–90. Hackensack, NJ: World Scientific.

Dowek, G. 2011. *Les Metamorphoses du Calcul. Dune Étonnante Histoire des Mathématiques.* Paris: Poche-Le Pommier

Doyle, M.W. 1986. "Liberalism and World Politics." *American Political Science Review* 804: 1151–1169.

Duffy, G. 1992. "Concurrent Interstate Conflict Simulations: Testing the Effects of the Serial Assumption." *Mathematical and Computer Modelling* 16(8–9): 241–270.

Durlauf, S. 2012. "Complexity, Economics and Public Policy." *Politics, Philosophy and Economics* 11(1): 45–75.

Dussutour, A., M. Beekman, S. Nicolis, and B. Meyer. 2009. "Noise Improves Collective Decision-Making by Ants in Dynamic Environments." *Proceedings of the Royal Society B* 276: 4353–4361 https://doi.org/10.1098/rspb.2009.1235

Easton, D. 1965. *A Systems Analysis of Political Life.* New York: Wiley.

Edwards, S., and S. Pratt. 2009. "Rationality in Collective Decision Making by Ant Colonies." *Proceedings of the Royal Society B* 276: 3655–3661.

Eguiluz, V.M., and M.G. Zimmermann. 2000. "Transmission of Information and Herd Behavior: An Application to Financial Markets." *Physical Review Letters* 85: 5659.

Ehrenfest, P., and T. Ehrenfest-Afanessjewa. 1912. "Begriffte Grundlagen der Statistschen Auffassunf in der Mechanik." In *Encyclopädie der Matematischen Wissenschaften*, edited by F. Klein and C. Müller, 4:3–90. Translated by M.J. Moravcsik. Leipzig: Teubner.

Eichengreen, B. 1999. "Kicking the Habit: Moving from Pegged Rates to Greater Exchange Rate Flexibility." *Economic Journal* 109: C1–C15.

Eichengreen, B. 2010. "Globalization and the Crisis." *CESifo Forum* 11(3): 20–24.

Eichengreen, B., A.K. Rose, and C. Wyplosz. 1996. "Speculative Attacks on Pegged Exchange Rates: An Empirical Exploration with Special Reference to the European Monetary System." In *The New Transatlantic Economy*, edited by M.B. Canzoneri, W. Ethier, and V. Grilli. Cambridge: Cambridge University Press.

Elkins, A.N., E.R. Muth, A.W. Hoover, A.D. Walker, T.L Carpenter, and F.S. Switzer. 2009. "Physiological Compliance and Team Performance." *Applied Ergonomics* 40: 997–1003.

Elliott, E., and L.D. Kiel. 2004. "A Complex Systems Approach for Developing Public Policy toward Terrorism: An Agent-Based Approach." *Chaos, Solitons, and Fractals* 20: 63–68.

Ellsberg, D. 1970. *Revolutionary Judo: Working Notes on Vietnam.* Santa Monica, CA: Rand Corporation. www.rand.org/content/dam/rand/pubs/documents/2006/D19807.pdf

Endsley, M.R. 1995. "Toward a Theory of Situation Awareness in Dynamic Systems." *Human Factors* 37: 32–64.

Endsley, M.R. 2015. "Situation Awareness Misconceptions and Misunderstandings." *Journal of Cognitive Engineering and Decision Making* 9: 4–32.

Eoyang, G. 1997. *Coping with Chaos: Seven Simple Tools.* Cheyenne, WY: Lagamo Corporation.

Epstein, J.M. 1985. *The Calculus of Conventional War: Dynamic Analysis Without Lanchester Theory*. Washington, D.C.: Brookings Institution Press.

Epstein, J.M. 1990. *Conventional Force Reductions: A Dynamic Assessment*. Washington, D.C.: Brooking Institution Press.

Epstein, J. 1999. "Agent-Based Computational Models and Generative Social Science." *Complexity* 4(5): 41–57.

Epstein, J., and Axtell, R. 1996. *Growing Artificial Societies: Social Science from the Bottom Up*. Washington, D.C. and Cambridge: Brookings Institution Press and MIT Press.

Epstein, J.M. 1997. *Nonlinear Dynamics, Mathematical Biology, and Social Science: Wise Use of Alternative Therapies*. 1st ed. Reading, PA: Perseus.

Epstein, J.M. 2002. "Modeling Civil Violence: An Agent-Based Computational Approach." *Proceedings of the National Academy of Sciences* 99 (3): 7243–7250.

Epstein, J.M. 2006. *Generative Social Science: Studies in Agent-Based Computational Modeling*. Princeton, NJ: Princeton University Press.

Epstein, J.M. 2014. *Agent Zero: Toward Neurocognitive Foundations for Generative Social Science*. Princeton, NJ: Princeton University Press.

Epstein, J.M., D.A. Cummings, S. Chakravarty, R. Singa, and D. Burke. 2004. "Toward a Containment Strategy for Smallpox Bioterror: An Individual-Based Computational Approach." In *Generative Social Science*, edited by J.M. Epstein, 277–306. Princeton, NJ: Princeton University Press.

Erdös, P., and A. Rényi. 1959. "On Random Graphs." *Publicationes Mathematicae* 6: 290–297.

Etcheson, C. 1989. *Arms Race Theory: Strategy and Structure of Behavior*. Santa Barbara, CA: Praeger Pub Text.

Ethiraj, S., and D. Levinthal. 2004. "Modularity and Innovation in Complex Systems." *Management Science* 50(2): 159–173.

Evans, C.R., and K.L. Dion. 1991. "Group Cohesion and Performance: A Meta-Analysis." *Small Group Research* 22: 175–186.

Fadiga, L., L. Fogassi, G. Pavesi, and G. Rizzolatti. 1995. "Motor Facilitation during Action Observation: A Magnetic Stimulation Study." *Journal of Neurophysiology* 73: 2608–2611.

Farjoun, M., and M. Levin. 2011. "A Fractal Approach to Industry Dynamism." *Organization Studies* 32(6): 825–851.

Farmer, J.D., and D. Foley. 2009. "The Economy Needs Agent-Based Modelling." *Nature* 460(7256): 685–686.

Farr, W. 1885. *Vital Statistics: A Memorial Volume of Selections from the Reports and Writings of William Farr*, edited by Noel A. Humphreys, 166–205. London: The Sanitary Institute of Great Britain.

Fatouh, M., S. Markose, and S. Giansante. 2019. "The Impact of Quantitative Easing on UK Bank Lending: Why Banks Do Not Lend To Businesses?" *Journal of Economic Behavior and Organization*. https://doi.org/10.1016/j.jebo.2019.02.023.

Fechner, G.T. 1860. *Elemente der Psychophysik*. Leipzig: Breitkopf and Härtel.

Feigenbaum, M. 1978. "Quantitative Universality for a Class of Non-Linear Transformations." *Journal of Statistical Physics* 19(1): 25–52.

Ferguson-Gow, H., S. Sumner, A.F.G. Bourke, and K.E. Jones. 2014. "Colony Size Predicts Division of Labour in Attine Ants." *Proc.R.Soc.B* 281(1793): 1–9.

Finkelstein, E.A., O.A. Khavjou, H. Thompson, J.G. Trogdon, L. Pan, B. Sherry, and W. Dietz. 2012. "Obesity and Severe Obesity Forecasts through 2030." *American Journal of Preventive Medicine* 42(6): 563–570.

Finkelstein, E.A., J.G. Trogdon, J.W. Cohen, and W. Dietz. 2009. "Annual Medical Spending Attributable to Obesity: Payer-and Service-Specific Estimates." *Health Affairs* 28(5): w822–w831.

Firth, T.W. 2014. "Toward a Computational Framework for Cognitive Biology: Unifying Approaches from Cognitive Neuroscience and Comparative Cognition." *Physics of Life Reviews* 11(2014): 329–364.

Fischer, S. 1994. "Modern Central Banking." In *The Future of Central Banking: the Tercentenary Symposium of the Bank of England*, edited by F. Capie, S. Fischer, C. Goodhart, and N. Schnadt, 262–330. Cambridge: Cambridge University Press.

Fitch, T. 2014. "Toward a Computational Framework for Cognitive Biology: Unifying Approaches from Cognitive Neuroscience and Comparative Cognition." *Physics of Life Reviews* 11: 329–364.

Fleener, M.J., and M.L. Merritt. 2007. "Paradigms Lost?" *Nonlinear Dynamics, Psychology, and Life Sciences* 11: 1–18.

Forrester, J. 1961. *Industrial Dynamics*. Cambridge: MIT Press.

Forrester, J. 1969. *Urban Dynamics*. Waltham, MA: Pegasus Communications.

Forslund, H.B., J.S. Torgerson, L. Sjöström, and A.K. Lindroos. 2005. "Snacking Frequency in Relation to Energy Intake and Food Choices in Obese Men and Women Compared to a Reference Population." *International Journal of Obesity* 29(6): 711–719.

Foster, J. 2005. "From Simplistic to Complex Systems in Economics." *Cambridge Journal of Economics* 29: 873–892.

Foster, D., and P. Young. 2006. "Regret Testing: Learning to Play Nash Equilibrium without Knowing You Have an Opponent." *Theoretical Economics* 1: 341–367.

Frank, K., and K. Fahrbach. 1999. "Organization Culture as a Complex System: Balance and Information in Models of Influence and Selection." *Organization Science* 10(3): 253–277.

Frank, L., M. Andresen, and T. Schmid. 2004. "Obesity Relationships with Community Design, Physical Activity, and Time Spent in Cars." *American Journal of Preventive Medicine* 27(2): 87–96.

Franks, N., A. Dornhaus, C. Best, and E. Jones-Gordon. 2006. "Decision Making By Small and Large House-Hunting Ant Colonies: One Size Fits All." *Animal Behavior* 72: 611–616.

Franks, N., A. Dornhaus, J. Fitzsimmons, and M. Stevens. 2003. "Speed Versus Accuracy in Collective Decision Making." *Proceedings of the Royal Society of London B* 270: 2457–2463.

Franks, N., E. Mallon, H. Bray, M. Hamilton, and T. Mischler. 2003. "Strategies for Choosing Between Alternatives With Different Attributes: Exemplified By House-Hunting Ants." *Animal Behavior* 65: 215–223.

Franks, N., T. Richardson, N. Stroeymeyt, R.W. Kirby, W. Amos, P. Hogan, J. Marshall, and T. Schlegel. 2013. "Speed-Cohesion Tradeoffs in Collective Decision Making in Ants and the Concept of Precision in Animal Behavior." *Animal Behavior* 85(6): 1233–1244. https://doi.org/10.1016/anbehav.2013.03.010

Franks, N., J. Stuttard, C. Doran, J. Esposito, M. Master, A. Sendova-Franks, N. Masuda, and N. Britton. 2015. "How Ants Use Quorum Sensing to Estimate the Average Quality of a Fluctuating Resource." *Scientific Reports* 5: 11890. https://doi.org/10.1038/srep11890

Freeman, W.J. 2000. *Neurodynamics: An Exploration of Mesoscopic Brain Dynamics.* New York: Springer-Verlag.

Frey, P.W., and R.J. Sears. 1978. "Model of Conditioning Incorporating the Rescorla-Wagner Associative Axiom, a Dynamic Attention Process, and a Catastrophe Rule." *Psychological Review* 8: 321–340.

Frieden, T.R., W. Dietz, and J. Collins. 2010. "Reducing Childhood Obesity through Policy Change: Acting Now to Prevent Obesity. *Health Affairs* 29(3): 357–363.

Friedman, J.W., ed. 1994. *Problems of Coordination in Economic Activity.* Boston: Kluwer.

Fung, W., D.A. Hsieh, and K. Tsatsaronis. 2000. "Do Hedge Funds Disrupt Emerging Markets?" *Brooking Wharton Papers on Financial Services* 2000: 377–401. https://doi.org/10.1353/pfs.2000.0009

Galán, J.M., L.R. Izquierdo, S.S. Izquierdo, J.I. Santos, R. Del Olmo, A. López-Paredes, and B. Edmonds. 2009. "Errors and Artefacts in Agent-Based Modelling." *Journal of Artificial Societies and Social Simulation* 12(1): 1–19.

Gallavotti, G. 1999. *Statistical Mechanics: A Short Treatise.* Berlin: Springer-Verlag.

Gallese, V. 2009. "Mirror Neurons, Embodied Simulation, and the Neural Basis of Social Identification." *Psychoanalytic Dialogues* 19(5): 519–536.

Gallese, V., L. Fadiga, L. Fogassi, and G. Rizzolatti. 1996."Action Recognition in the Premotor Cortex." *Brain* 119(2): 593–609.

Gallese, V., and C. Sinigaglia. 2011. "What is So Special about Embodied Simulation?" *Trends in Cognitive Sciences* 15(11): 512–519.

Ganco, M., and R. Agarwal. 2009. "Performance Differentials between Diversifying Entrants and Entrepreneurial Start-ups: A Complexity Approach." *Academy of Management Review* 34(2): 228–252.

Garey, M.R., and D.S. Johnson. 1979. *Computers and Intractability: A Guide to the Theory of NP-Completeness.* New York: W.H. Freeman.

Garud, R., J. Gehman, and A. Kumaraswamy. 2011. "Complexity Arrangements for Sustained Innovation: Lessons from 3M Corporation." *Organization Studies* 32(6): 737–767.

Gauss, C.F. 1809. "Theoria Motus Corporum Coelestium." In *Sectionibus Conicis Solem Ambientium.* Hamburg: Sumtibus Frid. Perthes et I.H. Besser.

Gayon, J. 2000. "History of the Concept of Allometry." *American Zoologist* 40(5): 748–758.

Geen, R.G. 1991. "Social Motivation." *Annual Review of Psychology* 42: 377–399.

Geeraerts, G. 1994. "War, Hypercomplexity and Computer Simulation." *Systems Research* 114: 53–66.

Gell-Mann, M. 1994. *The Quark and the Jaguar.* New York: W.H. Freeman.

Gelly, S., L. Koesis, M. Schoenauer, M. Sebag, D. Silver, C. Szepervari, and O. Teytaud. 2012. "The Grand Challenge of Computer Go: Monte Carlo Tree Search and Extensions." *Communications of the ACM* 55(3): 106–113.

Gershenfeld, N. 2012. "How to Make Almost Anything: The Digital Fabrication Revolution." In *The Fourth Industrial Revolution: The Davos Reader*, edited by G. Rose, 12–27. New York: Council on Foreign Relations.

Gibler, D.M., T.J. Rider, and M.L. Hutchison. 2005. "Taking Arms Against a Sea of Troubles: Conventional Arms Races during Periods of Rivalry." *Journal of Peace Research* 42(2): 131–147.
Gigerenzer, G. 2008a. "Why Heuristics Work." *Perspectives on Psychological Science* 3(1): 20–29.
Gigerenzer, G. 2008b. *Rationality for Mortals: How People Cope with Uncertainty*. New York: Oxford University Press.
Gigerenzer, G., and H. Brighton. 2009. "Homo Heuristicus: Why Biased Minds Make Better Inferences." *Topics in Cognitive Science* 1(1): 107–143.
Gilbert, N., and K. Troitzsch. 2005. *Simulation for the Social Scientist*. New York: McGraw-Hill Education UK.
Gilboa, I., A.W. Postlewaite, and D. Schmeidler. 2008. "Probability and Uncertainty in Economic Modeling." *The Journal of Economic Perspectives* 22(3): 173–188.
Gillespie, J., D. Zinnes, and G. Tahim 1976. "Deterrence as a Second Strike Capability: An Optimal Control Model and Differential Game Model." In *Mathematical Systems in International Relations Research*, edited by J. Gillespie and D. Zinnes, 47–69. New York: Praeger.
Gillespie, J.V., and D.A. Zinnes. 1975. "Progressions in Mathematical Models of International Conflict." *Synthese* 312: 289–321.
Girod, S., and R. Whittington, 2015. "Change Escalation Processes and Complex Adaptive System: From Incremental Reconfigurations to Discontinuous Restructuring." *Organizational Science* 26: 1520–1535.
Glattfelder, J. 2013. *Decoding Complexity Uncovering Patterns in Economic Networks*. New York: Springer.
Glazier, D.S. 2010. "A Unifying Explanation for Diverse Metabolic Scaling in Animals and Plants." *Biological Reviews* 85(1): 111–138.
Gleditsch, N.P., P. Wallensteen, M. Eriksson, M. Sollenberg, and H. Strand. 2002. "Armed Conflict 1946–2001: A New Dataset." *Journal of Peace Research* 39(5): 615–637.
Gleick, J. 1987. *Chaos: Making a New Science*. New York: Penguin Books.
Gode, D., and S. Sunder. 1993. "Allocative Efficiency of Markets with Zero Intelligence Traders: Markets as a Partial Substitute for Individual Rationality." *Journal of Political Economy* 101: 119–137.
Gödel, K. 1931. "On Formally Undecidable Propositions of *Principia Mathematica* and Related Systems." Translation of *Gödel's Theorem in Focus*, translated and edited by S.G. Shanker. London and Sydney: Croom Helm.
Goldin, D., S.A. Smolka, and P. Wegner, eds. 2006. *Interactive Computation the New Paradigm*. Berlin: Springer Verlag.
Goldin, D., and P. Wegner. 2008. "The Interactive Nature of Computing: Refuting the Strong Church–Turing Thesis." *Minds and Machines* 18(1): 17–38.
Goldreich, O. 2008. *Computational Complexity. A Conceptual Perspective*. Cambridge: Cambridge University Press.
Goldstein, J. 1994. *The Unshackled Organization*. Portland, OR: Productivity Press.
Goldstein, J. 2011. "Emergence in Complex Systems." In *The Sage Handbook of Complexity and Management*, edited by P. Allen, S. Maguire, and B. McKelvey, 65–78. Thousand Oaks, CA: Sage.

Golland, Y., Y. Arzouan, and N. Levit-Binnum. 2015. "The Mere Co-Presence: Synchronization of Autonomic Signals and Emotional Responses Across Co-Present Individuals Not Engaged in Direct Interaction." *Plos One* 10(5): e0125804. https://doi.org/10.1371/journal.pone.0125804

Goodhart, C. 1994. "Game Theory for Central Bankers: A Report to the Governor of the Bank of England." *Journal of Economic Literature* 32: 101–115.

Goodhart, C.A.E. 1981. "Problems of Monetary Management: The U.K Experience." In *Inflation, Depression and Economic Policy in the West*, edited by A.S. Courakis, 111–146. Lanham, MD: Rowman and Littlefield.

Goodman, N. 1955. *Fact, Fiction, and Forecast*. Cambridge: Harvard University Press.

Gore, R., C.J. Lynch, and H. Kavak. 2017. "Applying Statistical Debugging For Enhanced Trace Validation of Agent-Based Models." *Simulation* 93(4): 273–284.

Gore, R., P.F. Reynolds Jr., and D. Kamensky. 2011. "Statistical Debugging with Elastic Predicates." Paper presented at the 26th IEEE/ACM International Conference on Automated Software Engineering (ASE), 2011, Lawrence, KS. https://doi.org/10.1109/ASE.2011.6100107

Gore, R., P.F. Reynolds Jr., D. Kamensky, S. Diallo, and J. Padilla. 2015. "Statistical Debugging for Simulations." *ACM Transactions on Modeling and Computer Simulation (TOMACS)* 25(3): 16.

Gorman, J.C., P.G. Amazeen, and N. J. Cooke. 2010. "Team Coordination Dynamics." *Nonlinear Dynamics, Psychology, and Life Sciences* 14: 265–290.

Gorman, J.C., T.A. Dunbar, D. Grimm, and C.L. Gipson. 2017. "Understanding and Modeling Teams as Dynamical Systems." *Frontiers in Psychology* 8: 1053. https://doi.org/10.3389/psyg.2017.01053

Gotceitas, V., and P. Colgan. 1989. "Predator Foraging Success and Habitat Complexity: Quantitative Test of the Threshold Hypothesis." *Oecologia* 80(2): 158–166.

Gould, S.J. 2007. *Punctuated Equilibrium*. Harvard: Belknap Press

Grammer, K., B. Fink, and L. Renninger. 2002. "Dynamic Systems and Inferential Information Processing in Human Communication" *Neuroendocrinology Letters* 23(4): 15–22.

Griffiths, T.L., F. Lieder, and N. Goodman 2015. "Rational Use of Cognitive Resources: Levels of Analysis." *Topics in Cognitive Science* 7: 217–229.

Grobman, G.M. 2005. "Complexity Theory: A New Way to Look at Organizational Change." *Public Administration Quarterly* 29 (3/4): 350–382.

Groos, A., and A. Vallely. 2012. *Animals and the Human Imagination. A Companion to Animal Studies*. New York: Columbia University Press.

Gross, D., and R. Strand. 2000. "Can Agent-Based Models Assist Decisions on Large-Scale Practical Problems? A Philosophical Analysis." *Complexity* 5(6): 26–33.

Groves, K., C. Vance, and Y. Paik. 2008. "Linking Linear/Nonlinear Thinking Style Balance and Managerial Ethical Decision-Making." *Journal of Business Ethics* 80(2): 305–325.

Guastello, S. 1981. "Catastrophe Modeling of Equity in Organizations." *Behavioral Science* 26: 63–74.

Guastello, S. 1995. *Chaos, Catastrophe, and Human Affairs*. Mahwah, NJ: Erlbaum.

Guastello, S. 2002. *Managing Emergent Phenomena: Nonlinear Dynamics in Work Organizations*. Mahwah, NJ: Lawrence Erlbaum Associates.

Guastello, S. 2007. "Non-Linear Dynamics and Leadership Emergence." *The Leadership Quarterly* 19(4): 357–369.

Guastello, S. 2010. "Nonlinear Dynamics of Team Performance and Adaptability In Emergency Response." *Human Factors* 52: 162–172.

Guastello, S. 2014. *Human Factors Engineering and Ergonomics: A Systems Approach*, 2nd ed. Boca Raton, FL: CRC Press.

Guastello, S. 2015. "The Complexity of the Psychological Self and the Principle of Optimum Variability." *Nonlinear Dynamics, Psychology, and Life Sciences* 19: 511–528.

Guastello, S. 2016. "Physiological Synchronization in a Vigilance Dual Task." *Nonlinear Dynamics, Psychology, and Life Sciences* 20: 49–80.

Guastello, S. 2017. "Nonlinear Dynamical Systems for Theory and Research in Ergonomics." *Ergonomics* 60: 167–193.

Guastello, S., B.R. Bock, P. Caldwell, and R.W. Bond, Jr. 2005. "Origins of Coordination: Nonlinear Dynamics and the Role of Verbalization." *Nonlinear Dynamics, Psychology, and Life Sciences* 9: 175–208.

Guastello, S., and R.W. Bond, Jr. 2004. "Coordination in Stag Hunt Games with Application to Emergency Management." *Nonlinear Dynamics, Psychology, and Life Sciences* 8: 345–374.

Guastello, S., and R.W. Bond, Jr. 2007a. "The Emergence of Leadership in Coordination- Intensive Groups." *Nonlinear Dynamics, Psychology, and Life Sciences* 11: 91–117.

Guastello, S., A.N. Correro, II, and D.E. Marra. 2018. "Do Emergent Leaders Experience Greater Workload? The Swallowtail Catastrophe Model and Changes in Leadership in an Emergency Response Simulation." *Group Dynamics: Theory, Research, and Practice* 22(4): 200–222. https://doi.org/10.1037/gdn0000091

Guastello, S., and R.A.M. Gregson, eds. 2011. *Nonlinear Dynamical Systems Analysis for the Behavioral Sciences Using Real Data*. Boca Raton, FL: CRC Press.

Guastello, S., and D.D. Guastello. 1998. "Origins of Coordination and Team Effectiveness: A Perspective from Game Theory and Nonlinear Dynamics." *Journal of Applied Psychology* 83: 423–437.

Guastello, S., and E.A. Johnson. 1999. "The Effect of Downsizing on Hierarchical Work Flow Dynamics in Organizations." *Nonlinear Dynamics, Psychology and Life Sciences* 3: 347–377.

Guastello, S., and D.E. Marra. 2018. "External Validity and Factor Structure of Individual and Group Workload Ratings." *Theoretical issues in Ergonomics Science* 19: 229–253.

Guastello, S., D.E. Marra, J. Castro, M. Equi, and A.F. Peressini. 2017. "Turn Taking, Team Synchronization and Non-Stationarity in Physiological Time Series." *Nonlinear Dynamics, Psychology, and Life Sciences* 21: 319–334.

Guastello, S., D.E. Marra, J. Castro, M. Gomez, and C. Perna. 2017. "Performance and Participation Dynamics in an Emergency Response Simulation." *Nonlinear Dynamics, Psychology and Life Sciences* 21: 217–250.

Guastello, S., D.E. Marra, A.F. Peressini, J. Castro, and M. Gomez. 2018. "Autonomic Synchronization, Team Coordination, Participation, and Performance." *Nonlinear Dynamics, Psychology, and Life Sciences* 22: 359–394.

Guastello, S., D.E. Marra, C. Perna, J. Castro, M. Gomez, and A.F. Peressini. 2016. "Physiological Synchronization in Emergency Response Teams: Subjective Workload, Drivers and Empaths." *Nonlinear Dynamics, Psychology, and Life Sciences* 20: 223–270.

Guastello, S., and L. Mirabito. 2018. "Time Granularity, Lag Length, and Down-Sampling Rates for Neurocognitive Data." *Nonlinear Dynamics, Psychology, and Life Sciences* 22: 457–483.

Guastello, S., L. Mirabito, and A.F. Peressini. 2018. "Physiological Synchronization Under Three Task Conditions and Its Impact On Team Performance." Paper presented at the Annual International Conference of the Society for Chaos Theory in Psychology and Life Sciences, Raleigh, North Carolina. https://www.societyforchaostheory.org/conf/2018/about.cgi

Guastello, S., and A. Peressini. 2017. "Development of a Synchronization Coefficient For Biosocial Interactions in Groups and Teams." *Small Group Research* 48: 3–33.

Guastello, S., D. Pincus, and P.R. Gunderson. 2006. "Electrodermal Arousal Between Participants in a Conversation: Nonlinear Dynamics for Linkage Effects." *Nonlinear Dynamics, Psychology, and Life Sciences* 10: 365–399.

Guastello, S., K. Reiter, A. Shircel, P. Timm, M. Malon, and M. Fabisch. 2014. "The Performance-Variability Paradox, Financial Decision-Making, and the Curious Case of Negative Hurst Exponents." *Nonlinear Dynamics, Psychology, and Life Sciences* 18: 297–328.

Guerini, M., and A. Moneta. 2017. "A Method for Agent-Based Models Validation." *Journal of Economic Dynamics and Control* 82: 125–141.

Guevara, M., Cox, R.F.A., van Dijk, M., and van Geert, P. 2017. "Attractor Dynamics of Dynamic Interaction: A Recurrence Based Analysis." *Nonlinear Dynamics, Psychology, and Life Sciences* 21: 289–318.

Gully, S.M., K.A. Incalcaterra, A. Joshi, and J.M. Beaubein. 2002. "A Meta-Analysis of Team Efficacy, Potency, and Performance: Interdependence and Level of Analysis as Moderators of Observed Performance Relationships." *Journal of Applied Psychology* 87: 819–832.

Haken, H. 1984. *The Science of Structure: Synergetics*. New York: Van Nostrand Reinhold.

Haken, H., J.A.S. Kelso, and H. Bunz. 1985. "A Theoretical Model of Phase Transition in Human Hand Movements." *Biological Cybernetics* 51: 347–356.

Haldane, A. 2012. "Financial Arms Races." Bank of England. https://www.bis.org/review/r120426a.pdf

Hales, D. 2000. "Cooperation without Memory or Space: Tags, Groups and the Prisoner's Dilemma." In *International Workshop on Multi-Agent Systems and Agent-Based Simulation (MABS 2000)*, edited by S. Moss and P. Davidsson, 157–166. Berlin: Springer.

Hammond, R. A. 2009. "Complex Systems Modeling for Obesity Research." *Preventing Chronic Disease* 6(3): A97.

Hanappi, G. 2017. "Agent-Based Modelling. History, Essence, Future." *PSL Quarterly Review* 70(283): 449–472.

Handy, S., M. Boarnet, R. Ewing, and R. Killingsworth. 2002. "How the Built Environment Affects Physical Activity: Views from Urban Planning." *American Journal of Preventive Medicine* 23(2): 64–73.

Harris, J., and F. Benedict. 1918. "A Biometric Study of Human Basal Metabolism." *Proceedings of the National Academy of Sciences of the United States of America* 4(12): 370–373.

Hart, S.G., and L.E. Staveland. 1988. "Development of the NASA Task Load Index (TLX): Results of Experimental and Theoretical Research." In *Human Workload*, edited by P.A. Hancock and N. Meshkati, 138–183. Amsterdam: North Holland.

Hawking, S. 2010. "Ten Questions for Stephen Hawking." *Time Magazine*, November 15, 2010. http://content.time.com/time/magazine/article/0,9171,2029483,00.html

Hawking, S. 2015. "Research Priorities for Robust and Beneficial Artificial Intelligence: An Open Letter." *Future of Life Institute*, January 23, 2015. https://futureoflife.org/ai-open-letter/

Haxholdt, C., E. Larsen, and A. van Ackere. 2003. "Mode Locking and Chaos in a Deterministic Queueing Model with Feedback." *Management Science* 49(6): 816–830.

Hayek, F.A. 1948. *Individualism and Economic Order*. Chicago: University of Chicago Press.

Hayek, F.A. 1952. *The Sensory Order: An Inquiry into the Foundations of Theoretical Psychology*. Chicago: University of Chicago Press.

Hayek, F.A. 1960. *The Constitution of Liberty*. Chicago: University of Chicago Press.

Hayek, F.A. 1967. "The Theory of Complex Phenomena." In *Studies in Philosophy, Politics and Economics*, 22–42. London: Routledge and Kegan Paul.

Hazy, J. 2007. "Computer Models of Leadership: Foundations for A New Discipline or Meaningless Diversion?" *The Leadership Quarterly* 18(4): 391–410.

Healy, C., and S. Pratt. 2008. "The Effect of Prior Experience on Nest Site Evaluation by the Ant Temnothorax Curvispinosus." *Animal Behavior* 76: 893–899. https://doi.org/10.1016/anbehv.2008.02.016

Heath, R.A. 2002. "Can People Predict Chaotic Sequences?" *Nonlinear Dynamics, Psychology, and Life Sciences* 6: 37–54.

Helbing, D., and A. Kirman. 2013. "Rethinking Economics Using Complexity Theory." *Real- World Economics Review* 64: 23–52. http://dx.doi.org/10.2139/ssrn.2292370

Helbing, D., D. Brockmann, T. Chadefaux, K. Donnay, U. Blanke, O. Woolley-Meza, M. Moussaid, A. Johansson, J. Krause, and S. Schutte. 2015. "Saving Human Lives: What Complexity Science and Information Systems Can Contribute." *Journal of Statistical Physics* 158(3): 735–781.

Helm, J.L., D. Sbarra, and E. Ferrer. 2012. "Assessing Cross-Partner Association in Physiological Responses via Couple Oscillator Models." *Emotion* 12: 748–762.

Helton, W.S., G.J. Funke, and B.A. Knott. 2014. "Measuring Workload in Collaborative Contexts: Trait versus State Perspectives." *Human Factors* 56: 322–332.

Hempel, C. 1966. *Philosophy of Natural Science*. Englewood Cliffs, NJ: Prentice-Hall.

Hennessy, E., J.T. Ornstein, C.D. Economos, J.B. Herzog, V. Lynskey, E. Coffield, and R.A. Hammond. 2016. "Designing an Agent-Based Model for Childhood

Obesity Interventions: A Case Study of Child Obesity." *Preventing Chronic Disease* 13: E04.

Henning, R.A., W. Boucsein, and M.C. Gil. 2001. "Social-Physiological Compliance as a Determinant of Team Performance." *International Journal of Psychophysiology* 40: 221–232.

Hess, G.D. 1995. "An Introduction to Lewis Fry Richardson and His Mathematical Theory of War and Peace." *Conflict Management and Peace Science* 141: 77–113.

Hill, A.V. 1950. "The Dimensions of Animals and their Muscular Dynamics." *Science Progress* 38(150): 209–230.

Hinkelmann, F., D. Murrugarra, A.S. Jarrah, and R. Laubenbacher. 2011. "A Mathematical Framework for Agent-Based Models of Complex Biological Networks." *Bulletin of Mathematical Biology* 73(7): 1583–1602.

Hirschman, A. 1991. *The Rhetoric of Reaction: Perversity, Futility, Jeopardy.* Cambridge: Belknap Press.

Hirschman, A. 1995. *A Propensity to Self-Subversion.* Cambridge: Harvard University Press.

Hobbs, B., S. Ludsin, R. Knight, P. Ryan, J. Biberhofer, and J. Ciborowski. 2002. "Fuzzy Cognitive Mapping as a Tool to Define Management Objectives for Complex Ecosystems." *Ecological Applications* 12(5): 1548–1565.

Hofmann, M. 2005. "On the Complexity of Parameter Calibration in Simulation Models." *The Journal of Defense Modeling and Simulation* 2(4): 217–226.

Hoffmann, H., and D. Payton. 2018. "Optimization by Self-Organized Criticality." *Sci Rep* 8(1): 2358. https://doi.org/10.1038/s41598-018-20275-7.

Hofstadter, D. 1999. *Godel, Escher, Bach: An Eternal Golden Braid.* New York: Basic Books.

Högbladh, S. 2011. "Peace Agreement 1975–2011: Updating the UCDP Peace Agreement Dataset." *States in Armed Conflict* 55: 85–105.

Holland, J. 1992. "Complex Adaptive Systems." *Daedalus* 121(1): 17–30.

Holland, J. 1995. *Hidden Order: How Adaptation Builds Complexity.* New York: Basic Books.

Holland, J., and J. Miller. 1991. "Artificial Adaptive Agents in Economic Theory." *The American Economic Review* 81(2): 365–370.

Holldobler, B., and E. Wilson. 1990. *The Ants.* Cambridge: The Belknap Press.

Holt, R.P.F., J.B. Rosser, and D. Colander. 2011. "The Complexity Era in Economics." *Review of Political Economy* 23(3): 357–369.

Horgan J. 1995. "Trends in Complexity Studies: From Complexity to Perplexity." *Scientific American* 272:74–79.

Horgan, J. 1997. *The End of Science: Facing the Limits of Knowledge in the Twilight of the Scientific Age.* New York: Broadway Books.

Hove, M.J., and J.L. Risen. 2009. "It's all in the Timing: Interpersonal Synchrony Increases Affiliation." *Social Cognition* 27: 949–961.

Hoyert, M.S. 1992. "Order and Chaos in Fixed-Interval Schedules of Reinforcement." *Journal of the Experimental Analysis of Behavior* 57: 339–363.

Hunt, E., R. Baddeley, A. Worley, A. Sendova-Franks, and N. Franks. 2015. "Ants Determine Their Next Move at Rest: Motor Planning and Causality in Complex Systems." *Royal Society Open Science* 3: 150534. https://doi.org/10.1098/rsos.150534.

Ijiri, Y., and H. Simon. 1964. "Business Firm Growth and Size." *American Economic Review* 54: 77–89.

Ilachinski, A. 1997. *Irreducible Semi-Autonomous Adaptive Combat ISAAC: An Artificial-Life Approach to Land Warfare.* Center for Naval Analyses Research Memorandum CRM 97-61.10. http://citeseerx.ist.psu.edu/viewdoc/download?doi=10.1.1.219.6372&rep=rep1&type=pdf

Ilachinski, A. 2003. "Exploring Self-Organized Emergence in an Agent-Based Synthetic Warfare Lab." *Kybernetes* 32(1/2): 38–76.

Intriligator, M.D., and D.L. Brito. 1984. "Can Arms Races Lead to the Outbreak of War?" *Journal of Conflict Resolution* 28(1): 63–84.

Isard, W., C. Smith, and C.H. Anderton. 1988. *Arms Races, Arms Control, and Conflict Analysis: Contributions from Peace Science and Peace Economics.* Cambridge: Cambridge University Press.

Israel, Giorgio. 2005. "The Science of Complexity: Epistemological Problems and Perspectives." *Science in Context* 18, 1–31.

Itti, L., and P. Baldi. 2009. "Bayesian Surprise Attracts Human Attention." *Vision Research* 49(10), 1295–1306.

Iversen, G., and H. Norpoth. 1987. *Analysis of Variance.* Thousand Oaks: Sage.

Izquierdo, S.S., L.R. Izquierdo, and N.M. Gotts. 2008. "Reinforcement Learning Dynamics in Social Dilemmas." *Journal of Artificial Societies and Social Simulation* 11(2): 1–22.

Jacob, F. 1981. *Le Jeu des Possibles.* Paris: Librairie Arthème Fayad.

Jaeger, R.C., and T.R. Halliday. 1998. "On Confirmatory versus Exploratory Research." *Herpetologica* 54: S64–S66.

Jain, R., M.C. Rivera, and J.A. Lake. 1999. "Horizontal Gene Transfer among Genomes: The Complexity Hypothesis." *Proceedings of the National Academy of Sciences* 96(7): 3801–3806.

Janeway, C.A., P. Travers, M. Walport, and M.J. Shlomchik. 2005. *Immunobiology.* 6th ed. New York: Garland Science.

Janssen, M.A., and E. Ostrom. 2006. "Empirically Based, Agent-Based Models." *Ecology and Society* 11(2): 37–52.

Jarstad, A. D. Nilsson, and R. Sunderberg. 2012. "The IMPACT (Implementation of Pacts) Dataset Codebook." Version 2.0, Department of Peace and Conflict Research, Uppsala University. www.pcr.uu.se/data/

Jarvis, A., H.I. Reuter, A. Nelson, and E. Guevara. 2008. "Hole-Filled SRTM for the Globe: Version 4: Data Grid." CGIAR Consortium for Spatial Information. http://srtm.csi.cgiar.org/

Jensen, J.L.W.V. 1906. "Sur Les Fonctions Convexes et les Inégalités Entre les Valeurs Moyennes." *Acta Mathematica* 30(1): 175–193.

Jerant, A., and P. Franks. 2012. "Body Mass Index, Diabetes, Hypertension, and Short-Term Mortality: A Population-Based Observational Study 2000–2006." *Journal of the American Board of Family Medicine* 25(4): 422–431.

Jetter, A., and R. Sperry. 2013. "Fuzzy Cognitive Maps for Product Planning: Using Stakeholder Knowledge to Achieve Corporate Responsibility." In *Proceedings of the 46th Annual Hawaii International Conference on System Sciences*, 925–934. Computer Science Press. http://archives.pdx.edu/ds/psu/9851

Johansen, A., and D. Sornette. 2001. "Large Stock Market Price Drawdowns are Outliers." *Journal of Risk* 4(2): 69–110.

Jones, D. 2000. "Emerging Problems with the Basel Capital Accord: Regulatory Capital Arbitrage and Related Issues." *Journal of Banking and Finance* 24(1): 35–58.

Joosten, J.J., F. Soler-Toscano, and H. Zenil. 2011. "Program-Size versus Time Complexity, Speed-Up and Slowdown Phenomena in Small Turing Machines." *International Journal of Unconventional Computing* 7(5): 353–387. https://arxiv.org/abs/1102.5389

Joshi, M., J.M. Quinn, and P.M. Regan. 2015. "Annualized Implementation Data on Comprehensive Intrastate Peace Accords, 1989–2012." *Journal of Peace Research* 524: 551–562.

Joyce, A.A. 1989. "The Nuclear Arms Race: An Evolutionary Perspective." *Politics and the Life Sciences* 72: 186–202.

Kahneman, D. 2003. "Maps of Bounded Rationality: Psychology for Behavioral Economics." *American Economic Review* 93(5): 1449–1475.

Kahneman, D., and P. Egan. 2011. *Thinking, Fast and Slow*. New York: Farrar, Straus and Giroux.

Kahneman, D., and A. Tversky. 1979. "Prospect Theory: An Analysis of Decision under Risk." *Econometrica* 47: 263–291.

Kahneman, D., and A. Tversky. 1996. "On the Reality of Cognitive Illusions." *Psychological Review* 103: 502–591.

Kaiser, Ł., A. Gomez, N. Shazeer, A. Vaswani, N. Parmar, L. Jones, and J. Uszkoreit. 2017. "One Model to Learn Them All." https://arxiv.org/abs/1706.05137

Kalyvas, S.N. 2006. *The Logic of Violence in Civil War*. Cambridge: Cambridge University Press.

Kane, E.J. 2010. "Redefining and Containing Systemic Risk." In *Financial Market Regulation Legislation and Implications*, edited by J.A. Tatom, 107–20. New York: Springer.

Kant, I. 1965. *Immanuel Kant's Critique of Pure Reason*, translated by Norman Kemp Smith. New York: St. Martin's Press.

Kant, I. 2017. "Was Heisst: Sich im Denken Orientieren?" CreateSpace Independent Publishing Platform. www.hardpress.net

Kari, J. 2012. "Decidability and Undecidability in Cellular Automata." *International Journal of General Systems* 41(6): 539–554.

Kauffman, S. 1993. *The Origins of Order: Self-Organization and Selection in Evolution*. New York: Oxford University Press.

Kauffman, S. 1995. *At Home in the Universe. The Search for the Laws of Self-Organization and Complexity*. Oxford: Oxford University Press

Kauffman, S. 2000. *Investigations*. Cambridge: Cambridge University Press.

Kauffman, S., S. Pathak, P. Sen, and T. Choi. 2018. "Jury Rigging and Supply Network Design: Evolutionary 'Tinkering' in the Presence of Unknown-Unknowns." *Journal of Supply Chain Management* 54: 51–63.

Kaye-Blake, B., C. Schilling, and E. Post. 2014. "Validation of Agricultural MAS for Southland, New Zealand." *Journal of Artificial Societies and Social Simulation* 17(4): 1–15.

Kenny, D.A. 1994. *Interpersonal Perception*. New York: Guilford Press.

Keynes, J.M. 1921. *Treatise on Probability*. London: Macmillan.

Keynes, J.M. 1936. *The General Theory of Employment, Interest and Money.* London: Macmillan.

Keynes, J.M. 1938. "Professor Tinbergen's Method." *Economic Journal* 49(2): 558–568.

Kiel, L. 1993. "Nonlinear Dynamical Analysis: Assessing Systems Concepts in a Government Agency." *Public Administration Review* 53(2): 143–153.

Kiel, L., and E. Elliott, eds. 1996. *Chaos Theory in the Social Sciences: Foundations and Applications.* Ann Arbor: University of Michigan Press.

Kim, Y., T. Choi, T. Yan, and K. Dooley. 2011. "Structural Analysis of Supply Networks." *Journal of Operations Management* 29(3): 194–211.

Kim, T., E. McFee, D.O. Olguin, B. Waber, and A.S. Pentland. 2012. "Sociometric Badges: Using Sensor Technology to Capture New Forms of Collaboration." *Journal of Organizational Behavior* 33(3): 412–427.

Kindleberger, C.P. 1978. *Manias, Panics, and Crashes.* New York: Basic Books.

Kipnis, J. 2017. "Multifaceted Interactions between Adaptive Immunity and the Central Nervous System." *Science* 353(6301): 766–771.

Kipnis J., S. Gadani, and N.C. Derecki. 2012. "Pro-Cognitive Properties of T Cells." *Nat. Rev. Immunol.* 12: 663–669.

Kirstein, M. 2015. "From the Ergodic Hypothesis in Physics to the Ergodic Axiom in Economics." Paper presented at the conference of the Wintertagung of the ICAE, Linz, Austria.

Kishimoto, A., and M. Mueller. 2015. "Game Solvers." In *Handbook of Digital Games and Entertainment Technologies*, edited by R. Nakatsu, M. Rauterberg, and P. Ciancarini. Singapore: Springer.

Kleene, S.C. 1967. *Mathematical Logic.* New York: John Wiley and Sons.

Kleinberg, J., and E. Tardos. 2006. *Algorithm Design.* New York: Addison-Wesley.

Knight, F.H. 1921. *Risk, Uncertainty, and Profit.* Boston: Hart, Schaffer, and Marx.

Kohn, E. 2013. *How Forests Think. Toward an Anthropology Beyond the Human.* Berkeley: University of California Press.

Kolmogorov, A.N. 1965. "Combinatorial Foundations of Information Theory and the Calculus of Probabilities." *Russian Mathematical Surveys* 38(4): 29–40.

Koppl, R., S. Kauffman, T. Falin, and G. Longo. 2014. "Economics for a Creative World." *Journal of Institutional Economics* 11: 1–31.

Koppl, R., and J.B. Rosser, Jr. 2002. "All That I Have to Say Has Already Crossed Your Mind." *Metroeconomica* 53: 339–360.

Korn, H., and P. Faure. 2003. "Is There Chaos in the Brain? II. Experimental Evidence and Related Models." *C.R. Biologies* 326: 787–840.

Kosko, B. 1986. "Fuzzy Cognitive Maps." *International Journal of Man–Machine Studies* 24(1): 65–75.

Kott, A., and G. Citrenbaum. 2010. *Estimating Impact: A Handbook of Computational Methods, Models for Anticipating Economic, Social, Political, and Security Effects in International Interventions.* Berlin: Springer Science and Business Media.

Kozlowski, S.W.J., and D.R. Ilgen. 2006. "Enhancing the Effectiveness of Work Groups and Teams." *Psychological Science in the Public Interest* 7: 77–124.

Krugman, P. 1996. "Are Currency Crises Self-Fulfilling?" *NBER Macroeconomics Annual* 11: 345–78.

Kuhn, G.W. 1989. *Ground Forces Battle Casualty Rate Patterns: The Empirical Evidence*. McLean, VA: Logistics Management Institute. https://archive.org/details/DTIC_ADA306777

Kuhn, T. 1962. *The Structure of Scientific Revolutions*. Chicago: University of Chicago Press.

Kuhn, T. 1969. "Postscript-1969." In *The Structure of Scientific Revolutions*. 4th ed. Chicago: University of Chicago Press.

Kuhn, T. 1970. "Logic of Discovery or Psychology of Research?" In *Criticism and the Growth of Knowledge*, edited by I. Lakatos and A. Musgrave. Cambridge: Cambridge Univ. Press.

Küppers, G., and J. Lenhard. 2005. "Validation of Simulation: Patterns in the Social and Natural Sciences." *Journal of Artificial Societies and Social Simulation* 8(4): 1–13.

Kurzweil, R. 2005. *The Singularity is Near: When Humans Transcend Biology*. New York: Penguin Books

Kydland, F., and E. Prescott. 1977. "Rules Rather than Discretion: The Inconsistency of Optimal Plans." *Journal of Political Economy* 85(3): 473–492.

Kyewski, B., and L. Klein. 2006. "A Central Role for Central Tolerance" *Annual Review of Immunology* 24: 571–606.

Ladner, R.E. 1975. "On the Structure of Polynomial Time Reducibility." *Journal of ACM* 22: 151–171.

LaFree, G., and L. Dugan. 2007. "Introducing the Global Terrorism Database." *Terrorism and Political Violence* 192: 181–204.

Lakatos, I. 1968. "Criticism and the Methodology of Scientific Research Programmes." *Proceedings of the Aristotelian Society* 69: 149–186.

Lakens, D. 2015. "Estimating the Reproducibility of Psychological Science." *Science* 349(6251): 1–10.

Lanchester, F.W. 1956. "Mathematics in Warfare." *The World of Mathematics* 4: 2138–2157.

Landini, Simone, Mauro Gallegati, and J. Barkley Rosser, Jr. 2018. "Consistency and Incompleteness in General Equilibrium Theory." *Journal of Evolutionary Economics* 30(1): 205–230. https://doi.org/10.1007/s00191-018-0580-6

Landis, S.T. 2014. "Temperature Seasonality and Violent Conflict: The Inconsistencies of a Warming Planet." *Journal of Peace Research* 515: 603–618.

Langridge, E., N. Franks, and A. Sendova-Franks. 2004. "Improvement in Collective Performance with Experience in Ants." *Behavioral Ecology and Sociobiology* 56: 523–29.

L'Anson P., R. Gruter, W. Hughes, and S. Evison. 2016. "Symmetry Breaking In Mass Recruiting Ants: Extent of Foraging Biases Depends on Resource Quality." *Behavioral Ecology and Sociobiology* 70:1813–1820. https://doi.org/10.1007/s00265-016-2187-y

Latané, B., K. Williams, and S. Harkins. 1979. "Many Hands Make Light the Work: The Cases and Consequences of Social Loafing." *Journal of Personality and Social Psychology* 37: 822–832.

Laudan, L. 1978. *Progress and its Problems: Toward a Theory of Scientific Growth*. Berkeley: University of California Press.

Laughlin, R. 2005. *A Different World*. New York: Basic Books.
Lauren, M.K., and R.T. Stephen. 2002. "Fractals and Combat Modeling: Using Mana to Explore the Role of Entropy in Complexity Science." *Fractals* 1004: 481–489.
Lawson, T. 1997. *Economics and Reality*. London: Routledge.
Lebed, F., and M. Bar-Eli. 2013. *Complexity and Control in Team Sports*. New York: Routledge.
LeCun, Y., Y. Bengio, and G. Hinton. 2015. "Deep Learning." *Nature* 521: 436–444.
Lee, C. 2011. "Bounded Rationality and the Emergence of Simplicity amidst Complexity." *Journal of Economic Surveys* 25(3): 507–526
Leinster, T. 2014. *Basic Category Theory*. Cambridge: Cambridge University Press.
Lempert, R. 2002. "Agent-Based Modeling as Organizational and Public Policy Simulators." *Proceedings of the National Academy of Sciences* 99(3): 7195–7196.
Leonard, R.J. 1995. "From Parlor Games to Social Science: Von Neumann, Morgenstern, and the Creation of Game Theory 1928–1944." *Journal of Economic Literature* 33(2): 730–761.
Levina, A., J. Herrmann, and T. Geisel, 2007. "Dynamical Synapses Causing Self-Organized Criticality in Neural Networks." *Nature Physics* 3(12): 857. https://doi.org/10.1038/nphys758.
Levina, A., J. Herrmann, and T. Geisel. 2009. "Phase Transitions toward Criticality in a Neural System with Adaptive Interactions." *Physical Review Letters* 102(11): 118110. https://doi.org/10.1103/PhysRevLett.102.118110
Levinson, R.W., and J.M. Gottman. 1983. "Marital Interaction: Physiological Linkage and Affective Exchange." *Journal of Personality and Social Psychology* 45: 587–597.
Levinthal, D., and M. Warglien. 1999. "Landscape Design: Designing for Local Action in Complex Worlds." *Organization Science* 10(3): 342–357.
Levy, D. 1994. "Chaos Theory and Strategy: Theory, Applications, and Managerial Implications." *Strategic Management Journal* 15: 167–178.
Levy, J.S., and T.C. Morgan. 1984. "The Frequency and Seriousness of War: An Inverse Relationship?" *Journal of Conflict Resolution* 284: 731–749.
Lewes, G.H. 1875. *Problems of Life and Mind*. Boston: Houghton, Osgood and Company.
Lewin, R. 1994. *Complexity: Life at the Edge of Chaos*. Chicago: University of Chicago Press.
Lewis, A.A. 1985. "On Effectively Computable Realizations of Choice Functions." *Mathematical Social Sciences* 10: 43–80.
Lichtenstein, B., N. Carter, K. Dooley, and W. Gartner. 2007. "Complexity Dynamics of Nascent Entrepreneurship." *Journal of Business Venturing* 22(2): 236–261.
Lichtenstein, B., K. Dooley, and T. Lumpkin. 2006. "An Emergence Event in New Venture Creation: Measuring the Dynamics of Nascent Entrepreneurship." *Journal of Business Venturing* 21(2):153–175.
Lim, M., R. Metzler, and B.-Y. Yaneer. 2007. "Global Pattern Formation and Ethnic/Cultural Violence." *Science* 317(5844): 1540–1544.
Lindstedt, S.L., and W.A. Calder. 1976. "Body Size and Longevity in Birds." *The Condor* 78(1): 91–94.
Lindstedt, S.L., B.J. Miller, and S.W. Buskirk. 1986. "Home Range, Time, and Body Size in Mammals." *Ecology* 67(2): 413–418.

Linn, S., and N.N. Tay. 2007. "Complexity and the Character of Stock Returns: Empirical Evidence and a Model of Asset Prices Based on Complex Investor Learning." *Management Science* 53(7): 1165–1180.

Lipman, B.L. 1991. "How to Decide How to Decide How to … : Modeling Limited Rationality." *Econometrica* 59: 1105–1125.

Loasby, B.J. 1976. *Choice, Complexity and Ignorance*. Cambridge: Cambridge University Press.

Lopes, P. 2017. "Why are Behavioural and Immune Traits Linked?" *Hormones and Behavior* 88: 52–59.

Lorenz, E.N. 1963. "Deterministic Non-Periodic Flow," *Journal of Atmospheric Science* 20: 130–141.

Lorenz, H-W. 1992. "Multiple Attractors, Complex Basin Boundaries, and Transient Motion in Deterministic Economic Systems." In *Dynamic Economic Models and Optimal Control*, edited by G. Feichtinger, 411–430. Amsterdam: North-Holland.

Lucas, R. 1972. "Expectations and the Neutrality of Money." *Journal of Economic Theory* 4: 103–124.

Lucas, R. 1976. "Econometric Policy Evaluation: A Critique." *Carnegie-Rochester Conference Series on Public Policy* 1: 19–46.

Lumsden, C., W. Brandts, and L. Trainor. 1997. *Physical Theory in Biology: Foundations and Explorations*. Singapore: World Scientific.

Lumsden, J., L.K. Miles, M.J. Richardson, C.A. Smith, and C.N. Macrae. 2012. "Who Syncs? Social Motives and Interpersonal Coordination." *Journal of Experimental Social Psychology* 48: 46–751.

Luterbacher, U. 1975. "Arms Race Models: Where Do We Stand?" *European Journal of Political Research* 32: 199–217.

Lynch, C.J., H. Kavak, R. Gore, and D. Vernon-Bido. 2017. "Identifying Unexpected Behaviors of Agent-Based Models through Spatial Plots and Heat Maps." Paper presented at Swarmfest 2017, the 21st Annual Meeting on Agent-Based Modeling and Simulation, Swarm Development Group, Suffolk, Virginia.

Ma, Y., E.R. Bertone, E.J. Stanek, G.W. Reed, J.R. Hebert, N.L. Cohen, P.A. Merriam, and I.S. Ockene. 2003. "Association between Eating Patterns and Obesity in a Free-Living US Adult Population." *American Journal of Epidemiology* 158(1): 85–92.

Macal, C.M. 2016. "Everything You Need to Know About Agent-Based Modelling and Simulation." *Journal of Simulation* 10(2): 144–156.

MacIntosh, R., and D. MacLean. 1999. "Conditioned Emergence: A Dissipative Structures Approach to Transformation." *Strategic Management Journal* 20(4): 297–316.

MacKay, N.J. 2015. "When Lanchester Met Richardson, the Outcome was Stalemate: A Parable for Mathematical Models of Insurgency." In *OR, Defence and Security*, edited by R. Forder, 124–147. Basingstoke: Palgrave-MacMillian.

Macy, M.W., and J. Skvoretz. 1998. "The Evolution of Trust and Cooperation between Strangers: A Computational Model." *American Sociological Review* 63(5): 638–660.

Macy, M.W., and R. Willer. 2002. "From Factors to Actors: Computational Sociology and Agent-Based Modeling." *Annual Review of Sociology*: 28(1): 143–166.

Madden, L., D. Duchon, T. Madden, and D. Plowman. 2012. "Emergent Organizational Capacity for Compassion." *Academy of Management Review* 37: 689–708.
Maldonado, C.E. 2016a. "Transformación de la No-Complejidad en Complejidad." *Ingeniería* 2(3): 411–426.
Maldonado, C.E. 2016b. "Pensar Como la Naturaleza. Una Idea Radical." *Unipluriversidad* 16(2): 41–51. https://aprendeenlinea.udea.edu.co/revistas/index.php/unip/article/view/328311
Maldonado, C.E. 2017. "Hipercomputación Biológica y Comunicación entre los Seres Vivos." In *Un Festschrift para José Luis Villaveces*, edited by L.C. Arboleda, 109–124. Bogotá: Academia de Ciencias Exactas, Físicas y Naturales.
Maldonado, C.E. 2018a. "Biological Hypercomputation and Degrees of Freedom." In *Complexity in Biological and Physical Systems: Bifurcations, Solitons and Fractals*, edited by R. López-Ruiz. London: IntechOpen. https://doi.org/10.5772/intechopen.73179
Maldonado, C.E. 2018b. "Seis Tesis Sobre Complejidad y Salud." *Revista de Salud Universidad El Bosque* 8(1). https://doi.org//10.18270/rsb.v8i1.2370
Maldonado, C.E. 2018c. "Quantum Physics and Consciousness: A (Strong) Defense of Pansychism." *Trans/From/Acao* 41:101–118. https://doi.org/10.1590/0101-3173.2018.v41esp.07.p101
Maldonado, C.E. Forthcoming. "Las Matemáticas de la Complejidad son Matemáticas de Sistemas Discretos: Un Estudio Sobre Sus Consecuencias." In *Matemáticas y Complejidad*. Neiva, Colombia: Universidad Surcolombiana.
Maldonado, C.E., and N.A. Gomez. 2014. "Biological Hypercomputation: A New Research Problem in Complexity Theory." *Complexity* 20: 8–18.
Maldonado, C.E., and N. Mezza-García. 2016. "Anarchy and Complexity." *Emergence: Complexity and Organization* 18(1): 52–73.
Malinvaud, E. 1966. *Statistical Methods for Econometrics*. Amsterdam: North-Holland.
Mallon, E., S. Pratt, and N. Franks. 2001. "Individual and Collective Decision-Making During Nest Site Selection by the ant Leptothorax Albipennis." *Behavioral Ecology and Sociobiology* 50: 352–359.
Malnick, S.D., and H. Knobler. 2006. "The Medical Complications of Obesity." *QJM* 99(9): 565-579.
Mancuso, S. 2017. *El Futuro es Vegetal*. Barcelona: Galaxia de Gutenberg.
Mancuso, S., and A. Viola. 2015. *Brilliant Green. The Surprising History and Science of Plant Intelligence*. Washington, D.C.: Island Press.
Mandelbrot, B. 1977. *Fractals: Form, Chance, and Dimension*. San Francisco: W.H. Freeman and Co.
Mandelbrot, B. 1997. *Fractals and Scaling in Finance: Discontinuity, Concentration, Risk*. New York: Springer.
Manrique, P.D., M. Zheng, Z. Cao, E.M. Restrepo, and N.F. Johnson. 2018. "Generalized Gelation Theory Describes Onset of Online Extremist Support." *Physical Review Letters* 121(4): 048301.
Mantegna, R.N., and H.E. Stanley. 2000. *An Introduction to Econophysics*. Cambridge, UK: Cambridge University Press.
Markose, S. 1991. "End-Independent Rules and the Political Economy of Expanding Market Societies of Europe." *European Journal of Political Economy* 7: 579–601.

Markose, S. 2001. "Review of *Computable Economics: The Arne Ryde Memorial Lectures (Ryde Lectures)*, by Kumaraswamy Velupillai." *The Economic Journal* 111(472): F468–F470.

Markose, S.M. 2004. "Novelty in Complex Adaptive Systems (CAS): A Computational Theory of Actor Innovation." *Physica A: Statistical Mechanics and Its Applications* 344: 41–49.

Markose, S. 2005. "Computability and Evolutionary Complexity: Markets as Complex Adaptive Systems." *Economic Journal* 115: F159–F192.

Markose, S. 2013. "Systemic Risk Analytics: A Data-Driven Multi-Agent Financial Network (MAFN) Approach." *Journal of Banking Regulation* 14(3–4): 285–305.

Markose, S. 2017. "Complex Type 4 Structure Changing Dynamics of Digital Agents: Nash Equilibria of a Game with Arms Race in Innovations." *Journal of Dynamics and Games* 4(3): 255–284.

Markose, S. 2019. "The Digital Origins of Intelligence: How We Became Smart and Protean." Keynote Talk at the 2019 Bio-Inspired ICT Conference, Carnegie Mellon University, Pittsburgh, Pennsylvania. http://bionetics.org/keynotes/

Markose, S.M. 2021. "Genomic Intelligence as Über Bio-Cybersecurity: The Gödel Sentence in Immuno-Cognitive Systems." *Entropy* 23(4): 405. https://doi.org/10.3390/e23040405.

Markose, S., A. Alentorn, and A. Krause. 2004. "Dynamic Learning, Herding and Guru Effects in Networks." *IDEAS Working Paper Series from RePEc*.

Markose, S., B. Oluwasegun, and S. Giansante. 2012. "Multi-Agent Financial Network (MAFN) Model of US Collateralized Debt Obligations (CDO): Regulatory Capital Arbitrage, Negative CDS Carry Trade, and Systemic Risk Analysis." In *Simulation in Computational Finance and Economics: Tools and Emerging Applications*, edited by B. Alexandrova-Kabadjova, S. Martinez-Jaramillo, A.L. Garcia-Almanza, and E. Tsang, 225–254. Hershey, PA: IGI Global. https://doi.org/10.4018/978-1-4666-2011-7.ch012

Marks, M.A., M.J. Sabella, C.S. Burke, and S.J. Zaccaro. 2002. "The Impact of Cross-Training on Team Effectiveness." *Journal of Applied Psychology* 87: 3–13.

Marshall, N., A. Dornhaus, N.R. Franks, and T. Kovacs. 2006. "Noise, Cost, and Speed-Accuracy Trade-Offs: Decision-Making in a Decentralized System." *Journal of the Royal Society Interface* 3: 243–254. http://doi.org/10.1098/rsif.2005.0075

Masuda, N., T. O'Shea-Wheller, C. Doran, and N. Franks. 2015. "Computational Model of Collective Nest Selection by Ants with Heterogeneous Acceptance Thresholds." *Royal Society Open Science* 2: 140533. https://doi.org/10.1098/rsos.140533

Matthieu, J.E., T.S. Heffner, G.F. Goodwin, E. Salas, and J.A. Cannon-Bowers. 2000. "The Influence of Shared Mental Models on Team Process and Performance." *Journal of Applied Psychology* 85: 273–283.

Mattick, J. 2011. "The Central Role of RNA in Human Development and Cognition." *Federation of European Biochemical Societies* 585: 1873–3468.

Maturana, H., and F. Varela. 1972. *Autopoiesis and Cognition: The Realization of the Living*. Boston: Reidel.

Mayer-Kress, G. 1992. "Nonlinear Dynamics and Chaos in Arms Race Models." In *Modeling Complex Phenomena*, edited by L. Lam and V. Naroditsky, 153–183. New York: Springer.

Mayer-Kress, G., and S. Grossman. 1989. "Chaos in the International Arms Race." *Nature* 337(6209): 701–704.

Mayer-Kress, G., K.M. Newell, and Y.-T. Liu. 2009. "Nonlinear Dynamics of Motor Learning." *Nonlinear Dynamics, Psychology, and Life Sciences* 13: 3–26.

Maynard-Smith, J. 1982. *Evolution and the Theory of Games.* Cambridge: Cambridge University Press.

McClintock, B. 1984. "The Significance of Responses of the Genome to Challenge." *Science* 226(4676): 792–801.

McGinnis, M.D. 1991. "Richardson, Rationality, and Restrictive Models of Arms Races." *Journal of Conflict Resolution* 353: 443–473.

McKelvey, B. 1999. "Avoiding Complexity Catastrophe in Coevolutionary Pockets: Strategies for Rugged Landscapes." *Organization Science* 10(3): 294–321.

McKelvey, B. 2004. "Toward a Complexity Science of Entrepreneurship." *Journal of Business Venturing* 19: 313–341.

Meadows, D.H., D.L. Meadows, J. Randers, and W. Behrens, III. 1972. *The Limits to Growth: A Report to the Club of Rome.* New York: Universe Books.

Metzler, R., and J. Klafter. 2000. "The Random Walk's Guide to Anomalous Diffusion: A Fractional Dynamics Approach." *Physics Reports* 339(1): 1–77.

Meyer, A., V. Gaba, and K. Colwell. 2005. "Organizing Far from Equilibrium: Nonlinear Change in Organizational Fields." *Organization Science* 16(5): 456–473.

Miconi, T., J. Clune, and K.O. Stanley. 2018. "Differentiable Plasticity: Training Plastic Neural Networks with Backpropagation." https://arxiv.org/abs/1804.02464

Mihm, J., C. Loch, and A. Huchzermeier. 2003. "Problem–Solving Oscillations in Complex Engineering Projects." *Management Science* 49(6): 733–750.

Mihm, J., C. Loch, D. Wilkinson, and B. Huberman. 2010. "Hierarchical Structure and Search in Complex Organizations." *Management Science* 56(6): 831–848.

Miller, G.F. 1997. "Protean Primates: The Evolution of Adaptive Unpredictability in Competition and Courtship." In *Machiavellian Intelligence II: Extensions and Evaluations,* edited by A. Whiten and R.W. Byrne, 312–340. Cambridge: Cambridge Univ. Press.

Miller, J.G. 1978. *Living Systems.* New York: McGraw-Hill.

Miller, W.B. 2018. "Biological Information Systems: Evolution as Cognition-Based Information Management." *Progress in Biophysics and Molecular Biology* 134: 1–26.

Millonas, M. 1993. *Swarms, Phase Transitions, and Collective Intelligence.* New Mexico: Center for Nonlinear Studies and Theoretical Division, Santa Fe Institute. https://arxiv.org/abs/adap-org/9306002

Minsky, H. 1972. "Financial Instability Revisited: The Economics of Disaster." *Reappraisal of the Federal Reserve Discount Mechanism* 3: 97–136.

Mirowski, P. 2002. *Machine Dreams: Economics Becomes a Cyborg Science.* Cambridge: Cambridge University Press.

Mirowski, P., and E. Nik-Kah. 2017. *Knowledge We Have Lost in Information: The History of Information in Modern Economics.* New York: Oxford University Press.

Mitchell, M. 2009. *Complexity: A Guided Tour.* Oxford: Oxford University Press.

Mnih, V., A.P. Badia, M. Mirza, A. Graves, T. Lillicrap, T. Harley, D. Silver, and K. Kavukcuoglu. 2016. "Asynchronous Methods for Deep Reinforcement Learning." https://arxiv.org/abs/1602.01783

Moffat, J. 2003. *Complexity Theory and Network Centric Warfare.* Washington, D.C.: CCRP Publication Series.

Moglich, M. 1978. "Social Organization of Nest Emigration in Leptothorax (Hym., Form.)." *Insectes Sociaux* 25: 205–225.

Moglich M., U. Maschwitz, and B. Holldobler. 1974. "Tandem Calling: A New Kind of Signal in Ant Communication." *Science* 186: 1046–1047.

Mønster, D., D.D. Håkonsson, J.K. Eskildsen, and S. Wallot. 2016. "Physiological Evidence of Interpersonal Dynamics in a Cooperative Production Task." *Physiology and Behavior* 156: 24–34.

Mooney, C. 1997. *Monte Carlo Simulation, Quantitative Applications in the Social Sciences*. Thousand Oaks, CA: Sage.

Morel, B., and R. Ramanujam. 1999. "Through the Looking Glass of Complexity: The Dynamics of Organizations as Adaptive and Evolving Systems." *Organization Science* 10(3): 278–293.

Morland, K., S. Wing, R.A. Diez, and C. Poole. 2002. "Neighborhood Characteristics Associated with the Location of Food Stores and Food Service Places." *American Journal of Preventive Medicine* 22(1): 23–29.

Muller, M. 2002. "Computer Go." *Artificial Intelligence* 134: 145–179.

Must, A., J. Spadano, E.H. Coakley, A.E. Field, G. Colditz, and W.H. Dietz. 1999. "The Disease Burden Associated with Overweight and Obesity." *The Journal of the American Medical Association* 282(16): 1523–1529.

Nachbar, J.H., and W.R. Zame. 1996. "Non-Computable Strategies and Discounted Repeated Games." *Economic Theory* 8(1): 111–121.

Naeem, M., G. Prasad, D.R. Watson, and J.A.S. Kelso. 2012. "Electrophysiological signatures of intentional social coordination in the 10-12 Hz range." *Neuroimage* 59(2): 1795-1803.

Nagel, E., and J.R. Newman. 1958. *Gödels Proof*. New York: New York University Press.

Namatame, A., and S.H. Chen. 2016. *Agent-Based Modeling and Network Dynamics*. Oxford: Oxford University Press.

Nanetti, A., and S.A. Cheong. 2018. "Computational History: From Big Data to Big Simulations." In *Big Data in Computational Social Science and Humanities*, edited by S.-H. Chen, 337–363. New York: Springer.

Nataf, S. 2017. "Autoimmunity as a Driving Force of Cognitive Evolution." *Frontiers in Neuroscience* 11: 582.

Nestle, M., and M.F. Jacobson. 2000. "Halting the Obesity Epidemic: A Public Health Policy Approach." *Public Health Reports* 115(1): 12–24.

Newell, A, J.C. Shaw, and H. Simon. 1959. "Report on a General Problem-Solving Program." Report P-1584. Santa Monica: RAND Corporation.

Newell, A., and H. Simon. 1956. "The Logic Theory Machine: A Complex Information Processing System." Report P-868. Santa Monica: RAND Corporation.

Newell, A., and H. Simon. 1972. *Human Problem-Solving*. Englewood Cliffs, NJ: Prentice Hall.

Newell, K.M. 1991. "Motor Skill Acquisition." *Annual Review of Psychology* 42: 213–237.

Newman, M. 2005. "Power Laws, Pareto Distributions and Zipf's Law." *Contemporary Physics* 46(5): 323–351.

Newman, M. 2010. *Networks: An Introduction*. Oxford: Oxford University Press.

Nilsson, N.J. 2010. *The Quest for Artificial Intelligence: A History of Ideas and Achievements*. Cambridge: Cambridge University Press.

Noble, D. 2017. "Evolution Viewed from Physics, Physiology and Medicine." *Interface Focus* 7(5): 20160159.

Noia, J.M., and M.S. Neuberger. 2007. "Molecular Mechanisms of Antibody Somatic Hypermutation." *Annual Review of Biochemistry* 76: 1–22.

Norgan, N.G., and J.V. Durnin. 1980. "The Effect of 6 Weeks of Overfeeding on the Body Weight, Body Composition, and Energy Metabolism of Young Men." *The American Journal of Clinical Nutrition* 33(5): 978–988.

North, M.J., and C.M. Macal. 2007. *Managing Business Complexity: Discovering Strategic Solutions with Agent-Based Modeling and Simulation*. Oxford: Oxford University Press.

Nowak, M.A. 2011. *SuperCooperators: Altruism, Evolution, and Why We Need Each Other to Succeed*. New York: The Free Press

Nyarko, Y. 1991. "Learning in Mis-Specified Models and the Possibility of Cycles." *Journal of Economic Theory* 55: 416–427.

Obstfeld, M. 1996. "Models of Currency Crises with Self-Fulfilling Features." *European Economic Review* 40: 1037–1047.

O'Donnell, R.M. 2014–15. "A Critique of the Ergodic/Nonergodic Approach to Uncertainty." *Journal of Post Keynesian Economics* 37: 187–209.

Ogata, K. 1995. *Discrete-Time Control Systems*. 2nd ed. Englewood Cliffs, NJ: Prentice Hall.

Ogden, C.L., M.D. Carroll, B.K. Kit, and K.M. Flegal. 2014. "Prevalence of Childhood and Adult Obesity in the United States, 2011–2012." *The Journal of the American Medical Association* 311(8): 806–814.

Oneal, J.R., F.H. Oneal, Z. Maoz, and B. Russett. 1996. "The Liberal Peace: Interdependence, Democracy, and International Conflict, 1950–85." *Journal of Peace Research* 331: 11–28.

Oneal, J.R., and B. Russett 1999. "Assessing the Liberal Peace with Alternative Specifications: Trade Still Reduces Conflict." *Journal of Peace Research* 36(4): 423–442.

Ormans, L. 2016. "50 Journals Used in FT Research Rank." Financial Times, September 12, 2016. https://www.ft.com/content/3405a512-5cbb-11e1-8f1f-00144feabdc0

Orsucci, F.F., N. Musmeci, B. Aas, G. Schiepek, M. A. Reda, L. Canestri, G. de Felice, and A. Giuliani. 2016. "Synchronization Analysis of Language and Physiology in Human Dyads." *Nonlinear Dynamics, Psychology, and Life Sciences* 20:167–192.

Osborn, R., and J. Hunt. 2007. "Leadership and the Choice of Order: Complexity and Hierarchical Perspectives Near the Edge of Chaos." *The Leadership Quarterly* 18(4): 319–340.

O'Shea-Wheller, T.A., N. Masuda, A.B. Sendova-Franks, and N.R. Franks. 2017. "Variability in Individual Assessment Behavior and Its Implication for Collective Decision-Making." *Proceedings of the Royal Society B* 284: 20162237. https://doi.org/10.1098/rspb.20162237

Osipov, M. (1915) 1991. "The Influence of the Numerical Strength of Engaged Forces on their Casualties." Research Paper CAA-RP-91–2. Originally published in the *Tsarist Russian Journal, Military Collection*. Translated by R.L. Helmbold and A.S. Rehm. Bethesda: U.S. Army Concepts Analysis Agency.

Ottmann, M., and J. Vüllers. 2015. "The Power-Sharing Event Dataset PSED: A New Dataset on the Promises and Practices of Power-Sharing in Post-Conflict Countries." *Conflict Management and Peace Science* 323: 327–350.

Padilla, J.J., S.Y. Diallo, C.J. Lynch, and R. Gore. 2018. "Observations on the Practice and Profession of Modeling and Simulation: A Survey Approach." *Simulation* 94(6): 493–506.

Painter-Morland, M. 2008. "Systemic Leadership and the Emergence of Ethical Responsiveness." *Journal of Business Ethics* 82: 509–524.

Pais, D., P. Hogan, T. Schlegel, N. Franks, N. Leonard, and J. Marshall, 2013. "A Mechanism for Value-Sensitive Decision-Making." *PLoS One* 8(9): 73216. https://doi.org/10.1371/journal.pone.0073216

Palmer, R. 1982. "Broken Ergodicity." *Advances in Physics* 31: 669–736.

Palumbo, R.V., M.E. Marraccini, L.L. Weyandt, O. Wilder-Smith, H.A. McGee, S. Liu, and M.S. Goodwin. 2017. "Interpersonal Autonomic Physiology: A Systematic Review of the Literature." *Personality and Social Psychology Review* 21: 99–141.

Panchev, S., and N.K. Vitanov. 2008. "Mathematical Models of Intergroup Conflicts." https://arxiv.org/abs/0810.3818

Pannell, D. 1997. "Sensitivity Analysis of Normative Economic Models: Theoretical Framework and Practical Strategies." *Agricultural Economics* 16(2): 139–152.

Pathak, S., J. Day, A. Nair, W. Sawaya, and M. Kristal. 2007. "Complexity and Adaptivity in Supply Networks: Building Supply Network Theory Using a Complex Adaptive Systems Perspective." *Decision Sciences* 38(4): 547–580.

Pathak, S., D. Dilts, and G. Biswas. 2007. "On the Evolutionary Dynamics of Supply Network Topologies." *IEEE Transactions on Engineering Management* 54: 662–672.

Pentland, A. 2008. *Honest Signals: How They Shape Our World*. London: The MIT press.

Pepinsky, T.B. 2005. "From Agents to Outcomes: Simulation in International Relations." *European Journal of International Relations* 11(3): 367–394.

Perrin, J. 2005. *Brownian Movement and Molecular Reality*. New York: Dover.

Peters, O., and A. Adamou. 2018. "An Evolutionary Advantage of Cooperation. arXiv. org: 1506.03414v2 (nlin.AO) 24." https://arxiv.org/abs/1506.03414

Peters, O., and M. Gell-Mann. 2016. "Evaluating Gambles Using Dynamics." *Chaos: An Interdisciplinary Journal of Nonlinear Science* 2(6): 023103. https://doi.org/10.1063/1.4940236

Peterson, M., and M. Meckler. 2001. "Cuban-American Entrepreneurs: Chance, Complexity and Chaos." *Organization Studies* 22(1): 31–57.

Piccinini, N., D. Lambert, B.J. West, M. Bologna, and P. Grigolini. 2016. "Nonergodic Complexity Management." *Physical Review E* 93(6): 062301.

Pikovsky, A., M. Rosenblum, and J. Kurths. 2001. *Synchronization: A Universal Concept in Nonlinear Sciences*. Cambridge: Cambridge University Press.

Plowman, D., L. Baker, T. Beck, M. Kulkani, S. Solansky, and D. Travis. 2007. "Radical Change Accidentally: The Emergence and Application of Small Change." *Academy of Management Journal* 50(3): 515–543.

Poincaré, H. 1912. Chance. *The Monist* 221: 31–52.

Pollitt, H., and J.F. Mercure. 2018. "The Role of Money and the Financial Sector in Energy- Economy Models Used For Assessing Climate and Energy Policy." *Climate Policy* 18(2): 184–197.

Popper, K. 1959. *The Logic of Scientific Discovery*. New York: Basic Books.

Popper, K. 1963. *Conjectures and Refutations*. New York: Routledge and Kegan Paul.

Post, E. 1944. "Recursively Enumerable Sets of Positive Integers and Their Decision Problems." *Bulletin of American Mathematical Society* 50: 284–316.

Poulis, K., and E. Poulis. 2016. "Problematizing Fit and Survival: Transforming the Law of Requisite Variety Through Complexity Misalignment." *Academy of Management Review* 41(3): 503–527.

Powell, L., F. Chaloupka, and Y. Bao. 2007. The Availability of Fast-Food and Full-Service Restaurants in the United States: Association with Neighborhoods Characteristics. *American Journal of Preventive Medicine* 33(4): s240–s245.

Pramukkul, P., A. Svenkeson, P. Grigolini, M. Bologna, and B.J. West. 2013. "Complexity and the Fractional Calculus." *Advances in Mathematical Physics* 2013: 1–7. http://dx.doi.org/10.1073/pnas.0604801103

Pratt, S., and D. Sumpter. 2006. "A Tunable Algorithm for Collective Decision-Making." Proceedings of the National Academy of Sciences 103(43): 15906–15910. http://dx.doi.org/10.1155/2013/498789

Pratt, S., D. Sumpter, E. Mallon, and N. Franks, 2005. "An Agent-Based Model of Collective Nest Choice by the Ant Temnothorax Albipennis." *Animal Behavior* 70: 1023–1036.

Prigogine, I. 1980. *From Being to Becoming. Time and Complexity in the Physical Sciences*. San Francisco: W.H. Freeman and Co.

Prigogine, I., and I. Stengers. (1984) 2018. *Order Out of Chaos: Man's New Dialogue with Nature*. Toronto: Bantam Books.

Prokopenko, M., M. Harré, J. Lizier, F. Boschetti, P. Peppas, and S. Kauffman. 2019. "Self- Referential Basis of Undecidable Dynamics: From the Liar Paradox and the Halting Problem, to the Edge of Chaos." *Physics of Life Reviews* 31: 134–156. https://doi.org/10.1016/j.plrev.2018.12.003

Putra, H.C., H. Zhang, and C. Andrews. 2015. "Modeling Real Estate Market Responses to Climate Change in the Coastal Zone." *Journal of Artificial Societies and Social Simulation* 18(2): 1–16.

Pryor, F. 1995. *Economic Evolution and Structure: The Impact of Complexity on the U.S. Economic System*. New York: Cambridge University Press.

Quine, W. 1951. "Two Dogmas of Empiricism." *Philosophical Review* 60(1): 20–43. https://doi.org/10.2307/2181906.

Quine, W. 1953. *From a Logical Point of View*. Cambridge: Harvard University Press.

Quine, W., and J. Ullian. 1978. *The Web of Belief*. 2nd ed. New York: Random House.

Raleigh, C. 2015. "Urban Violence Patterns across African States." *International Studies Review* 171: 90–106.

Raleigh, C., A. Linke, H. Hegre, and J. Karlsen. 2010. "Introducing ACLED: An Armed Conflict Location and Event Dataset: Special Data Feature." *Journal of Peace Research* 475: 651–660.

Ramachandran, V.S. 2000. "Mirror Neurons and Imitation Learning as the Driving Force Behind the Great Leap Forward in Human Evolution: Conversation." EDGE, May 5, 2000. https://www.edge.org/3rd_culture/ramachandran/ramachandran_index.html

Ramenzoni, V.C., T.J. Davis, M.A. Riley, K. Shockley, and A.A. Baker. 2011. "Joint Action in a Cooperative Precision Task: Nested Processes of Intrapersonal and Interpersonal Coordination." *Experimental Brain Research* 211: 447–457.

Ramseyer, F., and W. Tschacher. 2016. "Movement Coordination in Psychotherapy: Synchrony of Hand Movements is Associated with Session Outcome: A Single-Case Study." *Nonlinear Dynamics, Psychology, and Life Sciences* 20: 145–166.

Rapoport, A. 1957. "Lewis F. Richardson's Mathematical Theory of War." *Conflict Resolution* 1(3): 249–299.

Reidpath, D., C. Burns, J. Garrard, M. Mahoney, and M. Townsend. 2002. "An Ecological Study of the Relationship Between Social and Environmental Determinants of Obesity." *Health and Place* 8(2): 141–145.

Reynolds, C.W. 1987. "Flocks, Herds, and Schools: A Distributed Behavioral Model." *Computer Graphics* 21: 25–34.

Richardson, L.F. 1935. "Mathematical Psychology of War." *Nature* 136(3452): 1025.

Richardson, L.F. 1948. "Variation of the Frequency of Fatal Quarrels with Magnitude." *Journal of the American Statistical Association* 43(244): 523–546.

Richardson, L.F. 1951. "Could an Arms-Race End Without Fighting?" *Nature* 168(4274): 567.

Richardson, L.F. 1960a. *Arms and Insecurity: A Mathematical Study of the Causes and Origins of War*. Pittsburgh: Boxwood Press.

Richardson, L.F. 1960b. *Statistics of Deadly Quarrels*. Pittsburgh: Boxwood Press.

Richardson, M.J., R.L. Garcia, T.D. Frank, M. Gergor, and K.L. Marsh. 2012. "Measuring Group Synchrony: A Cluster-Phase Method for Analyzing Multivariate Movement Time- Series." *Frontiers in Physiology* 3: 405. https://doi.org/10.3389/phys.2012.00405

Richardson, T., K. Christensen, N. Franks, H. Jensen, and A. Sendova-Franks. 2011 "Group Dynamics and Record Signals in the Ants Temnothorax Albipennis." *Journal of the Royal Society Interface* 8: 518–28.

Richardson, T., E. Robinson, K. Christensen, H. Jensen, N. Franks, and A. Sendova-Franks. 2010. "Record Dynamics in Ants." *PLoS ONE* 5(3): e9621. https://doi.org/10.1371/journal.pone.0009621

Richter, M., and K. Wong. 1999. "Non-Computability of Competitive Equilibrium." *Economic Theory* 14: 1–28.

Rico, R., M. Sánchez-Manzanares, F. Gil, and C. Gibson. 2008. "Team Implicit Coordination Processes: A Team Knowledge-Based Approach." *Academy of Management Review* 33: 163–184.

Rissanen, J. 1989. *Stochastic Complexity in Statistical Inquiry*. Singapore: World Scientific.

Rivkin, J. 2000. "Imitation of Complex Strategies." *Management Science* 46(6): 824–844.

Rivkin, J., and N. Siggelkow. 2007. "Patterned Interactions in Complex Systems: Implications for Exploration." *Management Science* 53(7): 1068–1085.

Rizzolatti, G., L. Fadiga, V. Gallese, and L. Fogassi. 1996. "Premotor Cortex and the Recognition of Motor Actions." *Cognitive Brain Research* 3: 131–141.

Roberts, D.C., and D.L. Turcotte. 1998. "Fractality and Self-Organized Criticality of Wars." *Fractals* 604: 351–357.

Robinson, E., O. Feinerman, and N. Franks. 2012. "Experience, Corpulence, and Decision Making In Ant Foraging." *Journal of Experimental Biology* 215(15): 2653–2659.

Robinson, E., O. Feinerman, and N. Franks. 2014. "How Collective Comparisons Emerge Without Individual Comparisons of the Options." *Proceedings of the Royal Society B* 281: 20140737. https://doi.org/10.1098/rspb.2014.0737

Robinson, E., N. Franks, S. Ellis, S. Okuda, and J. Marshall. 2011. "A Simple Threshold Rule is Sufficient to Explain Sophisticated Collective Decision-Making." *PLoS ONE* 6(5): e19981. https://doi.org/10.1371/journal.pone.0019981

Robinson, E., F. Smith, S. Sullivan, and N. Franks. 2009. "Do Ants Make Direct Comparisons?" *Proceedings of the Royal Society B* 276: 2635–2641. https://doi.org/10.1098/rspb.2009.0350

Rogers, H. 1967. *Theory of Recursive Functions and Effective Computability*. New York: McGraw-Hill.

Rogoff, K. 1985. "The Optimal Degree of Commitment to an Intermediate Monetary Target." *Quarterly Journal of Economics* 100(4): 169–190.

Rogowski, R., and S. Deakin. 2011. "Reflexive Labour Law, Capabilities and the Future of Social Europe." In *Transforming European Employment Policy: Labour Market Transitions and the Promotion of Capability*, edited by R. Rogowski, R. Salais, and Noel Whiteside, 229–254. Cheltenham, UK: Edward Elgar.

Romer, P. 2016. "The Trouble with Macroeconomics." *The American Economist* 20: 1–20.

Rosa, H. 2013. *Social Acceleration: A New Theory of Modernity*. New York: Columbia University Press.

Rosecrance, R.N. 1986. *The Rise of the Trading State: Commerce and Conquest in the Modern World*. New York: Basic Books.

Rosen, Robert. 1987. "Some Epistemological Issues in Physics and Biology." In *Quantum Implications*, edited by Basil Hiley and F. David Peat, 327–341. London: Routledge.

Rosenberg, A.L. 2010. *The Pillars of Computation Theory. State, Encoding, Nondeterminism*. Berlin: Springer-Verlag.

Rosser, J.B., Sr. 1936. "Extensions of Some Theorems of Gödel and Church." *Journal of Symbolic Logic* 1: 87–91.

Rosser, J.B., Jr. 1991. *From Catastrophe to Chaos: A General Theory of Economic Discontinuities*. Boston: Kluwer.

Rosser, J.B., Jr. 1996. "Chaos and Rationality." In Chaos Theory in the Social Sciences, edited by L. Douglas Kiel and Euel Elliott, 199–212. Ann Arbor: University of Michigan Press.

Rosser, J.B., Jr. 1998. "Complex Dynamics in New Keynesian and Post Keynesian Models." In *New Keynesian Economics/Post Keynesian Alternatives*, edited by R.J. Rotheim, 288–302. London: Routledge.

Rosser, J.B., Jr. 1999. "On the Complexities of Coplex Economic Dynamics." *Journal of Economic Perspectives* 13(4): 169–192.

Rosser, J.B., Jr. 2001. "Alternative Keynesian and Post Keynesian Perspectives on Uncertainty and Expectations." *Journal of Post Keynesian Economics* 23: 545–566.

Rosser, J.B., Jr. 2004. "On the Epistemological Implications of Economic Complexity." *Annals of the Japan Association for Philosophy of Science* 13: 45–57.

Rosser, J.B., Jr. 2010. "Constructivist Logic and Emergent Evolution in Economic Complexity," In *Computability, Constructive and Behavioural Economic Dynamics:*

Essays in Honour of Kumaraswamy (Vela) Velupillai, edited by S. Zambelli, 184–197. London: Routledge.

Rosser, J.B., Jr. 2012. "On the Foundations of Mathematical Economics." *New Mathematics and Natural Computation* 8: 53–72.

Rosser, J.B., Jr. 2015. "Reconsidering Ergodicity and Fundamental Uncertainty." *Journal of Post- Keynesian Economics* 38(3): 331–354.

Rosser, J. B., Jr. 2016. "Reconsidering Ergodicity and Fundamental Uncertainty." *Journal of Post Keynesian Economics* 38: 331–354.

Rosser, J.B., Jr. 2020a. "Reflections on Reflexivity and Complexity." In *History, Methodology and Identity for a 21st Social Economics,* edited by Wilfred Dolfsma, C. Wade Hands, and Robert McMaster, 67–86. London: Routledge,.

Rosser, J.B., Jr. 2020b. "The Minsky Moment and the Revenge of Entropy." *Macroeconomic Dynamics* 24: 7–23.

Rosser, J.B., Jr., C. Folke, F. Gunther, H. Isomaki, C. Perrings, and T. Puu. 1994. "Discontinuous Change in Multilevel Hierarchical Systems." *Systems Research* 11: 77–94.

Rosser, J.B., Jr., and M. Rosser. 2015. "Complexity and Behavioral Economics." *Nonlinear Dynamics, Psychology, and Life Sciences* 19: 67–92.

Rosser, J.B., Jr., M. Rosser, and M. Gallegati. 2012. "A Minsky-Kindleberger Perspective on the Financial Crisis." *Journal of Economic Issues* 45: 449–458.

Rouchier, J., C. Cioffi-Revilla, J.G. Polhill, and K. Takadama. 2008. "Progress in Model-to-Model Analysis." *Journal of Artificial Societies and Social Simulation* 11(2): 1–8.

Roza, A., and H. Shizgal. 1984. "The Harris Benedict Equation Reevaluated: Resting Energy Requirements and the Body Cell Mass." *American Journal of Clinical Nutrition* 40(1): 168–182.

Rummel, R.J. 1967. "Dimensions of Dyadic War, 1820–1952." *Journal of Conflict Resolution* 112: 176–183.

Russell, S., and P. Norvig. 2010. *Artificial Intelligence: A Modern Approach.* 3rd ed. New Jersey: Prentice Hall.

Saint-Simon, H. 1821. *Du Système Industriel.* Paris: Chex Antoine—Augustin Renouard.

Sakoda, J.M. 1971. "The Checkerboard Model of Social Interaction." *The Journal of Mathematical Sociology* 1(1): 119–132.

Sallans, B., A. Pfister, A. Karatzoglou, and G. Dorffner. 2003. "Simulation and Validation of an Integrated Markets Model." *Journal of Artificial Societies and Social Simulation* 6(4): 1–33.

Sallis, J., A. Bauman, and M. Pratt. 1998. "Environmental and Policy Interventions to Promote Physical Activity." *American Journal of Preventive Medicine* 15(4): 379–397.

Sallis, J., L.D. Frank, B.E. Saelens, and M.K. Kraft. 2004. "Active Transportation and Physical Activity: Opportunities for Collaboration on Transportation and Public Health Research." *Transportation Research Part A: Policy and Practice* 38(4): 249–268.

Saltelli, A., P. Annoni, I. Azzini, F. Campolongo, M. Ratto, and S. Tarantola. 2010. "Variance Based Sensitivity Analysis of Model Output. Design and Estimator for the Total Sensitivity Index." *Computer Physics Communications* 181(2): 259–270.

Samorodnitsky, G., and M.S. Taqqu. 1994. *Stable Non-Gaussian Random Processes: Stochastic Models with Infinite Variance.* New York: Chapman and Hall.
Sample, S.G. 1997. "Arms Races and Dispute Escalation: Resolving the Debate." *Journal of Peace Research* 341: 7–22.
Samuelson, L. 1997. *Evolutionary Games and Equilibrium Selection.* Cambridge: MIT Press.
Samuelson, Paul A. 1969. "Classical and Neoclassical Theory." In *Monetary Theory: Selected Readings*, edited by Robert W. Clower, 182–194. Hammondsworth, UK: Penguin.
Saperstein, A.M. 1984. "Chaos—a Model for the Outbreak of War." *Nature* 309(5966): 303–305.
Saperstein, A.M. 1986. "Predictability, Chaos, and the Transition to War." *Bulletin of Peace Proposals* 171: 87–93.
Saperstein, A.M. 1994. "Chaos as a Tool for Exploring Questions of International Security." *Conflict Management and Peace Science* 132: 149–177.
Saperstein, A.M. 1995. "War and Chaos." *American Scientist* 836: 548–557.
Saperstein, A.M. 1997. "Complexity, Chaos, and National Security Policy: Metaphors or Tools." In *Complexity, Global Politics, and National Security*, edited by D.S. Alberts and T.J. Czerwinski, 101–134. Washington, D.C.: National Defense University.
Saperstein, A.M., and G.E. Marsh. 1988. "SDI a Model for Chaos." *Bulletin of the Atomic Scientists* 448: 40–43.
Sargent, R.G. 1987. "An Overview of Verification and Validation of Simulation Models." In *Proceedings of the 19th Conference on Winter Simulation*, edited by Arne Thesen, Hank Grant, and W. David Kelton, 33–39. New York: ACM. https://doi.org/10.1145/318371.318379
Sargent, R.G. 2013. "Verification and Validation of Simulation Models." *Journal of Simulation* 7(1): 12–24.
Sarkar, S. 2000. "A Brief History of Cellular Automata." *ACM Computing Surveys* 32(1): 80–107.
Sarkees, M.R., and F. Wayman. 2010. *Resort to War: 1816–2007. Correlates of War.* Washington, D.C.: CQ Press.
Sasaki, T., and S. Pratt. 2011. "Emergence of Group Rationality from Irrational Individuals." *Behavioral Ecology* 22(2): 276–281. https://doi.org/10.1093/beheco/arq198
Sasaki, T., and S. Pratt. 2013. "Ants Learn to Rely on More Informative Attributes During Decision-Making." *Biology Letters* 9: 20130667. https://doi.org/10.1098/rsbl.20130667
Sawyer, R.K. 2005. *Social Emergence: Societies as Complex Systems.* New York: Cambridge University Press.
Schaeffer, J. 2000. "The Games Computers (and People) Play." *Advances in Computers* 52: 189–266.
Schaeffer, J., N. Burch, Y. Björnsson, A. Kishimoto, M. Müller, R.L.P. Lake, and S. Sutphen. 2007. "Checkers is Solved." *Science* 317: 1518–1522.
Schelling, T.C. 1971. "Dynamic Models of Segregation." *Journal of Mathematical Sociology* 12: 143–186.
Schiff, J. 2008. Cellular Automata: *A Discrete View of the World.* New York: Wiley.

Schindehutte, M., and M. Morris. 2009. "Advancing Strategic Entrepreneurship Research: The Role of Complexity Science in Shifting the Paradigm." *Entrepreneurship Theory and Practice* 33: 241–276.

Schmid, T.L., M. Pratt, and E. Howze. 1995. "Policy as Intervention: Environmental and Policy Approaches to the Prevention of Cardiovascular Disease." *American Journal of Public Health* 85(9): 1207–1211.

Schmidt-Nielsen, K. 1984. *Scaling: Why is Animal Size So Important?* Cambridge: Cambridge University Press.

Schmidt-Nielsen, K. 1997. *Animal Physiology: Adaptation and Environment.* Cambridge: Cambridge University Press.

Schneider, A., C. Wickert, and E. Marti. 2017. "Reducing Complexity by Creating Complexity: A Systems Theory Perspective on How Organizations Respond to Their Environments." *Journal of Management Studies* 54: 182–208.

Schrödinger, E. (1944) 2012. *What is Life? With Mind and Matter and Autobiographical Sketches* Cambridge: Cambridge University Press.

Schrodt, P.A. 1978. "Richardson's N-Nation Model and the Balance Of Power." *American Journal of Political Science* 22(2): 364–390.

Schrodt, P.A. 1981. "Conflict as a Determinant of Territory." *Behavioral Science* 26(1): 37–50.

Schumpeter, J.A. 1934. *The Theory of Economic Development: An Inquiry into Profits, Capital, Credit, Interest and the Business Cycle.* Cambridge: Harvard University Press.

Schuster, P. 2015. "Ebola—Challenge and Revival of Theoretical Epidemiology: Why Extrapolations from Early Phases of Epidemics are Problematic." *Complexity* 20(5): 7–12.

Schutte, S. 2017. "Violence and Civilian Loyalties: Evidence from Afghanistan." *Journal of Conflict Resolution* 618: 1595–1625.

Seeley, T.D. 2010. *Honeybee Democracy.* Princeton, NJ: Princeton University Press

Seger, C.A. 1994. "Implicit Learning." *Psychological Bulletin* 115: 163–196.

Sejnowski, T.J. 2018. *The Deep Learning Revolution.* Cambridge, MA: Cambridge University Press

Selden, P., and D. Fletcher. 2015. "The Entrepreneurial Journey as an Emergent Hierarchical System of Artifact-Creating Processes." *Journal of Business Venturing* 30(4): 603–615.

Semovski, S.V. 2001. "Self-Organization in Fish School." In *Nonlinear Dynamics in the Life and Social Sciences,* edited by W. Sulis and I. Trofimova, 398–406. Amsterdam: IOS Press.

Sen, P., and Chakrabarti, B.K., 2014. *Sociophysics: An Introduction.* Oxford: Oxford University Press.

Sendova-Franks, A., and N. Franks. 1995. "Division of Labour in a Crisis: Task Allocation During Colony Emigration in the Ant *Leptothorax Unifasciatus* (Latr.)." *Behavioral Ecology and Sociobiology* 36: 269–282.

Sendova-Franks, A., N. Franks, and N. Britton. 2002. "The Role of Competition in Task Switching during Colony Emigration in the Ant Leptothorax Albipennis." *Animal Behavior* 63: 715–725.

Seo, M.-G., L.L. Putnam, and J.M. Bartunek. 2004. "Dualities and Tensions of Planned Organizational Change." In *Handbook of Organizational Change and Innovation*, edited by M.S. Poole and A.H. Van de Ven, 73–107. New York: Oxford University Press.

Shackle, G.L.S. 1972. *Epistemics and Economics: A Critique of Economic Doctrines*. Cambridge: Cambridge University Press.

Shannon, C. 1950. "Programming a Computer for Playing Chess." *Philosophical Magazine* 41: 257–275.

Shapiro, E. 2012. "A Mechanical Turing Machine: Blueprint for a Biomolecular Computer." *Interface Focus* 2(4): 497–503.

Shapiro, J.A. 2013. "How Life Changes Itself: The Read–Write (RW) Genome." *Physics Life Review* 10(3): 287–323.

Shapiro, J.A. 2017. "Living Organisms Author Their Read–Write Genomes in Evolution." *Biology* 6(4): 42.

Shinkai, S., and Y. Aizawa. 2006. "The Lempel-Zev Complexity of Non-Stationary Chaos in Infinite Ergodic Cases." *Progress of Theoretical Physics* 116: 503–515.

Sibani, P., and P. Littlewood. 1993. "Slow Dynamics from Noise Adaption." *Physical Review Letters* 71(10): 1482–1485.

Siedliński, R. 2016. "Turing Machines and Evolution: A Critique of Gregory Chaitin's Metabiology." *Studies in Logic, Grammar and Rhetoric* 48(1): 133–150.

Siljak, D. 1977. "On the Stability of the Arms Race." In *Mathematical Systems in International Relations Research*, edited by J.V. Gillespie and D.A. Zinnes, 264–296. New York: Praeger.

Silver, D., A. Huang, C.J. Maddison, A. Guez, L. Sifre, G. van den Driessche, J. Schrittwieser, I. Antonoglou, V. Panneershelvam, and M. Lanctot. 2016. "Mastering the Game of Go With Deep Neural Networks and Tree Search." *Nature* 529: 484–489.

Silver, D., J. Schrittwieser, K. Simonyan, I. Antonoglou, A. Huang, A. Guez, T. Hubert, L. Baker, M. Lai, and A. Bolton. 2017. "Mastering the Game of Go Without Human Knowledge." *Nature* 550: 354–359.

Simaan, M., and J. Cruz 1975. "Formulation of Richardson's Model of Arms Race From a Differential Game Viewpoint." *The Review of Economic Studies* 421: 67–77.

Simon, H. 1947. *Administrative Behavior*. New York: Macmillan.

Simon, H. 1955. "A Behavioral Model of Rational Choice." *Quarterly Journal of Economics* 69(1): 99–118.

Simon, H. 1956. "Rational Choice and the Structure of the Environment." *Psychological Review* 63(2): 129–138.

Simon, H. 1957. *Models of Man: Social and Rational*. New York: John Wiley and Sons.

Simon, H. 1962. "The Architecture of Complexity." *Proceedings of the American Philosophical Society* 106(6): 467–482.

Simon, H. 1969. *The Sciences of the Artificial*. Cambridge: MIT Press.

Simon, H. 1976. "From Substantive to Procedural Rationality." In *25 Years of Economic Theory*, edited by T.J. Kastelein, 65–86. Boston: Springer.

Simon, H., and J. Schaeffer. 1992. "The Game of Chess." In *Handbook of Game Theory*, edited by Robert J. Aumann and S. Hart, 1:1–17. Amsterdam: Elsevier.

Simon, M.V., and H. Starr 2000. "Two-Level Security Management and the Prospects for New Democracies: A Simulation Analysis." *International Studies Quarterly* 443: 391–422.

Simulation Productions, Inc. 1979. *The Creature that Ate Sheboygan! Wreak Havoc with the Monster of Your Choice.* New York: SPI.

Simulated Society (SIMSOC) Group Simulation Game. 2018.

Singer, J.D. 1972. "The "Correlates of War" Project: Interim Report and Rationale." *World Politics* 242: 243–270.

Skarda, C., and W. J. Freeman. 1987. "How Brains Make Chaos in Order to Make Sense of the World." *Behavioural Brain Science* 10: 161–195.

Skinner, B.F. 1971. *Beyond Freedom and Dignity.* New York: Bantam Books.

Smith, A. 1759. *The Theory of Moral Sentiments.* London: Miller, Kincaid and Bell.

Smolin, L. 2001. *Three Roads to Quantum Gravity.* New York: Basic Books.

Smullyan, R. 1961. *Theory of Formal Systems.* Princeton, NJ: Princeton University Press.

Sokolowski, J.A., and C.M. Banks. 2010. *Modeling and Simulation Fundamentals: Theoretical Underpinnings and Practical Domains.* Hoboken, NJ: John Wiley and Sons.

Soler, L., K. Kok, G. Camara, and A. Veldkamp. 2012. "Using Fuzzy Cognitive Maps to Describe Current System Dynamics and Develop Land Cover Scenarios: A Case Study in the Brazilian Amazon." *Journal of Land Use Science* 7(2): 149–175.

Somit, A., and S. Peterson. 2003. *Human Nature and Public Policy: An Evolutionary Approach.* New York: Palgrave Macmillan.

Soros, G. 1995. *Soros on Soros: Staying Ahead of the Curve.* New York: John Wiley.

Soto, V., J. Tyson-Carr, K. Kokmotou, H., Roberts, S. Cook, N. Fallon, T. Giesbrecht, and A. Stancak. 2018. "Brain Responses to Emotional Faces in Natural Settings: A Wireless Mobile EEG Recording Study." *Frontiers in Psychology* 9: 1–15.

Speakman, J.R. 2005. "Body Size, Energy Metabolism and Lifespan." *Journal of Experimental Biology* 208(9): 1717–1730.

Spear, S. 1989. "Learning Rational Expectations under Computability Constraints." *Econometrica* 57: 889–910.

Sperber, D., ed. 2000. *Metarepresentations: A Multidisciplinary Perspective.* New York: Oxford University Press.

Stacey, R. 1992. *Managing the Unknowable.* San Francisco: Jossey-Bass.

Stadler, F. 1997. *Studien zum Wiener Kreis. Ursprung, Entwicklung und Wirkung des Logishen Empirismus im Kontext.* Frankfurt: Springer Verlag

Stefański, A. 2009. *Determining Thresholds of Complete Synchronization and Application.* Singapore: World Scientific.

Stevens, R., and T. Galloway. 2016. "Tracing Neurodynamic Information Flows During Teamwork." *Nonlinear Dynamics, Psychology, and Life Sciences* 20: 271–292.

Stevens, R., T. Galloway, and C. Lamb. 2014. "Submarine Navigation and Team Resilience: Linking EEG and Behavioral Models." *Proceedings of the Human Factors and Ergonomics Society* 58: 245–249.

Stevens, R., T. Galloway, and A. Willemson-Dunlap. 2016. "Intermediate Neurodynamic Representations: A Pathway toward Quantitative Measurements of Teamwork?" *Proceedings of the Human Factors and Ergonomics Society* 60: 1989–1993.

Stigler, G. 1961. "The Economics of Information." *Journal of Political Economy* 69: 213–225.

Stodder, J. 1995. "The Evolution of Complexity in Primitive Economies: Theory." *Journal of Comparative Economics* 20: 1–31.

Stroeymeyt, N., N. Franks, and M. Giurfa. 2011. "Knowledgeable Individuals Leads Collective Decisions in Ants." *The Journal of Experimental Biology* 214: 3046–3054. https://doi.org/10.1242/jeb.059188

Stroeymeyt, N., C. Jordan, G. Mayer, S. Hovsepian, M. Giurfa, and N. Franks. 2014. "Seasonality in Communication and Collective Decision-Making in Ants." *Proceedings of the Royal Society B* 281: 20133108. https://doi.org/10.1098/rspb.201303108

Stroeymeyt, N., E. Robinson, P. Hogan, J. Marshall, M. Giurfa, and N. Franks. 2011. "Experience-Dependent flexibility in Collective Decision Making by House-Hunting Ants." *Behavioral Ecology* 22(3) 535–542. https://doi.org/10.1093/beheco/arr007

Strogatz, S. 2003. *Sync: The Emerging Science of Spontaneous Order.* New York: Hyperion.

Sulis, W. 1995a. "Naturally Occurring Computational Systems." In *Chaos Theory in Psychology and the Life Sciences,* edited by R. Robertson, and A. Combs, 103–122. Mahwah: Erlbaum Associates.

Sulis, W. 1995b. "Causality in Naturally Occurring Computational Systems." *World Futures* 44(2–3): 129–148.

Sulis, W. 1997. "Fundamentals of Collective Intelligence." *Nonlinear Dynamics, Psychology, and Life Science* 1(1): 30–65.

Sulis, W. 1999. "A Formal Theory of Collective Intelligence." In *Dynamics, Synergetics, Autonomous Agents,* edited by W. Tschacher and J. Dauwalder, 224–237. Singapore: World Scientific.

Sulis, W. 2002. "Archetypal Dynamics: An Approach to the Study of Emergence." In *Formal Descriptions of Developing Systems,* edited by J. Nation, I. Trofimova, J. Rand, and W. Sulis, 185–228. Amsterdam: Kluwer.

Sulis, W. 2009. "Collective Intelligence: Observations and Models." In *Chaos and Complexity in Psychology: The Theory of Nonlinear Dynamical Systems,* edited by S. Guastello, M. Koopmans, and D. Pincus, 41–72. Cambridge: Cambridge University Press.

Sulis, W. 2017. "Modeling Stochastic Complexity in Complex Adaptive Systems: Non-Kolmogorov Probability and the Process Algebra Approach." *Nonlinear Dynamics, Psychology, and Life Sciences* 21(4): 407–440.

Sundberg, R., and E. Melander 2013. "Introducing the UCDP Georeferenced Event Dataset." *Journal of Peace Research* 504: 523–532.

Sutherland, S. 1992. *Irrationality: The Enemy Within.* London: Constable.

Swinburn, B.A., I. Caterson, J.C. Seidell, and W.P.T. James 2004. "Diet, Nutrition and the Prevention of Excess Weight Gain and Obesity." *Public Health Nutrition* 7(1a): 123–146.

Takadama, K., T. Kawai, and Y. Koyama. 2008. "Micro-and Macro-Level Validation in Agent-Based Simulation: Reproduction of Human-Like Behaviors and Thinking in a Sequential Bargaining Game." *Journal of Artificial Societies and Social Simulation* 11(2): 1–17.

Takadama, K., Y.L. Suematsu, N. Sugimoto, N.E. Nawa, and K. Shimohara. 2003. "Cross- Element Validation in Multiagent-Based Simulation: Switching Learning Mechanisms in Agents." *Journal of Artificial Societies and Social Simulation* 6(4): 1–17.

Taleb, N. 2007. *The Black Swan: The Impact of the Highly Improbable.* New York: Random House.

Tanriover, O., and S. Bilgen. 2011. "UML-Based Conceptual Models and V and V." In *Conceptual Modeling for Discrete-Event Simulation,* edited by S. Robinson, R. Brooks, K. Kotiadis, and D.J. Van Der Zee, 383–422. Boca Raton, FL: CRC Press.

Tasa, K., S. Taggar, and G. Seijts. 2007. "The Development of Collective Efficacy on Teams: A Multi-Level and Longitudinal Perspective." *Journal of Applied Psychology* 92(1): 17–27.

Terra, L.A., and J.L. Passador. 2016. "Symbiotic Dynamic: The Strategic Problem from the Perspective of Complexity." *Systems Research and Behavioral Science* 33(2): 235–248.

Thaler, R. 2018. "From Cashews to Nudges: The Evolution of Behavioral Economics." *American Economic Review* 108(6): 1265–1287.

Thiele, J.C., W. Kurth, and V. Grimm. 2014. "Facilitating Parameter Estimation and Sensitivity Analysis of Agent-Based Models: A Cookbook Using NetLogo and 'R'." *Journal of Artificial Societies and Social Simulation* 17(3): 1–45.

Thietart, R. 2016. "Strategy Dynamics: Agency, Path Dependency, and Self-Organized Emergence." *Strategic Management Journal* 37: 774–792.

Thietart, R., and B. Forgues. 1995. "Chaos Theory and Organization." *Organization Science* 6: 19–31.

Thom, R. 1972. *Structural Stability and Morphogenesis: An Outline of a General Theory of Models.* Reading, PA: Addison-Wesley.

Thurner, S., J.D. Farmer, and J. Geanakoplos. 2012. "Leverage Causes Fat Tails and Clustered Volatility." *Quantitative Finance* 12(5): 695–707.

Thurner, S., R. Hanel, and P. Klimek. 2018. *Introduction to the Theory of Complex Systems.* Oxford: Oxford University Press.

Tinbergen, J. 1937. *An Econometric Approach to Business Cycles.* Paris: Hermann.

Tinbergen, J. 1940. "On a Method of Statistical Business Research: A Reply." *Economic Journal* 50: 41–54.

Tofts, C. 1993. "Algorithms for Task Allocation in Ants: A Study of Temporal Polyethism Theory." *Bulletin of Mathematical Biology* 55(5): 891–918.

Tognoli E., J. Lagarde, G. DeGuzman, and S. Kelso. 2007 "The Phi Complex as the Neuromarker of Human Social Coordination." *Proceedings of the National Academy of Sciences of the USA* 104(19): 8190–8195.

Tolk, A., ed. 2012. *Engineering Principles of Combat Modeling and Distributed Simulation.* Hoboken, NJ: John Wiley and Sons, Inc.

Tolk, A., S. Y. Diallo, J.J. Padilla, and H. Herencia-Zapana. 2013." Reference Modelling in Support of MandS—Foundations and Applications." *Journal of Simulation* 7(2): 69–82.

Tomochi, M., and M. Kono. 1998. "Chaotic Evolution of Arms Races." *Chaos: An Interdisciplinary Journal of Nonlinear Science* 84: 808–813.

Tourish, D. 2018. "Is Complexity Leadership Theory Complex Enough?" *Organization Studies* 40(2): 219–238.

Trofimova, I. 2002. "Sociability, Diversity and Compatibility in Developing Systems: EVS Approach." In *Formal Descriptions of Developing Systems*, edited by J.S. Nation, I. Trofimova, J. Rand, and W. Sulis, 231–248. Amsterdam: Kluwer.

Trofimova, I. 2016a. "The Interlocking Between Functional Aspects of Activities and a Neurochemical Model of Adult Temperament." In *Temperaments: Individual Differences, Social and Environmental Influences and Impact on Quality of Life*, edited by M.C. Arnold, 77–147. New York: Nova Science Publishers.

Trofimova, I. 2016b. "Phenomena of Functional Differentiation (FD) and Fractal Functionality (FF)." *International Journal of Design and Nature and Ecodynamics* 11(4): 508–521.

Trofimova, I. 2017. "Functional Constructivism: In Search of Formal Descriptors." *Nonlinear Dynamics in Psychology and Life Sciences* 21(4): 441–474.

Trofimova, I. 2019. "An Overlap between Mental Abilities and Temperament Traits." In *General And Specific Mental Abilities*, edited by D. McFarland, 77–114. Cambridge: Cambridge Scholars Publishing.

Tromp, J., and G. Farnebäck. 2007. "Combinatorics of Go." In *Computers and Games*, edited by H.J. van den Herik, P. Ciancarini, H.H.L.M. Donkers, eds. *Lecture Notes in Computer Science*. Heidelberg: Springer.

Trust for America's Health and Robert Wood Johnson Foundation. 2012. *F as in Fat: How Obesity Threatens America's Future*. Princeton, NJ: The Robert Wood Johnson Foundation. https://www.rwjf.org/en/library/research/2013/08/f-as-in-fat--how-obesity-threatens-america-s-future-2013.html

Tsuda, I. 2014. "Logic Dynamics for Deductive Inference—Its Stability and Neural Basis." In *Chaos, Information Processing and Paradoxical Games: The Legacy of John S Nicolis*, edited by N. Gregoire and B. Vasilios, 355–373. Hackensack, NJ: World Scientific Publishing Co. Pte. Ltd. https://doi.org/10.1142/9789814602136_0017

Tucker, Paul. 2011. "Macro and Microprudential Supervision." Speech given at the British Bankers' Association Annual International Banking Conference, London, UK. www.bis.org/review/r110704e.pdf

Turcotte, D.L. 1992. *Fractals and Chaos in Geology and Geophysics*. Cambridge: Cambridge University Press.

Turing, A. 1937a. "Computability and λ-Definability." *Journal of Symbolic Logic* 2: 153–163.

Turing, A. 1937b. "On Computable Numbers, With an Application to the Entscheidungsproblem." *Proceedings of the London Mathematical Society* 50: 230–265.

Turing, A. 1953. "Digital Computers Applied to Games." In *Faster than Thought*, edited by B.V. Bowden. London: Pitman Publishing.

Turvey, M.T. 1990. "Coordination." *American Psychologist* 45: 938–953.

Tversky, A. 1972. "Elimination by Aspects." *Psychological Review* 79: 281–299.

Tversky, A., and Kahneman, D. 1973. "Availability: A Heuristic for Judging Frequency and Probability." *Cognitive Psychology* 5: 207–232.

Uffink, J. 2006. "A Compendium of the Foundations of Classical Statistical Physics." Ph.D. diss., University of Utrecht, Netherlands. http://philsci-archive.pitt.edu/2691/1/UffinkFinal.pdf

Uhl-Bien, M., and R. Marion. 2008. *Complexity Leadership*. Charlotte, NC: IAP.
Uhl-Bien, M., R. Marion, and B. McKelvey. 2007. "Complexity Leadership Theory: Shifting Leadership from the Industrial Age to the Knowledge Era." *Leadership Quarterly* 18: 298–318.
United States Department of Health and Human Services. 2012. *Overweight and Obesity Statistics*. Bethesda, MD: The National Institute of Diabetes, Digestive, and Kidney Diseases.
United States Department of Health and Human Services and National Institutes of Health, National Heart, Lung, and Blood Institute. 2005. *Aim for a Healthy Weight*. (NIH Publication No. 05-5213). Bethesda, MD: National Institutes of Health.
Vainio, H., and F. Bianchini. 2002. *Weight Control and Physical Activity*, vol. 6 in *International Agency for Research (IARC) Handbooks of Cancer Prevention*. Lyon: IARC Press.
Valiant, L.G. 1984. "A Theory of the Learnable." *Communications of the ACM* 27(11): 1134–1142.
Valiant, L.G. 2013. *Probably Approximately Correct*. New York: Basic Books.
Van Cauwenberg, J., I. De Bourdeaudhuij, F. Meester, D. Van Dyck, J. Salmon, P. Clarys, and B. Deforche. 2011. "Relationship between the Physical Environment and Physical Activity in Older Adults: A Systematic Review." *Health and Place* 17(2): 458–469.
Van de Ven, A.H., and M.S. Poole. 1995. "Explaining Development and Change in Organizations." *Academy of Management Review* 20: 510–540.
Van Eck, P.S., W. Jager, and P.S. Leeflang. 2011. "Opinion Leaders' Role in Innovation Diffusion: A Simulation Study." *Journal of Product Innovation Management* 28(2): 187–203.
Van Heijinoort, Jean. 1967. *A Source Book of Mathematical Logic*. Cambridge: Harvard University Press.
van Vliet, M., K. Kok, and T. Veldkamp. 2010. "Linking Stakeholders and Modellers in Scenario Studies: The use of Fuzzy Cognitive Maps as a Communication and Learning Tool." *Futures* 42(1): 1–14.
Varela, F. 1989. *Autonomie et Connaissance: Essai Sur Le Vivant*. Paris: Seuil.
Varela, F., E. Thompson, and E. Rosh. 1992. *The Embodied Mind: Cognitive Science and Human Experience*. Cambridge: The MIT Press.
Varghese, S., J.A.A.W. Elemans, A.E. Rowan, and R.J.M. Nolte. 2015. "Molecular Computing: Paths to Chemical Turing Machines." *Chemical Science* 6(11): 6050–6058.
Vedral, V. 2010. *Decoding Reality: The Universe as Quantum Information*. Oxford: Oxford University Press.
Velupillai, K. 2000. *Computable Economics*. Oxford: Oxford University Press.
Velupillai, K., ed. 2005. *Computability, Complexity and Constructivity in Economic Analysis*. Hoboken, NJ: Wiley-Blackwell.
Velupillai, K. 2007. "The Impossibility of an Effective Theory of Policy in a Complex Economy." In *Complexity Hints for Economic Policy*, edited by M. Salzano and D. Colander, 273–290. Milan: Springer.
Velupillai, K. 2010. *Computable Foundations for Economics*. London and New York: Routledge.

Velupillai, K. 2019. "Classical Behavioural Finance Theory." *Review of Behavioral Economics* 6: 1–18.

Velupillai, K., and Y.F. Kao. 2014. "Computable and Computational Complexity Theoretic Bases for Herbert Simon's Cognitive Behavioral Economics." *Cognitive Systems Research* 29(1): 40–52. https://doi.org/10.1016/j.cogsys.2013.07.005

Vetter, G., M. Stadler, and J.D. Haynes. 1997. "Phase Transitions in Learning." *Journal of Mind and Behavior* 18: 335–350.

Vink, R., M.L. Wijnants, A.H.N. Cillessen, and A.M.T. Bosman. 2017. "Cooperative Learning and Interpersonal Synchrony." *Nonlinear Dynamics, Psychology, and Life Sciences* 21: 189–216.

Vogt, M., N.-C. Bormann, S. Rüegger, L.-E. Cederman, P. Hunziker, and L. Girardin. 2015. "Integrating Data on Ethnicity, Geography, and Conflict: The Ethnic Power Relations Data Set Family." *Journal of Conflict Resolution* 597: 1327–1342.

von Bertalanffy, L. 1951. "General System Theory—A New Approach to Unity of Science." *Human Biology* 23: 303–361.

von Bertalanffy, L. 1968. *General System Theory: Foundations, Development, Applications*. New York: George Braziller.

Boltzmann, L. 1884. "Über die Eigenschaften Monocyklischer und Andere Damit Verwander Systeme." *Crelle's Journal für Due Reine und Augwandi Matematik* 100: 201–212.

von Clausewitz, C. 1976. *On War*. Translated by Michael Howard and Peter Paret. Princeton, NJ: Princeton University Press

von Neumann, J. 1932. "Proof of the Quasi-Ergodic Hypothesis." *Proceedings of the National Academy of Sciences* 18: 263–266.

von Neumann, J., and O. Morgenstern. 1953. *Theory of Games and Economic Behavior*. Princeton, NJ: Princeton University of Press.

Waldrop, M. 1992. *Complexity: The Emerging Science at the Edge of Order and Chaos*. New York: Simon and Shuster.

Wallace, M.D. 1979. "Arms Races and Escalation: Some New Evidence." *Journal of Conflict Resolution* 231: 3–16.

Wang, Y., M. Beydoun, L. Liang, B. Caballero, and S. Kumanyika. 2008. "Will All Americans Become Overweight or Obese? Estimating the Progression and Cost of the U.S. Obesity Epidemic." *Obesity* 16(10): 2323–2330.

Wang, Y., H. Xue, H.J. Chen, and T. Igusa. 2014. "Examining Social Norm Impacts on Obesity and Eating Behaviors Among US School Children Based on Agent-Based Model." *BMC Public Health* 14(1): 923–934. https://doi.org/10.1186/1471-2458-14-923

Watkins, N., G. Pruessner, S. Chapman, N. Crosby, and H. Jensen. 2016. "25 Years of Self-Organized Criticality: Concepts and Controversies." *Space Science Reviews* 198(1): 3–44.

Watts, D. 2002. "A Simple Model of Global Cascades on Random Networks." *Proceedings of the National Academy of Sciences* 99(9): 5766–5771.

Weick, K., and D. Gilfillan. 1971. "Fate of Arbitrary Traditions in a Laboratory Microculture." *Journal of Personality and Social Psychology* 17: 179–191.

Weidlich, A., and D. Veit. 2008. "A Critical Survey of Agent-Based Wholesale Electricity Market Models." *Energy Economics* 30(4): 1728–1759.

Weidmann, N.B., and I. Salehyan. 2013. "Violence and Ethnic Segregation: A Computational Model Applied to Baghdad." *International Studies Quarterly* 571: 52–64.

Weisburd, D., A.A. Braga, E.R. Groff, and A. Wooditch. 2017. "Can Hot Spots Policing Reduce Crime in Urban Areas? An Agent-Based Simulation." *Criminology* 55(1): 137–173.

Werner, G. 2010. "Fractals in the Nervous System: Conceptual Implications for Theoretical Neuroscience." *Frontiers in Physiology* 1: 1–28. https://doi.org/10.3389/fphys.2010.00015

West, B.J. 2010. "Fractal Physiology and the Fractional Calculus: A Perspective." *Frontiers in Physiology* 1: 1–17. https://doi.org/10.3389/fphys.2010.00012.

West, B.J. 2016a. *Fractional Calculus View of Complexity: Tomorrow's Science*. Boca Raton, FL: CRC Press.

West, B.J. 2016b. "Information Forces." *Journal of Theoretical and Computational Science* 3(2): 1–5. https://doi.org/10.4172/2376-130x.1000144

West, B.J. 2017. *Nature's Patterns and the Fractional Calculus*. Leiden: De Gruyter.

West, B.J., E.L. Geneston, and P. Grigolini. 2008. "Maximizing Information Exchange between Complex Networks." *Physics Reports* 468(1–3): 1–99.

West, B.J., and P. Grigolini. 2011. *Complex Webs: Anticipating the Improbable*. Cambridge: Cambridge University Press.

West, D., and B.J. West. 2012. "On Allometry Relations." *International Journal of Modern Physics B* 26(18): 1230010.

West, D., and B.J. West. 2013. "Physiologic Time: A Hypothesis." *Physics of Life Reviews* 10(2): 210–224.

West, G. 2017. *Scale: The Universal Laws of Growth, Innovation, Sustainability, and the Pace of Life in Organisms, Cities, Economies, and Companies*. New York: Penguin Press.

West, G.B., and J.H. Brown. 2004. "Life's Universal Scaling Laws." *Physics Today* 57(9): 36-43.

West, G.B., J.H. Brown, and B.J. Enquist. 1997. "A General Model for the Origin of Allometric Scaling Laws in Biology." *Science* 276(5309): 122–126.

Wheatley, M. 1992. *Leadership and the New Science: Learning about Organization from an Orderly Universe*. Oakland, CA: Berrett-Koehler Publishers.

Wheeler, W. 1911. "The Ant Colony as an Organism." *Journal of Morphology* 22(2): 307–325.

Whitehead, A. 1978. *Process and Reality*. New York: The Free Press.

Whitner, R., and O. Balci. 1989. "Guidelines for Selecting and Using Simulation Model Verification Techniques." In *Proceedings of the 21st Conference on Winter Simulation*, 559–568. Washington, D.C.: ACM.

Whittle, P. 2010. *Neural Nets and Chaotic Carriers*. 2nd ed. London: Imperial College Press.

Wholleben, P. 2016. *The Hidden Life of Trees. What They Feel, How They Communicate*. Vancouver/Berkeley: Greystone Books.

Wiener, N. 1948a. *Cybernetics: Or Control and Communication in the Animal and the Machine*. Cambridge: MIT Press.

Wiener, N. 1948b. "Time, Communication, and the Nervous System." *Annals of the New York Academy of Sciences* 50(1): 197–220.

Wigmore, J., ed. 1913. *The Principles Of Judicial Proof: As Given by Logic, Psychology, and General Experience, and Illustrated in Judicial Trials*. New York: Little, Brown.

Wigner, E.P. 1960. "The Unreasonable Effectiveness of Mathematics in the Natural Sciences." *Communications on Pure and Applied Mathematics* 13: 1–14.

Wilson, E.O. 1971. *The Insect Societies*. Cambridge: The Belknap Press.

Wilson, E.O. 1975. *Sociobiology*. Cambridge: Harvard University Press.

Wilson, E.O. 1998. *Consilience: The Unity of Knowledge*. New York: Vintage Books.

Wilson, E.O. 2012. *The Social Conquest of Earth*. New York-London: W.W. Norton and Company.

Windrum, P., G. Fagiolo, and A. Moneta. 2007. "Empirical Validation of Agent-Based Models: Alternatives and Prospects." *Journal of Artificial Societies and Social Simulation* 10(2): 1–19.

Winfree, A.T. 1987. *The Timing of Biological Clocks*. New York: Scientific American Press.

Wissner-Gross, A.D., and C.E. Freer. 2013. "Causal Entropic Forces." *Physical Review Letters* 110(16): 168702.

Witmer, F.D. 2015. "Remote Sensing of Violent Conflict: Eyes From Above." *International Journal of Remote Sensing* 369: 2326–2352.

Witt, U. 2007. "Why Novelty is Essential for Economic Evolution – and Why it is so Hard to Analyze." Paper presented at the EAEPE Conference, Porto Max-Planck-Institute of Economics Evolutionary Economics Group, Jena, Germany.

Wolfram, S. 1988. *Emerging Syntheses in Science: Proceedings of the Founding Workshops of the Santa Fe Institute*. Santa Fe, NM: Santa Fe Institute.

Wolfram, S. 2012. *A New Science*. Champaign, IL: Wolfram Media.

Wolfson, M., A. Puri, and M. Martelli. 1992. "The Nonlinear Dynamics of International Conflict." *Journal of Conflict Resolution* 361: 119–149.

Wong, Y.H., and R. Chan. 1999. "Relationship Marketing in China: Guanxi, Favouritism and Adaptation." *Journal of Business Ethics* 22: 107–118.

Wu, Y., Z. Zheng, Y. Jiang, L. Chess, and H. Jiang. 2009. "The Specificity of T-Cell Regulation that Enables Self-Nonself Discrimination in the Periphery." *Proceedings of the National Academy of Sciences* 106(2): 534–539.

Wyatt, S.B., K.P. Winters, and P.M. Dubbert. 2006. "Overweight and Obesity: Prevalence, Consequences and Causes of a Growing Public Health Problem." *The American Journal of the Medical Sciences* 331(4): 166–174.

Yuan, Y., and B. McKelvey. 2004. "Situated Learning Theory: Adding Rate and Complexity Effects Via Kauffman's NK Model." *Nonlinear Dynamics, Psychology, and Life Sciences* 8: 65–101

Zambelli, S. 2004. "Production of Ideas by Means of Ideas: Turing Machine Metaphor." *Metroeconomica* 55: 155–179.

Zaslavsky, G.M. 2002. "Chaos, Fractional Kinetics, and Anomalous Transport." *Physics Reports* 371(6): 461–580.

Zeeman, E. 1974. "On the Unstable Behavior of the Stock Exchanges." *Journal of Mathematical Economics* 1: 39–44.

Zhang, J., L. Tong, P.J. Lamberson, R.A. Durazo-Arvizu, A. Luke, and D.A. Shoham. 2015. "Leveraging Social Influence to Address Overweight and Obesity Using Agent-Based Models: The Role of Adolescent Social Networks." *Social Science and Medicine* 125: 203–213.

Zimmerman, B., and D. Hurst. 1993. "Breaking the Boundaries: The Fractal Organization." *Journal of Management Inquiry* 2(4): 334–355.

Zolotarev, V.M. 1986. *One-Dimensional Stable Distributions*. Providence, RI: American Mathematical Society.

Zuboff, S. 2019. *The Age of Surveillance Capitalism: The Fight for a Human Future at the New Frontier of Power*. New York: Public Affairs Books.

Contributors

Saikou Diallo is Research Associate Professor in the Virginia Modeling, Analysis and Simulation Center (VMASC) at Old Dominion University. He is VMASC's lead researcher in Modeling and Simulation Science where he focuses on applying Modeling and Simulation as part of multidisciplinary teams to study social phenomena, religion and culture. Dr. Diallo has over one hundred publications in the form of peer-reviewed conferences, journals and book chapters.

Kevin J. Dooley is a Distinguished Professor of Supply Chain Management in the WP Carey School of Business at Arizona State University. He is also Chief Scientist of The Sustainability Consortium, and a Senior Sustainability Scientist in the Julie Ann Wrigley Global Institute of Sustainability. His current research addresses complexity science, sustainable supply chains and innovation.

Euel Elliott is Professor of Public Policy and Political Economy at the University of Texas at Dallas, where he has taught and served in various administrative positions for nearly thirty years. He has contributed numerous articles and book chapters on the topic of complex systems and nonlinear dynamics, as well as co-editing with L. Douglas Kiel three volumes on topics related to nonlinear dynamics and complex adaptive systems, and their application to the social and behavioral sciences.

Ross Gore is a Research Assistant Professor at the Virginia Modeling, Analysis and Simulation Center (VMASC) at Old Dominion University. He holds a Ph.D. and a master's degree in Computer Science from the

University of Virginia and a bachelor's degree in Computer Science from the University of Richmond. His current work focuses on data science and predictive analytics.

Patrick Grim is Philosopher in Residence at the Center for the Study of Complex Systems at the University of Michigan. He is editor of the *American Philosophical Quarterly*, founding co-editor of the *Philosopher's Annual* and author of *The Incomplete Universe*, *The Philosophical Computer* and other works. His research interests include ethics, formal modelling, complex systems and the philosophy of science.

Stephen J. Guastello is Professor of Psychology at Marquette University where he specializes in industrial-organizational psychology and human factors. He is the author or co-author of six books on applications of nonlinear dynamics in psychology, author of numerous articles in the same general area, and founding Editor-in-Chief of *Nonlinear Dynamics, Psychology, and Life Sciences*.

James R. Harrington is Associate Professor of Public and Nonprofit Management at the University of Texas at Dallas. His research interests include policy analysis, accountability and performance management in government, program evaluation and education governance.

Joshua Kavner graduated from the University of Michigan in 2020 with a Bachelor of Science in Data Science Engineering. His contributions toward this work include the computational modeling of networked information cascades. Joshua is currently a Ph.D. student in the computer science department at Rensselaer Polytechnic Institute studying multiagent systems, algorithmic game theory and reinforcement learning.

L. Douglas Kiel is Professor of Public and Nonprofit Management at the University of Texas at Dallas. Kiel's publications are cited in academic journals ranging across fields as diverse as public administration, economics, psychology, engineering, music and nuclear science. Kiel and his colleague, Euel Elliott, have co-edited three volumes on topics related to nonlinear dynamics and complex adaptive systems, and their application to the social and behavioral sciences.

Cassey Lee is Senior Fellow at the Institute of Southeast Asian Studies (ISEAS) –Yusof Ishak Institute, Singapore. Prior to joining ISEAS, Dr. Lee held academic appointments at the University of Wollongong, Nottingham University Business School (Malaysia) and University of Malaya. Dr. Lee received his Ph.D. (Economics) from the University of California, Irvine, and specializes in industrial organization.

Christopher J. Lynch is a Lead Project Scientist at the Virginia Modeling, Analysis and Simulation Center (VMASC) at Old Dominion University (ODU). He received his Ph.D. in Modeling & Simulation from ODU. He leads the Data Analytics Working Group at VMASC, and his research interests include exploring and developing techniques for analyzing real data and simulation data to inform model development, inform decision making and support simulation credibility.

Carlos Eduardo Maldonado is Professor of Medicine at the Universidad El Bosque in Bogota, Colombia. He has published extensively in the area of complex systems and sustainability, and is the recipient of numerous academic awards. He has also received numerous awards in recognition of his scholarly achievements, and has a chair in his name at UAEM (Mexico). Professor Maldonado has in recent years been a visiting scholar at the University of Pittsburgh (USA), the Catholic university of America (Washington, DC) and the University of Cambridge.

Sheri Markose has a Ph.D. from the London School of Economics and is Professor of Economics at the University of Essex, UK. As the founding director (2002–2009) of the Centre for Computational Finance and Economic Agents, Sheri pioneered a multi-disciplinary curriculum covering agent-based computational economics and complexity sciences. Sheri is Associate Editor of *Frontiers of AI and Robotics: Computational Intelligence*.

John R. McCaskill is Clinical Professor of Public and Nonprofit Management at the University of Texas at Dallas. His research investigates the behaviors of organizations under conditions of resource scarcity. His doctoral dissertation employed agent-based modeling to examine complex humanitarian interventions. This work led to his receipt of the Network of Schools of Public Policy, Affairs and Administration's Dissertation of the Year Award (2012).

Jose J. Padilla, Ph.D. is Research Associate Professor at the Virginia Modeling, Analysis and Simulation Center at Old Dominion University. Dr. Padilla's research focuses on developing approaches that facilitate the formulation, specification and simulation design of problem situations. Current work ranges from the development of simulation platforms (cloudes.me) to in-country data collection toward the development of theories through modeling (storymodelers.org).

John Barkley Rosser, Jr. is Professor of Economics at James Madison University. He is well known for the application of catastrophe theory, chaotic and nonlinear dynamics to understanding economic dynamics. He has produced more than 200 publications as well as numerous books, and has served as editor and co-editor of leading journals, and is the recipient of numerous awards for his contributions to the field of economics.

Lloyd Shatkin graduated from the University of Michigan in 2019 with a master's degree in Computer Science and Engineering. Prior to enrolling in his graduate program, he attended UM as an undergraduate where he studied Data Science and Philosophy, leading to his participation in Complex Systems research. Shatkin currently works as a Software Engineer at JP Morgan Chase.

Maxime Stauffer is Research Assistant at the Graduate Institute Geneva, collaborator at the Geneva Science Policy Interface, founder of the Social Complexity Lab Geneva, founder and Research Director at Effective Altruism Geneva and adviser to the European Commission. He applies complexity theory and agent-based modeling to household behavior and malnutrition, collective decision-making in policy contexts and systemic resilience.

William Sulis, M.D., FRCPC (Psychiatry, Geriatric Psychiatry), Ph.D. (Mathematics), Ph.D. (Physics) is Associate Clinical Professor and Director of the Collective Intelligence Laboratory at McMaster

University. He has published on subjects ranging from transient induced global response synchronization and dynamics of collective intelligence systems, to foundations of quantum mechanics and the relationship between Trofimova's Functional Ensemble of Temperament model and mental illness.

Manjari Trivedi is an undergraduate at the University of Michigan studying Physics, Mathematics and Computer Science. In her freshman year, she participated in the Undergraduate Research Opportunities Program, during which she contributed to the Paradigm Shifts project. Her current research is focused on network monitoring and diagnostics and, specifically, analysing network topology.

Bruce J. West is the Senior Scientist Mathematics (ST) in the Army Research Office (1999–present). He was Physics Professor (1989–1999) and contract researcher (1974–1989); published 300 articles, 35 book chapters and 22 books; and has 19,000 citations with an h-factor of 67. He is an Elected Fellow of multiple societies, received numerous scientific awards and, in 2017, was honored with the Presidential Distinguished Rank Award.

Index

Page numbers in italics indicate tables and figures.

Abbott, A., 19, 69, 70, 82
ABM. *See* agent-based modeling
Abney, D.H., 59
Acanthomyops claviger, 268, 271
Accard, P., 73
acceptance threshold, 279, 280, 292
Adamou, A., 199
adaptation, 19, 29, 34, 42, 44, 62, 92, 105, 203, 263, 329
adaptive behavior, 34–39, 62, 88, 137, 246–247, 268
   background, 34–35
   complex adaptive systems, 35–39
      agent fitness, 39
      agent interaction, 37–38
      irreversibility and emergent order, 38–39
      problem-solving and conflict, 38
      schemata and agents, 36–37
adaptive immune system, 128, 130, 131, 132, 133, 135, 135n27, 136, 151
affiliation and synchronization, 58–59
Agarwal, R., 75
agent-based complexity, 329
agent-based modeling (ABM), 4–5, 79, 293, 325, 347
   challenges and prospects, 22–23, 183–203
      academic communities, 186–189
      critiques, 193–194
      emerging prospects, 201–203
      evolution, 189–190
      learning challenge, 190–193
      public policy, 199–200
      verification and validation challenges, 194–199
   data, 104
   entrepreneurial processes, 78
   inter-state conflict, 84, 94 (*see also* inter-state conflict)
   intra-state conflict, 100–103 (*see also* intra-state conflict)
   methods, 105, 106
   obesity and policy implications, 23, 203–238, *224*, 235
      background, 206–210
      calibration experiment, 219–222, 224
      cross-model validation, 208, 209–210, 219, 222–226, 236
      future policies, 226–236
      model description, 211–215
      projections of states, *230–233, 234*
      sensitivity analysis experiment, 217–219
      trace experiment with statistical debugging, 215–217
      validation, 209–210, 219
      verification, 208–209, 215
   payoff, 140, 142n32

agent-based modeling (ABM) (*Continued.*)
  simulating complexity, 8–11, 22–23
  stock market, 140, 142
agent fitness, 39
  agent interaction, 37–38
AidData, 98
Alentorn, A., 140
Allen, P., 42
allometry, 24–25, 248, 249, 255
  allometry/information hypothesis, 245–247
  temporal relations, 250–251
  time, 243–245
AlphaGo Zero, 169–170
alternative schema, 36, 38, 188
Alvarez, M., 339
AMAR, 97
Amazeen, P.G., 47
American Society for Public Administration, 67
analytical blindness, 85, 88
Anasazi project, 8n1, 207
Anderson, P., 72
Andresen, B., 242
Andresen, M., 211
anomalies, 309–311, 315, 317–318
Ant House Hunting Algorithm, 291
ants, 24, 25, 263, 265, 270
  army, 264
  comparison judgment, 276–277
  foraging, 281, 284, 294
  homogenous, 190
  nest exiting, 285, 286, 287
  nest location, 294
  nest population, 293
  nest selection, 274
  speed, 289–290
  See also Leptothorax albipennis; social insect colony
architectural complexity, 78
Aristotle, 271, 326, 356
  Posterior Analytics, 302
armed conflict and complexity science, 19–20, 83–108
  complexity and conflict, 84–86
  formalization, 86, 90, 91, 105, 334

friction, 87
future, 103–106
  data, 104–105
  methods, 105–106
  theory, 103–104
past—prior to 2000, 86–94
  computational models of armed conflict, 93–94
  data, 89–90
  mathematical models of armed conflict, 92
  mathematical models of arms races, 90–92
  methods, 90–94
  theory, 87–89
present—2000–2019, 94–103
  agent-based model of tra-state conflict, 100–103
  data, 96–98
  methods, 98–103
  modeling patterns of insurgent conflict, 98–100
  theory, 95–96
Armed Conflict Location and Event Data Project, 96
Arthur, W.B., 119, 140–141, 142, 329
artificial intelligence, 159–162
  categories, *160*
  rationality and bounded rationality, *162*
  toward bounded rationality or rationality, 161–162
Ashby, W.R.
  Law of Requisite Variety, 19, 37, 72, 73, 80, 82
Ashmos, D., 73
asymptotic stability, 44, *45*, 46
attractor, 76, 291, 331, 332
  dynamic, 65, 327
autonomic arousal, 54, 55, 57, 59, 60, 61
  synchronized, 62–63
autonomous agents, 191
Autonomous Agents and Multi-Agent Systems, 191
autonomous work groups, 35
Axelrod, R., 83, 156, 187, 316

Axtell, R., 8, 9, 13, 207
  Growing Artificial Societies: Social Science from the Bottom Up, 185–186, 190

Bak, P.
  sandpile model, 65, 72, 73, 80, 322
balance-of-power, 85n1
Bar-Eli, M., 59
Barker, J.
  Future Edge, 67
Barro, R., 120
Bateson, G., 65
Bauman, A., 205
Baumann, O., 75
Baumol, W., 112n4
Bayesian, 15, 126n21, 191, 302, 325, 335
Beran, J., 249
Bernheim, D., 156
Bhatt, M., 117n11
Bhavani, R., 84, 96, 101, 102
Big Bang of Immunology, 115, 122, 155
big data, 23, 105, 202, 284
Billinger, S., 75
Binmore, K., 117, 147n36, 332, 334, 335
biological hypercomputation (BH), 17, 37, 343–363
  complexity science and freedom, 346–349
  computational understanding, 354–357
  first-hand approach, 349–353
  social and political implications, 358–362
biological time, 241, 242, 243
bio-psycho-social information, 201–202
Bir, E., 13n2
Birkhoff, G.D., 340
Biswas, G., 80
Bloomquist, K.M., 210
Blume, L. 334
board games, 51, 53
  artificial intelligence, 162, 163, 165, 168
  complexity, *163*
  knowledge, 164, 165
  search, 165
Bohorquez, J.C., 98
Boisot, M., 37, 73
Boltzmann, L., 339
Bond, R.W., Jr., 51
Borill, P.L., 11
bottom-up
  destabilization, 39
  self-organization, 34
  social interactions, 186, 283
bounded rationality, 15, 21, 105, 157–159, 173–174, 192, 327, 328, 341
  artificial intelligence, 159–162, *162*
  complexity foundation and limited knowledge, 337–338
  definition, 159
  go-playing computers, 162–170
  knowledge, 164–165
  learning, 168–170
  search, 165–168
Britton, N., 291
Brock, W.A., 332, 333, 334
Brody, S., 245
broken ergodicity, 269
broken symmetry, 269
Brown, R., 309
Brown, S., 66
Brownian motion, 309
Burgelman, R., 72
Burke, S., 34
Buskirk, S.W., 243
Busy Beaver Function, 119n12
butterfly effect, 26, 82, 327, 330
Byrne, R., 136

Calder, W.A., 243, 244
Camerer, C., 117n11, 156
Caplow, T. 34
Carnap, R., 302
Caroll, Lewis
  Alice Through the Looking-Glass, 112n4
CAS. *See* complex adaptive systems

cascades, 321, 325
  anomalies, *310*, 310–311
  falsification, 305, 306, 308, 310, 314
  global, 311, 314
  paradigm-shift, 310
  size, 306, *306*, 307, *307*, 309, 311–319, *312*, *313–314*, *318*, *319*, 323, *324*
catastrophe theory, 65, 66, 79, 330, 333, 334
CDC. *See* Centers for Disease Control
Cederman, L.E., 83, 100
Centers for Disease Control (CDC), 219
  Behavioral Risk Factor Surveillance System (BRFSS), 222, 224
  experimental data points, *220*
cellular automata, 4, 8, 22, 113n6, 158, 170–173, *171*, *172*, 174, 189
Chaitin, G., 119, 119n12, 329
chaos theory, 2, 18, 66, 84, 88, 91, 95, 341
  See also Society for Chaos Theory in Psychology and Life Sciences
Cheng, Y., 66
chess, 158, 160, 162–163, 164, 168, 169, 174
Child, J., 73
Chiles, T., 76, 77
Choi, T., 80, 101, 102
Church, A., 2, 12, 335
  Church–Turing Thesis, 16, 17, 27, 343
civil, 86, 101, 102
Civil Mediation dataset, 98
classical logic, 10, 11, 193, 194
Clauset, A., 99, 100
Climate Change and African Political Stability Project, 97
Clinton Parameters, 102
"clockwork universe," 266
Club of Rome, 185
cognitive behavioral economics, 14
cognitive roadmaps, 14, 15
Cohen, I., 117n10

cohesion
  group, 59, 62, 277
  speed, 277, 293
  team, 58
Colander, D., 156
Colbert, B., 72
collective intelligence, 5, 24, 25, 41, 263–297
  adaptive complex systems, 266–271
  broken ergodicity, 269
  broken symmetry, 269
  collective intelligence modeling, 290–296
  compatibility and the Mutual Agreement Principle, 271
  complex systems methods use, nest emigrations, 264, 284–288
  complex systems methods use, universality, 288–290
  complex system methods utility, 282–284
  decision-making, 271–274
  interactive determinism, 268
  nondispersive temporal evolution, 269
  nonrepresentational contextual dependence, 268
  pattern isolation and reconfiguration, 270
  phase transitions, critical, and control parameters, 269
  salience, 270–271
  self-organization, 268
  social insect colony, 263–266
    decision-making, 274–282
  stochastic determinism, 268
colony-level effect, 279, 292
Colwell, K., 76
combat, 94
comparison judgement, 276
compatibility, 271
complex adaptive systems (CAS), 2, 5, 19, 21, 22, 27, 34, 35–39, 65, 192, 266, 267
  agent fitness, 39
  agent interaction, 37–38

collective intelligence, 268, 283
  (*see also* collective intelligence)
combat, 94
definition, 6–7
dissipative model, 76 (*see also* dissipative systems)
guanxi, 72
informal dynamics, 79
interacting agents, 156
irreversibility and emergent order, 38–39
nonlinear dynamics, 66
novelty production, 113
problem-solving and conflict, 38
schemata and agents, 36–37
total quality management, 66
"complexity arrangements," 72
"complexity in a bottle," 22
complexity sciences, 1, 2, 3, 4, 18, 24, 27, 28, 29, 111, 111n2, 183, 203, 243, 343, 344, 345, *346*, 348, 353, 360, 361, 362, 363
  freedom, 346–349
complexity sciences and organization sciences, 64–82
  evolution and revolution in scientific paradigms, 68–70
  methods, 70–71
  publications, 72–78
  roots, 64–68
complexity science and armed conflict, 19–20, 83–108
  complexity and conflict, 84–86
  future, 103–106
    data, 104–105
    methods, 105–106
    theory, 103–104
  past—prior to 2000, 86–94
    computational models of armed conflict, 93–94
    data, 89–90
    mathematical models of armed conflict, 92
    mathematical models of arms races, 90–92
    methods, 90–94

theory, 87–89
present—2000–2019, 94–103
  agent-based model of intra-state conflict, 100–103
  data, 96–98
  methods, 98–103
  modeling patterns of insurgent conflict, 98–100
  theory, 95–96
complicated system, 84, 326
computational complexity, 6, 12, 13, 14, 15, 16, 71, 192, 193, 246, 327, 328, 329, 334, 337, 341
  knowledge problems, 334–336
computer simulation, 41, 93–94, 103, 105, 184, 186, 187, 267, 291
conceptual schemes, 26, 301, 302, 303
conflict
  civil, 86, 101, 102
  complexity, 84–86
  inter-state, 84, 86, 89, 92, 94, 95, 96, 99, 100, 103
  intra-state, 83, 84, 86, 95, 96, 98, 100–103
  problem-solving, 38
  See also armed conflict and complexity science
contrarian payoff structure, 120, 141, 142, 142n32
control parameter, 54, 55, 269
Conway, J., 189
Cooke, N.J., 47
coordination, group dynamics, 39–54
  animal models, 41
  dynamics and groups size, 53–54
  evolutionary Stag Hunt games, 50–53
  intersection experiments, 44–48, *45*, *47*
  nonlinear dynamics, 40–44
    implicit learning, 44
    learning processes, 42–44
    game theory, 41–42
    self-organization, 40–41
  self-efficacy, 50
  shared mental models, 40
  social loafing, 49
  Stag Hunt games, 48–49

coordination acquisition, 40, 44, 46, 47, *47*
corpulence, 281, 286, 287
Correlates of War project, 89
Courdier, R., 208
Crawford, V., 138
Credit Default Swaps, 153
critical parameter, 187, 269, 288
cross-model validation, 208, 209–210, 219, 222–226, 236
Cukierman, A., 146n35, 147
Cuvier, G., 245

da Costa, N.C.A., 13, 13n2
Danone, 77
Darwinian learning, 42
Davidson, P., 328, 338–239, 340, 341
Davidsson, P., 186
Day, R., 328
decision-making, 274–282
  irrational, 274, 279
decoy effect, 274, 275
deep learning, 169, 191, 191, 192, 356
Demetrius, L., 253
Derbinski, J., 125
Descartes, R., 302, 352, 358
Diaconis, P., 335
dialectic strategy, 38
Diallo, S.Y., 5, 23, 207, 211
Dilts, D., 80
directed networks, 316–322, *320*, *321*
dissipative systems, 72, 75–76, 77–78, 80–81, 82
"disciplinary matrices," 301–302
dissipative systems, 72, 75–76, 77–78, 80, 81, 82
Dobzhansky, T., 155
Dooley, J., 4, 18, 19, 36, 66
  event history, 78
  nonlinear dynamics, 73–74
  supply chains, 80
Doria, F.A., 13, 13n2
Dornhaus, A., 291
dualism, 351–352

Duffy, G., 94
Durlauf, S., 119, 329
Dussutour, A., 294
Dawkins, 117
dynamic complexity, 328–334, 341
dynamic decisions, 88
Dynamic Structures General Equilibrium, 184

Eciton burchelli, 268, 269
Edwards, S., 274–275
EEG, 54, 57, 61, 202
Ehnts, D., 339
Ehrenfest, P., 339, 340
Ehrenfest, T., 339
Eichengreen, B., 149, 150, 154
Eisenhardt, K., 66
electrodermal time series, *56*
El Farol game, 142
elimination by aspects, 274
Elkins, A.N., 59
Elliott, E., 5, 8, 22, 188
  Chaos Theory in the Social Sciences, 2, 30
embodied offline simulation, 125, 126n21, *139*
emergence, 2, 5, 9, 34, 68, 71, 72, 76–78, 82, 84, 98, 103, 112, 126, 160, 266–268, 291, 296, 323, 344, 346, 350
  emergent order and irreversibility, 38–39
Emergence: Complexity and Organization, 67
emergency response, 50, *56*
  team, 51, 52, 53, 60
emigration, nest, 284–288
enaction, 354, 355, 359, 361
energy expenditure, 23, 206, 211, 212, 213, 227–228, *228*, 229, 234
energy intake, 23, 206
entrepreneurism, 77–78
entropy, 19, 36, 37, 39, 61, 242, 245, 246–247, 252, 253, 254
  informational, 328

Eoyang, G., 66, 81
Epstein, J.M., 8, 9, 92, 101, 193
   Agent_Zero, 190
   Growing Artificial Societies: Social Science From the Bottom Up, 185–186, 190
equal weight heuristic, 274
Erfahrung, 352n2
ergodicity, 198–199, 328, 339–341
   broken, 269
   knowledge, 338–331
   nonergodicity, 27, 327, 333, 338, 341–342
Erlebnis, 352n2
ERM. *See* European Exchange Rate
ESS. *See* evolutionarily stable states
European Exchange Rate (ERM), 147, 148, *148*, 149, 150n37, 153
evolution and revolution in scientific paradigms, 68–70
evolutionarily stable states (ESS), 40, 41–42
evolutionary biology, 112n4, 189, 272
evolutionary theory, 15
experience, recent, 281
experimental data points, *220*
expert systems, 356
explicit learning, 40, 44, *45*, 55, 62, 86, 101, 103–104, 106, 107, 113n6, 136, 146, 165

Facebook, 359
falsifiability, 305
falsification
   Kuhnian, 309, 310, 311, 314
   Popperian, 304–305, *305*, 306–307, 308–309, 311, 314–315, *315*
far-from-equilibrium, 65, 72, 73, 75–77, 78, 80, 82
Farjoun, M., 74
Farmer, J.D., 187, 188
Farr's Law, 254
Faure, P., 137
feedback loops, 8, 34, 38, 54, 55, 85, 87

Feigenbaum, M., 288–289
Feinderman, O., 276, 281
Financial Times, 70, 79, 80
Fink, B., 137
Finkelstein, E.A., 224, *224*
Fischer, S., 144
Fitch, T., 126n21
fitness, 42, 74, 272, 273
   agent, 39
   landscape, 75, 273
FKE. *See* fractional kinetic equation
FPE. *See* Fokker-Planck equation
Fleener, M.J., 33
Fletcher, D., 78
flicker noise, 323
Fokker-Planck equation (FPE), 247, 248, 261
Foley, D., 187, 188
forbidden codes, 129–130
Ford Motor Company, 77
Forgues, B., 66
formal systems, 2, 129
   Gödel, 116, 117, 118, 130
Forrester, J., 22, 65, 66
   Urban Dynamics, 184–185
Foster, D., 142
Foster, J., 112, 119, 119n13
Fractal Functionality, 25, 297
fractional kinetic equation (FKE), 247, 249
   solution to FKE, 260–262
Frank, K., 74
Franks, N., 265, 274, 276, 277, 280, 281, 284, 290
free-lunch theorem, 146, 153, 353n3
Freedman, D., 335
freedom, 346–349
Frydman, R., 111n1, 147n36
Functional Differentiation, 297

Gaba, V., 76
Gallavotti, G., 340
Gallese, V., 126
Galloway, T., 61

game theory, 138, 151, 162, 163, 190, 335
  classical, 165
  combinatorial, 158n4
  evolutionary, 62
  extant, 117, 135, 156
  group dynamics, 41–42
  mainstream, 121
  monetary, 146, 147
  perspective, 40
  standard, 112, 117
  von Neumann, 189
Ganco, M., 75
Garey, M.R., 193
Garud, R., 72
Gauss, C.F., 245
Gaussian distribution, 250, 251, 283, 294
Gayon, J., 248
Gehman, J., 72
Gell-Mann, M., 36, 199
Gelly, S., 167n12
general systems theory, 18, 64, 65
generative social science, 9, 193
Genomic Nash Equilibrium, 115, 115n8, 117
GeoEPR, 97
giant component, *308*, 308–309, 311, 314, 320, 323
Gigerenzer, G., 14, 192
Gilboa, I., 15
Girod, S., 77
Giurfa, M., 279
Gleditsch, K.S., 83, 99, 100
Gleick, J., 189
  Chaos: Making of a New Science, 66
Global Terrorism Database, 96
go, game of, 157–174
  cellular automat, 170–173, *171*, *172*
  go-playing computers and bounded rationality and evolution, 162–170, 176–179
    knowledge, 164–165
    learning, 168–170
    search, 165–168
  rules, 175
  See also artificial intelligence; bounded rationality
go board, 165, *166*, *167*, 169, 170
Gode, D., 336
Gödel, K.
  archetype of Liar, 116, 117
  complexity, 12, 16
  endogenous novelty production, 17
  formal systems, 118
  incompleteness, 2, 17, 21, 113n6, 117, 118, 122, 127, 128, 129, 130, *130*, 135n28, *139*, 145, 152, 155, 329, 335
  logic, 138, 143, *145*, 147n36, 335
  meta-mathematics, 16, 114, 122, 154
  meta-representation, 124, *127*
  numbers, 123
  sentence, 134–137, 135n28
  substitution, 115, 124
  undecidable proposition, 130, *130*
Gödel-Turing-Post (G-T-P), 21, 111n1, 113–115, 115n8, 116–118, 117n10, 119, 120, 126n19, 126n21, 135, 138, *139*, 140, 144, 147, 155
G-T-P logic condition and evidence from genomic evolution of Self-Ref and Self-Rep, 121–128
  online self-assembly with Self-Ref, machine execution and offline Self-Rep in immuno-cognitive systems, 122–128
  Self-Ref machinery, 123–124
  Self-Rep mirror system, 124–128
G-T-P logic condition and the Liar strategy/malware, contrarian structures, and who do you need to surprise?, 128–132
  Liar/malware strategy f_p, 132
  malware/Liar strategy function and V-D-J-based T-cell detection of non-self pathogens, 131–132
  self-halting machines, 124–130

Goldstein, J., 66
"good enough" strategy, 278, 293
Goodhart, C., 146, 146n35, 150
  Law, 120, 144
Goodman, N., 302
Google, 359
  DeepMind AlphaGo, 157, 169, 173
Gordon, D., 120
Gore, R., 5, 23
Gorman, J.C., 47
Grammer, K., 137
graph theory, 11, 73, 80
Great Leap Forward, 122, 155
Gridded Population of the World, 97
Griffiths, T.L., 162
Grim, P., 5, 26
Gross, D., 210
"group," 34, 36
group cognition process, 34, 35, 61
group dynamics, 4, 19, 33–63
  adaptive behavior, 34–39
    background, 34–35
    complex adaptive systems, 35–39
      agent fitness, 39
      agent interaction, 37–38
      irreversibility and emergent order, 38–39
      problem-solving and conflict, 38
      schemata and agents, 36–37
  coordination, 39–54
    dynamics and groups size, 53–54
    evolutionary Stag Hunt games, 50–53
    intersection experiments, 44–48, 45, 47
    nonlinear dynamics, 40–44
      implicit learning, 44
      learning processes, 42–44
      game theory, 41–42
      self-organization, 40–41
    self-efficacy, 50
    shared mental models, 40
    social loafing, 49
    Stag Hunt games, 48–49
  synchronization, 54–62, 56
    measurement, 55–57
    principles, 54–55
    team performance, 57–62
      synchronization and affiliation, 58–59
      synchronization and performance, 59–62
  group-level outcome, 34
  group/team emergency response, 51, 52, 53, 60
  group/team performance, 19, 33, 47, 50, 53, 55, 57–62, 63
  group/team size, 49, 53, 54, 100
    dynamics, 53–54
  Group Workload (GWL) Ratings, 60, 62
Grove, A., 72
Groves, K., 72
G-T-P. *See* Gödel-Turing-Post
Guastello, D.E., 44
Guastello, S., 4, 18, 19, 33, 44
  catastrophe theory, 66, 79
  The Creature that Ate Sheboyan, 51–53
  metric of time series data, 56
  properties of S_E, 57
guanxi, 72
Guerini, M., 198
Guevara, M., 59

Haken, H., 65
Harrington, J., 5, 8, 22
Hawking, S., 29, 257
Haxholdt, C., 74
Hayek, F.A., 13, 121, 152, 333
Hayekian Austrians, 333
Healy, C., 279
heart rate, 202, 243, *244*
Helbing, D., 156
Heller, J.
  Catch 22, 138n30
Helm, J.L., 58
Hempel, C., 302
Hennessy, E., 200
Henning, R.A., 59
Hess, G.D., 90n2
heuristics, 14, 15, 105, 106, 159, 192, 245, 273–274, 316, 337
  equal weight, 274
  lexicographic, 274

430 Index

Hilbert space, 347
Hill, A.V., 242
Hirschman, A., 120–121, 153
Holland, J., 2, 186
Holmes-Moriarty problem, 335
Hommes, C., 332, 333, 334
homogeneity, 57, 140, 141n31, 141–142, 189, 190, 248, 280, 340–341, 342
honeybee, 264
  emigration, 294
Horgan, J.
  The End of Science, 328
Hoyert, M.S., 43
human interactions, 4, 11, 55, 184
Human System Dynamics (REF), 81
Hunt, E., 290
Hurst, D., 66
hypercomputation, 5, 16–17, 27, 343–363
  biological (BH), 17, 27
    complexity science and gaining degrees of freedom, *346*, 346–349
    computational understanding, 354–357
    first-hand approach, 349–353
    social and political implications, 358–363
    timeline, *351*
  non-classical, 17
hyper-rational, 335, 342

IBM
  Deep Blue, 158, 167
  Ilgen, D.R., 33
immuno-cognitive system, 17, 111n1, 115–116, 117, 122, 134, 136, 138, *139*, 155, 156
mirror systems, *127*
Implementation of Pacts, 98
implicit learning, 40, 44, *45*, 46, 55, 62, 94, 103, 107, 246
incompleteness, 2, 17, 21, 113n6, 117, 118, 122, 127, 128, 129, 130, *130*, 135n28, *139*, 145, 152, 155, 329, 335

individual acceptance, 279, 280, 292
individual differences, 34, 36, 49, 283
informal dynamics, 79
information cascades, 321, 325
  anomalies, *310*, 310–311
  falsification, 305, 306, 308, 310, 314
  global, 311, 314
  paradigm-shift, 310
  size, 306, *306*, 307, *307*, 309, 311–319, *312*, *313–314*, *318*, *319*, 323, *324*
information stability, 252–253
innate immune system, 116, 116n9
interacting agents, 41, 156, 332
interactive determinism, 268
intersection, 4, 44–54, *47*, 165, 175
inter-state conflict, 84, 86, 89, 92, 94, 95, 96, 99, 100, 103
intra-state conflict, 83, 84, 86, 95, 96, 98, 100–103
irrational, 273, 274, 279
irrelevance, 270–271
irreversibility and emergent order, 38–39, 254

Johnson Foundation, Robert Wood, 224, *225–226*
Jones, D., 154
Journal of Artificial Societies and Social Simulation, 22, 207

Kahneman, D., 14, 22, 159, 192
Kane, E.J., 153
Kant, I., 121, 151–152, 355–356, 358
Kantian
  end-neutral rules, 152, 153
  principles, 21
Kao, F., 14
Kasporov, G., 158, 167
Kauffman, S., 2, 72
  rugged landscape NK model, 74, 75, 80, 81
  tinkering, 80
Kavner, J., 5
Kenny, D.A., 50
Keynes, J.M., 334, 335, 338, 339, 340, 341

Keynesian, 198, 199, 328, 333, 335, 339
Kiel, L.D., 5, 8, 22, 66, 188
  Chaos Theory in the Social Sciences, 2, 30
Kindleberger, C.P., 334
Kirman, A., 156
Kirstein, M., 198
Knight, F.H., 338, 341
Knightian uncertainty, 199
knowledge and complexity, 326–342
  complexity foundation and limited knowledge, 337–338
  computational complexity problems, 334–337
  dynamic complexity, 329–334
  ergodicity, 338–341
  forms, 328–329
Koehler, M., 210
Koppl, R., 16, 17, 334, 335
Korn, H., 137
Kosko, B., 316
Kovacs, T., 291
Kozlowski, S.W.J., 33
Krause, A., 140
Krugman, P., 146, 150n37
Kuhn, T.S., 70, 319
  disciplinary matrix, 302
  scientific change, 19, 26, 309, 314–315, *316*, 321, 323
  shared paradigm, 325
  The Structure of Scientific Revolutions, 68–69
Kuhnian dynamics, 309–314, 315, 319, 323
Kuhnian falsification, 309, 310, 311, 314
Kumaraswamy, A., 72
Kurzweil, R., 357
Kydland, F., 120

Lanchester, F.W., 92, 94
Lane, D., 329
Langridge, E., 265
Larsen, E., 74
Lasius alienus, 268, 271

Lasker, E., 157
Latin Hypercube Sampling, 208
Laudan, L., 302
Law of Requisite Variety, 19, 37, 72, 73, 80, 82
learning
  challenge, 190–193
  Darwinian, 42
  deep, 169, 191, 191, 192, 356
  explicit, 40, 44, *45*, 55, 62, 86, 101, 103–104, 106, 107, 113n6, 136, 146, 165
  go playing computers, 168–170
  implicit, 40, 44, *45*, 46, 55, 62, 94, 103, 107, 246
  machine, 15, 106, 168, 356
  multi-agent, 191
  nonlinear dynamics, 42–44
  processes, 42–44
Lebed, F., 59
Lee, C., 4, 8, 21–22
Leibniz, 302
Lempert, R., 199
Leptothorax albipennis, 264, 265, 274, 291
Levin, M., 74
Levinthal, D., 74
Levy, D., 66
Lévy distribution, 250, 261
Lewes, H., 84
Lewin, R., 66
Liar/hacker/antigen, 122, 144, 131, 134, 136, *145*, 146, 147n36, 149–150, 151, 152, 153, 155, 156
  archetype, 116, 117
  G-T-P logic condition and the Liar strategy/malware, contrarian structures, and who do you need to surprise?, 128–132
  Liar/malware strategy f_p, 132
  malware/Liar strategy function and V-D-J-based T-cell detection of non-self, 131–132
  Soros, 147
Lindstedt, S.L., 243, 244

Linn, S., 74
local minima, 273
local observer view, 10, 193–194
logic, 271–272
Lichtenstein, B., 78
Lloyd, S., 328
log-time Poisson distribution, 287
loose theoretical framework, 72
Lorenz, E., 330
Lorenz, H-W., 331
Lotz, M., 133n24
Lucas, R., 144n34
   Critique, 144, *145*, 153
   policy ineffectiveness, 120
   surprise strategy, 120n15, 121, 140, 143–147, *145*
   thesis on surprise policy strategy and widespread policy failure, 143–150
Lumpkin, T., 78
Lyapunov exponent, 46, 52, 53, 90n2
Lynch, C.J., 5, 23

Macal, C.M., 188, 189, 195, 196, 197, 198, 202
Machiavellian intelligence, 112, 136, 155
machine learning, 15, 106, 168, 356
Macintosh, R., 76
Maclean, D., 76
Madden, T., 76
Maldonado, C.E., 5, 16, 21, 27
Malebranche, 302
Malinvaud, E., 340
Mallon, E., 265
Marion, R., 79
Markose, S.M., 111n1
   agent-based model, 27, 140, 142, 143
   cellular automata, 4, 8, 16, 17, 20–21, 22
   diagonal elements, 124–125
   digital agents, 113
   G-T-P conditions, 114–116, 129, 131, 155
   identical recursive machinery, 122
   Kantian end-neutral rules, 152
   Liar strategy, 132
   meta-representation, 136
   non-trivial recursive reduction function, 136
   offline simulation, 125
   regulatory rules, 153
   surprise strategy function, 131
   T-cell training, 133
Marshall, J., 291
Martelli, M., 85n1
Marti, E., 73
mass action, 268
Masuda, N., 293
Maturana, H., 65
McCaskill, J, 5, 8, 22
McClintock, B., 113, 113n5, 119, 155
McKelvey, B., 37, 73, 74, 78, 79
MECH, 195
Meckler, M., 72
Merritt, M.L., 33
metabolic time, 241
meta-stability, 37
Meyer, A., 76
Mihm, J., 75
Miller, G.F., 137
Miller, J., 2, 243
Miller, W.B., 117n11
Millonas, M., 269
Mindwalk, 67
Minority game, 142
Minsky, H., 334
Mirowski, P., 336
mirror
   genomic, 127, *130*
   immune systems, 123, *127*
   mapping, 130
   m-TEC, 132
   neuron system, 114, 115, 115n8, 116–117, 119, 122, 126, 126n20, 127, 128, 137n29
   self-referential, 155
   self-rep, 124–128, 155
Mishra, B., 111n1, 115n8
mixed motivation games, 42
Monomerium Pharaonis, 268
Mønster, D., 59

Monte-Carlo Tree Search (MCTS),
  166–167, 167n12, 169,
  222–223
Morel, B., 73
Morris, M., 78
multi-agent learning, 191
multiscenario simulation, 199–200
Mutual Agreement Principal, 271

Nachbar, J.H., 135n28
NASA
  Shuttle Radar Topographic Mission,
    97
  Task Load Index, 60
Nash equilibrium, 16, 41, 42, 117n11,
  118, 124, 131, 136, 138,
  138n30, 144, 145, 149, 151,
  155, 327, 335
  Genomic, 115, 115n8, 117
National Heart, Lung, and Blood
  Institute, 213
National Institutes of Health, 213
negentropy, 348–349
nest emigrations, 264, 284–288
network degree, *318*
Newell, A., 43
New England Complexity Systems
  Institutes, 67
Newton, I., 258
  calculus, 358
  "clockwork universe," 266
  dynamics, 242
  law of motion, 254
Nik-Kah, E., 336
non-classical logic and mathematics, 10,
  17, 354
nondispersive temporal evolution, 269
nonergodicity, 27, 327, 333, 338,
  341–342
non-halting codes, 130
Non-Halting Problem, 162, 173
*Nonlinear Dynamics in Psychology and
  Life Sciences*, 67
nonlinear dynamic systems (NDS),
  26–27, 33–63, 66, 185
  coordination, 40–44

implicit learning, 44
learning processes, 42–44
game theory, 41–42
self-organization, 40–41
non-rational, 273, 276
nonrepresentational contextual
  dependence, 268
Non-State Actors, 97
Nonviolent and Violent Campaigns and
  Outcomes Dataset, 97
"normal science," 68, 82
North, M.J., 189, 195, 196, 197, 198
novelty production, 111–156
  Gödel sentence, 134–137
  G-T-P logic condition and evidence
    from genomic evolution
    of Self-Ref and Self-Rep,
    121–128
  online self-assembly with Self-Ref,
    machine execution and offline
    Self-Rep in immuno-cognitive
    systems, 122–128
  Self-Ref machinery, 123–124
  Self-Rep mirror system, 124–128
  G-T-P logic condition and the Liar
    strategy/malware, contrarian
    structures, and who do you
    need to surprise?, 128–132
  Liar/malware strategy f_p, 132
  malware/Liar strategy function and
    V-D-J-based T-cell detection
    of non-self pathogens,
    131–132
  self-halting machines, 124–130
  Kant, Hayek, and Hirschman,
    150–154
  oppositional structures and innovative
    rule breaking, 137–150
  currency peg collapse, 147–150,
    148
  Gödel logic on Liar-like structures,
    145
  Lucas's thesis on surprise policy
    strategy and widespread policy
    failure, 143–150
  methodological differences, *139*

novelty production (*Continued.*)
   self-reflexive stock market games and contrarian/minority payoff structures in Arthur, 140–143
   price trends and winner determination, *143*
   Soros Liar strategy, 147–150
   T-cells, 133–134
NP-problems, 12–13, 16, 193

obesity and policy implications, agent-based model of, 23, 203–238, *224, 235*
   background, 206–210
   calibration experiment, 219–222, 224
   cross-model validation, 208, 209–210, 219, 222–226, 236
   future policies, 226–236
   model description, 211–215
   parameters, *214*
   projections of states, *230–233, 234*
   sensitivity analysis experiment, 217–219, *218–219*
   statistical debugging, 208, 209, 215–217, 219, 229, 236, 237
   trace experiments, 208, 215–217
   validation, 209–210, 219
   verification, 208–209, 215
Obstfeld, M., 147
O'Donnell, R.M., 328, 339, 340
Ogata, K., 90n2
ontological issues, 5, 26–27, 104, 106, 199, 339
optimum variability, 19, 37
organizational theory, 18, 82
Organization Science, 78
organization sciences and complexity sciences, 64–82
   evolution and revolution in scientific paradigms, 68–70
   methods, 70–71
   publications, 72–78
   roots, 64–68
orientation trait, 273
O'Shea-Wheller, T., 280
Osipov, M., 92
"other," 117n10

PAC learnability, 15
Padilla, J., 5, 23
Paik, Y., 72
Painter-Morland, M., 79
pair-wise comparison, 273
Pais, D., 294
Palmer, R., 269
paradigm shift, 2, 33, 67, 68–69, 98, 266, 304, 310, 314, 315, 321, 323
Parma Group, 115, 115n8, 126
partial recursive function, 9, 125, 193
Pathak, S., 80
patterned-oriented modeling approach, 197
pattern isolation, 270
pattern recognition, 177
Paulson, J., 153
PCM. *See* Principle of Complexity Management
Peace Accords Matrix Implementation Dataset, 98
Pelligrini, P., 153
Pentland, A., 201
Peressini, A.F., 56, 57
Peters, 199
Peterson, M., 72
phase transition, 43, 85, 111n2, 269, 271, 284, 288, 308, 323, 330, 332, 341
philosophy of science, 5, 302, 303, 305, 322, 325
physiologic time, 24, 241, 242, 243–244, 245, 247, 249, 251, 252, 253, 261
Piccinini, N., 242
Plato, 302
Plexus Institute, 67
Plowman, D., 76–77
P-NP problem, 9, 11, 12, 13, 20
Poisson distribution, 285–286, 287
Popper, K., 26, 302, 325
   falsification, 304–305, *305,* 306–307, 308–309, 311, 314–315, *315*
   scientific change, 314–315, *315,* 321

Post, E., 113, 118, 129, 130, 131, 135, 135n28
Postlewaite, A., 15
Poulis, E., 73
Poulis, K., 73
Power-Sharing Event Dataset, 98
Pratt, M., 205
Pratt, S., 265, 274, 275, 279, 291
preponderance-of-power, 85n1
Prescott, E., 120
Prigogine, I., 66, 80
    Nobel Lecture, 254
    Order Out of Chaos, 65, 72, 75, 81–82
Principle of Complexity Management (PCM), 242, 254
probabilistic processing, 15, 94, 167, 256, 273
probability density function (PDF), 245, 246, 247, 248–249, 250, 251, 252, 253, 254, 256, 257, *257*, 258, 259, 260, 261
probably approximately correct (PAC), 15
problem-solving and conflict, 38
Process Algebra, 25, 297
Process Theory, 267
productive function, 118, 130, 131, 135n28
progressive integration, 303, *304*
Prokopenko, M., 111n1, 113, 113n6
psychological safety, 35
Puri, A., 85n1

Quine, W., 302–303
quorum sensing, 280
quorum threshold, 264–265, 281, 291, 292, 296

Ramachandran, V.S., 122, 126, 126n20
Ramanujam, R., 73
Ramenzoni, V.C., 59
rational decision-making, 273, 274, 294
    irrational, 273, 274, 279
    non-rational, 273, 276
recent experience, 281
record dynamics, 286, 287

recursive reduction, 136
Red Queen, 112, 112n4, 114, 156
Renninger, L., 137
Requisite Variety, Law of, 19, 37, 72, 73, 80, 82
RFID, 276, 281, 285, 291, 292
Richardson, L.F., 83, 88, 90–91, 92
Rivkin, J., 74, 75
Robert Wood Johnson Foundation, 224, *225–226*
Robinson, E., 276, 281, 292
Rogers, H., 115, 123, 124
Rogoff, K., 146
Romer, P., 112
Rosa, H., 203
Rosen, R, 267
Rosser, J.B., Jr., 5, 26, 199
    bit tent view of dynamic complexity, 329
    bottom-up destabilization, 39
    catastrophe theory, 334
    computational complexity, 334
    ergodicity, 328
    "Holmes-Moriarty" problem, 335
routinizing, 37
rugged landscape model, 72, 74, 80, 81
Rungtusanatham, M., 80

Saint-Simon, H., 28, 29
Sakoda, J.M., 187
Salehyan, I., 101, 102
salience, 270–271
    ethnic, 96, 104
Sallis, J., 205
Samuelson, L., 332
Samuelson, P., 338–339
sandpile model, 65, 72, 73, 80, 322
Santa Fe Institute, 65
    Swarm, 188
Saperstein, A.M., 88, 91, 91n3, 92n4
Sasaki, T., 275, 279
satisficing, 14, 15, 94, 192, 274, 337
Schaeffer, J., 158
scaling, 5, 6, 183, 243, 247–251, 252, 253, 254, 261
    allometric laws, 7

scaling (*Continued.*)
  definition, 23
  laws, 7
  self-organization, 23–25
schema, 39, 72
  alternative, 36, 38, 188
  Wolfram-Chomsky, 16, 113
schemata
  and agents, 36–37
  change, 37
Schindehutte, M., 78
Schmeidler, D., 15
Schneider, A., 73
Schneider, S., 157
Schrödinger, E., 190
  "negentropy," 348–349
  What is Life?, 363
Schumacher, T., 75
Schumpeter, J.A., 112, 112n3, 198
scientific change, 26, 301, 302, 304
  Kuhn, 309, 314, *316*, 321, 323
  Popper, *315*, 321
scientific paradigms, 68–70, 301–302, 303–304
  directed networks, 316–322
scientific theory, 303, 316
  integrated, 315
seasonality, 281
Selden, P., 78
self-assembly, 116, 121, 123, 124, 132
self-efficacy, 49, 50, 52, 53–54
self-halting machines, 124–130
self-organized criticality, 72, 73, 74, 80, 85, 88
  and science, 322–324
self-organization, 34, 35, 39, 40–41, 44, 45, 62, 65–66, 323, 333, 344
  definition, 23–24
Self-Ref, 114, 118, 119, 155
  G-T-P logic condition, 121–123
  machinery, 123–124
Self-Rep, 114, 118, 119, 122, 133, 155
  mirror system, 124–128
Sendova-Franks, A., 265, 291
sensitivity analysis experiment, 217–219, *218–219*
shared mental model, 40, 48, 62

"sharing economy," 81
Shatkin, L., 5
Siggelkow, N., 75
Silver, D., 169
Simon, H., 14–15, 22, 24, 65, 157–158, 159–160, 163, 165, 170, 192, 272, 327, 328, 337–338, 341
Sinigaglia, C., 126
Skinner, B.F., 28
small-tent complexity, 329, 332
small-world simulation, 9, 75, 193
Smolin, L., 10, 11
social insect colony, 263–266
  decision-making, 274–282
social loafing, 35, 49, 53
Society for Chaos Theory in Psychology and Life Sciences, 67
sociometer, 201–202
sociotechnical systems theory, 35
Sodel, L., 158, 169
Soros, G., 147, 147n36, 153
Spear, S., 141
speed-cohesion tradeoff, 277, 293
Spinoza, 302
Stacey, R., 66
Stag Hunt games, 48–49, 50–53, 60
statistical debugging, 208, 209, 215–217, 219, 229, 236, 237
Stauffer, M.H.T., 4, 18, 19–20
Stenger, I., 80
  Order Out of Chaos, 65, 72, 75, 81–82
Stevens, R., 61
Stieglitz, N., 75
Stigler, G., 338
stochastic determinism, 268
Strand, R., 210
strategic innovation, 112, 117, 121, 131
strictly cooperative games, 42
Stroeymeyt, N., 278, 279, 281
Strong Church–Turing Thesis, 16, 17
Structural Vector Autoregression, 198
subordination, 249, 256–259, *257*
Sugarscape, 187
Sulis, W., 5, 24, 25, 263, 264, 291
Sumpter, D., 291
Sunder, S., 336

"supply chain," 70, 80
supply networks, 68, 80
"surprises," 21, 111, 112, 118, 120, 120n15, 121, 131, 136, 138, 144, *145*, 146, 156
symmetry breaking, 36, 39, 269, 270
system dynamics, 1, 65, 66, 101, 104, 185, 248
synchronization
  group dynamics, 54–62, *56*
    measurement, 55–57
    principles, 54–55
    team performance, 57–62
      synchronization and affiliation, 58–59
      synchronization and performance, 59–62

Tang, C., 322
Tasa, K., 50
task allocation, 263, 268
Tay, N.N., 74
"team," 33, 34
  See also "group"
team/group emergency response, 51, 52, 53, 60
team/group performance, 19, 33, 47, 50, 53, 55, 57–62, 63
team/group size, 49, 53, 54, 100
  dynamics, 53–54
team orientation, 35
telogical mode, 38, 64, 73, 119n12
temnothorax albipennis, 264, 276, 277, 278, 280, 289, 291, 292, 297
temperament, 273, 283
temporal allometry relations, 250–253
  information stability, 252–253
Tesfatsion, L., 10, 194
Thaler, R., 22, 159
theoretical frameworks, 3, 17, 26, 72, 80, 95–96, 301–302, 303, 305
thermodynamics, 65, 75–76, 243, 246–247, 254, 266, 282, 348
Thietart, R., 66, 77
Thom, R., 65

Thymus Medulla, 115n8, 116, 119, 122, 124, 129, *130*
time, 241–262
  allometry, 243–245
  allometry/information hypothesis, 245–247
  biological, 241, 242, 243
  fractional probability calculus, 247–250
  metabolic, 241
  physiologic, 24, 241, 242, 243–244, 245, 247, 249, 251, 252, 253, 261
  solution to FKE, 260–262
  subordination, 256–259, *257*
  temporal allometry relations, 250–253
    information stability, 252–253
Tinbergen, J., 340–341
tinkering, 80, 352, 353
total body mass (TBM), 25, 242, 243, 245, 247, 249, 250–251, 253, 254, 261
Tourish, D., 79
transitivity, 272, 274
Trivedi, M., 5
Trust for America's Health, 224, *225–226*
Tsuda, I., 127–128
Tucker, P., 120n14
Turing, A., 113, 163, 193
  Award, 157–158, 158n2
  Church–Turing Thesis, 2, 16, 17, 27, 343
  computable, 9, 17, 27, 193
  machine (TM), 12, 16–18, 27, 121, 129, 135, 135n28, 193, 335, 336, 341, 342, 343, 348, 350, 351, 352, 357, 359, 363
  test for AI, 170
  Universal Turing Machine (UTM), 161–162, 173
  See also Gödel-Turing-Post
Tversky, A., 14, 22, 159, 192

UCDP. *See* Uppsala Data Program
Uhl-Bien, M., 79
unfreeze-move-refreeze model, 66

universality, 24, 113, 284, 288–290
Universal Turing Machine (UTM),
    161–162, 173
unknown-unknowns, 80
Uppsala Data Program (UCDP), 96
    Peace Agreement Dataset, 98
urban dynamics, 184
urban violence, 101, 102, 103
US Department of Health and Human
    Services, 213
utility, 23, 105, 199, 272
    complex systems methods, 282–284
    maximization, 14, 15, 192
UTM. *See* Universal Turing Machine

Valiant, L.G., 15
validation, 209–210, 219
    cross-model, 222–226
    micro-level, 210
    See also verification and validation
van Ackere, A., 74
Vance, C., 72
Van de Ven, A.H., 66, 73–74
VandV. *See* verification and validation
Varela, F., 65, 355
Velupillai, K., 9, 14, 147n36, 199, 334
verification, 208–209, 215
verification and validation (VandV),
    206, 207, 210, 213, 215, 237,
    238
    challenges, 194–199
Vink, R., 60
von Bertalanaffy, L., 64
von Clausewitz, C.
    On War, 87
von Neumann, J., 161, 162–163, 168,
    171, 340
    cellular automata, 189
    Game Theory, 189

Warglien, M., 74
Watts, D., 311
Weber's Law, 270, 296

Weidmann, N.B., 83, 101, 102
weighted additive strategy, 274
Weighted Calculus of Communicating
    Systems, 297
Werker-Brenner approach, 207
West, B.J., 5, 24, 25
Wheatley, M., 66
Whitehead, A., 267
Whiten, A., 136
Whittington, R., 77
Wickert, C., 73
Wiener, N., 64, 242, 246
Wiener/Shannon information, 246, 247,
    252, 254
Wiesenfeld, K., 322
Wigmore, J.
    "chart method," 316, *317*
Wigner, E.P., 114
Wilson, E.O., 3, 28, 268
Witt, U., 112
Wolfram, S., 8
    Rule 110, 113n6
Wolfram-Chomsky schema, 16, 113
Wolfram-Chomsky Type IV cellular
    automata, 22
Wolfson, M., 85n1
workload
    cognitive, 60
    Group Workload (GWL) Ratings,
        60, 62
    subjective, 60
World War I, 86
World War II, 86, 89, 138
    post, 336

Young, M., 99
Young, P., 142

Zame, R., 135n28
Zaslavsky, G.M., 247, 249
Zeeman, E., 333
Zeitgeist, 345
Zimmerman, B., 66